Democratic Oversight and Reform of the Security Sector in Turkey

2005/2006 Status Report

edited by
Ümit Cizre

LIT

Bibliographic information published by the Deutsche Nationalbibliothek
The Deutsche Nationalbibliothek lists this publication in the Deutsche Nationalbibliografie; detailed bibliographic data are available in the Internet at http://dnb.d-nb.de.

ISBN 978-3-03735-234-2 (Schweiz)
ISBN 978-3-8258-0969-0 (Deutschland)

A catalogue record for this book is available from the British Library

Dufourstr. 31
CH-8008 Zürich
Tel. +41 (0) 44-251 75 05
Fax +41 (0) 44-251 75 06
e-Mail: zuerich@lit-verlag.ch
http://www.lit-verlag.ch

LIT VERLAG Dr. W. Hopf
Berlin 2007
Auslieferung/Verlagskontakt:
Fresnostr. 2
D-48159 Münster
Tel. +49 (0)251–62 03 20
Fax +49 (0)251–23 19 72
e-Mail: lit@lit-verlag.de
http://www.lit-verlag.de

Auslieferung:
Schweiz/Österreich: Medienlogistik Pichler-ÖBZ GmbH & Co KG
IZ-NÖ, Süd, Straße 1, Objekt 34, A-2355 Wiener Neudorf
Tel. +43 (0) 2236/63 535 - 290, Fax +43 (0) 2236/63 535 - 243, e-Mail: mlo@medien-logistik.at
Deutschland: LIT Verlag Fresnostr. 2, D-48159 Münster
Tel. +49 (0) 2 51/620 32 - 22, Fax +49 (0) 2 51/922 60 99, e-Mail: vertrieb@lit-verlag.de

Distributed in the UK by: Global Book Marketing, 99B Wallis Rd, London, E9 5LN
Phone: +44 (0) 20 8533 5800 – Fax: +44 (0) 1600 775 663
http://www.centralbooks.co.uk/acatalog/search.html

Distributed in North America by:

Transaction Publishers
New Brunswick (U.S.A.) and London (U.K.)

Transaction Publishers
Rutgers University
35 Berrue Circle
Piscataway, NJ 08854

Phone: +1 (732) 445 - 2280
Fax: + 1 (732) 445 - 3138
for orders (U. S. only):
toll free (888) 999 - 6778
e-mail:
orders@transactionspub.com

Democratic Oversight and Reform of the Security Sector in Turkey

edited by
Ümit Cizre

Geneva Centre for the
Democratic Control of Armed Forces
(DCAF)

LIT

CONTENTS

Acknowledgments

The editor would like to thank Aji Buchanan, Stefan Imobersteg and Vahan Galoumian without whose competent assistance and cooperation this book would not have been published. Thanks also go to the authors whose contributions will help to achieve a better understanding of the current state of the Turkish security sector, identify security sector reform needs in short and the long term, and remove the shroud of secrecy that surrounds the security institutions, by presenting reliable information which will now be available to legislators, media professionals and civil society-at-large.

Preface

Since the founding of the modern, secular Republic of Turkey in 1923, the Turkish Armed Forces have maintained a highly influential stature in both military and political spheres. Turkey has one of the largest standing armies in the world, is the second largest army in NATO after the United States, and has toppled four civilian governments in the last four decades. Turkey's army is therefore not only a potential force on the battlefield, but also a real force in day-to-day politics.

The inequity between the Turkish military's role and principles of democratic governance have become even more apparent as EU-Turkey negotiations gained momentum at the end of 1990's. Whilst the prospect of European Union (EU) membership has been a major driving force behind Turkey's reforms, media freedom, judicial independence, and civilian control of the military have – in European eyes – not yet been fully consolidated in the Turkish system.

This disproportionate and dominating role played by the military in the country's politics and society and the need for increased accountability, transparency and civilian control mechanisms are undoubtedly one of the major causes for concern in aligning Turkey's security sector with EU practices. This concern was noted in the European Commission's 2006 Progress Report: 'Overall, limited progress has been made in aligning civil-military relations with EU practices. Statements by the military should only concern military, defence and security matters and should only be made under the authority of the government, while the civilian authorities should fully exercise their supervisory functions in particular as regards the formulation of the national security strategy and its implementation, including with regard to relations with neighbouring countries.'

There is upon this view a need for further harmonisation of Turkish Civil-Military (CMR) with democratic standards, which would be best achieved by a healthy cooperation between the government, parliament and security sector institutions (the armed forces, the police department, the gendarmerie, and others) with the assistance of expert opinion, and by taking into consideration the demands stemming from civil society. In addition, there is an urgent requirement for the implementation of a substantive Security Sector Reform (SSR) process, involving the establishment of democratic oversight of all governmental security institutions and democratic decision taking on their functions, general policies, strategies, and budgets.

Founded in 2000, the Geneva Centre for the Democratic Control of Armed Forces (DCAF) has worked to promote good governance and reform of the security sector in accordance with democratic standards. DCAF, as an International Foundation with 49 member governments, conducts research on good practices, encourages the development and promotion of relevant norms at the national and international levels, makes policy recommendations and provides in-country advice and practical assistance programmes to all interested actors. The Centre works with governments and civil society to foster and strengthen the democratic and civilian control of security sector organisations such as police, intelligence agencies, border security services, paramilitary forces, and armed forces.

Since 2003, DCAF has been working with the Turkish Economic and Social Studies Foundation (Türkiye Ekonomik ve Sosyal Etüdler Vakfı, TESEV), which is one of Turkey's leading NGOs among those involved in security sector reform and issues related to the challenges of democratisation. TESEV has played a pioneering role in sensitising the public to security issues; creating a security-conscious community capable of monitoring and overseeing the sector; and in establishing the norms and principles of the issues of democratic governance and oversight of the security sector. The foundation carries out studies in Turkey for the development of independent thinking, the establishment of the principle of transparency, the democratisation of the country as part of the process of European harmonisation and to help strengthen the country's role in the region.

Published as part of the DCAF-TESEV Book Series in Security Sector Studies, 'Democratic Oversight and Reform of the Security Sector in Turkey – 2005/2006 Status Report' provides an informative and critical analysis of all Turkey's security sector actors, covering their history, current status and advances, as well as the remaining challenges they face. This report – based entirely on publicly available sources - aims to raise awareness among elected members of the Parliament, and to continue to build up the relevant expertise among civilians, to better understand the issues of civilian and democratic oversight and security sector governance and to tackle the challenges of their security sector reform.

I would like to thank Dr. Ümit Cizre, Associate Professor at Bilkent University and cherished International Advisory Board member of the Geneva Centre for the Democratic Control of Armed Forces for conceptualising and editing this important status report, along with the contributors, for some of which the publication of the Turkish version was unfortunately coupled with rather unpleasant surprises.

Geneva, October 2007

Philipp Fluri, Ph.D.
Deputy Director

Introduction
Creating Public Interest, Sensitivity and Engagement as Part of Security Sector Reform

Ümit Cizre[*]

This is the 'first' Almanac ever to be published about the 'Security Sector' in the history of the Turkish Republic. Although it is centred on the year 2005, the historical, strategic, political and legal features of the security units it covers are valid for almost all times. The Almanac presents the reader with an account of each agency responsible for providing security, ranging from the military to non-military ones, as well as the actors responsible for their oversight such as the parliament and executive. These accounts comprise their brief history; organisational features; declared and undeclared operational principles and activities; hierarchical structures; accountability levels; the legal framework they operate under; basic trends that were observed in their practices in the year 2005; the impact of international developments and the transformations they underwent in the process of aligning their practices with those of the European Union in accordance with the requirements of full membership, which has become a more realistic prospect since 17 December 2004.

The security actors covered in this Almanac are, in contemporary parlance, members of Turkey's 'security sector.' There is a burgeoning consensus that the security sector refers to all agencies which have the legitimate authority to order, use, and/or threaten to use force to provide external and internal security of the state and its citizens. These agencies include the armed forces, paramilitary forces, police and gendarmerie, intelligence services, border/coast guard formations and defence ministries. Non-state private security actors are also included in the sector. In this Almanac, the four forces of the Armed Forces, namely Land, Air, Naval Forces and the Gendarmerie, the Police, the Coast Guard Command, Police and Gendarmerie Intelligence organisations, Special Operations Units, National Intelligence Organisation, National Defence Council, security-related activities of Turkey's Legislative and Executive branches, Military Judicial System, Village Guards, Private Security System, Civil Society-Security and Media-Security links, are studied by experts based on available objective data and in a dynamic framework in conjunction with current domestic and international strategic developments.

---

* Professor, Bilkent University, Political Science Department

Essentially, this Almanac aims to provide objective and reliable knowledge about Turkey's security sector agencies, in an analytical format, in order to trigger public interest and sensitivity on security, defence and strategy issues and agencies. It also aims to help provide the background information required for opening a public space for enlightened debate. In other words, this Almanac reflects the new international thinking which believes that an effective and democratic oversight of the security institutions entails a civilian 'empowerment' dimension, which can only be achieved by spreading the knowledge and expertise of security from the 'state' to wider society. Empowerment is about building up the awareness, sensitivity, and expertise of civilians, regarding matters of defence, security and strategy. Civilians will then be able to monitor and oversee the security agencies' performance of their statutory functions, to deliver security efficiently and effectively in an environment consistent with democratic principles. Most importantly, this publication aims at making a healthy contribution towards changing Turkey's security culture as part of the process of security sector reform (SSR), in line with international norms of transparency, accountability and human-security.

Conceptual Underpinnings

This Almanac can best be appreciated through an understanding of the current meaning and importance attached globally to its object of study, which is that of the 'security sector' and the establishing of its democratic accountability as part of its reform. The overriding goals of security sector reform are a more efficient use of resources to improve the proficiency of the security forces together with the achievement of effectiveness in terms of openness, clarity and partnership rather than rivalry between the security agencies. In enhancing the technical capacity of the security units, it is important that there should be no overlapping authority and inter-agency competition in the sector. The chapters in this Almanac on the police and gendarmerie amply demonstrate the corrosive effects of a problematic division of functions between these units.

Re-conceptualising Civilian Control/Oversight

This Almanac reflects the shift of concern in the post-Cold War era from the structural and institutional features of security-providing units to issues dealing with the consolidation of norms and procedures of accountability in the security realm to ensure that the security institutions provide effective security in an environment which has internalised democratic values and practices at both political and social levels. Therefore, in identifying the characteristics of the security sector of Turkey, this study accepts the pillar principle of democratic governance of the security sector. This principle promotes the democratic accountability of a professional and effective security structure to the democratically-elected political representatives in the parliament, with both civil society and media being instrumental in the process.

Democratic governance of the security sector is applicable for both democratic western states and those which aspire to move on the continuum to democracy. It has a special and invaluable role to play in post-conflict and post-authoritarian transitions, peacekeeping and long-term peacebuilding and development programmes. However, while the democratic states have the capacity to initiate the revision and reform of their security agencies, the political impulse to undertake the improvement and management of security sectors, based on international norms of transparency, accountability and the rule of law in the rest of the world, is largely driven by external conditions. However, this is not negating national ownership, or implying that democratic governance of the sector is an entirely 'western' concept which is imported to the rest of the world for western benefit regardless of its effects on the effectiveness and legitimacy of local security systems.

It follows that the starting point of the Almanac is the 'new' concept of democratic civilian oversight/control which revolves around setting up procedures of accountability which transcend the bureaucratic mechanisms of oversight and adopt a more inclusive approach. Control/oversight no longer means an exclusive domination by constitutionally elected civilian bodies over a unified military structure, but includes a decentralised and diffused strategy involving civil society, think-tanks, universities and a community of interested and informed civilians. To be more explicit, democratic civilian control, in this approach for example, is not to be conceptualised as a twofold split between the armed forces and civilian authorities whereby the latter simply prevails over the former. Rather, it implies a move from the classic but deficient concept of 'civil-military relations' to 'democratic governance of civil-military affairs.' This is a move from an imperfect and unequal distribution of knowledge and power between the two sides –usually in the military's favour in our part of the world-- to the internalisation of democratic values and practices on the part of both the civilian and military sides at both political and social levels.[1]

The creation of a domestic political environment, i.e., local ownership of reform, in which SSR can be sustained, is more important than sheer external pressures to produce that end. Since 1999, for instance, the emerging paradigm of SSR in Turkey has been largely centred around the military. The reason for this is the Turkey-specific 'guardian' role of the military, which requires that the military plays a predominant role in the defining of what qualifies within the remit of national security threats, and retains primary responsibility for formulating security policy responses to them. In countries where the military has historically guarded over the national interests and objectives, there is little expertise, intellectual interest and knowledge on the civilian side to understand, take an interest in and discuss defence and security issues. However, the new conceptual focus in civil military relations redefines the civil-military interface around a more egalitarian dialogue between the two sides and immediately raises the parallel problem of bridging the knowledge gap between the two sides about threats and security policy instruments before a healthy partnership can be achieved: Even in advanced western democracies, 'asymmetry of knowledge' is a major problem in the establishment of national policy and budgetary frameworks of control by elected civilian authorities.

---

1 Timothy Edmunds, (2002): 'Promoting Democratic Control of Armed Forces in Central and Eastern Europe: Lessons Learnt and Future Research Agendas,' in H. Born, M. Caparini and P. Fluri (eds.) *Security Sector Reform and Democracy in Transitional Societies* , Baden Baden: Nomos Verlagsgesellschaft, p. 102.

This Almanac, therefore promotes the principle of democratic civilian oversight/control by acknowledging that the knowledge gap between the security sector and the civilian members of the society creates a communication deficiency resulting in a 'monologue' rather than a dialogue. In most countries where Almanacs are published, the political objective is to establish an egalitarian and dynamic interaction between the overseeing civilians and the agencies of the security system. The Turkish Almanac is no different. Let us also note that one of the intended consequences is to increase the self-confidence of civilians responsible for monitoring and oversight, to enable them simply to carry out their task of overseeing with an equal level of strategic 'grammar' and technical 'vocabulary' of the various units involved in the security sector. This is also expected to lead to the emergence of collaboration and harmony between the security agencies and civilian overseers, or between the agencies themselves, thus removing intra-sectoral conflicts, rivalry and struggles.

These expectations are markedly relevant in Turkey where any civilian role expansion in security affairs also creates an opportunity for the political class to regain its self-confidence, problem-solving ability, and its capacity to influence the political fate of the society. Among other things, this Almanac serves the objective of boosting the 'political effiectiveness' of the overall civilian groups, not just the governments or parliaments.

It is therefore correct to say that this Almanac is published on time, and at the right juncture to empower the political, civil and economic society in terms of enhancing their interest, knowledge and engagement in the process of making security actors efficient, responsive and accountable in the performance of their duties.

Human Security

The writers of the Almanac have taken pains to incorporate in their accounts the presence and/or absence of instances of a 'human security' imperative in Turkey's democratic management of the security sector. This perspective helps the readers to understand the political sources and nature of conflict and violence revolving around 'internal threats' and the political dynamics that have sustained them in the last two decades. The contemporary shift of focus of security from revolving around the 'military'/ hard security of the 'state' to the protection of the life, liberty, and welfare of the man in the street, finds an echo in this Almanac because it stresses these important aspects.

The suggestions of the EU Commission's Regular Report of 2004 and Progress Report of 2005 that Turkey's civilians should start to take a more active role in the formulation of national security strategy, reflects the thinking that traditional military approach/ 'security of the state' has limited utility in meeting the contemporary security problems of a non-military nature. These problems include: poverty/ deprivation, infringements of freedom of expression, mass/forced migration, conflictive politics of ethnicity and religious identity, organised crime, human trafficking, and abuse of women and children.

The human security concept can help understand the catalysts, salience, and directions of the reform of the security sector, not only in Turkey, but in many non-Western contexts: As stated so succinctly by the Director of the UN Institute for

Disarmament Research (UNDIR), 'effective reform of the security sector requires an appreciation that security sector reform links with human rights and human security. At the core of SSR is the concept of human security....'[2] When we remember that during the 1990s, the effectiveness of the military bureaucracy in Turkey was achieved against an internal conflict/enemy, it becomes clear that Turkey is one of those countries which have wide experience of the kind of tensions that can arise between the security sector's effectiveness and the fundamental rules of human rights.

The Role of the EU

The EU Helsinki Summit of 1999, which extended the candidate status to Turkey, provided the impetus for preparing a National Plan for the Adoption of the Acquis adopted in 2001, which was revised in 2003. Political reforms to align Turkey's laws with the EU have been introduced through two major constitutional reforms in 2001 and 2004 and 8 legislative packages introduced between February 2002 and July 2004.

Since the Summit, the possibility of EU accession has become the main driving force for democratic reforms in the security sector and civil-military relations. The EU's use of pre-conditionality is being used as an effective instrument for the promotion of democratic civilian oversight mechanisms over the security sector. As part of the accession process, the European Commission has been assessing Turkey' s progress, based on the fulfilment of the political criteria set out in the Copenhagen European Council meeting of 1993. Although SSR or civil- military relations are not explicitly referred to in the Criteria, the 'political criteria' inscribed in the Accession Partnership Document (drawn up by the EU in 2000 and most recently revised and adopted in January 2006) and the EU's regular progress reports since 1998, have suggested the need for structural changes in the organisation of civil-military relations to enhance democratic civilian control and bring the institutional structure in line with EU standards. Moreover, in the regular progress reports of the European Commission on Turkey, certain institutional areas of civil-military relations are specifically marked out as requiring reform. It is common for the Annual Reports to repeatedly emphasize the EU Commission's view that 'Turkey should work towards greater accountability and transparency in the conduct of security affairs in line with Member States' best practice. In particular,statements by the military should only concern military, defence and security matters and should only be made under the authority of the government.' The latest Annual Report of 8 November 2006 again dwells on the deficiencies of democratic civilian oversight over the formulation of threats and national security policies: 'overall, limited progress has been made in aligning civil-military relations with EU practices... the civilian authorities should fully exercise their supervisory functions in particular with regard to the formulation

---

2 Patricia Lewis, (2003) "Requirements for Effective Security Sector Reform," in *Security Sector Reform:Its Relevance for Conflict Prevention, Peace Building and Development,* Geneva: United Nations in Geneva and Geneva Center for Democratic Control of Armed Forces, p.27.

of the national security strategy and its implementation, as well as taking into account relations with neighbouring countries.'[3]

It seems that the changes to be made in Turkey's security sector to align them with the good practices of the EU, boil down to three conceptual foci: the key concern is centred on the need to alter the 'threat' perception and the 'security policy responses' to this. One implication here is that in taking significant steps towards interpreting the threats in a less militaristic manner, greater participation is required during the preparations of the National Security Policy Document. This is mainly due to the fact that this document is considered to be 'the secret constitution' of the country. The second perspective is a redefinition and expansion of what is understood by civilian oversight/control which relies on sensitising governmental and non-governmental civilian sectors to security by spreading better knowledge. The process also encourages the broader democratisation/reform process by way of removing 'secrecy and taboos' automatically identified with security and defence issues. The media plays an important part in diffusing this information, and in providing a venue for questioning and debating defence, security and strategy issues. The final focus dwells on civilian 'empowerment' as the fundamental prerequisite for establishing a workable/healthy/normal balance between civilians and the security agents, and especially the military. It seems a must therefore that in order to achieve a democratic, yet effective, system of management of post-Cold War defence and security issues, it is crucial to build up 'an effective strategic community, encompassing academics and other interest groups who can provide a dynamic debate on security and defence issues to the benefit of the armed services and the wider public.'[4]

General Political Dynamics

Even though the civilian capacity to debate and shape the security issues and policies remained limited, and the fact that security was still regarded as an instrument of state control of the society in Turkey in 2005, current public debates on various aspects of security sector in the country go to show that the critical threshold of 'voicing opinions' on the almost taboo topics of security has passed. A new consciousness, awareness and sensitivity has started to dominate international as well as Turkey's public opinion, who have become more and more aware that factors labelled as threats by social groups are constructed through discourse. There is now a higher appreciation that more transparency and better channels of accountability about the principles, policies and issues of security such as military expenditure - which are still somewhat hidden behind the curtain of secrecy--, threat perception, procurement, force deployment, strategic planning, senior appointments and promotions, can make a positive contribution to strengthening peace and stability in the

---

[3] European Commission, Commission Staff Working Document, Turkey 2006 Progress Report.

[4] Christopher Dandeker, (2003) 'Military and Society: The Problem, the Challenges and Possible Answers', in A. Bryden and P. Fluri (eds.), Security Sector Reform: Institutions, Society and Good Governance, Baden Baden: Nomos Verlagsgesellschaft, p. 149.

country and in the region as well as the legitimacy of the security agents and state. Professor Robin Luckham, a prominent researcher in the field of the Security Sector, notes that the problem of 'democratic oversight' is not the mere implementation of civilian control over military and non-military units, it is inculcating the tradition of democratic accountability in the sector to end the persistence of military policies behind the formalities of civilian democratic governments.[5]

As of 2005, significant segments of civil society and think-tanks were engaged in activities bridging the asymmetry of knowledge between the security community and civilian parties. That they are not yet conspicuously effective, should not obscure the fact that the precepts that shape national security policies are increasingly being debated by civilian bodies. In this regard, a new venue has been created by the beginning of a collaboration, since 2004, between one of Turkey's prominent think-tanks, the Turkish Economic and Social Research Foundation (TESEV) and the Geneva Centre for the Democratic Control of Armed Forces (DCAF). The consortium operates through conferences, workshops, publications and training sessions for media and parliamentarians. The consortium has launched a Series in Security Sector Studies in May 2004 in an international workshop promoting the Turkish translation of the Handbook for Parliamentarians- Parliamentary Oversight of the Security Sector: Principles, Mechanisms and Practices.[6] Subsequent publications and activities since then,[7] which culminates in the publication of this Almanac, serve to show that civil-military relations part of security system in Turkey is characterised by greater dynamism than the historical-cultural frame allows for.

The Justice and Development Party (JDP) government, in its first term in office (2002-2007), has made a commitment to reduce considerably the political role of the military in non-military spheres, as part of its compliance with the full membership requirements of the European Union. The EU was instrumental in the JDP's plans to introduce reforms which involve society and include concern for citizens. If EU entry requirements have provided one external impetus for the JDP government's attempts to reshape military-civilian relations, the international community's approval of its Islamic credentials has provided another. This trend stems from the West's security concerns about the regions' Islamic movements and regimes. It has effected positively the ruling party's choice of embarking on its plan to be a full member of the EU and its inclusion in its political reform agenda the alteration of the existing system of civil military relations in favour of civilians.

---

5 Gavin Cawthra and Robin Luckham (2003) 'Democratic Control and the Security Sector, the Scope for Transformation and Its Limits,' in Gavin Cawthra and Robin Luckham (eds.) Governing Insecurity, Democratic Control of Military and Security Establishments in Transitional Democracies, London and New York: Zed Books, p. 14.

6 The book was published jointly by DCAF and Interparliamentary Union in 2003 in Geneva.

7 These publications and activities cover the spectrum of security sector activities and agencies as well as 'good practices' elsewhere. The latest output is ALMANAC TURKEY 2005: Security Sector and Democratic Oversight, edited by Umit Cizre. For detailed information see: http://www.tesev.org.tr/events/democ_hor.php

The government divested considerable energy into the landmark democracy package of 7 August 2003 designed to bring Turkey in line with the EU criteria. That package included a major constitutional amendment designed to curb the powers of the National Security Council (NSC), considered to be Turkey's parallel government, and convert it into an advisory body. The European Commission's evaluation in October 2004 of Turkey's progress in accession laid out that '... The Commission considers that Turkey sufficiently fulfills the political criteria and recommends that accession negotiations be opened.'[8]

However, there are two distinct phases in the JDP government's policies on the security sector, notably that of the military since 2002, with opposite contents and outcomes. The first phase spans approximately the first three years of the government's life from the 2002 elections to the launching of negotiations with the EU, in October 2005, to fulfill Ankara's bid for full membership. In this time period, true enough, the JDP's democratic mandate, provided by the dynamism of the 2002 electoral process, acted as powerful forces behind the government's drive to curtail the TAF's political prerogatives and tutelage as a major leg of the reform agenda. The democratic package of August 2003, which tipped the balance in the civilians' favour comes in this period.

In the second phase from 2005 onwards (until the general elections in 2007), despite the momentous legal and constitutional changes the JDP made in its bid for EU membership since 2002, international criticism of the government escalated on the grounds that it failed to act expeditiously on the reforms to get a start-date for negotiations on 3 October 2005. There was also criticism that the JDP had allowed the Islamist agenda to creep into the amendments to the Penal Code in September-October 2004 and in June 2005.[9] At the same time, the State Department and the Pentagon expressed their displeasure with the resurgence of anti-American sentiments and policies in Ankara which they believed had begun souring the relationship between the two countries since the advent of 'subtle yet insidious Islamism of the Justice and Development Party... and a combination of old leftism and new Islamism.'[10]

---

8 Recommendations on the 2004 Regular Report on Turkey's Progress towards Accession (Commission of the European Communities, 6 October 2004), p., 2. European Council of Heads of State of 25 member countries in December 2004 decided to open accession negotiations with Turkey on 3 October 2005.

9 Just before the EU Commission issued its annual report on Turkey in October 2004, the government, in an amendment clause to the Penal Law criminalized adultery. After a wave of protests by the Union and internal opposition, the clause was withdrawn. The second controversy arose in the next round of amendments to the Penal Code in June 2005 on the clauses constraining the freedom of the press and decreasing the maximum sentences against those who run illegal educational institutions. Impelled by the fear that this provision would encourage the opening of illegal Koran courses that would infringe on the secular foundations of the educational system, the President vetoed the amendment.

10 Robert L. Pollock, 'The Sick Man of Europe- Again,' The Wall Street Journal, 16 February 2005.

Although the entry talks were launched in October 2005, the government's resolve to hang onto the agenda of democratising reforms and keep the 'military question' within its remit has weakened. Turkey's strong coalition of secular forces led by the military were locked in their 'radical doubt' over the JDP's 'Islamic' aspirations. The unfettered strength of this coalition caused a loss of a sense of normality within the JDP's political leadership in its relationship with the military. The EU's Common Position Paper, issued after Turkey-EU Partnership Council meeting on 12 June 2006, maintains that progress has been made but 'the pace of change has slowed in Turkey in the last year.' Therefore, the Position Paper recommends significant further efforts regarding the implementation of reforms in human rights; civil-military relations; security affairs; fundamental freedoms; torture and ill-treatment; non-violent expression of opinion; freedom of religion; cultural rights; protection of minorities; domestic violence and honor killings and the normalisation of relations between Turkey and EU members including the Greek Cypriot government.[11]

The somewhat negative signals coming from the European Commission about Ankara's membership, combined with the JDP's domestic and foreign policy discourse which widened the chasm between Turkey and the EU and the USA, led to a decline in the JDP's democracy discourse. This was instead replaced by some repackaged conservative nationalist reactions leading to a new convergence with the military's policy priorities on key issues. More importantly, the re-emergence of the war against the Kurdish seperatist movement, and the renewed importance that was attached to internal security threats, once more promoted the position of the military as being pivotal in the internal security crackdown as well as in foreign policy.

In line with its general strategy towards the military in the second phase, which emphasises the absence of tensions or rows in civil-military relations, the government has tried hard to sustain a concordant relationship with the army on a number of issues. These include the primacy of state-centred security considerations and hard-line approach towards the Kurdish question, Northern Iraq and the EU sidelining human security approach. The JDP's management of the armed forces of avoiding actual confrontation, let the military sector voice seem stronger than it should have been. To avoid any open collision with the secular establishment and especially with General Buyukanit, the Chief of the General Staff since 2006, the ruling party spent considerable energy to smooth over the sharply critical tone of the public statements of the high-echelon; to pretend to read these statements in a positive light; and to keep the military out of limelight by constantly placating it.

The military hierarchy levelled harsh criticisms against the government in their defence of secularism. It seems clear that the presidential elections in May 2007, which loomed large in 2005 and 2006, played the most crucial role in the military's adoption of a pointedly assertive political profile to prevent the likelihood of an Islamic-oriented president coming to power. The Istanbul based NGO, TESEV, which was by then actively engaged in promoting the cause of democratic

---

[11] The EU Common Position Paper's online address is: http://www.turkishpress.com/news.asp?=128408

oversight of the security agencies including the military,[12] and even the former representative of the European Commission in Ankara, Hansjoerg Kretschmer, who said at a meeting that the armed forces do not respect the legal and constitutional order[13] also became the targets of strongly-worded critiques of the high command.

It is clear that once the EU-driven democracy agenda faltered, effective democratic alterations in the civil-military equation were postponed if not abandoned forever. The important point to note here is that the JDP government has considered the civil-military balance as a small part of wider political reform which includes democratisation, rather than turning this around to correct the imbalance and to continue wider political reform simultaneously with reform in the national security realm.

The Turkish experience supports the view that the prime movers of a government's capacity to alter the security sector balance through a serious reform programmes, are neither entirely technical nor entirely external impositions, but are a combination of global opportunities with the initiatives of local actors, forces and processes. The momentous reform package of August 2003 shows quite clearly that the best formula to generate the capacity for elected and non-elected civilian centres in the democratic governance of the security sector, is a new strategic context created not just by external circumstances but also by the political will, i.e., the gathering momentum of a government's own policies.

---

12 In October 2006, a few days after the first English edition of TESEV's publication of 'Almanac Turkey 2005 Security Sector and Democratic Oversight', the chief of General Staff General Buyukanit publicly attacked TESEV, the Almanac and its contributors on the grounds that the attempt was directed at undermining the military.

13 Kretchmer made this remark as a keynote speaker in the launching of the English edition of Almanac Turkey 2005 on 18 September 2006.

Turkish Grand National Assembly (TBMM)

Ahmet Yıldız[*]

The Grand National Assembly of Turkey (Türkiye Büyük Millet Meclisi, TBMM, usually referred to simply as Meclis – 'the Parliament') is the unicameral parliament of Turkey which is the sole body given the legislative prerogatives by the Turkish Constitution.

Historical Background

The relationship between the military and civilian sectors constitutes the most critical aspect of the Turkish political system, and it undoubtedly needs to be restructured, in order to reinforce democratic governance in Turkey. The central problem originates from the underlying concept of state power which provides the military sector with an autonomous domain within the state. In this sense, the military is independent of state control, to a certain extent, and is endorsed as the primary guardian of the Republic. In brief, the functions of political execution and control are assigned to the military. This development, which dates back to the second constitutional period, has caused a permanent separation between the fields of activity and authority of the government and the military sector. It has, in fact, created a fault line with a tremendous effect on Turkish politics. The tradition of preserving the position of the military sector in an almost autonomous domain of power, elevates its authority and involvement in many areas of internal politics, ranging from international relations to education and basic rights. The incompatibility of this model with the contemporary idea of democratic governance, has become one of the most resonant problems in Turkish politics.

In Turkey, the military has assumed an active role within politics via the National Security Council (Milli Güvenlik Kurulu, MGK) and the media; within industry and trade via foundations and the Army Solidarity Institution (Ordu Yardımlaşma Kurumu, OYAK); and within the judicial system via the military judiciary. At present, obligatory military service spreads military values throughout society and these values are shaped by nationalism, as opposed to a democratic political culture. Therefore, complete parliamentary control of military expenditure cannot be established and the democratisation of the status and functions of the Turkish Armed

* PhD, Turkish Grand National Assembly (TBMM) Research Centre.

Forces (Türk Silahlı Kuvvetleri, TSK) remains a major roadblock in the process of European Union (EU) accession.

In the EU reform process, that began with Turkey acquiring the status of a candidate country in December 1999, and particularly with the 7th EU Harmonisation Package, the Turkish Grand National Assembly (Türk Silahli Kuυυetleri,TBMM) made radical amendments in Law No. 2945 on the MGK and its General Secretariat and in Article 118 of the 1982 Constitution, which provides the MGK with executive powers over the government. The MGK was defined accordingly as a consultative organ which makes decisions on issues related to the development and exercise of the national security policy to be recommended to the government, as foreseen in the 1961 Constitution. The following points ensued from the legal modifications of the period:

- The practice of appointing military members to the Council of Higher Education (Yükseköğretim Kurulu, YÖK), to the Turkish Radio and Television Corporation (Türkiye Radyo ve Televisyon Kurumu, TRT), and to State Security Courts (Devlet Güvenlik Mahkemeleri) was discontinued.
- In the MGK, where decisions depend on a majority consensus, the number of civilian members increased so as to surpass the number of military members.
- For the first time, a civilian secretary general was appointed to the MGK.
- The MGK's Department of Psychological Operations, which showed evidence of active psychological war planning in the period of 28 February, was abolished and its functions were transferred to the office of the prime minister.
- For the first time, military supplies were placed under the control of the Supreme Court of Accounts (Sayıştay).
- Legal regulations were established allowing specific military hospitals to admit a certain ratio of civilian patients to make use of idle capacity.
- Students dismissed from Gülhane Military Medical Academy (Gülhane Askeri Tıp Akademisi, GATA) were given the opportunity of being transferred to other medical schools.
- Prohibited military zones were opened for the purpose of tourism, pending approval by the general staff.
- Private security services were reorganised.
- A new regulation was put in force with Law No. 5201 on the Control of Industrial Organisations Manufacturing Arms, Explosives and Munitions of War. The Law covers all industrial institutions in the private and public sectors working in the manufacture of arms and munitions, and provides them with mechanisms for control.
- In 2004 and, perhaps, for the first time in the history of the Turkish Republic, the share allotted for security expenditures, which had always been the largest budgetary item, was surpassed by the share allotted for the budget of the Ministry of Education. The same was true for the 2005 budget.

From a general point of view, the legal reforms limited the autonomous status of the armed forces within the state and represented the first steps toward the establishment of the primacy of civilian authority. Although various factors contributed to the creation of the reforms, the realisation of the amendments was undoubtedly linked to the requirements of the EU accession process.

The legislative branch establishes laws regulating and defining the security sector, the scope of its authority, and approves related budgetary allowances. It also executes parliamentary oversight and control of the security sector. This chapter studies the laws that were passed during the 22nd Legislative Period in the 3rd Legislative Year[1] (1 October 2004 – 30 September 2005), which have created meaningful results in terms of parliamentary oversight and control of the security sector. The methods of control will be analysed, the function, authority and membership structure of the National Defence Committee will be evaluated, and the role of the Plan and Budget Committee, in the process of the preparation and approval of the defence budget, will be examined. Parliamentary oversight and control of the security sector and orientation of security policy will be discussed, specifically in relation to the democratisation process in Turkey. The level of parliamentary oversight and control attained by the military (the TSK and gendarmerie) and non-military (the police and intelligence agencies to some extent) domains of the security sector will also be studied.

Legislative Power, Defence and Security

In terms of parliamentary oversight and control of the security sector, how might the present condition of our subject matter be evaluated in accordance with modern conceptions of security, that is, with a focus on the security of the individual and society (human security), instead of exclusively on state security? When the position of the Turkish Grand National Assembly as the holder of legislative power is assessed, the general picture can be delineated as follows:

Does the Parliament Discuss and Approve the National Security Policy Document?

The concept of national security is defined in the Frequently Asked Questions section of the Ministry of National Defence's (Milli Savunma Bakanliği) website as follows: The protection of the state's constitutional order, national existence and integrity, all of its political, social, cultural and economic interests and its treaty rights in the international arena, against both internal and external threats.'[2] This document, which formulates the national security strategy in such a way as to en-

---

1 The Turkish Grand National Assembly (TBMM) Rules of Procedure Article 1: 'A legislative period is the time period between two general elections of MPs for the Turkish Grand National Assembly, which lasts five years unless it is extended in acccordance with the Constitution or new elections are called. A legislative year is the period from 1 October to 30 September.' See *TBMM Kanunlar ve Kararlar Müdürlüğü, Türkiye Cumhuriyeti Anayasası ve Türkiye Büyük Millet Meclisi İçtüzüğü* (Ankara, 2005), p. 17. The TBMM Rules of Procedure is also available at http://www.tbmm.gov.tr/ictuzuk.htm

2 See http://www.mgk.gov.tr/sss.html, [Access Date: 01.02.2006].

compass the whole political arena, is recommended to the Council of Ministers upon a ruling by the MGK. It becomes equivalent to a decree by the Council of Ministers following its approval by the latter. Known by the mainstream media as the Red Book/Code, the National Security Policy Document (Milli Güvenlik Siyaseti Belgesi, MGSB), is considered a state document with a degree of secrecy and is not submitted to the members of the TBMM for their perusal.[3] This document bears greater importance than that of any ordinary decree by the Council of Ministers because of the importance attached by the public to it, and the fact that it has the power to shape the political arena as it defines basic internal and external threats as witnessed in the 28 February case.

It cannot be claimed that the parliament has any influence in discussions concerning the concept of security and the determination of related parameters, particularly in terms of the composition and implementation of the National Security Policy Document.

Are Military Expenditures Subject to the Control of the TBMM?

Law No. 4963, dated 30 July 2003, drastically reformed the control of military supplies. It foresaw that control would be chaperoned by the Supreme Court of Accounts, acting on behalf of the TBMM, under the premise that it be kept secret.[4] According to Article 160 of the Constitution and Articles 1 and 28 of Law No. 832 on the Supreme Court of Accounts: 'The Supreme Court of Accounts is responsible for controlling all revenues, expenses and properties of social security institutions and public administrations included in the central administrative budget, in passing final judgment concerning the accounts and transactions of those in charge, and in executing the functions of examination, control and decision given by law on behalf of the Turkish Grand National Assembly.'

Currently, this control also extends to the military. All the revenues, expenses and properties of the military are subject to the control of the Supreme Court of Accounts. In the same vein, the statements which exempted military supplies from control in Article 10 of Law No. 5170 dated 7 May 2004 and in Article 160 of the Constitution, have been abolished. However, this was not reflected in the Law of the Supreme Court of Accounts. The regulation foreseen in Appended Article 12 has yet to be introduced, as the institutions mentioned therein failed to reach an agreement over the statement of concern. The preparations of a new draft for the Law of the Supreme Court of Accounts, which will include this amendment, are underway.

---

3 Ibid.

4 See Appended Article 12 of Law No. 832 on the Supreme Court of Accounts enacted on 21.02.1967 (Appendix: 30.07.2003–4963/7 Art.): 'The control of state properties held by the Armed Forces will be executed following the principles of secrecy necessitated by the national defence services. The principles and methods pertaining to the execution of this control are delineated by a 'secret' regulation prepared by the Ministry of National Defence respecting the opinion of the General Staff and the Supreme Court of Accounts and approved by the Council of Ministers.'

What is the Role of the General Assembly and the Parliamentary Committees in the Process of Preparation and Approval of the Defence Budget? Does the National Defence Committee of the TBMM Have Adequate Authority and Capacity to Influence Defence and Security Policies?

The TBMM's Plan and Budget Committee is responsible for examining the TSK's yearly budget and placing restrictions on its expenditure. However, over time, parliament members have readily left the discussion of military issues to the general staff and the government, and have accepted the information detailed in the draft budget and the minister of National Defence's introductory address as sufficient. As the Ministry of National Defence does not present any information of an adequate technical level on military matters to committee members, and as the members do not request such information, then the defence budgets, have to date, been the most unproblematic budget item. In other words, it comes as a package and is approved almost without change.

The National Defence Committee, which was established on 27 April 1920, is one of the permanent special committees in the TBMM's Rules of Procedure. The present National Defence Committee is composed of members elected at the seventh meeting of the General Assembly of the TBMM on 19 October 2004. These include a chairman, vice chairman, spokesperson and secretary.

The National Defence Committee consists of 24 members, 16 of whom are from the Justice and Development Party (Adalet ve Kalkınma Partisi, AKP) and eight of whom are from the main opposition Republican People's Party (Cumhuriyet Halk Partisi, CHP). Only one committee member is a woman, and she is İnci Özdemir (AKP, Istanbul and the daughter of a soldier). One of the members, Vahit Erdem (AKP, Kırıkkale) is the ex-undersecretary of the Defence Industry. The man who was elected as the first chairman of the committee on 3 December 2002, Ramazan Toprak (AKP, Aksaray), resigned on 8 January 2003, following media revelations about his dismissal from the armed forces by the Supreme Military Council (Yüksek Askeri Şura, YAŞ). Cengiz Kaptanoğlu (AKP, Istanbul, and ship-owner by profession) was subsequently elected Chairman on 5 February 2003.

In the Rules of Procedure, the committee's role is to 'examine the draft laws and law proposals concerning national security, defence, civilian defence and military service.'[5] The draft laws and law proposals that are submitted to the TBMM Chairman on the aforementioned subjects, are transferred to this committee and following debate are conveyed to the General Assembly. Therefore, the committee does not have the authority to examine and control the budgets of the Ministry of National Defence and the Turkish Armed Forces.

The committee does not play a direct role in the formation of defence policy as Turkey's defence policy is, in essence, shaped by the General Staff, the Ministry of Foreign Affairs and the National Security Council (MGK). The role of the MGK in determining defence policy is to accept and recommend the MGSB (in which the priority of internal and external threats is specified) to the government. Members of

---

[5] Rules of Procedure of 5 March 1973; Justification No. 763. See http://www.tbmm.gov.tr/ictuzuk.htm

parliament (MPs) can comment individually on defence policies, and can exercise means of control either together or individually. In Turkish parliamentary law the committee is not authorised to submit a proposal as a legal entity.

The Ministry of National Defence does not seek the opinion of the committee when preparing the draft budget. Committee members can participate in debates pertaining to the budget of the Ministry of National Defence, in the Plan and Budget Committee, and present their opinions or suggestions. During debates on the defence budget for the fiscal year 2005, several members, and in particular Onur Öymen and Birgen Keleş (the representatives of CHP, the chief opposition party), voiced their concerns over restrictions on deputies who are not permitted to criticise the defence budget. Some deputies requested that the secret aspect of military expenditure be removed (Kemal Kılıçdaroğlu, CHP), whilst others asked that the parliament be periodically informed on these issues (Birgen Keleş, CHP). Ironically, the same deputies presented highly ideological addresses supporting the armed forces, specifically in relation to the army's mission to protect secularism. As a case in point, the minister of National Defence makes decisions about the dismissal of army personnel in association with YAŞ, without recourse to higher judicial authorities.

It is wholly apparent that this approach supports the military's adoption of the mission of protecting the qualities of the Republic, on their own initiative. For example, committee member Mustafa Özyürek (CHP, Mersin) claimed that some circles lead campaigns to discredit the army.[6] As the Rules of Procedure imply, the committee can only examine the draft laws and law proposals and, therefore, it does not have input in the procurement of the arms, tools and munitions required by the military. Likewise, the committee neither suggests alternatives nor voices objections over these issues. Whereas in many democratic countries the parliament reviews and/or approves major projects for the procurement of arms, the TBMM has no authority over this issue.

Similarly, the parliament has no authority over the appointment of top officials in the security sector, for example the chief of the general staff and the force commanders, the police chiefs and the chiefs of the intelligence agencies. Likewise, the role of the Defence Committee in relation to issues such as the determination of the physical size of the military bureaucracy, remuneration policies, education, working and living conditions, is limited to negotiating and accepting or refusing the drafts prepared by the government and submitted to the parliament, along with private member's bills, a rare occurrence.

6 For the minutes of the debates of the 2005 budget of the National Defence Ministry at the Plan and Budget Committee see 2005 Mali Yılı Genel ve Katma Bütçe Kanun Tasarıları ile 2003 Mali Yılı Genel ve Katma Bütçe Kesin Hesap Kanunu Tasarılarının Plan ve Bütçe Komisyonu Görüşme Tutanakları, Printed Minutes, pp. 11–35.

Numerical Data Pertaining to the 3rd Legislative Year Defence Budget

Functional Classification of the Allowances of Fiscal Year 2005

In the functional classification of the allowances of fiscal year 2005, the largest share (YTL 22.692.241.681) was allocated to social security and social aid while the share allocated to education (YTL 18.865.285.398) was the second largest, followed by defence (YTL11.035.360.187), and public order and security (YTL 8.509.544.328). The share allocated to health was YTL 6.013.195.823 YTL.

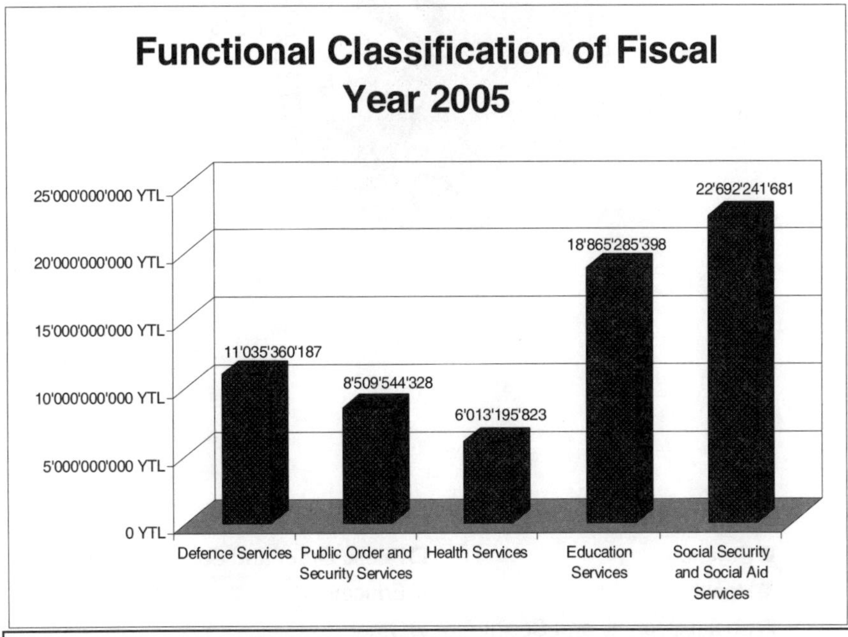

The budget for fiscal year 2005 in terms of institutional allowances shows that the largest share (YTL 14.882.259.500) was allocated to the Ministry of National Education, followed by the Ministry of National Defence (share of YTL 10.977.067.000). The Ministry of Health ranked third (YTL 5.462.974.750). The institutions that received the largest allocations following the aforementioned are the Directorate General of Security, the Gendarmerie General Command, the Ministry of Internal Affairs, the National Intelligence Organisation and the Coast Guard Command. The Ministry of Education received the largest budget allocation in 2005 as well as in 2004. (Source: Naciye Aslıhan Tuncer and Baran Kuşoğlu, 'Eğitim, Sağlık ve Güvenlik Harcamalarının Bütçe Payları,' TBMM Araştırma Servisi Bilgi Notu, October 2005).

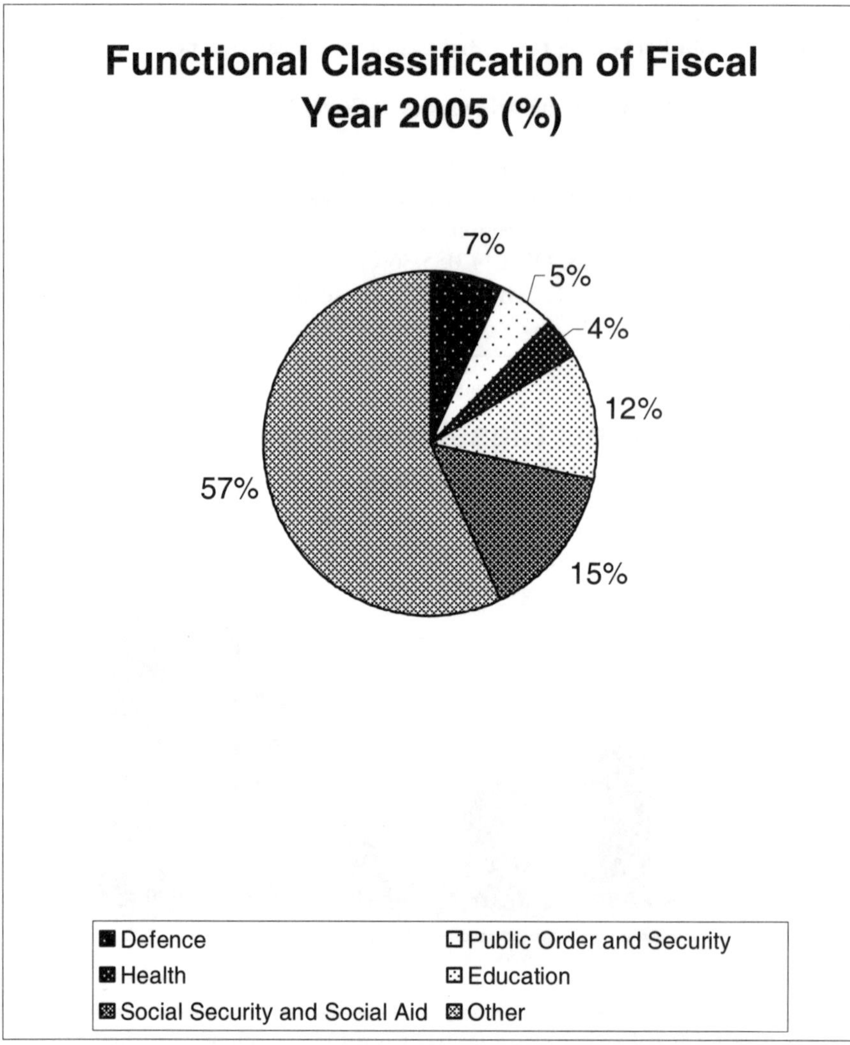
Functional Classification of Fiscal Year 2005 (%)
7%
5%
4%
12%
15%
57%
Defence
Public Order and Security
Health
Education
Social Security and Social Aid
Other

'Budget's Done, Hail to the Army'

The fact that Mustafa Kemal Atatürk, the founder of the Republic of Turkey, was a soldier, and the general acceptance in society that the Turkish Armed Forces is the guardian of the republic, in addition to the fact that military service is embraced by popular culture, have ensured that the budget of the Ministry of National Defence traditionally regarded as falling within the domain of state power, remains outside the realm of politics. With the dominant effect of the prevailing political culture that centres on the idea that the armed forces have come from the bosom of and are identified with the nation and which, therefore, positions the armed forces above TBMM in terms of legislative power, the Ministry of National Defence budget has been treated almost ceremonially ever since the inauguration of the one-party period. Criticizing the budget is seen as akin to criticizing TSK, which is viewed as an institution beyond reproach. This has created a sort of symbolic ceremony wherein, following the approval of the Ministry of National Defence budget in the General Assembly without any debate, all the political parties, either individually or in unison, present expressions of thanksgiving expressing the 'gratitude of TBMM to the Turkish Armed Forces.' This ceremony is known as 'done with the budget, hail to the army.' What is interesting is that this practice that emerged during the one-party period survived until 1989 during the multi-party system, though with some minor interruptions. The transfer of all TSK-related matters from the sacred to the mundane and understanding of the issue as one related to democratic fields of human activity evolved during the second half of the 1980s and, especially, in the first half of the 1990s.

The exact minutes of the 1989 gratitude to the army ceremony are presented below:

VI – THANKS, CONGRATULATIONS AND WISHES

1. The common proposal of the Deputy Chairs of the parliamentary groups of political parties concerning the communication of the feelings of endearment, respect and confidence of the Turkish Grand National Assembly to our armed forces on the occasion of the approval of the Ministry of National Defence budget.

CHAIRMAN – Esteemed members of the parliament; Deputy Chairs of the parliamentary groups of the three political parties represented in the assembly have submitted a note addressed to us. I will have it read out:

'To the Chairman of the Turkish Grand National Assembly,

On the occasion of the debate and approval of the 1989 budget for the Ministry of National Defence by our Grand Assembly, we propose the communication of the feelings of endearment, respect and confidence of the Turkish Grand National Assembly to all the members of our powerful, glorious and heroic armed forces who are the determined guardians of our country and nation and the assurance of our national security.'

Mükerrem Taşçıoğlu

Deputy Chair, Motherland Party Parliamentary Group

Onur Kumbaracıbaşı

Deputy Chair, Social Democratic People's Party Parliamentary Group

Vefa Tanır

Deputy Chair, True Path Party Parliamentary Group

CHAIRMAN – The Chairmanship will act accordingly and inform the valued members of the Turkish Armed Forces. (Applause)

I pray once more for the budget of the Ministry of National Defence to be auspicious.

(Source: TBMM Tutanak Dergisi, Period 18 (1988), Vol. 21, p. 200 [Legislative Year: 2, 19 December 1988, Meeting: 47, Sitting: 21).

Laws Passed in 2005 Concerning Control of the Security Sector

In reviewing the laws that were passed during the 3rd legislative year from 1 October 2004 – 30 September 2005, only two stand out as noteworthy in terms of parliamentary control of the security sector.

The first of these is Law No. 5365 enacted on 16 June 2005, entitled the Law Amending TSK Internal Service Law; TSK Personnel Law; Gülhane Military Medical Academy Law; and the Law Concerning the Establishment and Management of Circulating Capital in Institutions Attached to the Ministry of National Defence and to the Land, Naval and Air Forces.' This law, among other articles, stipulates that military hospitals with circulating capital admit civilian patients at a ratio or number to be determined yearly by the General Staff, up to ten percent of the number of beds and on the condition that vacancies exist. The reason for this amendment is the discovery of a large amount of idle capacity in the 42 military hospitals, as well as the desire to make the technology of those military hospitals available to civilian patients when required. There is no restriction for military personnel using the services of civilian health institutions (either state or private) in cases of emergency. The costs of such medical services will be reimbursed by the armed forces and the Ministry of National Defence (Milli Savunma Bakanlığı, MSB).

Law No. 5397 entitled the Law Concerning the Amendment of Some Laws is also significant. It was introduced on 23 July 2005 after the realisation that the new Code of Criminal Procedures (Ceza Muhakelesi Kanunu, CMK) No. 5271, which was introduced in 2004, did not allow all electronic communications to be tapped by the National Intelligence Organisation (Milli İstihbarat Teşkilatı, MİT) and the police. Accordingly, this law permits a centralised operation of intelligence activities, on a technical level, which is hosted by the Telecommunications Authority. It also regulates the handling of legal interception by the agencies in charge.

Although no concrete steps have been taken concerning the limitation of intelligence activities to the National Intelligence Organisation (MİT), the police and the gendarmerie, to the exclusion of the military, an important development has nevertheless taken place. This concerns the Gendarmerie Intelligence Organisation, which is known to the public as the Gendarmerie Intelligence and Anti-Terror Organisation (Jandarma İstihbarat ve Terörle Mücadele Teşkilatı, JİTEM). JİTEM is thought to be responsible for many illegal acts of violence, which the government has thus far denied even though JİTEM has been referred to in this text as a legal entity, and has been allowed to intercept communications through a court order. Whilst the law allowed police and gendarmerie to tap communications only in cases of organised crime, no such limitation was placed on the MİT.

The gendarmerie's request for authority to intercept telephone calls nationwide was rejected by the Internal Affairs Committee. Meanwhile, three committee members – deputies of the governing party – indicated that they viewed Article 2, which grants the authority of political intelligence to the gendarmerie, as a nerve ending where the military sector and the government meet. They consequently voiced their objections.[7]

Legislative Activities in 2005 Concerning Parliamentary 'Control' of the Security Sector

During the third legislative year of the 22nd period, it was clear that, in terms of parliamentary control of the security sector, deputies preferred to receive written questions and tended to apply this practice most frequently. Very few of the other resources that were made available to parliamentary members by the Rules of Procedure were utilised, such as general debate, parliamentary inquiry, interpellation and parliamentary investigation. During the process of control, vis-à-vis parliamentary questions enquiries concerning the abuse of authority and mistreatment by the gendarmerie were commonly left unanswered.

During this period, only one oral question worthy of note was submitted. In his Motion No. 6/1371 dated 9 December 2004, Hüseyin Güler, member of the CHP (Mersin), requested information from the minister of internal affairs, Abdulkadir Aksu, concerning actions taken against those police officers responsible for preventing teachers from exercising their democratic rights, even though all of them were members of the education union Eğitim-Sen. The Minister of Internal Affairs answered this question at the 73rd meeting on 22 March 2005, stating that Eğitim-Sen members had been taken into custody for attempting to organise a demonstration after making a declaration to the press at the Kadıköy Port Square on 8 December 2004. This action was not permitted, on the grounds that 'it displayed qualities associated with illegal meetings and demonstrations.'

Only eight of the written motions submitted during the third legislative year contributed to the enhancement of parliamentary control of the security sector. One of the motions was submitted by Emin Şirin (Independent, İstanbul) and another by Musa Uzunkaya, (AKP, Samsun). The remaining six were submitted by CHP depu-

---

7 The reason for AKP Kastamonu Deputy Sinan Özkan's reservation is meaningful from this perspective: 'The authority and mission of executing intelligence activities, which has a political aspect to it, is given to the gendarmerie, which has organic relations with the armed forces and operates completely within the principles determined by the armed forces on issues such as ranks, promotion, recruitment and records. If the conditions of our country make it an indispensable necessity for the gendarmerie, who performs the duties of maintaining law and order and security in the provinces, to execute the task of intelligence-gathering, this organisation must first of all be attached to civilian authority on all issues (promotion, rank, compensation, employment of personnel, records, etc.), as is the case in EU member countries, in order to be able to perform this task which has a political aspect, and, subsequently, it must use this authority within its own province, and it must even cooperate with the police as one single security unit (with different fields of responsibility) in the performance of its duties and responsibilities.' See Yalova Deputy Şükrü Önder's, Bazı Kanunlarda Değişiklik Yapılmasına Dair Kanun Teklifi ve İçişleri Komisyonu Raporu (2/546), TBMM Tutanak Dergisi, Period 22 (2005), Vol. 91, p. 8 [Legislative Year: 2, 3 July 2005, Meeting: 47]. The text is also available at http://www.tbmm.gov.tr/develop/owa/tutanak_g_sd.birlesim_baslangic

ties. Questions pertained to the gendarmerie's mistreatment of citizens, the excessive powers granted to the police and gendarmerie by law, the activities and authority of the armed forces, and the contents of the National Security Policy Document. The proposals have been classified as follows:

Questions Concerning Allegations of Mistreatment and the Excessive Authority of the Gendarmerie

The first written question was submitted by Emin Koç (CHP, Yozgat), no. 7/4515 dated 22 December 2004, where Koç addressed the following questions to Abdulkadir Aksu:

1. Is it true that the police and gendarmerie records pertaining to crimes committed before 31 December 1982 have been deleted, in order to protect the rights of the people and protect them from grievances?
2. What is the number of people who will benefit from this deletion?
3. What are the start and end dates of the period covered?
4. How many people have suffered grievances due to erroneous records? How have such grievances been redressed?
5. What kind of system will your Ministry follow henceforth concerning criminals?

Aksu submitted the following response no. 7/45 dated 7 February 2005:

1. The records kept by the police and the gendarmerie in the computer system of the Contraband, Intelligence Operations and Data Collection Department (Kaçakçılık İstihbarat Harekât ve Bilgi Toplama Daire Başkanlığı, as KİHBİ) pertaining to crimes committed before 31 December 1982, have been deleted.
2. Records relating to 111'515 people concerning crimes committed before the aforementioned date have been deleted.
3. The deletion covers records dating from the adoption of the Law on Amnesty in 1974 – 31 December 1982.
4. The deletion of records was deemed appropriate, due to concerns that they might have caused in terms of unnecessarily taking individuals into custody or their use in security investigations. This practice aims at avoiding suffering and grievances by the people.
5. The records that are kept today about people, are based on a request by the judiciary or military authorities and contain a Republic of Turkey Identity Number, correct registry data and are revised in accordance with the juridical decisions taken.'

The second motion was submitted by Musa Uzunkaya (AKP, Samsun) on 3 January 2005, no. 7/4682. Uzunkaya inquired about the degree of truth in allegations that village Imams had been filed by the gendarmerie in the Yuva municipality in Elmalı district, Antalya. Uzunkaya stated that Imams were brought by force to the station under the supervision of soldiers and interrogated about their political views. Uzunkaya asked whether any action had been, or would be taken, against those responsible.

As the question concerning mistreatment and the abuse of authority by the gendarmerie was not answered in due time, it was published in the Received Papers List, which aims at exposing unanswered questions for public view. This action represents the sole sanctioning tool that is capable of being effectively implemented in such cases.

The third question, no. 7/54 of 25 March 2005, was submitted by Ali Kemal Deveciler (CHP, Balıkesir), who was asking Aksu whether an investigation had been launched concerning those responsible for the infringement of the code of secrecy of the Public Prosecutions Office during Operation KOD SÜRGÜ 5, which was undertaken by the Gendarmerie Regiment Commands of Balıkesir. This concerned the actions of the mayor and municipal employees in the Municipality of Pelitköy in the Burhaniye district, which had caused the public employees concern over their loss of credibility. Deveci replied with the question 'was the option of transferring the gendarmerie personnel who had taken it upon themselves to act as police force, prosecutor, judiciary and executive authority ever considered?' Since the motion was not answered within a ten-day period following the fifteen days allocated in the Rules of Procedure, it was published in the Received Papers List.

The fourth question, (no. 7/54, dated 17 May 2005), was submitted by Atilla Kart (CHP, Konya). Kart inquired about the reason for the dismissal of Kenan Güzelgün and Hayati Karadağ from the Gendarmerie's non-commissioned officer vocational college in Konya Ereğli, where the two concerned were first-year students. Kart asked why the students and their families were informed verbally instead of by a written notice. Kart questioned the grounds for the infringement of Article 5 of Law No. 4982 on the Right to Information, and whether this was related to a consideration based on a confidential document or on an event concerning a state secret scenario.

The minister of national defence, Vecdi Gönül, replied by stating that the question should be referred to the Ministry of Internal Affairs. Gönül requested that he be informed of any information obtained by the Ministry. From an administrative standpoint, the gendarmerie is, in fact, attached to the Ministry of Internal Affairs. On 4 June 2005, Minister of Internal Affairs Abdulkadir Aksu, presented the following response: 'The individuals concerned were dismissed from the gendarmerie's non-commissioned officer vocational college based on '[Ref] (b) Article 31, entitled Discipline and Dismissal of the Law and [Ref] (c) Article 61, entitled Conditions of Admission of the Regulations. They were informed of the decision via a written notification. However, the information and documents constituting the grounds for the decision were not disclosed as they were regarded as secret. There was no infringement of Article 5 of Law No. 4982 on the Right to Information, as no claim or application was made concerning the issue.

Motions Concerning the Turkish Armed Forces (TSK)

In his written question no. 7/4473 dated 16 December 2004, Şefik Zengin (CHP, Mersin) addressed the prime minister with the following questions concerning TSK military hospitals, which had been asked to admit civilian patients, within the limits of certain quotas, to the Gülhane Military Medical Academy (GATA) and the Turkish Armed Forces Rehabilitation Centre in Bilkent:

1) What is the numeric data on civilian patients admitted to GATA and what examinations are carried out?
2) What is the social status of civilians serving in GATA and the TSK Rehabilitation Centre?
3) What are the opinions of the doctors working therein about this practice?
4) Will military personnel be given the opportunity of utilising the services of civilian hospitals likewise?'

These questions addressed the concern that the practice of admitting civilian patients to military hospitals created discrimination against military personnel.

Minister of National Defence Vecdi Gönül, replied to these questions on behalf of the prime minister on 25 January 2005, stating that data on the number of people admitted to GATA demonstrated that the hospital was overloaded. The ratio of idle capacity among provincial hospitals was also significant. There was no information provided on the social status of patients in military hospitals as no such records were kept. As a final note, military personnel had already been given the right to utilise civilian hospitals.

This was the only parliamentary question concerning the Turkish Armed Forces (TSK) that was submitted during the third legislative year. Questions pertaining to the National Security Council were similarly lacking.

Parliamentary Questions Concerning the National Security Policy Document

Emin Şirin (Independent, Istanbul), submitted a number of questions, no. 7/4250 dated 25 November 2004. Those of relevance are as follows:

1) Who is responsible for the preparation of the National Security Policy Document, and which law assigns the individual(s) responsible with this authority?
2) What are the criteria involved in the formulation of this document?
3) Will this document be presented to members of parliament (MPs) in a closed sitting of the TBMM either at the stage of preparation or after having been prepared, in order to ensure that the MPs are informed about the document of concern, which is also known as the secret constitution.
4) Does the government share the judgment of the Chief of the General Staff who stated that 'Turkey thinks that countries no longer constitute a threat against one other'?
5) If the principal threat covered by the National Security Policy Document is asymmetric terrorism, is the fight against this kind of terrorism the responsibility of the TSK or the police?
6) It has been reported in the media, that the issue of reactionary and separatist activities is the priority target in the National Security Policy Document, which appears to be already in force. Has the desired result against reactionary activities been achieved? What is the actual status of each of the 18 recommendations submitted by the MGK on 28 February?

Şirin's questions were published in the Received Papers List pending a formal response. In fact, Şirin had also submitted a question on the same subject in the second legislative year, again addressing the prime minister, but the question remained unanswered.

The second question, no. 7/4507, concerning the National Security Policy Document was submitted by MP Ali Rıza Gülçiçek (CHP, Istanbul) on 22 December 2004. Based on a report published in Hürriyet, he asked whether the National Security Policy Document defined Alevism as a dangerous sect, and pressed the prime minister on the subject. The Minister of National Defence, Vecdi Gönül, responded on behalf of the prime minister on 25 January 2005, arguing that the document did not include 'any points that could bring our Alevi citizens under suspicion.'

Conclusion

As the legislative authority, the TBMM executes oversight and control over the security sector. When 2005 is examined in its entirety, the parliament's position was not effective in the enactment of legislation and in the utilisation of methods of control. This reinforces the fact that it failed to play a meaningful role in the formation of defence and security policies, and as such, in the resolution of threats and appointments at the highest echelons of the security sector. In addition, the control of military supplies and expenditures by the Supreme Court of Accounts, acting on behalf of the TBMM, has yet to be realised.

Likewise, parliament has no direct influence over the share of the budget allocated for the procurement of arms. The purchase of arms exceeding a certain amount is not even submitted for approval by the parliament. Therefore, in the case of the defence budget, the representatives of the nation who should be involved in the allotment of the country's resources, do not/cannot perform an essential political function. There is no data pertaining to 2005 which shows that the parliament achieved effective oversight of the security sector, particularly along the lines of accounting for its decisions or in establishing transparent methodologies.

A related 'detail' was uncovered by the press in 2005: the TBMM's external security is provided by the Battalion of the Parliament attached to the Presidential Guard Regiment, while its presence is unrelated to security requirements. The article entitled 'A More Civilian Outlook,' by Resul Tosun (AKP, Tokat),[8] triggered reactions by the General Staff who described it as 'individual raving.'[9] This happened to be a tell-tale incident revealing the hindrances incurred and reactions provoked by deputies, when they proposed to modify issues that are unbefitting to the civilian character of the assembly.

8 Resul Tosun, 'Daha sivil bir görüntü,' Yeni Şafak, 7 December, 2005.

9 'Genelkurmay'dan tepki: Muhafız alayı teklifi hezeyan,' Radikal, 9 December, 2005.

Government

Zühtü Arslan[*]

Background: National Security and Government

In democratic countries, and in accordance with the principle of democratic accountability, governments are responsible for the formulation and the implementation of security policies. Governments must take measures to ensure security and peace in the country. They are also responsible for formulating and implementing policies to defend the country against external threats. Governments will accept technical support from public servants and experts whilst formulating security and defence policies, however, political decision-making and responsibility are ultimately vested in the government.

On the legal side, the constitution and the rule of law empower governments to determine, change and implement security and defence policies. Thus, according to Article 117 of the 1982 Constitution: 'the Council of Ministers is accountable to the Turkish Grand National Assembly (Türkiye Büyük Millet Meclisi, TBMM) for ensuring national security and preparing the armed forces for national defence.' Moreover, Article 118 of the Constitution, together with the amendment of 3 October 2001, defines the duty of the National Security Council (Milli Güvenlik Kurulu, MGK) in the following way: to submit the recommendations for determination and implementation of national security policy of the state to the Council of Ministers. Decisions regarding the measures mandated by the MGK to protect the existence and independence of the state, the integrity of the country and the peace and security of the public are evaluated by the Council of Ministers. Therefore, the Council of Ministers has the authority to make decisions related to national security and to implement them accordingly. However, despite this constitutional principle, relations between civil and military organisations are different in practice. The military sector is far more effective in determining national security policy.

The broader definition of national security in Turkey, apart from its classical and technical meanings, is to strengthen the autonomy/independence of the military sector and to improve its monitoring of the government through the MGK. According to Article 2 of Law No. 2945 on the MGK and the MGK general secretariat, 'national security' implies: '... preservation and protection of the constitutional order of the state, its national existence, integrity, all of its political, social, cultural and economic interests and contractual rights in the international arena, against the

---

* Associate Prof., Police Academy, Faculty of Security Sciences, Lecturer of Constitutional Law

collective internal and external threats.' This definition highlights that the MGK is responsible for the preservation of Turkey's social, political and economic interests, a point which was criticised by the Commission of the European Union in its regular Progress Report on Turkey. According to the report, the rule of law provides Turkey's National Security Council with 'a broad definition of national security, which — depending on interpretation — could cover almost any policy field.'[1]

The clear restrictions on the government and consequential empowerment of the MGK have been the characteristic state of play since the council's inception. During discussions in parliament which established the MGK law in 1962, the deputy prime minister of the time, Turhan Feyzioğlu, clearly indicated how the limits of national security policy were to be understood. According to Feyzioğlu, 'national security policy — not only in Turkey but also in all other countries — cannot focus exclusively on military policy. The council also deals with issues such as health, trade, education, industry, agriculture, transportation and public works policies.'[2]

To impart such an indeterminate interpretation to national security, invariably allows the armed forces to function as an ideological state instrument, through its involvement in issues not directly related to national security. In brief, this nonspecific idea of national security extends the use of controlling power by the MGK. The constitutional provisions which authorise the government to formulate and implement national security policies therefore exist solely on paper.

Steps Taken by the Government on National Security Issues During the EU Harmonisation Process

The Justice and Development Party (Adalet ve Kalkınma Partisi, AKP), which has been in power since 2002, attaches great importance to its relationship with the European Union (EU), and identifies full EU membership as its primary objective. Important steps have been taken to ensure democratic control of the security sector and democratisation of the political system, especially prior to the commencement of negotiations between the two bodies on 3 October 2005. The initiatives that were introduced at the time of the 2001 constitutional amendment, reinforced the preeminence of democratic political government.

The 2001 amendment to the constitution, modified the structure and functions of the National Security Council by increasing the number of civilian members and declaring that the decisions of the council were thereafter to be considered as recommendations. The legal amendments of 2003 restricted the authority of the MGK General Secretariat and lowered its budget and number of units. It was decided that the secretary general should be a civilian and that the MGK would convene once every two months. These amendments endeavoured to mould the MGK into an advisory organisation consisting of more civilian members. In fact, the

---

1 See Commission of the European Communities, Turkey: 2004 Progress Report, Brussels, 6 October 2004, SEC (2004) 1201, p.18; Turkey: 2005 Progress Report, Brussels, 9 November 2005, SEC (2005) 1426, p.14.

2 Millet Meclisi Tutanak Dergisi, Period 1 (1962), Volume: 8, p.190-191. Hikmet Özdemir, Rejim ve Asker, (İstanbul: Afa Yayıncılık, 1989), p.109-110.

changes were effective not only in theory but also in practice, and in August 2005 the MGK appointed its first civilian secretary general.

Numerous steps were also taken to reduce the influence of the military sector over the judiciary and other civilian authorities. Following the decisions of the European Court of Human Rights against Turkey, a constitutional amendment banning military judges from serving in the State Security Courts (Devlet Güvenlik Mahkemeleri, DGM), went into effect. In 2004, these courts were abolished altogether. Moreover, the authority of the MGK General Secretariat and armed forces to appoint members to the Council of Higher Education (Yükseköğretim Kurulu, YÖK) and the Higher Council of Radio and Television (Radyo Televizyon Üst Kurulu, RTÜK) were abolished.

One of the most important measures to provide parliamentary oversight of the military sector was taken during the 2004 constitutional amendment, with the repeal of the provision that exempts the expenditure of the armed forces from the inspection of the Supreme Court of Accounts (Sayıştay).

While judged as positive initiatives, these amendments were, nonetheless, deemed insufficient in terms of establishing the necessary criteria for Turkey's full membership to the EU. In its progress reports, the EU noted that the direct and indirect impact of the armed forces on civilian politics was still an issue.

The National Security Policy Document and Government

The National Security Policy Document (Milli Güvenlik Siyaseti Belgesi, MGSB) is one of the most discussed, but least known documents, on civil-military relations in Turkey. Little is known about the preparation methods and content of the document which has been labelled as the secret constitution, deep constitution, red constitution and red book. Moreover, the legal basis of this document is a controversial issue and some assert that its legal basis is established in Clause 2 of Article 2 of the Law on the National Security Council and its General Secretariat. In this law, national security policy is defined as, 'a policy which includes the principles related to internal, external and defence-type operations determined by the Council of Ministers, shaped by the MGK, with the objective of providing national security and attaining national goals.'

Therefore, the MGSB is a document incorporating principles determined by the council of ministers in accordance with the opinions of the MGK. Here, the term shows that the framework of this document is determined by MGK. The logical result is that the Council of Ministers is not permitted to act outside this framework and has the authority of evaluation within its limits. The only official information about the scope and method of preparation of this document is stated in the FAQ section of the MGK General Secretariat's website: 'The MGSB is prepared by the National Security Council General Secretariat, in coordination with the related ministries, institutions and organisations, and drafted for submission to the National Security Council. When the document is agreed by the National Security Council, it is submitted to the Council of Ministers for approval. Once that approval is finalised, it is named as the National Security Policy Document and becomes effective. The implementation of the MGSB is vested in the Council of Ministers.' The MGSB is defined as a 'document of the Council of Ministers,'[3] even though it is the MGK General Secretariat and not the council which is responsible for the preparation of the document. In addition, neither Article 118 of the Constitution nor any article of law on the MGK grants such authority to the MGK General Secretariat.

The question of the government's contribution to the document's preparation is significant in terms of the principle of the civilian authority's supremacy. The preparation of the most recent MGSB, and its leakage to the press following an MGK meeting, was controversial. The 2005 Progress Report on Turkey, which was prepared by the Commission of the European Union, states that the government participated in the preparation process by a letter. According to this report, the prime minister sent a letter to the National Security Council's General Secretariat in January 2005 stressing that it was the government's responsibility to maintain national security before the parliament. It was subsequently requested that the MGSB be shortened and kept to the essentials.[4] According to the news, the government and the MGK held opposing views in relation to the content of the document. Hence, related debates were postponed in the MGK meeting of 23 August 2005. In the meeting of 24 October 2005, the document was accepted with the inclusion of various issues by the general staff.

Both the leaking of the document to the press and the content of the MGK-approved document resulted in a debate. It was a cause of irritation to the government that the document had surfaced in the media despite its classification as confidential. The Deputy Prime Minister and Foreign Minister Abdullah Gül gave instructions to the National Intelligence Organisation to find those responsible. When the Commander of the Land Forces stated, 'Beware of where the MGSB has been published after Monday's MGK meeting,' journalists, military figures and politicians alike began to argue about who was responsible for leaking the document.

The content of the MGSB was discussed almost as much as its leakage to the press. According to the news, the new document confirmed that the armed forces were responsible for protecting the domestic order of the country and stated that while right-wing extremism was no longer a threat, fundamentalists and separatists were 'threatening factors.' In addition it stated that Greece's tendency to extend the limits of its territorial waters was a casus belli. What must be underlined is that the Turkish Armed Forces (Türk Silahlı Kuvvetleri, TSK), was commissioned with the task of safeguarding domestic order/security whenever necessary and this is what ultimately defined its role and position within the system.

When these expressions from the document were evaluated, together with Article 35 of the TSK Internal Service Law, the legitimacy of the guardianship of the armed forces over the political and administrative systems became wholly ap-

---

3 In the official website of MGK General Secretariat, the MGSB is defined as follows: 'the National Security Policy Document is a document of the Council of Ministers that includes the essentials regarding internal and external security and defence policies to be pursued in accordance with the national interests and national objectives of the Turkish Republic.' See http://www.mgk.gov.tr/sss.html

4 European Commission, Turkey: 2005 Progress Report, Brussels, 9 November 2005, SEC (2005) 1426, p.14.

parent. In the EU's 2005 Progress Report, attention was drawn both directly and indirectly to the issue of guardianship. The government was also advised to heed the EU's warning about the lack of a pre-eminent civilian authority. In the final paragraph of the civil-military relations section of the report, the EU's counsel read as follows: 'Turkey should work toward greater accountability and transparency in the conduct of security affairs in line with Member States' best practices. In particular, statements by the military should only concern military, defence and security matters and should only be made under the authority of the government, whilst the civilian authorities should fully exercise their supervisory functions, in particular with regard to the formulation of the national security strategy and its implementation, and including relations with neighbouring countries.'[5]

The Supreme Military Council and the Government

One of the fundamental structures which has strengthened the institutional and political autonomy of the Turkish Armed Forces is the Supreme Military Council (Yüksek Askeri Şura, YAŞ). The YAŞ was established to act only in peacetime, in accordance with Law No. 1612, during the period of the interim regime that was launched by the military memorandum (muhtıra) of 12 March 1971. According to the Law on the Establishment and Duties of the Supreme Military Council, the members of the council are the prime minister, the chief of the general staff, the minister of national defence, force commanders, the commander of the armed forces, the commander of the gendarmerie, the commander of the navy and the generals and admirals of the armed forces. The YAŞ meets bi-annually under the chairmanship of the prime minister. In addition to its legal duties, it decides on promotion, retirement and disciplinary measures regarding armed forces personnel.[6] Article 2 of Law No. 1612 stipulates that: the YAŞ members' votes and evaluative notes of the armed forces' staff carry equal weight in promotions. In addition, according to Article 5 of this law, decisions shall be taken by a simple majority vote by the members. In the event of a tie, the chairman's vote shall be the decisive one. Elections shall be open-ballot unless otherwise decided.

It is well known that since the establishment of the first AKP Government, there have been debates between the government and the military during YAŞ meetings. It is significant that the prime minister and the minister of national defence submitted opposing annotations regarding the discharge of military personnel as a

---

5 Ibid, p. 14-15.

6 Article 3 of Law No. 1612 on the duties of YAŞ reads: 'a) to deliver an opinion regarding review when necessary and determination of the military strategic concept prepared by the General Staff b) to deliver an opinion regarding the objectives and main program of the armed forces c) to deliver an opinion about laws, regulations and directives regarding the armed forces d) to deliver an opinion regarding the armed forces when the prime minister, the commander of the general staff and the minister of national defence requires it e) to conduct other duties in other issues.' See Resmi Gazete (Official Gazette) dated 26 July 1972.

result of disciplinary problems. These annotations were also included in the regular meetings of 2005.

At the YAŞ meetings of 1-4 August 2005 and on 1 December 2005, 15 personnel, which included four TSK members, were expelled due to undisciplined behaviour. The prime minister and the minister of national defence submitted opposing comments on this decision. The fact that the YAŞ — which is constitutionally under the government's authority — takes disciplinary measures against the prime minister's vote may be in line with the law on the YAŞ. Nonetheless, concerns should be raised about democratic oversight and the ability of the YAŞ to manoeuvre independently of the government. Moreover, despite the fact that the YAŞ meetings are held under the chairmanship of the prime minister, the chief of the general staff sits next to the prime minister creating an impression that both civilian and military authorities are on an equal footing.

According to Article 125 of the constitution, the YAŞ decisions are not subject to judicial review. This demonstrates that one of the major organisations within the security sector is exempt from judicial monitoring. However, one of the essential rules of law is that any action and function of the administration be subject to judicial monitoring on which the higher courts agree. The chairmen of the High Court of Appeals, the Council of State (Danıştay) and the Constitutional Court (Anayasa Mahkemesi), have stated that in light of the fact that the YAŞ decisions are not subject to judicial monitoring, constitutional provisions stand in contradiction to the concept of a state based on the rule of law. On the 137th anniversary of the foundation of the Council of State, which is the superior court for administrative justice, its Chairman, Ender Çetinkaya, stated: 'It is obvious that the exemption of the YAŞ decisions and some administrative acts from judicial monitoring are in contradiction of the principle of the rule of law of our Republic.'[7] President Ahment Necdet Sezer, who is the chief executive and who chairs the council of ministers if required, affirmed in his speech as chairman of the Constitutional Court, that the YAŞ decisions should be subject to judicial monitoring.[8]

---

7 The President of the High Court of Appeals—in his speech on the opening of the 2004 judicial year—also stated that Article 125/2 of the Constitution should be repealed. See the speeches in www.danistay.gov.tr and www.yargitay.gov.tr

8 Ahmet Necdet Sezer emphasised the state of law in his speech at the inauguration ceremony of the symposium organised for the 38th Anniversary of the Establishment of the Constitutional Court and he also criticised the constitutional provisions that inhibit the judgement of administrative actions and processes such as YAŞ decisions and the president's individual acts. According to Sezer; restrictions in the constitution for the control of administrative judgment damages the principle of state of law. See Anayasa Yargısı, Volume: 17 (Ankara, 2000), p. 9.

Important Events of 2005

The Southeast Issue and the Government's Policy of Balance

In 2005, the government attempted to pursue a balanced policy on the southeast issue. In relation to the terrorist dimension, Prime Minister Erdoğan tried to isolate the PKK from politics, in addition to organisations that were allegedly linked to the PKK (i.e. ROJ TV in Denmark). Security measures were considered and efforts were made to resolve sociological matters. In stressing the integrity of the nation and the state, the prime minister rejected separatist policies. Erdoğan also explored solutions by conducting open discussions with members of the intelligentsia.

A group of academics, Non-Governmental Organisation (NGO) leaders, columnists and others, met with the prime minister on 10 August 2005, to discuss the possibility of initiating a new policy on the southeast question. At this meeting, the prime minister stated that, 'from our point of view, the Kurdish issue and so many other matters are problems of democratisation for us.' This position was reiterated during the prime minister's visit to Diyarbakır. Initial debate centred on the controversial issue of 'supra' and 'sub' [national] identities. In his speeches, the prime minister stressed that being a citizen of the Republic of Turkey is the 'supra' [national] identity (üst kimlik) and that different ethnic groups function within their own cultures as 'sub' [national] identities (alt kimlik). To strike a balance, the prime minister pledged his dedication to fight terrorism and emphasised that the integrity of the nation and the state would not be neglected. Concurrently, it was reiterated that regressions in the area of democratisation would not be tolerated, and that terrorist organisations would not be permitted to exploit the newly-found freedoms. The prime minister spoke of the importance of the struggle against terrorism in his speech at the 10th EU-Mediterranean Summit on 28 November 2005. Attention was directed to the obligation of inhibiting attempts by terrorist organisations to exploit the freedoms of democracy: 'freedom of speech, thought and the press cannot be permitted to become a shelter for terrorist organisations that try to gain undue advantage by creating an atmosphere of fear and by killing innocent people arbitrarily. The advocates of terrorism, who agitate for freedom of speech for their supporters, should not forget that they disregard the right to life of the people they shoot dead.' Considering the timing of this speech, the prime minister seemed to be directing his message to the prime minister of Denmark, who allows ROJ TV to broadcast in Denmark, as well as towards any other country that allegedly offered support to the PKK.

The spontaneous reactions and particular sensitivities exhibited by other state institutions at the time, might explain the government's adoption of a balanced policy. The prime minister's views on citizenship in the Republic of Turkey as a 'supra' [national] identity, and on the concept of constitutional citizenship (anayasal vatandaşlık), were criticised by opposition parties and became subject to 'fine-tuning' by both the MGK and the president. The MGK's statement of 23 August 2005, included a reminder to the effect that the duty of any government is 'preservation of the independence and integrity of the nation and unity of the country.' The president addressed the matter of identity in his New Year's message of 2005.

Şemdinli Events and the Government

The bombing of a bookstore in Şemdinli, in the Hakkari province on 9 November 2005, which resulted in the deaths of two people, created widespread public suspicion that a Susurluk-type scandal was behind the incident. The bookstore was owned by an alleged former PKK member and was presumably bombed by members of the Gendarmerie Intelligence Organisation (Jandarma İstihbarat Teşkilatı, JİT[9]). The event became a source of tension in Şemdinli, in the wider region and throughout the entire country. On 15 November, the demonstrations in Şemdinli broadened to Yüksekova where three people were killed and 16 wounded. One day later in Hakkari, a group of demonstrators confronted the police and as a result 20 people were wounded, including five policemen. On 21 November 2005, Prime Minister Erdoğan went to Hakkari, Şemdinli and Yüksekova to visit the bombed bookstore and he insisted that the damages would be compensated. One week after the prime minister's visit to the region, two JİT non-commissioned officers were arrested under suspicion of involvement in the incidents in Şemdinli.

During the judgement process, the government maintained a stern stance and pledged to launch an unbiased investigation. The prime minister, along with other ministers, stressed that Turkey was a state governed by the rule of law, that no suspect would be protected, that the criminals would be punished, and that no such incidents aimed at the separation of state and society would be tolerated. The government also vowed to conduct a thorough follow-up investigation in the event of any similar actions in the future. In his speech to the parliament, Erdoğan declared, 'There are those who try to change the illegal into the legal. (…) Some like foggy weather. I had the opportunity to witness this phenomenon. But we will clear this fog. A state governed by rule of law shall not have grey areas.' In a further demonstration of its resolve, the government sent two civil inspectors to the region and changes were made to the governorship of Hakkari and the district governorships of Yüksekova and Şemdinli.

On 25 November 2005, the ministers of foreign and internal affairs, the minister of justice, the chief of the general staff, the commander of the armed forces and the commander of the gendarmerie held a meeting on terrorism, upon the invitation of the prime minister. According to the official announcement, 'it was underlined that state organisations, NGOs and everyone bearing responsibility should contribute to the judicial process to proceed properly.'

Controversies on Security Issues within the Government

It is well known that members of the cabinet do not always agree with each other and that differences of opinion arise at times. The nationalist and security hard-liner position of the Minister of Justice, Cemil Çiçek, toward the Armenian issue and the

---

9 The unit in charge of intelligence in the gendarmerie is referred to as the 'Intelligence Presidency of the Gendarmerie General Command' according to Article 2 of Law No. 5397 dated 3 July 2005 and Supplementary Article 5 of the Law on the Establishment, Duties and Jurisdiction of Gendarmerie.

amendment of the Anti-Terror Law (Terörle Mücadele Kanunu, TMK), is not shared by the prime minister who adopts a more liberal stance. This is probably in response to the restrictive approach of the minister of justice. In his speech to the General Assembly of the TBMM on 24 May 2005, the minister of justice characterised the conference planned for 25-27 May 2005 at Bosphorus University, entitled Ottoman Armenians in the Period of the Fall of the Empire, as 'a dagger thrust into the back of the Turkish nation.' Çiçek concluded his speech with the following words: 'If it were within my jurisdiction, I would begin prosecution procedures immediately. I wish that as minister of justice, I had not relinquished my authority to prosecute. I wonder what the YÖK will do now. I wonder what Bosphorus University will do now. I wonder, we wonder, our nation wonders. We must put an end to this cycle of irresponsibility, insincerity, treason, insult and propaganda, conducted against this nation by those who carry this nation's identity cards. The conscience of this nation is perturbed.'[10]

On the day after Çiçek's speech, Bosphorus University announced that the conference had been postponed. However, when it was rescheduled to take place in September, the Istanbul Administrative Court No. 4 banned the conference. The prime minister criticised the decision of the court, stating that the opinions of the minister of justice were his own and that differing viewpoints needed to be expressed. The minister of foreign affairs stated that he would have attended the conference if his agenda had allowed for it. As an interesting and ironic consequence, the minister of justice stated that the Administrative Court No. 4 had not banned the conference but merely changed its venue. Ultimately, however, the Armenian conference was held in Bilgi University from 24-25 September 2005, with the unwitting support of the government.

Another controversial point concerned the Code of Criminal Procedure (Ceza Muhakemesi Kanunu, CMK) which was approved on 4 December 2004 and introduced on 1 June 2005. The CMK shifted some of the security forces authority to public prosecutors. It was criticised by the Ministry of Internal Affairs and the General Directorate of Security, who claimed that it would turn Turkey into 'a paradise for criminals.' In response, Çiçek sternly reprimanded the police: 'Do not keep criticising the law, just implement it!' He added that the security forces should perform under new conditions and renounce old methods. The Minister of Internal Affairs, Abdulkadir Aksu, thus responded by saying: 'Our security forces are not making excuses. They are striving to perfect their performance.' Aksu also stated that laws which introduce fundamental changes might cause confusion and that uncertainty could be resolved by circulars from the relevant ministries and through on-site training and seminars.

Following these discussions, several amendments were made to the Code of Criminal Procedures No. 5353 dated 25 May 2005, to the effect that in cases where delay is unfavourable and where the public prosecutor cannot be reached, police officers are authorised to search and confiscate upon the written authorisation of the

---

10 Minutes of the General Assembly, TBMM, 22nd Period, 3rd Legislative Year, 101st Sitting (24 May 2005), p.18. See. www.tbmm.gov.tr

police superintendent (CMK, Article 119/1, 127/1). Thus, as a result of this policy balance, matters discussed by the ministries were effectively settled.

Finally, the amendment to the TMK, which was included in the agenda from the second half of 2005, is of significance. The TSK authorities claimed that they had limited resources to confront terrorism. As a result, they asked for a review of the TMK, which is in line with the model of the British anti-terrorism law. Consequently, under the aegis of the ministry of justice, the commission drafted a new anti-terror law in September 2005. However, the text of this draft was not released to the public. According to critics in the media, the draft included ratification of the formerly repealed Article 8, concerning 'imprisonment for a minimum of one and a maximum of three years for proclamations, demonstrations or marches aiming to separate the integrity of the nation and state of the Republic of Turkey.' Critics also expressed fears that once these broad definitions were left open to interpretation they could represent 'the sword of Damocles' against freedom of speech.[11]

With the TMK amendment, differences of opinion arose between government members. While the minister of justice defended the use of restrictive amendments, the prime minister and the minister of foreign affairs maintained that setbacks in the democratisation process and conformity to the Copenhagen criteria were unthinkable.

The Security Sector's Share of the Budget

The security sector's share of the budget, and especially that of the defence sector, is almost always an issue for debate. It dropped to second place compared with other public sectors for the first time in 2004, and this trend continued in the 2005 and 2006 budgets. Shown in the following tables are the appropriations of the security sector in the 2005 budget, the increase and decrease of expenditures and the budgetary distribution, as per organisation.

When the treasury allowance of YTL 7'652'237'552 is extracted, the consolidated central government budget reaches YTL 174'339'990'202. The budget appropriation to law enforcement and the security services stands at a total of YTL 21'136'727'894.

---

[11] Editor's Note: The sword of Damocles is a reference to the legend of Damocles. It represents 'the insecurity of those with great power due to the possibility of that power being taken away suddenly, or, more generally, any feeling of impending doom,' as cited in the online wikipedia resource, see http://en.wikipedia.org/wiki/Damocles

Security in the Work Plan of the 59th Cabinet

On 19 March 2002, Prime Minister Erdoğan underlined that the TBMM government programme put the security sector in a priviledged position. 'Distinguished members of parliament, in parallel with the contributions of Turkey to NATO, have taken its deserved place in the European Security and Defence Identity (ESDI) which was established within the framework of the European Defence Strategy in the first AKP cabinet. Our government gives priority to the development of facilities required for the activities of our armed forces — which play an important role in preventing possible threats and in ensuring regional and global peace, stability and security — in international organisations, especially NATO and the United Nations. In this context, I would like to emphasise our understanding of the concept of security. Security is the essential and crucial function of a state. When the geographical position of Turkey and regional developments are considered, our government is not going to be insensitive to security and defence issues. Whatever is required for our security and defence, will be fulfilled by our government.'

Table 1: The Share and Increase of 'Defence Services' and 'Public Order and Security Services' in the 2004 and 2005 Budgets.[12]

Functions	2004 Annual Budget YTL	Share %	2005 Annual Budget YTL	Share %	Increase %
Defence Services	10'044'014'591	6.7	11'035'360'187	7.1	10
Public Order and Security Services	7'309'703'987	4.9	8'494'259'328	5.5	16
Total	17'353'718'768	11.6	19'529'649'515	12.6	12.53

[12] It is useful to specify the service units included in Defence Services and Public Order and Security Services shown in the budget. Defence Services includes: military defence, civil defence, external military aid, research and development regarding defence, non-classified defence. Public Order and Security Services include: security, fire prevention, courts, prison management, research and development regarding public order and security and non-classified public order and security services. See: Directorate General of Budget and Fiscal Control http://www.bumko.gov.tr/proje/proje1/fonksinif.mht

Table 2: Defence and Security Expenditures in the Non-interest Budget as per 15 December 2005

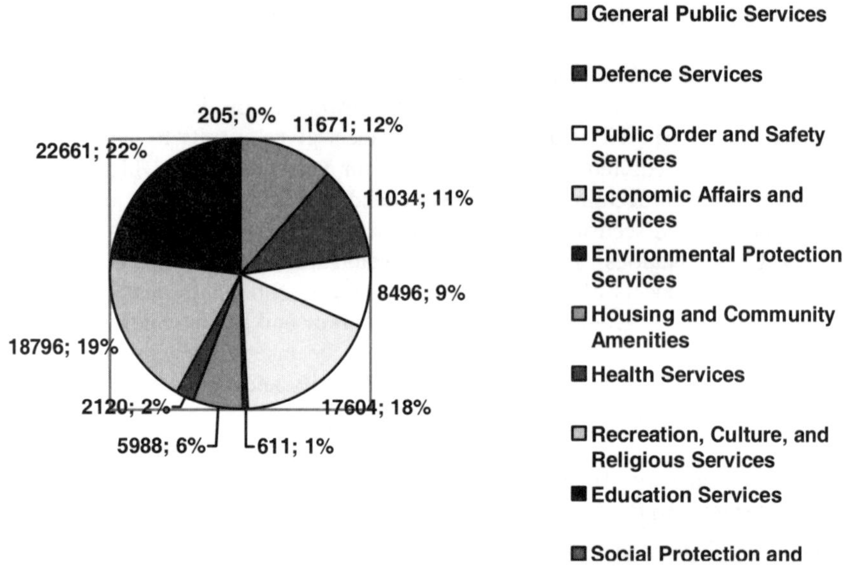

Reference: Republic Of Turkey General Directorate of Budget and Fiscal Control, http://www.bumko.gov.tr/chart/data.htm
Reference: Republic Of Turkey General Directorate of Budget and Fiscal Control, http://www.bumko.gov.tr

Table 3: Appropriations and Rates for Defence Services and Public Order and Safety Services in the 2006 Central Government Budget

	Budget Appropriation (YTL)	Rate %
Defence Services	11'926'587'182	6.84
Public Order and Security Services	9'210'140'712	5.28
Total	21'136'727'894	12.12

Table 4: Appropriations Made for the Institutions of the Security and Defence Sector in the 2004, 2005, 2006 Budgets

Institutions	2004 (TL)	2005 (YTL)	2006 (YTL)
Ministry of National Defence	10'889'575'000'000'000	10'976'455'418	11'877'533'000
Undersecretariat of the Defence Industry		38'009'366	23'440'000
Gendarmerie General Command	2'279'671'000'000'000	2'371'673'385	2'571'561'000
Coast Guard Command	162'360'000'000'000	174'658'857	194'459'000
General Directorate of Security	3'370'350'000'000'000	4'236'257'718	4'804'713'000
Undersecretariat of the National Intelligence Organisation	301'000'000'000'000	296'108'500	352'570'000
National Security Council General Secretariat	9'768'152'000'000	11'739'574	10'971'000

National Security Council

Gencer Özcan[*]

Historical Background

Founded on 24 April 1933, the Higher Defence Council (Yüksek Müdafaa Meclisi, YMM), was a predecessor of the current National Security Council (Milli Güvenlik Kurulu, MGK). The YMM was organised under the chairmanship of the prime minister, or the president if he/she so wished, with the participation of the chief of the general staff and the members of the council of ministers. Its activities were regulated by decree and its mission was specified as 'developing and coordinating the national security policy of the state of the Turkish Republic.'

The YMM was later replaced by the National Defence Higher Council (Milli Savunma Yüksek Kurulu, MSYK), which was founded on 3 June 1949. The MSYK consisted of the prime minister as chairman, ministers proposed by the prime minister and elected by the cabinet, the minister of defence, the chief of the general staff, and the president, who was automatically considered a member of the MSYK. With the council of ministers decree of 1 July 1949, the following ministers became council members: internal affairs, foreign affairs, finance, public works, economy, commerce, transportation, and agriculture and enterprises. The same decree stipulated that the commander of the Turkish Armed Forces (Türk Silahi Kuvvetleri, TSK) would only be a member of the council in times of war. The MSYK was given the following duties: 'To prepare the essentials of the National Defence Policy that will be followed by the government, define the national defence duties and missions that are to be carried out by governmental organisations, private institutions/enterprises, citizens, and to prepare the Total National Mobility Plan in times of peace and to ensure its full application whenever necessary.'

With the 1961 Constitution, the MSYK was transformed into the MGK, and as such, the council was elevated into a constitutional institution. Article 111 of the 1961 Constitution redefined the MGK's structure and duties, and stipulated that the council's members should consist of ministers, which would be defined by law, the chief of the general staff and various armed forces representatives. In this way, the influence of the military wing was considerably increased in the MGK. According to this Article, the MGK's mission is to 'declare the necessary basic concepts concerning national security to the Cabinet, to assist in the decision-making process, and to provide coordination.' Following the Memorandum of 12 March, Article 111 was

* Associate Professor, Yıldız Technical University, Faculty of Economics and Administrative Sciences, Department of Political Science and International Relations.

amended on 20 September 1971. The changes stipulated that the members should be the 'commanding officers of the army' instead of 'representatives of various armed forces.' Additionally, the council would 'give advice on the necessary basic concepts to the cabinet in the national security decision making process, and provide for coordination.' The MGK's decisions were thus strengthened and took on the form of 'recommendations.'

After the regulations of 12 September 1980, the MGK's authority and duties were expanded, and the military wing within the MGK gained a determining influence over the council's decisions.

The Situation post-1980

The MGK is situated at the centre of the state security structure, which was reviewed by the military administration between 1980 and 1983, in order to legalise the preventive measures to be taken against domestic and foreign threats. With the 1982 Constitution and Law No. 2945 of the National Security Council and National Security Council General Secretariat, dated 9 November 1983, the MGK's authorities and duties, as well as its decision-making process, were strengthened in a way that increased the military's influence. A strong MGK General Secretariat was established under the supervision of the general staff, with expansive authority and many opportunities for the staff. Through the establishment of other legal regulations during the post-coup period, the institution's central role within the governmental mechanism was strengthened even further. On the one hand, the military had the opportunity of exerting influence over developments that were regarded as national security problems during the regular monthly MGK meetings, and, on the other hand, they managed to play a key role in the preparation of the National Security Policy Document (Milli Güvenlik Siyaseti Belgesi - MGSB), regarded by some observers as the 'Secret Constitution' or the 'god of laws.' In this way, the MGK has functioned as a military mechanism within the government for the past twenty years, supported by a General Secretariat which has been granted with expansive authority and a broad national security approach.

The MGK's structure, authority and duties are generally defined by Article 118 of the 1982 Constitution. According to this article, the MGK consists of the president, the prime minister, the chief of the general staff, the ministers of national defence, internal affairs, foreign affairs, commanders of the land, naval and air forces and the gendarmerie. The distribution of the council members demonstrates that a careful balance has been established between the military and the politicians. During times of coalition governments, possible conflicts between ministers from different political parties increases the military wing's chances of having its views accepted. Similarly, when the support of the president has been assured, the balance is tipped in favour of the military. Article 118 also regulates the MGK's position in reference to the council of ministers: the MGK 'declares its views to the Council of Ministers, concerning the decisions to be made regarding the determination and implementation of the national security policy and the coordination this requires,' and in return, 'the measures that the council deems necessary are taken as a priority consideration by the council of ministers.' The fact that the cabinet has to 'take [the decisions of the MGK] into consideration as a priority,' is an important indicator of the way the political regime functions, and shows that the council has been raised to the same level as that of the Council of Ministers.

MGK after the Helsinki Summit of 1999

After the European Union (EU) Helsinki Summit of 1999, regulations were made to shape Turkey's national security policies in a more democratic way. The legal regulations directly concerning the MGK can be analysed under three main headings. The first and foremost of these regulations is the amendment to Article 118 which made the MGK into a constitutional institution. According to the amendment dated 3 October 2001, the MGK consists of 'the prime minister, the chief of the general staff, deputy prime ministers, ministers of justice, national defence, internal affairs, foreign affairs, land, naval and air forces commanders and the commander of gendarmerie, under the lead of the president.' This allows most of the members to come from the government wing. Again, with this amendment, it was stipulated that the MGK's decisions must be 'evaluated' by the Cabinet and not 'taken into consideration as a priority.' The amendments also stressed the fact that the MGK's decisions possess the character of a 'recommendation.'

The second regulation refers to the amendments made to the Law of National Security Council and the National Security Council General Secretariat, No. 2945, on 7 August 2003, in order to make it compliant with the constitution. With these amendments, it was stipulated that the general secretary be appointed by the prime minister and that the vast authorities of the council be limited. Law No. 2945 gave the General Secretariat the authorities of following and controlling the practices and regulating, directing and coordinating activities. This made the MGK General Secretariat into a unit that functioned as the memory and action centre of the government, where intelligence coming from all governmental institutions was gathered single-handedly. The secretary general, whose duty was to provide continuity in the government, became the 'brain' of the MGK – 'the secret Prime Minister.'[1] The General Secretariat's authority to 'follow and control the practices,' implemented as per MGK decisions, was transferred to the deputy prime minister. As part of the same amendment, the council meetings are to be held every two months instead of every month, and personnel with a non-military background can now be appointed as secretary general.

The third amendment refers to the abolition of the secret regulation defining the duties and working principles of the MGK's General Secretariat, through a new regulation dated 29 December 2003. An important step towards transparency of the political regime, is the fact that this regulation – which permitted the General Secretariat to function as an autonomous executive power, through the extraordinary authorities it gave to the secretary general – was abolished. Decision No. 6688, which detailed the restructuring of the General Secretariat and the redefining of its duties, authority and staff, was narrowed. The regulation was accepted by the Council of

---

1 Ali Bayramoğlu, 'Asker ve Siyaset,' Birikim, August – September 2002, p. 44.

Ministers on 29 December, and the organic ties between the organisation and the general staff were severed.[2] Additionally, the number of intermediary service units was decreased from eleven to six. This led to the closure of units, such as the 'Community Relations Presidency' (Toplumla İlişkiler Başkanlığı, TİB), which had been responsible for conducting psychological operations.

In 2005, reflections of the changes made to the MGK's duties and authority, as part of the EU compliance laws, were observed in different practices. The demilitarisation/transparency efforts, aimed to make the MGK an institution that no longer exerted military power over the political regime. However, the military wing continued to deliver messages about sensitive subjects to the government during its meetings and, as was seen in the August meeting, continued to issue warnings. Nonetheless, with the increase of civilian members at the MGK and its ongoing structural changes, the council lost, to a certain extent, its use as a platform in which the wishes of the military were legalised. This generated claims that the function had been transferred to the Supreme Military Council (Yüksek Askeri Şuri, YAŞ).

The differences in the declaration that was released following the Supreme Military Council meeting of 30 November 2004, both in their content and format, justify the claims of the MGK's function being transferred to the YAŞ.' According to the declaration, during the YAŞ meeting, 'the threats and risks in the region were analysed and the surrounding countries' disarmament and modernisation activities were compared; in this context, the status of the important project concerning the TSK's maintenance of the power of deterrence was assessed, the importance of the allocation of necessary resources for the realisation of these projects was stressed, the status quo in Iraq, the impact of possible further developments on Turkey, and the related preventive measures taken were discussed. An assessment of the fight against terrorism and fundamentalism was made, the issue of the total fight against terror in all areas was discussed, fundamentalist activities against the secular republic were evaluated and the preventive measures that should be taken were reviewed. In addition, information was presented about the establishment activities of the Centre of Excellence for Defence Against Terrorism, that was proposed to NATO by Turkey.'[3] During the YAŞ meeting of 1 December 2005, Prime Minister Erdoğan was informed in detail by the general staff's Operations and Intelligence Units about increasing activities made by the fundamentalists against the secular republic in recent times. A presentation was also made by the general staff's Planning and Prin-

2 Journalist Murat Yetkin wrote that with the decrease in some service units and the number of consultants, the number of retired officers working in the General Secretariat will also decrease, contributing to the demilitarisation of the organisation. 'Right now, there is a staff of around 950 people. According to statistics, most of the personnel are of civilian origin but when you take out the secretaries and office clerks, most of the remaining civilians are retired officers. The government plans a soft transfer of the excess personnel to the General Staff or other government agencies.' Murat Yetkin, 'Bayramdan Sonra Sivil MGK Geliyor,' Radikal, 28 November 2003.

3 'Açıklamaya Dikkat,' Hürriyet, 1 November, 2004.

ciples Department concerning the latest developments in the Middle East, the status quo in Iraq and the impact of possible developments on Turkey.[4]

MGK Activities in 2005

In 2004, important developments concerning the National Security Council were observed. These developments were observed, in the process of redefining both the MGK and the General Secretariat's duties and authority, as part of the legal amendments made in order to meet the Copenhagen Criteria. Firstly, as a result of the changes made in Law No. 2945, the working mechanisms of the MGK that had been in effect since 1983, were changed as of December 2004. Secondly, the amendments concerning the changes to the authority, duties and administration of the MGK General Secretariat went into effect in the second half of the year. As of August 2004, the General Secretariat was led by a non-military administrator and coverage of the 1984 secret regulation, defining the working principles of the organisation, was greatly narrowed. With the release of a new regulation, the General Secretariat commenced a process of visible demilitarisation and transparency. As part of the same amendment, the MGK representatives in institutions such as the RTÜK, the TRT and the YÖK, were retracted. The review of the National Security Document (2005) should also be evaluated as part of these developments.

Agenda Headlines

Generally, the most important external security issues that are discussed by the council involve Cyprus, Greece and developments in Iraq, however, domestic security is also discussed in great detail. Topics include public order problems such as separatist terrorism, fundamentalist threats and petty theft, reasons for domestic migration and the problems it causes in big cities, the implementation of a national science and technology strategy, 'the effective use of water resources' and 'energy security.' Moreover, after 'separatism' and 'fundamentalism' were classified as top priority threats in the 1990s, issues involving domestic security have more frequently made their way onto the council's agenda.

The evaluation of issues that were included in the MGK agenda in 2005 commenced with the regular meeting held in the last days of 2004. In the meeting of 30 December 2004, the EU summit decisions of 16-17 December were assessed, and the two reports prepared by the Ministry of Foreign Affairs and the EU General Secretariat were opened for discussion. The organisation of a schedule for full membership negotiations was a positive development. However, the 'removal of some negative aspects' and 'proceeding with the negotiations in a way that is not discriminating to Turkey, that is unconditional and that is sustainable' were stressed as a precondition. Concerning the PKK/KONGRA GEL activities, that are classified as part of domestic security issues, it was stated that after the organisation declared a supposed restart of its attacks in the region, it failed to be as effective as it aimed to

---

4 Uğur Ergan, 'En Az İhraç,' Hürriyet, 2 November 2005.

be. In relation to foreign security issues, developments such as the Iraqi elections of late January and the killing of the Baghdad Embassy security staff were discussed.

The first meeting of 2005 was held on 25 February. The declaration that followed showed that the council gave priority to the status quo after Iraq's elections. It is interesting to note the importance given in the declaration to the participation by all, in the creation of the new constitution for national integrity in Iraq. Also, of significance is the appeal in the declaration to international opinion, for the recognition of the existence of the Republic of Northern Cyprus after it held elections. The declaration also stressed that a 'detailed evaluation was made concerning the level reached in the defence industry and how much of the modernisation needs of the Turkish Armed Forces it meets, as well as the measures required with regard to the development of a sufficient national defence industry.'

The second meeting scheduled for 25 April was held on 18 April because of the presidential elections in the KKTC, and the Armenian Genocide claims that returned to the spotlight on the 90th anniversary (24 April). Topics of discussion included foreign security issues such as EU relations, Iraq's transition period and problems with the United States. Soft security issues were also discussed, such as international migration to Turkey, domestic migration and the status of the energy sector. The minister of energy and natural resources, Hilmi Güler, was invited to give a presentation at the meeting.

It was interesting to note that following the meeting, besides the Cyprus issue, the emphasis was placed on soft security issues. 'The reasons for domestic migration and the problems it causes in big cities' were highlighted and a call was made for the immediate implementation of solutions to problems faced by cities experiencing population growth and decline due to migration. It was also pointed out that 'a detailed evaluation of the country's energy security has been developed, together with the status quo of the sector, its potential, energy planning for the future, as well as the required investment demands and restructuring work.'

The MGK meeting in June received much attention due to the debates concerning the MGSB update. Despite the news that the MGSB would be finalised in the meeting held on 21 June, its completion had to be postponed due to a lack of consensus between the military sector and the government.

The review of the MGSB, in light of new threat assessments, caught the public's attention in August. Due to new reports stating that the preparations for a new document were in their final stage, that would prioritise asymmetrical threat factors because of the increase in PKK assaults in the months of summer, the debates about who should determine threat priorities, and in which way, intensified again. The news based on general staff resources about the fundamentalist threat maintaining top priority was criticised by circles close to the government. Yet despite these debates, the MGSB was not included in the agenda of the August meeting.

A report prepared by the MGK General Secretariat, following the increase in PKK attacks, was distributed to council members prior to the August meeting. The report strives to answer the question why the PKK's terrorist activities, that were at a relatively low level after 1999, rose again in May 2005. The rise in question was related to a variety of reasons, such as the PKK's internal struggles due to inactivity and leadership conflict, and whether developments in the Middle East, especially in

Iraq, and the relations between Turkey with the EU were about to take a new turn. The report proposed new legal measures to be taken in order to eliminate problems faced by the security forces in their fight against terror, but stated that Turkey should refrain from measures, such as a state of emergency, that would harm the EU [membership] process.[5] The increase in PKK attacks, as well as the debates about the 'main identity' that began in the month of August, made the Kurdish problem the most important item on the agenda of the 23 August meeting.

The military members brought to the attention of the council the use of the expression the 'Kurdish problem', in speeches made by Prime Minister Erdoğan prior to his meeting with a number of opinion leaders on 10 August and in Diyarbakır on 12 August. During the meeting, the military members asked the prime minister questions such as 'what exactly does he mean by the Kurdish problem, what kind of a plan does he have for its resolution, and what does he mean by a democratic republic?.' The declaration following the 23 August meeting, was assessed as a 'post-modern' warning by the military to the government, because of its content and the format used.[6] Article 2 of the declaration justifies these assessments. Statements such as 'the main idea behind the founding philosophy of the Republic of Turkey, or protecting the independence and integrity of the nation, the indivisibility of the country, and protecting the republic that is a democratic, secular and social state governed by the rule of law' reflect a well-known style that is frequently used by the armed forces:

> 'In compliance with the main idea behind the founding philosophy of the Republic of Turkey, the characteristics of the Republic have been defined in the constitution; protecting the independence and integrity of the nation, the indivisibility of the country, and protecting the republic that is a democratic, secular and social state governed by the rule of law; providing the peace, welfare and happiness for the society without discriminating against people based on language, religion, ethnic background and gender, were listed as the main purposes and duties of the state. The first and foremost purpose of the governments of the republic is to achieve this aim by carrying out the duties as stipulated in the constitution. There is no doubt that this aim will be achieved by protecting the independence and integrity of the nation and the indivisibility of the country'.

---

5 Murat Yetkin, 'Konuyu Kim Açar?,' Radikal, 15 August 2005.

6 Yetkin claimed that President Ahmet Necdet Sezer 'earmarked almost every sentence' of the declaration. Murat Yetkin, 'Geniş Açıdan Bakınca,' Radikal, 25 August 2005. During the press conference he held on 26 August 2005, AKP Deputy Secretary General Dengir Mir Mehmet Fırat answered a question about whether the declaration was a warning in the following manner: 'The party reads it just like a declaration that was released by a constitutional institution. No one doubts the validity of the constitution. We know, just like everybody else knows, what the characteristics of the state are. Beside, there is no definition, nor forcing in this declaration. (...) Therefore, what we have here is a suggestion. We have not seen and do not see anything of a warning nature in the MGK declaration.'

The public also showed great interest in the MGK meeting of 24 October, which took place with the participation of the new force commanders which were appointed on 30 August, namely the commander of the Naval Forces, Yener Karahanoğlu, and Air Force commander, General Faruk Cömert. The fact that the meeting coincided with the start of negotiations with the EU regarding full membership is significant. In the meeting of 24 October, the council pointed out that the water issue was the casus belli of the future in the Middle East, and discussed the necessary measures to avoid shortages in Turkey over the next 20-30 years. The council's inclusion of matters such as energy security and water problems in its agenda was also noteworthy.[7] The fact that a 'soft security' issue, such as water shortage, was analysed not only from the point of view of the problems it causes in relations with Syria and Iraq, but also from a technical viewpoint, was seen as a novelty belonging to MGK General Secretary Alpogan's time in office.

Furthermore, during the 24 October meeting there was also news about the work starting on a new assessment of Northern Iraq and 'terrorism', with the approval of President Ahmet Necdet Sezer. Entitled the East and Southeast Action Plan, this work, that was to be a part of the agenda of the December meeting, is as a result of this request by Sezer.[8] The increase in PKK assaults and the Şemdinli incidents that started on 9 November were the main points on the agenda of the 29 December meeting. Indeed, it was interesting to note that the issues that were debated – such as developments in Iraq, the fight against the PKK, internal migration and the economic problems stemming from it – were always somehow related to the problem of the Kurdish separatist movement. In the words of a journalist, the MGK is not concerned about the citizens of Rize migrating to İstanbul, but about the citizens of Diyarbakır, Şırnak, Hakkari and Batman migrating to İstanbul, Mersin, Bursa or Ankara.[9] During the meeting, the East and Southeast Action Plan that was prepared for Iraq, and the Kurdish separatist movement problem were presented to the government. However, in the declaration that followed, no information was given about whether the plan had been discussed by the Council. The Action Plan stipulated that a separate secretariat be established within the Anti Terror Higher Council (Terörle

---

7 The Minister of Energy and Natural Resources Hilmi Güler and the Director General of the State Hydraulic Works (Devlet Su Işleri, DSI) Veysel Eroğlu made a presentation during the MGK meeting and in their presentation, they pointed out that Turkey is not a water-rich country and can therefore have problems in the future due to the increase in the population. In order to avoid water problems, it was decided that all relevant government institutions will coordinate and follow a long-term strategy, and it was foreseen that in the target year 2023 'a water capacity of 38.5 billion cubic meters be reached for drinking, daily usage and industry.' In the declaration following the meeting, it was stressed that 'in order to ensure an efficient use of our water resources; for the irrigation of agricultural areas, meeting the water needs of the cities and the industry, for the complete usage of the technical and economic hydroelectric production potential, the measures to be taken until the year 2023 and the immediate completion of dams on border-crossing waters' were discussed.

8 Murat Yetkin, 'Irak ve Kürt federasyonu MGK'da,' Radikal, 25 December 2005.

9 Murat Yetkin, '29 Aralık MGK'sının Önemi,' Radikal, 31 December 2005.

Mücadele Yüksek Kurulu, TMYK), responsible for coordination between government bodies. In accordance with the proposal, it was decided that the TMYK, led by Deputy Prime Minister Abdullah Gül, should be responsible for the coordination of the general staff, the ministries of internal affairs, foreign affairs, justice, national intelligence organisation and other related ministries, especially in matters concerning the Kurdish problem.[10]

Updating the MGSB

The updating of the MGSB was on the agenda throughout the year, and became the most important item of the 24 October meeting. During the MGK meeting in June 2004, it was decided to make an amendment to the document, which was last updated in 2001. The prospect of a change for the first time since the AKP had come to power, led to a struggle between the centres that shared political power and this was often clearly seen by the public. The threats and how they would be prioritised in the document, became the most controversial points. The document was expected to be shorter than its predecessors and it was foreseen that the section containing the external threats against national security would undergo a change. The forecasts that were based on information from government resources, took into consideration developments such as Syria no longer posing a threat, increasing concerns about the future of Iraq, and Iran's attempts to gain nuclear power. In the MGSB draft prepared by the MGK General Secretariat, the main reason for the update was defined as the global terrorism as part of asymmetrical threat currently within Turkey in the form of bomb attacks in Istanbul.[11]

There are two changes worth mentioning in the preparation process of the MGSB. The first is the simplification of the document from its original 90 pages to 25 pages, upon the request of Prime Minister Erdoğan. The second involves the suggestions concerning changes to the tone of the document in the update prepared by the Ministry of Foreign Affairs. In news based on explanations made by the ministry' officials, the new tone was defined as follows: We put together a simple text. Instead of vague expressions, we made clear definitions of Turkey's benefits, and the threats. We expressed clearly the measures that could be taken against the threats. We wrote in clear terms what should be done and why. We put an end to military logic. There was no use of vague expressions that could be freely interpreted by anyone, such as 'various measures will be taken', 'whatever is necessary will be done' and 'is open to threats.'[12] The MGSB did not include comments about the impossibility of opening the Heybeliada Clergy School in the final draft, as offi-

---

10 Murat Yetkin, 'PKK'yla Mücadelede Yeni Patron,' Radikal, 4 January 2006. The Council that made it once again into the spotlight, following Chief of Staff Özkök's statements about the necessity of establishing a new institution that worked under the prime minister and provided coordination between security circles and the government, held its first meeting in September 2005. Murat Yetkin, 'Terörle Mücadelenin Başına Dışişleri Bakanı,' Radikal, 27 September 2005.

11 Fikret Bila, 'Milli Güvenlik Siyaset Belgesi,' Milliyet, 25 November 2004.

12 Hilal Köylü, 'Patrikhane Tehdit Değil,' Radikal, December 28, 2004.

cials had stated such details were unnecessary in a document containing the general guidelines of the national security policy.[13]

The most important change to the document is the removal of the definition of the extreme right wing movement as a threat. It is interesting to note, however, that along with separatist terrorism and fundamentalist activities, the extreme left wing also kept its place in the document as a threat factor.[14] In the new 25-page document that was handed over to the cabinet, separatism, fundamentalism and the extreme left wing remained as priority threats, whereas the extreme right was no longer classified as a threat, but defined only as a factor that should be monitored. In the chapter on terrorism, that has apparently led to controversy between the government and the military, the expression 'terrorist organisations that employ religious motifs' was used. As part of this definition, organisations such as Al-Qaida and Hezbollah were openly named.[15]

In the document, Cyprus was defined as one of the foundation blocks of Turkey's security in the Eastern Mediterranean, and the protection of rights and advantages in Cyprus was stressed as a priority target. As part of the asymmetrical threat assessment, that was employed for the first time in the MGSB, problems such as international terrorism, drug and human trafficking and factors such as weapons of mass destruction, were also taken into consideration. In addition to the issues that have an influence on public order, problems of an economic nature such as unemployment, the imbalance in wealth distribution and differences in the level of development amongst the regions were also listed. Another feature of importance was the mention once again of the water problem, which was noted as a possible casus belli in the Middle East in the future. The water problem is now officially recorded as a matter of national security.[16] Additionally, there was news that the new MGSB had kept the section containing the expression 'the use of the army against domestic security threats and their authority to take over the administration when deemed necessary in order to eliminate the threats'.[17]

---

13 Deniz Zeyrek, 'Gerekirse Asker Yine 'Göreve', Radikal, 28 October 2005.

14 In the Domestic Security Strategy Document, domestic threat was defined as 'a threat the roots and provoking resources of which are within the borders and abroad, consisting of extreme left, extreme right, separatist and minority activities, aiming at abolishing the government system defined by the Constitution and replacing it with a system compliant with its own ideology and dividing the country through dangers that disturb the domestic security.' Ali Sali, 'MGSB'de İlk Tehdit Yine Terör,' Yeni Şafak, 24 October 2005.

15 Turan Yılmaz, 'Aşırı Sağ Artık Tehdit Değil,' Hürriyet, 25 October 2005. This article by Turan Yılmaz caused severe reactions, especially in the government circles. Foreign Minister Gül declared that he instructed MİT to find those responsible for leaking the document and defined the leakage as irresponsibility. Ertuğrul Özkök, 'O Haber Niye Hürriyet'e 'Sızdırıldı',' Hürriyet, 1 November 2005.

16 After the water problem was assessed as a security problem, TBMM Foreign Affairs Committee Chair Mehmet Dülger complained that the parliament was not sufficiently informed. Kemal Saydamer, 'Dülger: Water Strategy Vital To Turkey,' Turkish Daily News, 30 October 2005.

17 Deniz Zeyrek, 'Gerekirse Asker Yine 'Göreve,' Radikal, 28 October 2005.

In the section concerning external security, the threats were not placed in any priority order, and only the influence of neighbouring countries on Turkey's security strategy was assessed. In the assessment concerning Greece, it was pointed out that no compromise should be made and that a decisive policy should be followed over the issue of the ownership of the islands, which remains a controversial point. It was stated in the document that the possibility of Greece extending its territorial waters beyond six miles was unacceptable for Turkey, and that such a possibility would be considered as an act of war.[18] This statement caused tension in relations with Greece and Prime Minister Karamanlis, who postponed his visit to Turkey once again. Government circles reacted severely to the MGSB's changes being leaked to the press. Prime Minister Erdoğan claimed that the leak came from some MGK General Secretariat employees during the preparation process,[19] whereas Minister of Foreign Affairs Gül stated that the leak was handled irresponsibly, and that MİT had been instructed to find the persons responsible for the incident. Chief of the General Staff Özkök argued that journalists should have more sense than to print everything they receive.[20]

During the revision process, subjects that had been kept under a veil of secrecy were opened to debate, albeit in a limited fashion, and the government and the armed forces effectively tried to mobilise the public. As a result of this, discussions that had once remained on the MGK's agenda were now brought onto centre stage in the public arena and topics that had been considered taboo became publicly discussed political issues. The debate in the second half of 2004 concerning the opening of the Fener Greek Patriarchate and Clergy School is a case in point. Although the general staff assessed the opening of the Heybeliada Clergy School as an objectionable development during its update to the MGSB,[21] the judgement prepared by the Ministry of Foreign Affairs stated that the patriarchate did not pose a threat.[22] In what was reportedly the view of government circles, news articles stated that the Clergy School would be permitted to open if 'more Turkish teachers are sent to Komotini [Greece] Celâl Bayar High School in return.'[23]

A problem emerges, however, when the developments concerning the MGSB are taken as a whole, and despite some positive developments in the preparation process of the documents. In Western democracies, similar documents prepared by the government and the security sector, state the necessary precautions and the gen-

---

18 Barkın Şık, 'Aşırı Sağ Tehdit Değil,' Milliyet, 26 October 2005. According to news based on MGK sources, it is interesting to note that some conditions were put on the table in order to remove the casus belli decision that led to debates in the last days of October. 'As long as the Greek Parliament's 1994 decision about '19 May 1919 being the genocide day of the Pontus Greeks', its decision of '25 April 1996 recognizing the Armenian genocide', and its 1998 decision about '14 September 1922 being the day of Asia Minor genocide' are not abolished, the decision of the Turkish parliament cannot be abolished either.' Ibid.

19 Ergun Aksoy, 'Kırmızı Kitabı Kim Medyaya Sızdırdı?. Erdoğan: MGK Genel Sekreterliği Çalışanları,' Sabah, 2 November 2005.

20 'Özkök Cool Towards YÖK Stance,' Turkish Daily News, 31 October 2005.

21 Uğur Ergan, 'Heybeli Açılmasın,' Hürriyet, 28 April 2005.

22 Hilal Köylü, 'Patrikhane Tehdit Değil,' Radikal, 28 November 2004.

23 'Güvenlik Anayasası Masada,' Cumhuriyet, 21 June 2005.

eral action plan for national security as general principles. Whereas in Turkey, when we take into consideration the preparation process, content and political impact of the MGSB, we see that the document is designed predominantly by the military sector in a way that limits the authorities of various executive and legislative organs. During the preparation phase, the General Staff and the MGK General Secretariat play a predominant role, as opposed to the Council of Ministers which should be in the centre of the process. When the content is analysed, political decisions and problems that should be left to the responsibility of governments and the oversight of parliaments, are taken out of the political process with the justification that they are issues of state security. As for the political impact, the MGSB is seen as a document that analyses problems that could be evaluated and handled differently by different governments, in a way that is binding not only for the government of the time but also for other governments that will come to power at a later date. This effect has the result of burdening governments with the responsibility of decisions for which they are not liable.

In this manner, regular political processes are interrupted for the sake of 'protecting state secrets,' and in the execution phase, decisions that were accepted by one government are imposed upon another in the name of continuity of state administration. These procedures do not comply with the established practices of modern western democracies. As long as the preparation, implementation and revision of the MGSB are unchanged, steps taken for the demilitarisation of the MGK and the MGK General Secretariat will remain superficial.

MGK General Secretariat

Although the General Secretariat was established directly under the prime minister, prior to the radical amendments in August 2003, its personnel were military. According to Law No. 2945, the General Secretariat was given duties and authorities which include the follow-up and supervision of practices, organisation, guidance and coordination of activities. Article 9 gave the General Secretariat the duty of informing the president, the prime minister and the MGK when an MGK decision did not become a council of ministers decision. The secretariat, whose duties included carrying out all kinds of study, research, analysis and assessment, and presenting these along with recommendations to the president, prime minister and the National Security Council', practically had the first say in putting the agenda together. Clause (b) of Article 13 states that the secretariat was responsible for cooperation, follow-up and supervision of practices, organisation, guidance and coordination of activities in the implementation of the council's decisions. In Article 14, the secretariat was authorised on behalf of the president, prime minister and the MGK, in the carrying out, follow-up, control and supervision of the duties as defined in the previous article. Article 15 states that the secretary is appointed from among TSK members, and promoted to the rank of general/vice admiral 'by the council of ministers decision, upon a letter of recommendation by the chief of the general staff and the proposal of the prime minister.'

The duties of the National Security Council General Secretariat were regulated by a secret by-law – i.e., 'the MGK General Secretariat By-Law that went into effect on 10 February 1984, with the Cabinet Decision Number 84/776.' Article 17 defines the MGK General Secretariat's duties and authorities concerning the MGK decisions that are adopted as cabinet decisions as the following: 'It follows and controls the practices. It undertakes all necessary actions for the realisation of activities and procedures in compliance with the decision's content. When necessary, it enters into cooperation with ministries, institutions and organisations, and carries out organisational, guidance and coordination activities between ministries, institutions and organisations in the name of the prime minister.' The most striking aspect of the by-law is the authority it gives to the General Secretariat for conducting psychological operations. The authorities of the Community Relations Presidency (Toplumla İlişkiler Başkanlığı,- TİB), which was part of the General Secretariat, clarify how the community should be guided in compliance with national security objectives. The TİB defines all kinds of psychological operational demands nationwide, prepares long/mid/short-term plans in accordance with national policies and objectives, ensures that the plans develop according to the necessities brought about by daily circumstances, carries out the secretary general's Approved Psychological Operations Plan, follows up and controls the practices of the executive units and carries out coordination duties, as stipulated by the by-law.[24]

The restructuring of the General Secretariat in a way that pursued and controlled all aspects of social and political life is significant. The National Security Office within the General Secretariat consists of the following under-secretariats: Special Politics, Social Politics, Political Economy, Education and Culture, Politics and Science and Technology Politics. Furthermore, the establishment of sub-units under the Community Relations Presidency, such as a Print Media, Audiovisual Media and Internet under-secretariats, and most interesting of all, a Non-Governmental Organisations' under-secretariat can be seen as examples of an attempt to adapt Cold-War centred activities to the post-Cold War era.

MGK General Secretariat after the Legal Amendments of 7 August 2003

The secret by-law regulating the working principles of the MGK General Secretariat was abolished in January 2004. The new by-law, regulating the authorities of the General Secretariat by a single article, brought about important limitations to its authority and radical changes to its organisational structure. The most striking of these changes involved the termination of the psychological operations authority within the organisation. The by-law of 32 articles, abolished the most controversial units of the General Secretariat, such as national security policy, community relations, information gathering, and total defence civil services. The by-law was announced in the Official Gazette (Resmi Gazette), and unlike its predecessor it represented a significant change.

Following the changes in the legal authority and definition of the duties and organisational structure of the General Secretariat, it was observed that some of the organisation's functions were transferred to other institutions. For instance, the unit

---

24 'Milli Güvenlik Kurulu Genel Sekreterliği Yönetmeliği,' Humanite, December 2003 – January 2004, p.147.

named the community relations presidency, which was responsible for psychological operations, was put under the general staff, and a series of news articles published in November 2004 contain interesting details about this transfer of duties. According to the news, and shortly before Yiğit Alpogan's appointment as secretary general, a type of 'spring clean' took place, in which the security profiles of unfavourable persons and institutions, and psychological operation plans were destroyed, so that when the new secretary general took over the post, he found the institution devoid of these profiles and plans.'[25] Whether the intelligence profiles were actually destroyed continued to dominate discussions over the following days. A commentary, referring to the possibility of the transfer of the archives in question to another institution, pointed out that in order to understand where they went, it was necessary to answer the question of which government institution the staff of Board of Community Relations and the Board of Intelligence Gathering Group were transferred to.[26]

The appointment of Ambassador Yiğit Alpogan, through his transfer from the Embassy in Athens to the head of the General Secretariat in August 2004, represents an important step towards the demilitarisation of the security apparatus in accordance with the EU compliance process. When taken into consideration with the legal amendments made in the same vein, the appointment of an official who was not a member of the general staff, demonstrates that an institution of key importance in the development of national security policies enjoys a more harmonious relation with governments. In statements made by Alpogan in the days following his appointment, signs supporting this view were observed. Alpogan stressed that he started his job with a wish to make the General Secretariat's Organisation 'an institution that produces policies and strategies and serves its 'clients', i.e. its members. He also stated that in matters of national security he would direct the organisation towards following developments abroad, as opposed to following just domestic developments.[27] As an organisation with an intensive interest in mundane security matters, this statement is a sign that under the Alpogan administration, the organisation would no longer be concerned with daily political problems, but would instead inaugurate a new era by focusing its attention abroad. How exactly this tendency might reflect on the organisation's practices can only be understood by future developments.

The Alpogan administration gave special importance to press relations, providing interviews to journalists specialising in security issues, organising periodical press conferences and informing the public of its non-confidential activities. Alpogan's first step towards 'transparency' was the press conference organised on 30 December 2004. The conference was a first after the founding of the High Defence Council in 1933, and was widely covered in the press. During the conference, Alpogan defined his view of the General Secretariat Organisation as follows: 'We see our organisation as an institution that carries out long-term projects on domestic and foreign threats and one that generates ideas. Our main task is to serve the higher

---

[25] Deniz Zeyrek ve Serkan Demirtaş, 'Yeni MGK'dan İlk İcraat: Fişler İmha,' Radikal, 18 November 2004.

[26] Murat Yetkin, 'Kuşlar Nereye Uçtu?,' Radikal, 19 November 2004.

[27] 'Sivil MGK Perdelerini Açıyor,' Hürriyet, 25 November 2004.

council consisting of military and civilian members. We provide the decision makers with the necessary material and our work ends there. The MGK is not an executive institution, but a consultative one.'

In the press conference, Alpogan stressed that some of the controversial activities from the past would no longer be carried out, and that activities such as work concerning Turks living abroad had been terminated.[28] In his statements, Alpogan stated that a total of 294 people were employed by the organisation, of which 279 were civilians and 15 were uniformed soldiers. The community relations presidency had been abolished, its duties were taken away from the General Secretariat and, in its place, a think-tank had been established. On the other hand, it was also noted that although Alpogan gave the number of uniformed soldiers in his statement, he refrained from saying that 71 percent of the undersecretaries were retired soldiers.[29] The fact that two diplomats from the ministry of foreign affairs, namely Kenan İpek and Gürsel Demirok, were appointed as chief consultants to Alpogan, and that the contracts of 20 out of the 53 retired military personnel were not renewed in 2005 did, however, represent small but meaningful steps towards the 'demilitarisation' of the organisation.[30]

The structural transformation of the MGK's General Secretariat under the Alpogan administration is another important development. The new structure of the Research and Assessment Presidency (Araştırma Değerlendirme Başkanlığı, Ar-De), which was responsible for writing the security assessment reports that were presented in the MGK meetings, now consisted of three separate units. Accordingly, the presidency included one unit that was made responsible for the coordination of economic, cultural, scientific and educational research, and two units that were delegated responsibility for issues concerning domestic and foreign security, respectively. The appointment of Gürsel Demirok - a career diplomat in the Ministry of Foreign Affairs - as the vice-president of the Foreign Security Unit under the Ar-De presidency, is an attempt at changing the military nature of the organisation. Another development that can be seen as meaningful is the restructuring of the foreign security vice-presidency into six group presidencies – i.e. EU, Middle East, Russia-Caucasus, Greece-Cyprus-the Balkans, United States-Far East and International Institutions – as is the case in the ministry of foreign affairs. Additionally, Alpogan's visits to Israel in April 2005 and to the United States in January 2006, point to the possibility that the organisation will also function in a similar way to that of the Ministry of Foreign Affairs. The realisation of this possibility can be seen as a positive step towards a more democratic implementation of national security policies in Turkey.

In 2005, the MGK General Secretariat was also involved in the organisation of a strategy drawn up between 21-23 December aimed at managing a possible crisis

---

28 'Şeffaflaştık,' Hürriyet, 1 December 2004.

29 Faruk Mercan, 'Kırmızı Kitaplar Yenileniyor,' Aksiyon, 6 December 2004.

30 It is interesting to note that high officials, such as retired Major General Emin Ersan, who was first assistant to the General Secretary, Research Department President Erol Kırışoğlu and Department President in charge of Secretariat Services, retired Brigadier-General Enver Var, were among those whose contracts were terminated.

following an earthquake in the Marmara region. The purpose of the 2005 Disaster Crisis Management Manoeuvre, supervised by the prime minister's Crisis Management Centre, was made responsible for testing the efficiency of the national crisis management system, contributing to the development of disaster plans, testing the civilian-military cooperation and security alarm measures, and providing training in disaster management. The Elite Observer Briefing, that was part of this Disaster Crisis Management Manoeuvre, took place in the MGK General Secretariat with the participation of Prime Minister Erdoğan. The briefing was also attended by Chief of the General Staff Hilmi Özkök, Foreign Minister Gül, Deputy Prime Minister Ali Şahin, Minister of Internal Affairs Abdülkadir Aksu, Minister of Energy and Natural Resources Hilmi Güler and the commanders of the Armed Forces.

An important step in the demilitarisation process was the implementation of a structure that would work directly under the prime minister, and that would take over the tasks and authority of the prime minister's Crisis Management Centre. The Crisis Management Centre was founded in 1997 to work as part of the MGK General Secretariat and the Total Defence Civilian Services Office. According to the bill of the Turkish Emergency Management General Secretariat, the new institution would take the necessary precautions to ensure the realisation of efficient emergency management nationwide, in cases of such a scale that threaten the national security and the welfare of the people. These include natural disasters, disasters of human origin, terrorism, domestic and foreign threats, severe economic depression, dangerous epidemics, migration and population movements. It would also coordinate and define the principles of civil-military cooperation and create and implement related policies.[31]

Another important aspect of the new regulations of the Alpogan administration involved an increase in the ratio of female employees to 40 percent.[32] Institu-

---

31 The institution that is planned to have a structure similar to the Federal Emergency Administration Agency in the US will work directly under Prime Minister Erdoğan in order to provide coordination between units, increase the intervention capabilities, and organise the currently distributed emergency-management under a single administration. According to the draft, the main service units of the institution will consist of risk, damage decrease, preparation and improvement, intervention and emergency administration centre, fire services, education, operational services and standards, strategic planning of international and civil society relations, evaluation and information technologies, resource planning and administration, and security and civilian-military cooperation presidencies. It is stipulated that the secretariat, which will be authorised and responsible for cooperation and coordination with the General Staff, ministries, government bodies, universities, local administrations, non-governmental organisations and the private sector in their respective subjects of expertise, will employ contract personnel, have a separate budget and will not be subject to the Government Bidding Law in matters of procurement. Ufuk Hiçyılmaz, 'Başbakanlık Krize Talip,' Aksiyon, 2 May 2005.

32 Utku Çakırözer, 'MGK'da Kadın Yönetici Devri,' Milliyet, February 21, 2005. Füsun Arslantosun was appointed as Deputy President of the Board of Press and Public Relations, Asuman Orhan was appointed as Deputy President of the Personnel Department, and together with Emel Budak who was appointed to the Legal Undersecretariat, three female experts assumed key administrative roles for the first time in MGK history.

tional transformation was also reflected in the publishing of the 'Promotion and Title Change By-Law' in the Official Gazette on 28 August 2005.

It is clear that the attempts of the Alpogan administration at demilitarising the organisation and transforming it into an intellectual institution, aimed to change the view that the MGK General Secretariat merely represented an extension of the general staff operating as an executive institution. However, if 'demilitarisation' is to be defined as purging the government bodies and its essential institutions of a militarist outlook both legally and functionally, then institutional demilitarisation goes beyond ridding an institution of uniformed officials and bringing in non-uniformed executives. This should not be understood as undermining the legal changes that make it possible to appoint civilians, instead of executives with a military background, as well as the appointments made as the result of such legislation. Although the appointment of civilian officials to key positions within the security sector represents one of the most important and necessary steps toward demilitarisation, it is far from being sufficient.

Conclusion

2005 witnessed the opening of national security problems to public debate. The public viewed the changes taking place within the MGK in an effort to understand the true nature of the relations between the armed forces and the government. Prior to MGK meetings, debates about which matters would make it onto the agenda, and which issues would cause internal conflict, were widely analysed in the press. Judging from public interest in the developments concerning the MGK, it seems that the organisation is viewed as a barometer which displays how much the military sector limits political power. Debates over its agenda have ultimately served a positive function by establishing the discussion of security matters, which were once considered taboo, as ordinary political problems.

When analysing the transformation process of the MGK and its General Secretariat, the demilitarisation process emerges clearly alongside a decrease in the number of staff with a military background. 2005 certainly ushered in a period of greater transparency: the public was informed of the General Secretariat's activities and the publishing of appointment and promotion by-laws were observed. Furthermore, the appointment of diplomats as secretary generals and heads of various research units, as well as the restructuring of some units parallel to that of the Ministry of Foreign Affairs, leads one to assume that the Ministry of Foreign Affairs will have an increasing influence on the MGK in the future.

Initial attempts to modify images of a military institution, that carries out secret activities, to that of a civilian and transparent institution, have been largely successful. Nonetheless, it is still too early to say that the process of debating, developing and implementing national security policies is running in a democratic way. This statement does not, however, negate the fact that the steps taken towards the demilitarisation of the MGK and its General Secretariat are too important to ignore. Moreover, to think that a structure which took decades to emerge could be abolished in the near future, would be tantamount to denying the political realities of our country, to say the least. The development of national policies in the direction of the demilitarisation of the security apparatus, and their implementation and revision, which leads to civilian oversight of the security sector, should be seen as commonplace by the basic organs and institutions of the government. These policies should also be accepted by the public. In light of this, however, Turkey has a long way to go before it achieves a democratic and politicised national security structure and function.

Military Judiciary

Ümit Kardaş[*]

The Historical Background of the Military Judiciary in Turkey

Today, the existence of a military judiciary is recognised by the constitutions of many countries.[1] Constitutional articles generally leave the authority of decision-making concerning the establishment, and the span of authority of the military judiciary, to the legislative body. However, some constitutions do not make any provisions for the institution of any military judiciary, at least in times of peace.[2]

Whilst some countries do not make any provisions for a military judiciary, others consider its abolition, and in some cases a military judiciary exists where civil judges are given positions in military courts (civilianisation). These facts demonstrate that the very concept of a military judiciary is undergoing a process of change at the international level.[3] The military judiciary is brought to the fore, by the ideals of basic human rights and freedoms that are gaining ground in the 21st century, along with considerations concerning the principle of the independence of judges as guarantors of these rights and freedoms.

In the Ottoman Empire, the military class was a privileged one. It was composed not only of those who went to war and worked in military uniforms, but also included those in public service. Anyone who was appointed with the Sultan's warrant ('berat') to any government/state office was considered to be part of the military.[4] When there was a question of dereliction of duty or oppression by a person belonging to the military class, the accused was sent to a military council. In the case of senior state officials, the Sultan himself chaired the council. In general, the Imperial Chancery of State ('Divanı hümayun') functioned as a court and the rules

---

* PhD., Lawyer, Retired Military Judge and Prosecutor.

1 Article 105 of the Belgian Constitution of 1831, Article 116 of the Dutch Constitution of 1887, Articles 107 and 120 of the Brasilian Constitution of 1967, Article 145 of the Turkish Republic Constitution of 1982.

2 The Constitution of the Federal Republic of Germany may be cited as an example. The Constitution of Austria has foreseen no military judiciary either in times of peace or war.

3 Antonio Intelisano, 'Independence of Military Judges, Judges Advocates and Public Prosecutors,' VIIIth International Congress (Ankara, 1979), p. 4.

4 Ahmet Mumcu claims that the reason the word 'military' encompasses all public service in the Ottoman State is worth examining, and proposes that this may have originated from the fact that the state organisation was based on military aims in the interest of the foundation. For more information, see Ahmet Mumcu, Osmanlı Devletinde Siyaseten Katl (Ankara: Birey ve Toplum Yayınları, 1963), p. 55-57; Mumcu, Coşkun Üçok, Türk Hukuk Tarihi (Ankara: Savaş Yayınevi, 1982), p. 198-199.

imposed by Islamic law were not strictly abided by in the judgment of the military class. The Sultan, or his representative, could lead an investigation on their own initiative, in cases in which it was deemed necessary, and could use the authority of political execution without obtaining a fatwa.[**] Many examples throughout Ottoman history illustrate how this procedure led to illegal applications, unjust prosecution and death.

In relation to the trial of janissaries,[5] which was a disciplined military force attached to the central authority, the rule was that a janissary could only be judged by his commandant and within his barracks. Even the vizier, who had exclusive judiciary power, was not permitted to judge or punish a janissary.[6]

In 1914, after the constitutional period, a Military High Court of Appeals (Divan-ı Temyizi Askerî – Askerî Yargıtay) was established in Istanbul under a provisory law. The president of the court, who possessed the authority of a corps commander, was elected by the minister of war and appointed by the sultan. The court also consisted of seven members, of whom four were high-ranking officers and three were jurists.[7] This represented the first incident of jurists participating in a military court. In 1916, the Military High Court of Appeals was reorganised in greater detail through a provisory law. This was abolished by decree in 1920, leaving the authority of appeals investigations to an administrative institution, which comprised a committee attached to the Bureau of Military Justice of the Ministry of War (Harbiye Nezareti Askerî Adliye İdaresi). The committee, which was composed of three officers and two civilian jurists, was abolished after a short period and the Military High Court of Appeals was re-established.[8] After the establishment of the Turkish Grand National Assembly, the Military High Court of Appeals was initiated, in which the president and two of its members were soldiers and the two others were jurists, in accordance with Law No. 237 of 1922.[9]

---

5 Tarık Zafer Tunaya, Siyasi Müessesler ve Anayasa Hukuku, Siyaset İlmi Serisi 9 (İstanbul, 1969), p. 265; Mumcu, Üçok, Türk Hukuk Tarihi, p. 237.

** Editor's Note: Fatwa is a legal opinion based on Iaslamic law, issued by a mufti (jurisconsult), on a particular matter.

6 Sahir Erman, Askerî Ceza Hukuku, (İstanbul: İ.Ü. Hukuk Fakültesi Yayınları, 1974), p.14 -15. When the Janissary Corps was abolished by Mahmud II (Vakayi Hayriye), the rules concerning janissaries were also abolished, and a new code of law named Kanunname-i Asakiri Muhammediye (Law of Muhammedan Military Force) was put in force in 1829, following which the practice of court martials consisting of seven persons was established according to the law called Cezaname (Penal Code) dated 1838. The president in these court martials was to be either a colonel or a major of cavalry or infantry whereas the members consisted of two captains, one first-lieutenant, one lieutenant and one noncommissioned officer. Furthermore, an officer of the rank of captain (örf zabiti) would perform the role of prosecutor. Later, court martials of which the formation could change according to the rank of the accused but which always consisted of a president and four members, were established with Imperial Military Penal Code of 1870.

7 Fahri Çoker, 'Askerî Yargıtayın Tarihçesi,' Askerî Adalet Dergisi (1966), p. 39.

8 Vasfi Raşit Seviğ, Askerî Adalet (Ankara, 1955), p. 300.

9 Sahir Erman, Askerî Ceza Hukuku, (İstanbul: İ.Ü. Hukuk Fakültesi Yayınları, 1974), p.308.

Following the declaration of the Republic, Law No. 1631 on the Military Trial Procedure (Askerî Muhakeme Usül Yasası) was passed on 22 May 1930. It was prepared with recourse to German and French laws. In accordance with this law, the military courts established within the regiments or equivalent posts, were composed of a president and two members.[10] This law set up regimental (alay) military courts, as well as military courts attached to each division (tümen, or its equivalent); to the army corps (kolordu, or its equivalent); and to higher command posts. These courts consisted of a military judge and two military officers, in addition to the military judge who acted as prosecutor,[11] whilst the Military High Court of Appeals consisted of two departments, in which four military officers and four jurists presided as members in each department. The members elected from among the military officers holding the rank of Brigadier General or higher, were appointed by decree for a period of two years, whilst the jurists were elected from amongst Colonel level. The President and Vice-President of the Military High Court of Appeals were elected from among military officers with the rank of Lieutenant General or higher and were appointed for a period of two years, by decree from the Council of Ministers.[12] It is, therefore, impossible to assert that the independence and immunity of military judges was assured within the system established by Law No. 1631.

The Situation Following the Law of the Establishment and Trail Procedures of Military Courts No. 353, Dated 1963

The Constitution of 1961, Article 138, clause 4, requires that the majority of the members of the military court possess the qualifications of a judge. In Article 2 of Law No. 353, prepared in accordance with the aforementioned provision from the 1961 Constitution, it was pronounced that military courts were to be composed of two military judges and one military officer.[13] However, as a result of the lack of a specific provision in the 1982 Constitution concerning the establishment of military courts, lawmakers established military courts independently and disregarded the requirement that the majority of military court members possess the qualifications of

---

10 Hilmi Özarpat, Askerî Yargılama Usulü Hukuk, (Ankara, 1950), p. 32; Erman, Askerî Ceza Hukuku, p. 316.

11 Özarpat, Askerî Yargılama Usulü Hukuk, p. 33-35; Erman, Askerî Ceza Hukuku, p. 316-318.

12 Özarpat, Askerî Yargılama Usulü Hukuk, p. 39-40.; Erman, Askerî Ceza Hukuku, p. 342-343.

13 According to Article 1 of Law No. 353, military courts are founded near division, army corps and force commandants and the general staff. However, military courts founded near divisions have been abolished with an amendment to the same law, but with a temporary clause they have been allowed to serve until their abolition becomes final. See Resmi Gazete (Official Gazette) No. 17229, dated 23.01.1981. Again, an amendment has been made to Article 2 of Law No. 353 with Law No. 2538 dated 16.10.1981, which stipulates that in hearings against 200 or more persons, the military court must be composed of four judges and a military officer. See http://www.msb.gov.tr/Birimler/AsAdIsB/AsAdIsB353Kanun.htm

a judge. Obviously, setting such a precedent made the military judiciary even more controversial.

The General Staff Military Court (Genelkurmay Askerî Mahkemesi) consists of three military judges and two generals or admirals, and it is here that the cases against generals and admirals are heard. The disciplinary courts established in accordance with Law No. 477 on the Establishment of Disciplinary Courts, where cases of disciplinary crimes committed by military persons are heard, consist of a chairman and two members, all of whom are military officers. During the trials of non-commissioned officers and privates, one of the member positions is filled by a non-commissioned officer. The Military High Court of Appeals is made up of five departments. The members of the Military High Court of Appeals are elected from candidates who are first-class military judges with the rank of Lieutenant Colonel or above. Each vacant position requires three candidates, with the vote of the absolute majority of the total number of members of the General Council of Military High Court of Appeals, who are then appointed by the President of the Republic.

What are the Problems Concerning the Military Judiciary?

As modified in line with the constitution, Article 9 of Law No. 353 on the Establishment and Trial Procedures of Military Courts defines the extent of authority of military courts in relation to military personnel. In addition to military crimes committed by military personnel, these courts also try crimes committed by military personnel against other personnel, on military premises, or in relation to their military duties and service. Certain crimes committed by civilians are also considered within the span of authority of military courts.[14] Articles 12 and 13 of the same law pertain to cases of military and civilian persons committing a crime in concert, as well as to cases where a person has committed crimes subject to military trial and crimes subject to judicial trial. Due to these regulations, it is advisable to discuss the subject matter for military persons and civilians separately.

Problem 1: What Is a Military Crime? How Should It Be Defined?

There is no definition in the Military Criminal Code (Askerî Ceza Kanunu, ACK) as to what constitutes a military crime. However, the need for such a definition remains of utmost importance, as other spheres of duty are determined with respect to this definition. Crimes committed by civilians in agreement with military personnel are considered military crimes, which constitutes the grounds for their trial in military courts and causes them to fall under a different and separate jurisdiction from their normal civil court.

Clearly, the civilian and military judiciary systems in Turkey are different from one another; they are based on different procedures and the independence as well as immunity of the judges are arranged differently in each system. This creates incongruity with regard to the unity of jurisdiction. Therefore, it is of tremendous

[14] Article 11 of Law No. 353 on the Establishment and Trial Procedures of Militar Courts.

importance that the concept of military crime be clearly defined, with well-defined limits that leave no room for interpretation. An example which illustrates the urgent need for this definition comes from Article 54 of the ACK; based on clauses 125 to 145 of the Turkish Criminal Code (Türk Ceza Kanunu, TCK), inserted into the ACK and henceforth defined as military crimes. The crimes these clauses refer to are of a political nature and, therefore, it is imprudent at best to transform them into military crimes. Besides artificially expanding the parameters of military crime, this also results in the fact that military personnel and civilians who commit these crimes together will both fall within the purview of military jurisdiction and thus be separated from their 'civilian judges.'

Military crimes must be defined more narrowly so as to encompass military matters only. In other words, military crimes should be those crimes committed by military personnel and related to military duty and service alone. These must be defined as those acts that directly affect military discipline and infringe upon military service and duty. These crimes must be the principal criterion in determining the range of authority of military courts. Based on this, few crimes specified in the ACK could be considered military crimes. It is of utmost importance to clearly stress that once the range of authority of military jurisdiction is defined, with respect to the aforementioned criteria, it will not be possible for civilians to be judged in military courts.

What are the Legal Foundations for Trials of Civilians in Military Courts?

The trial of civilians in military courts is regulated in Article 11 of Law No. 353. A parallel regulation was effected by Article 6 appended to the ACK on 25 May, 1972, and Article 55 of the ACK entitled War Treason refers to Article 129/1 of the TCK. This article stipulates that persons who conspire with foreigners to facilitate the military manoeuvres of the enemy at the expense of the state of Turkey, damage the military operations of the state of Turkey, or commit acts toward the aforementioned purposes, will be punished. Articles corresponding to these crimes will be applied in the new TCK.

Article 56 of the ACK, which refers to Articles 133, 136/last, 127/3 of the TCK, has been named Treason to National Defence. In the new TCK, articles corresponding to these crimes will be applied. Article 57 of the ACK is entitled Acts Against National Defence and, at the same time, refers to Article 135 of the TCK, which covers the crime of espionage in secret military zones. Crimes referred to herein are covered in Chapter 1 of the TCK, entitled Crimes Against the Personality of the State. Articles 127/3, 129, 133, 136/3, are comprised in the first part of Chapter 1, entitled Crimes Against the International Personality of the State. In the new TCK, articles corresponding to these crimes will be applied.

Article 63 of the ACK regulates the crimes of absentee conscription, absentee conscription by way of late accession, call-to-duty desertion, and total desertion. The punishment of reserve officers and military employees who do not report for duty when called, is regulated in Article 64 of the ACK. Article 81 of the ACK regulates the Crime of Fraud in Order to Avoid Military Service. Article 93 of the ACK pertains to the punishment of those inciting provocation, Article 94 to the punishment of incitation of mutiny, Article 95 to the punishment of those negotiating military affairs or gathering for military purposes without authority, whereas Articles 100, 101 and 102 regulate the crimes of military mutiny. Non-military persons who commit any of the crimes mentioned in clause (B) of Article 11 of Law No. 353 in primary military forbidden zones, guardhouses, outposts, military headquarters and barracks, military institutions or places where soldiers reside or are billeted will be tried in military courts. In addition, non-military persons who attack, curse or insult soldiers, or resort to violence or threat in order to force them to perform, or not, the functions related to their military duties in the aforementioned places, are removed from their 'natural courts' and subjected to a military judiciary.

Clause (C) of Article 11 of Law No. 353, covers the crimes named in the Articles 188, 190, 191, 254, 255, 256, 257, 258, 260, 266, 267, 268, 269, 271, 272 and 273 of the TCK committed by non-military persons against soldiers performing sentry, guard, patrol, and outpost duty or military police, military traffic, police or rescue and aid work. The authority of hearing such cases is left to the military judiciary. Again, articles that correspond to these crimes in the new TCK will be applied. Clause (E) of Article 11 of Law No. 353 also posits that civilians can be judged in military courts in circumstances described in other laws. For example, civilians who commit crimes delineated in the code of martial law, crimes which instigated the declaration of martial law, or crimes that are related to a crime heard by the court of martial law will be tried in military courts.

Problem 2:– Jurisdiction as to Location

In addition to the ACK, a crime committed by military personnel may also be covered in the TCK by Law No. 6136, or, by another special law. However, a crime committed on military premises falls under military jurisdiction. Upon examination of the decrees of the Military High Court of Appeals, which were established in light of Articles 12, 21 and 100 of the Law of Internal Service, military premises can be constituted as places where soldiers are educated, where they carry out their duties or manoeuvres and where they live or are billeted. These places include detachments, headquarters, military institutions (military hospitals, schools, officers' clubs, factories, clothing factories, recruiting offices, supply bases and warehouses), which are identified in Article 12 of the Law of Internal Service.

Places deemed within the military's jurisdiction have been 'named' in this article. However, a definition for what is to be understood by the expression 'place of military jurisdiction' , i.e. the scope of the military courts' authority has not been provided. Neither Law No. 353 nor Law No. 211 on Internal Service provides a definition; definitions are only provided in reference to the aforementioned places. For example, in Article 12 of the Law of Internal Service, the term 'military institution' has been defined. Military personnel are separated from their 'natural courts' and from their 'natural judges', solely on the basis that a crime has been committed in a place considered within the military's jurisdiction. The fact that a definition does not exist, paves the way for an application of this criterion which is much too broad.

Problem 3: Why Is the Criterion of 'Crimes Committed by Military Personnel Against Military Personnel' Problematic?

Whilst the military judiciary is responsible for cases involving military personnel, these need not be military crimes as predicated in the ACK. It is sufficient that the alleged actions be committed against military personnel.

Military personnel who commit theft, fraud, forgery or property violation against a military person will be judged in a military court. However, these crimes have not even been referred to by the ACK. In other words, they do not even possess the attributes of a semi-military crime. The fact that they fall under the authority of the military judiciary, merely because they have been committed against military personnel, is not a sound premise on which to determine the extent of the court's authority. These arrangements are contrary to the principle of 'normal jurisdiction.' Accepting the authority of military judiciaries merely on the grounds that both the perpetrator and the victim are military personnel, and refraining from handing such cases over to civilian courts, can only be interpreted as the military's effort to conceal internal matters and keep them private. This problem has significantly expanded the court's authority.

Important Developments in 2005

There has been no discussion of the aforementioned points, nor have any legal modifications been made as of 2005, due to the assumption that the problems herein fall under the dominion of military issues that cannot be addressed. However, these are problems pertaining to the judiciary at large, which need to be solved in light of the principles of 'normal jurisdiction,' unity of jurisdiction and judicial independence. The only modification that has taken place in this domain, is the clause appended to Article 11 of Law No. 353, with Law No. 4963 dated 30 July 2003, and this was unfortunately insufficient. This clause stipulates that cases concerning crimes covered by Article 58 of the ACK (TCK 153, 161, 155) will not be heard in military courts if they are committed in times of peace by civilians.

A Holistic Evaluation of the Problems Related to Military Jurisdiction

The issue of defining the jurisdiction of military courts is problematic. Different opinions within the judicial system itself have elicited disagreements between judicial institutions. The related decrees of the Department of Punishment of the Court of Jurisdictional Disputes clearly indicate the parameters of the conflict between the military and civilian judiciaries. Under present regulations, the authority of military courts has substantially increased. Military courts hear cases of military crimes and also cases of common offences committed by military personnel. This is contrary to their raison d'être. Thus, military courts have become the sole place for the trial of soldiers, and as such they are insulated from the 'civilian courts.' It is important to bear in mind that as Turkish citizens, all military personnel are also subject to common law.

The military court is a completely separate institution in terms of its structure, procedures, jurisdiction and treatment of attenuating circumstances. This is particularly evident when the special procedures of its jurisdiction are considered, such as the appointment of judges, punishments imposed and the dependency of military judges on the commander with whom they are in a hierarchical relationship. Military personnel are not only isolated from their 'civilian jurisdiction' but are also in a different realm of jurisdiction by being placed under a military authority for committing common offences. Clearly, the authority of the military judiciary, comprising local military courts and the Military High Court of Appeals, must be determined with the utmost precision and sensitivity.

The most striking aspect of this issue is the inclusion of non-military personnel into this system. It is obvious that crimes that elicit the trial of civilians in military courts, are not crimes directly or indirectly related to the procurement of national defence, to the execution of military service, or to the protection of discipline. However, claims that certain crimes committed by civilians are impairing the military cannot be made, as these crimes are typically of a political rather than a military nature. The trial of civilians in military courts equates to their removal from 'civilian courts.' Thus, the politicising of military courts has many drawbacks.

Last but not least, is the fact that military judges are not independent and immune. Military judges dress in military uniforms and are part of the hierarchical structure. Commanders effect the promotion of military judges, whereas the force commander to whom they report is responsible for their appointment. Judges are evaluated by the review committee attached to the Ministry of National Defence. The minister of national defence can impose disciplinary action upon them. In this situation, a combatant officer appointed by the commander acts with the authority of a judge. It is obvious that the trial of civilians who commit certain crimes - even in times of peace - in courts which do not fit into any democratic and legal framework, violates the right to a fair trial. The presence of military judges also hinders the financial situation of civilian judges. Financial and social benefits considered for civilian judges have been stalled and limited in order not to affect the hierarchy within the ranks of military judges. Furthermore, such partiality emanates from the armed forces which act with the imperative of protecting its own hierarchy in mind. In a state governed by the rule of law and administered by a pluralist democracy, it is not even conceivable to think of such impediments to civilian judges.

Comparative Law and the Establishment of Military Courts

The basic characteristic of the military judiciary in countries following the Anglo-Saxon system of law, is the presence of ad hoc military courts which combine to hear a single case or a determined number of cases and are dismissed after declaration of the verdict. In Britain, the military court is composed of military officers and a 'judge advocate,' whereas in the United States, the court consists of military officers and a 'military judge' who also participates in the hearings. However, the military judiciary has no authority whatsoever over civilians.

In Germany, Sweden, Denmark and Norway a military court is non-existent in times of peace. Austria has no military court even in times of war. In France, Belgium, the Netherlands, Switzerland and Spain, civilian judges participate in the establishment of military courts, paving the way for demilitarisation. In Algeria, Morocco and Tunisia, civilian judges take part in the establishment of military courts. Furthermore, no Military High Court of Appeals exists in Belgium, Britain, France, the Netherlands, Greece, Canada, Russia, Algeria or Tunisia.

Turkish Armed Forces

Lale Sarıibrahimoğlu[*]

Introduction

The Turkish Armed Forces (Türk Silahlı Kuvvetleri, TSK) consists of the land, naval and air forces working under the General Staff. In times of war, the General Command of the Gendarmerie and the Coast Guard Command also operate under the land and naval forces, even though they are responsible the Ministry of Internal Affairs in times of peace.

As stipulated by Article 117 of the Constitution, the chief of the general staff is appointed by the president upon the Council of Minister's proposal, and his/her duties and authorities are regulated by law. In times of war, he/she carries out the duty of commander-in-chief on behalf of the president. The chief of the general staff's duties are: to define the principles and programmes for personnel, intelligence, operations, organisation, training/education and logistical support services, in order to command and prepare the armed forces for war. He/she also directs the TSK's relations with other countries and the North Atlantic Treaty Organisation (NATO).[1]

As specified by Article 117, the chief of the general staff works closely with the Ministry of National Defence (Milli Savunma Bakanlığı, MSB), but he/she is accountable to the prime minister, and not to the minister of national defence. The chief of the general staff's status was established following the coup of 1960 and with the 1961 Constitution. However, the constitution fails to define to whom the chief of the general staff is responsible, while he/she conducts his/her duties. Former President Süleyman Demirel argued that this condition worked against the principles of a state governed by rule of law.[2]

The TSK's special status constitutes one of the most significant obstacles for Turkey in relation to its efforts to achieve compatibility with the European Union's (EU) political criteria in its negotiations for full membership. The EU demands that the Turkish chief of the general staff works under the minister of defence, as in Western democracies. Turkey is the only member state of NATO whose chief of the general staff is still answerable to the prime minister.

---

* Journalist, Defence, Specialist

1 See http://www.tsk.mil.tr

2 Yavuz Donat's interview with Süleyman Demirel: 'Demokrasi'de ordunun yeri,' Sabah, 3 November 2005.

The second most significant problem regarding the role, authority and position of the chief of the general staff is the TSK's tradition of proscribing elected civilian governments. This was demonstrated by the three military coups, and the 'indirect intervention' of 28 February 1997 known as the 'post-modern coup', that have taken place in the 82 years since the founding of the Republic of Turkey. What made the 28 February intervention post-modern was the mobilisation of an army of civilian allies who voluntarily defended the military over 'fundamentalism' by evoking the reactions of the press and many Non-Governmental Organisations (NGOs). The TSK carried out the aforementioned coups based on article 35 of the Internal Service Law.[3] The problem with Article 35 is that the authority to appoint the duty of protection and supervision is designated to the TSK as opposed to a civilian political authority.[4]

The turning point in the public debating of subjects that were considered taboo in Turkish politics, which started with the TSK, was prompted by the EU Helsinki Summit of December 1999 and the granting of candidate status to Turkey by the EU. The first serious efforts to democratise the civilian and military sectors were initiated in the aftermath of a grave financial crisis of February 2001. After the financial crisis, a number of reforms were initiated and paved the way for good governance, such as the TSK's diminishing active role in the political domain, parliamentary supervision of the MSB budget and the extra budgetary resources allocated to defence through the Supreme Court of Accounts. These reforms were implemented by the Justice and Development Party (Adalet ve Kalkınma Partisi, AKP), which came into power as the sole ruling party in November 2002, and was supported by the Republican People's Party (Cumhuriyet Halk Partisi CHP), the opposition party of the time.

2002 was also the year when the current chief of the general staff, General Hilmi Özkök, took over from General Hüseyin Kıvrıkoğlu in a rather unpleasant fashion. The prime minister of the time, Bülent Ecevit, made a proposal on 15 July 2002[5] to extend Kıvrıkoğlu's period of duty, even though the legal period[6] had ended. Ecevit's justification to continue with the current chief of the general staff, centred on the possible negative impact of the US-led invasion of Iraq in March 2003 and the potentially critical developments in Cyprus.

The proposal to extend Kıvrıkoğlu's period of duty was supported by the TSK's high-ranking generals, dubbed the Eurasianists, who preferred to act in coalition on issues concerning Iran, Russia and Central Asia, instead of improving relations with the US and the West. The majority of these generals have since retired.

---

3 The Internal Service Law, which was accepted after the 1960 coup, gives TSK the duty of protecting and watching over the Turkish Homeland and the Turkish Republic as defined by the constitution.

4 Yavuz Donat's interview with Süleyman Demirel, '35. Madde Kalkmalı,' Sabah, 31 November 2005. In this interview, Demirel stresses that Article 35, which gives TSK the authority for carrying out a coup, does not exist anywhere else in the world.

5 Sedat Ergin, 'Ordu ile oynamak,' Hürriyet, 9 December 2003.

6 Despite some exceptions, chiefs of general staff have a legal period of duty for four years and are required to be under the age of 67 for any extension of this period to be possible.

However, President Ahmet Necdet Sezer did not favour the proposal despite Ecevit's insistent attempts, due to the possibility that such an extension might undermine the commanding principles of the TSK and turn the hierarchy upside down.[7] Ecevit's attempts were halted by the former chief of general staff, General İsmail Hakkı Karadayı, and following a meeting held with President Sezer in 2002, Özkök became the new chief of the general staff.[8]

In 2003 and 2004, three important laws took effect which diminished the TSK's influence in the political domain and paved the way for its supervision by a civilian authority. The first is the Law Concerning the Amendment of Laws No. 4963 of 30 July 2003, known as the Seventh Harmonisation Package, which introduced amendments to several articles of the National Security Council (Milli Güvenlik Kurulu MGK), as well as the MGK General Secretariat's founding Law No. 2945, dated 19 November 1983. The amendments, which were published in the Official Gazette (Resmi Gazete) on 8 January 2004, were introduced by a decree that was accepted by the cabinet on 29 December 2003. With this decree, the MGK's activities and decisions, which provide the legal grounds for the influential role the TSK plays in political life, were reduced to the level of 'recommendations to the Council of Ministers.' In addition, a civilian was appointed as the MGK general secretary for the first time, and although five military members were to remain in the MGK, the number of civilian members was increased to seven. As a result of these amendments, the TSK's membership to the Council of Higher Education (Yüksek Öğrenim Kurumu, YÖK) and Higher Council of Radio and Television (Radyo ve Televizyon Üst Kurulu, RTÜK) was abolished.

The second significant law is the Public Financial Administration and Control Law (Kamu Mali Yönetimi ve Kontrol Kanunu, KMYKK) which was accepted in December 2003 and which took effect in January 2005. This law stipulates the parliamentary supervision of the TSK's budget —consisting of the military budget allocated through the MSB and the extra budgetary resources allocated to defence — through the Supreme Court of Accounts. With a decree that was passed in February 2004 based on this law, the road was opened for the Supreme Court of Accounts to supervise military expenditure, and any extra budgetary defence expenditure, by demand of the president of the parliament.

The third regulation that stipulated civilian supervision of military expenditure was implemented as a constitutional amendment. With the legal adjustment

---

7 Sedat Ergin, 'Sivil darbe mi, askerî tasfiye mi,' Hürriyet, 7 December 2003.

8 The writer's interview at the time with well informed military sources. On the other hand, there are important indications that the US played a role in the events that emerged with failure of the Kıvrıkoğlu operation and Özkök's becoming Chief of General Staff. In this context, the article written by ret. US Lieutenant Colonel Steve Williams for the American think tank Western Policy Center, dated 30 October 2002 and entitled, 'The New Face of the Turkish Army' is worthy of attention. The fact that the writer plasters Özkök with praise, whereas he criticizes Kıvrıkoğlu, drawing attention to the fact that Kıvrıkoğlu never visited the US during his term of office but went to China, and defining him as a recluse, creates the impression of US lobbying activities for preventing the operation against Özkök. Indeed, Özkök visited the US one day after the 3 November elections which brought AKP to power.

publicly known as the Eighth Harmonisation Package, an amendment was made to the last paragraph of Article 160 of the Constitution on 7 May 2004. The principle of auditing the TSK-held state property, through the Supreme Court of Accounts in the name of Turkish Grand National Assembly (Türkiye Büyük Millet Meclisi, TBMM), was legalised with this amendment which went into effect following its publication in the Official Gazette on 22 May 2004. This was clearly another step towards lifting the veil of secrecy on this matter. However, it is significant that due to the TSK's ongoing objections, the regulatory statute necessary for the Supreme Court of Accounts to conduct this audit has yet to be passed.

During this period, the TBMM also made an attempt to initiate a democratic oversight mechanism over fraudulent acts in the area of weapons procurement. In 2003, the TBMM's Corruption Investigation Committee launched an investigation, with the claim that the state had sustained a loss of USD 180 million in the procurement of Airborne Early Warning and Control (AEW&C) systems. However, the investigation was terminated and the government approved the purchase of four AEW&Cs worth USD 1.5 billion. The termination of the investigation was yet another example of the parliamentary, and governmental, inhibition and reticence to scrutinise military bids.

These reforms, which made the military sector more accountable to taxpayers, and partly diminished its dominant role in politics, were inextricably tied to Turkey's expectations that the country would be granted a definitive date for the commencement of full EU membership negotiations on 3 October 2005.

However, these steps, which were taken for the sake of harmonisation with the EU's democratic criteria, triggered criticism, particularly from General Özkök, who defined the AKP's coming into power as a democratic process and was credited with paving the way for the reforms. Indeed, anti-EU groups both within and outside of the armed forces held Özkök responsible by claiming that he 'made concessions to secularism and was close to a party with a strong Islamist base – the AKP.'

Important Developments in 2005

In 2005, problems were experienced in relation to Turkey's internalisation process, i.e. the acceptance and implementation of a series of reforms that were passed to harmonise Turkish legislation with that of the EU.

The Commanders' Public Speeches

As criticised in the EU's Progress Report of 9 November 2005, the TSK continued to influence politics. High-ranking commanders regularly expressed their views on domestic as well as foreign policy matters. One of the most concrete examples was the 45-page speech delivered by Özkök on 20 April 2005 on the occasion of the opening of the War College Command. With this detailed speech on both domestic and foreign policy matters, made on behalf of the TSK which does not have any political responsibility, Özkök has proven that the TSK still continues to make binding speeches on political issues.[9]

Yet another example of the TSK's influence on national policies was the speech made by Land Forces Commander General Yaşar Büyükanıt's subsequent to the bookstore bombing, which was allegedly carried out against PKK convict Seferi Yılmaz in Şemdinli-Hakkâri on 9 November 2005. However, reactions were swift because of the TSK's influence on the judiciary. In reference to Gendarmerie NCO Ali Kaya, Büyükanıt stated that he 'knew him well and that he is a good soldier, but if necessary he could be tried.'[10] Kaya was apprehended with NCO Özcan İldeniz under suspicion of involvement in the bombing and for 'disrupting the unity of the state.'

Another example of the behaviour of high-ranking commanders was highlighted by Samsun Garrison Commander, Major General Naci Beştepe's visit to the Ondokuz Mayıs University (OMÜ) President, Ferit Bernay, who was heavily involved in debates on secularism with the AKP.[11] General Hurşit Tolun retired from his post as Commander of the First Army Corps in the Supreme Military Council (Yüksek Askeri Şura, YAŞ), and another high-ranking military official who politically-driven speeches during his retirement. Tolun delivered a speech at the village support practice, which was organised by the Fifth Army Corps in Önerler village of Çorlu-Tekirdağ. At this event, he appeared as the leader of a political formation of approximately 40 retired generals, and claimed that the supporters of shari'a, who are determined to turn the basic principles of the Turkish Republic upside down, have been involved in a systematic attack against those individuals and the institutions who want attempts to introduce Islamic laws in Turkey to be stopped.[12]

The custom of high-ranking commanders making public speeches on domestic and foreign policy matters was sustained most obviously by Özkök and Büyükanıt. While a recent decrease in such behaviour has been observed, the fact remains that the TSK continues to influence domestic and foreign policy, both of which should ultimately be shaped by the government.

---

9 See http://www.tsk.mil.tr (especially: Basın Yayın Halkla İlişkiler, Konuşmalar ve Yazılı Mesajlar, 2005 Yılı Konuşmalar ve Yazılı Mesajlar).

10 It is expected that General Büyükanıt will take over as chief of general staff in the Supreme Military Council (Yüksek Askeri Şura), YAŞ meeting of August 2006, and to continue this duty until his retirement in 2008. It is not known whether the government will interfere with Büyükanıt, who exhibits behaviour that intervenes with civilian politics. However, when asked whether Büyükanıt's assumption of this duty will be blocked a high-level AKP Deputy said 'Let's see what the new day will bring' and expressed his displeasure with the future chief of general staff.

11 'Tümgeneral Beştepe'den OMÜ'ye destek ziyareti,' Cumhuriyet, 21 January 2006.

12 'Tolon: Terör konusunda Türkiye'ye çifte standart uygulandı,' Anadolu Ajansı, 24 July 2005.

National Security Policy Document

The National Security Policy Document (Milli Güvenlik Siyaseti Belgesi, MGSB) is a roadmap that identifies the domestic and foreign threats faced by Turkey and delineates the policies which have been established in order to avoid these threats. Despite a number of legal reforms that stipulate civilian oversight of the military sector, it cannot be said that the National Security Policy Document is prepared completely under the initiative of a civilian authority. Although they might take a different form, the roadmaps in EU countries also analyse threat perceptions in domestic and foreign security matters and summarise policy recommendations. However, these roadmaps, which are prepared by civilian authorities working directly under the prime minister and with the contribution of the military, are widely available to the public. It is also possible to obtain information about the details of the structures of the military forces of those countries, in particular through material openly published on their web sites. Nonetheless, it is also apparent that every country retains information that is classified as secret, and that classified materials are naturally not open to public debate. At this juncture, the critical aspect of the practice of secrecy in Turkey is the fact that some of the information that is classified secret is not considered so in countries that are more advanced, especially in reference to military technology.

Since the contents of such files are kept secret, information can only be obtained by news leaked to the press and from various high-level sources. Given that the public has dubbed the National Security Policy Document as the secret constitution, it is possible to summarise developments regarding the document in 2005 as follows: in 2005, there was a desire to prepare the MGSB, perhaps for the first time, with the meaningful guidance and participation of the civilian authority.[13] However, the document was published in October 2005, following a delay stemming from the military wing's objections concerning domestic and foreign threat assessments and with an emphasis placed on the views of the military sector.[14] It was observed in the MGK meeting of October 2005 that the government made attempts to influence the shaping of the MGSB. It appears as though the government will lead the way in the perception of domestic threats, beginning with the fight against PKK terrorism which is on the rise again.[15] However, the document was published only after the

13 A long time before the debates on whether the civilian authority can shape the MGSB, it followed an active policy regarding Cyprus in 2004 and played a leading role in changing the Cyprus policy that is shaped with the influence of the military.

14 A high-level official who was interviewed by this writer stated that, as opposed to claims in the press, MGSB was not published the way the military wanted, but was accepted with a slight change that the official could not disclose.

15 Indeed, when speaking about the General Staff's demand for a new legal regulation in the fight against terrorism, the Minister of Foreign Affairs Abdullah Gül stated, 'The armed forces and the police get their instructions from the government. This global fight also has other aspects. Freedoms should not be limited,' reiterated the need for the government to play the leading role in the shaping of policies. ('Gül: Terörle mücadelede direktifi hükûmet verir,' Milliyet, January 4, 2006). Mir Dengir Fırat, one of the leading figures of AKP said: 'The General Staff, Gendarmerie Intelligence and Anti-Terror Organisation

inclusion of a series of statements from the TSK, which considered the extension of Greece's territorial waters in the Aegean to 12 miles as a casus belli.

Parliament and its related committees do not participate in the preparation of the MGSB. According to Article 118 of the Constitution, the duty of assessing whether the TBMM should be informed about the MGSB rests with the cabinet, which is responsible for national security. However, a high-level general, who wished to remain anonymous, noted that 'We (the military) prepare the MGSB, and send it to the prime minister's office for printing' thereby confirming that the TSK is, in fact, the authority preparing this document.

Similarly, the president does not play a role in the preparation of the MGSB, and as chairman of the MGK, he is only permitted to make suggestions at MGSB-related meetings.

The White Book

As in other NATO-member countries, the MSB also publishes a White Book. The purpose of this book is to provide information to the public about the country's domestic and foreign threat perceptions, its defence policies and structures. The White Book is published with a frequency which varies from country to country. For instance, in Germany and France it was published for the last time in 1994, after the dissolution of the Soviet Union. These countries are currently making preparations for a new White Book following the terrorist attacks of September 11, assessing 'asymmetrical threat' perceptions concerning threats of an unknown origin.

In Turkey, the White Books are traditionally published every two years.[16] However, this tradition has not been observed since 2000, for reasons which apparently centre on various technical problems.

Although it is possible for the public to find informative content in the White Books of other NATO and EU countries, information in Turkey's White Books are cut and pasted from previous editions. For instance, detailed information regarding the army structures of other NATO countries cannot be found in the MSB's White Book. This Almanac, however, presents diagrams pertaining to the organisational structure of the TSK that are not contained in the White Book, but were obtained from a number of specialised foreign publications and compiled from their sources (see. Diagrams 1–17).

The government is preparing to publish a report entitled the 'National Strategic Concept' (Ulusal Stratejik Konsept, USK). Prepared with the coordination of the Ministry of Foreign Affairs, it is stated that the report analyses which global developments might influence Turkey in the decades to come and that it embraces a long-term viewpoint.

The USK, expected to be completed next year, is intended to represent an umbrella document that will be placed above the MGSB, the White Book, and the

(Jandarma İstihbarat ve Terörle Mücadele Teşkilatı, MİT) are of no importance to us. We are the boss,' hinting that the draft for the Anti-Terror will be prepared by the government. ('Genelkurmay, JİTEM bizi bağlamaz,' Milliyet, 16 September 2005).

16 See http://www.msb.gov.tr

National Military Strategic Concept (Milli Askerî Strateji Konsepti), and which will provide the basis for the re-structuring of the armed forces.

Domestic and Foreign Threats

Article 2a of the MGK was identified by the 2005 EU Progress Report as problematic, in light of its broad definition and interpretation of national security.[17] For instance, the desire of the Joint Staff to close down the Teachers' Union (Eğitim-Sen), an organisation representing teachers who advocate education in one's mother tongue (for instance in Kurdish) was allegedly due to a broad threat perception.[18]

Both the TSK and the government believe that the PKK, the extreme-left Revolutionary People's Liberation Party/Front (Devrimci Halk Kurtuluş Partisi/Cephesi, DHKP/C), Hizbullah[**] and Al-Qaeda (an organisation which is determined to establish local links in Turkey) are important domestic threats. However, the government and the TSK disagree over the definition of what constitutes an internal threat and also disagree on whether the TSK should deal with domestic threats or if its role should be limited to protection against external threats.

The signals that the TSK has been giving, in which they perceive the ruling AKP as an indirect threat to secularism, represents another interesting development. It undermines the idea that the elected government is the determining authority of threat perceptions.

The TSK conflicts with the government on the issue of perceptions of foreign threats. Despite the Cyprus problem and the unresolved border conflicts in the Aegean between Greece and Turkey, the possibility that EU-candidate Turkey will go to war with EU-member Greece over these issues is practically non-existent. Nonetheless, the fact that the TSK considers that Greece's extension of its Aegean territorial waters by 12 miles as a casus belli[19] reflects a certain level of paranoia.

---

17 According to this article, national security entails the protection of the state's constitutional order, its national existence, its integrity, all of its interests in the international realm including the political, social, cultural and economic against all manner of domestic and foreign threats.

18 European Commission, Turkey 2005 Progress Report, 9 November 2005. See http://www.abgs.gov.tr

19 The fact that Greece's possible extension of her territorial waters to 12 miles is considered a casus belli led to the shelving of the idea of dissolving the Aegean army, which was established as a deterrent against Greece. This idea first emerged in May 2000 from former Naval Forces Commander Admiral Güven Erkaya, who was a consultant to then Prime Minister Ecevit. The same proposal came last year from TBMM Chairman Bülent Arınç. However, following TSK's reaction, the idea of dissolving the Aegean army was abandoned. The reasoning for this was the expectation that following the dissolution of the Aegean army, Greece would make a mollifying diplomatic gesture and also give up her armaments policy in the eastern Aegean islands. The Aegean army was established as the 4th Army Corps immediately after the Cyprus peace operation on 20 May 1975. It contains six brigades, four regiments, nine battalions, air defence troops, aerial and artillery batteries and logistics-support detachments.

The government, on the other hand, is expecting to overcome this impasse and is trying to find a solution through diplomatic means.

Ironically, following the September 11 attacks, the TSK's threat perception did not undergo significant changes. Due to its long fight against the terrorist activities of the Kurdistan Workers' Party (Partiya Karkerên Kurdistan, PKK), the TSK states that it is already prepared for asymmetrical threats which might come from irregular sources.

Therefore, the TSK perceives the problems that it identifies, which include symmetrical risks, as extensions of the Cold War era that might have a negative effect on Turkey's security and as such lead to a high-intensity conventional conflict. This includes possible instability in neighbouring countries, the establishment of a separate Kurdish state in northern Iraq, weapons of mass destruction as well as asymmetrical risks and threats, such as separatist and fundamentalist activities, and joint threats, such as international terrorism and illegal migration.[20]

The resulting impression is that in relation to domestic and foreign threat perceptions, the government does not boast a comprehensive threat perception either. According to a western expert, it appears that the government conducts diplomacy with temporary solutions in mind, while handing security matters over to the military.

The Problem of Downsizing the Army

The TSK, which did not significantly alter its threat perceptions after September 11, has not experienced a downsizing of any kind or initiated plans to move towards a fully professional army, which might allow for a more rapid response to such threats. Instead, the TSK plans to adopt a mixed system over time, consisting of both professional soldiers and compulsory military service personnel (conscripts).[21]

According to a western military expert, the TSK, with its four forces, ten army corps, special forces command and two infantry divisions, maintains a structure similar to that which existed during the Cold War (see Box 1). Another criticism of the TSK's structure came from CHP Istanbul Deputy Şükrü Elekdağ. Elekdağ stated that the threat perceived by Turkey equates to approximately one fourth of the threat it faced in 1988-1998, that conventional threats have significantly decreased and yet no important changes had been observed in the TSK's structure. Highlighting that the Turkish Armed Forces is the largest force within NATO after the United States, Elekdağ pointed out that the TSK should reduce its size, arguing

---

** Editor's Note: Hizbullah, or the Party of God, is a militant Islamist Sunni group unrelated to the Lebanon-based Shi'ite Hezbollah.

20 For the speech made by Chief of General Staff Özkök on 20 April 2005 at the War Academies Command see http://www.tsk.mil.tr

21 Askere Alma Daire Başkanlığı (ASAL); bkz. http://www.msb.gov.tr

that a decrease in the number of soldiers would allow for serious savings on expenditure.[22] (For an evaluation of the cost of a single soldier, see Sidebar 2).

According to official figures, the number of soldiers in Turkey stands at 820'000, and the largest segment is in the Land Forces Command (Kara Kuvvetleri Komutanlığı KKK) (See Sidebar 3). However, according to unofficial figures, the number is actually closer to one million. The number of soldiers is approximately 800'000, whilst commissioned officers (including generals) form a small part of the aforementioned total. In contrast, Germany only has a total of 248'305 soldiers, in spite of having a population of over 70 million which is similar to that of Turkey.

Western military experts believe that the TSK's delay in strengthening its capacity to respond to the new kind of threats that emerged after September 11, is related to its focus on domestic threat-perceptions such as fundamentalist activities and the PKK. According to this view, which is also adhered to by some Turkish military experts, the main obstacles to a meaningful reduction of the TSK, relate to the TSK's desire to play a leading role in determining domestic threats, even though their main duty is to protect the homeland against foreign threats. Furthermore, and although this is not officially stated, the TSK wants to keep the definition of what constitutes a domestic threat as broad as possible, to the point of including the ruling Justice and Development Party as an indirect threat to secularism. This is perceived by many to be one of the most important obstacles to the downsizing of the TSK.

On 23 June 2003, the period of duty for conscripts was reduced from 18 months to 15 for soldiers and from 16 to 12 months for officers. In May 2004, the TSK dissolved the 4th Brigade (Sidebar 4). These decisions, however, were rather symbolic as a means to reduce the number of military personnel and render the army more flexible. Chief of the General Staff General Özkök, stated in his speech of 20 April 2005 that, as a result of dissolving the Fourth Brigade, the number of military personnel would be reduced by 150'000 and that until the modernisation project had been completed, there would be no further downsizing of the TSK.

The speed with which a meaningful reduction and move towards fully professional armed forces might be conducted in the future undoubtedly depends on the nature of relations between the government and the armed forces.

It is also claimed that, in this context, the AKP government gained political prestige by the TSK's participation in several international Peace Corps operations.[23] In order to increase its strategic activity on the international level, the TSK assumed command of the International Security Assistance Force (ISAF) in Afghanistan twice in 2004, and again in February 2005. The TSK also hosts three of the Centres of Excellence established as part of the re-structuring of NATO in response to new

---

22 Elekdağ made this speech to the TBMM Plan and Budget Committee during the MSB budgetary meetings ('CHP'li Elekdağ'dan 'TSK yeniden yapılandırılsın' çağrısı,' Anadolu Ajansı, 8 November 2004).

23 However, it is also observed that there is a difference in the policy of obtaining prestige solely with the power of TSK within the government. Indeed, Minister of Foreign Affairs Abdullah Gül said 'Even if TSK is very powerful, or our economy is powerful, if [our] democracy is not within universal standards, [we] cannot become a strong country' ('Gül: TSK yetmez,' Milliyet, 26 December 2005).

threats. These are the Counter-Terrorism Centre, the Partnership for Peace Training Centre and the Third Army Corps in Istanbul, which has been allocated to NATO's Emergency Intervention Force.

The TSK's EU Strategy

In 2005, in various statements and presentations, the TSK demonstrated that it was not in favour of EU membership, which began heavily influencing the TSK's privileged and autonomous structure. At the opening of the naval forces military school for its 233rd educational year on 3 October 2005, which was the same date given for Turkey's negotiations for full membership to the EU, Naval Forces Commander Admiral Yener Karahanoğlu stated: 'I believe we will have to count our fingers after shaking hands with the EU.' These words epitomised the TSK's opposition to and scepticism of the EU.

General Tolun, who retired from commanding the First Army Corps in 2005, continued to cause controversy on account of his outspoken opposition to the AKP as well as Turkey's projected EU membership. Tolun is considered to be one of the leaders of the Back to the Defence of Rights Movement (Yeniden Müdafa-i Hukuk Hareketi), a political formation consisting of a group of academics and retired generals. Claiming that Turkey was moving away from secularism, Tolun maintained that the Western interventions were intended to protect the long-term benefits of EU countries and the United States and represent the root of all the problems Turkey faces, such as minority rights, attacks against the Aegean, Cyprus, the republican regime along with fundamentalist extreme tendencies.[24]

The TSK stated that it would favour Turkey's admission into the EU, as long as it retained its privileged status. Knowing, however, that membership under such circumstances was unrealistic, the TSK has instead embraced an ambiguous approach.

The TSK and Foreign Policy

Under the present government, and perhaps for the first time, Turkey has parted from the status quo mentality. The most telling example of this has been the important step taken by the government to solve the Cyprus problem which has been ongoing for over 40 years.

Whilst a majority of Turkish Cypriots accepted the Annan Peace Plan on 24 April 2004, the Greek Cypriots rejected it. This plan is named after UN General Secretary Kofi Annan and stipulates modalities for the reunification of the island. In May 2004, the EU not only accepted Greek Cypriots as full members, even though they had refused the solution plan, but also failed to remove the economic embargo on Turks using the Greek veto as an excuse. As a consequence, frustration was expressed by many different sections of Turkish society and this, perhaps, was the reason for the slowing down of the reform process in Turkey.

---

24 'Türkiye laiklikten uzaklaştırılıyor,' Cumhuriyet, 10 December 2005.

While the TBMM's refusal to open a second front over Turkey for US forces during the invasion of Iraq led to tensions in US-Turkey relations, it could also be viewed as a turning-point. The TSK played an important role in the rejection of the proposal and incurred significant damage in its relationship with the United Sates. As a result of this situation, Turkey became an observer of the developments that were taking place next door in Iraq, and that have the potential to influence the whole of the Middle East.

However, while the government and the TSK have taken important steps to improve relations with the United States, and to follow concessionary policies towards Iraq, the US administration — despite the existence of a group of people vengeful of the rejection of the motion of 1 March — began to re-invest in its policy of improving relations with Turkey. The United States depends heavily on Turkey for its own national interests within the region.

Nevertheless, problems have surfaced between Turkey and the United States over the procurement of weapons. Turkey's policy of increasing national material in its procurement of arms, together with stricter US policies on the transfer of technology to developing countries, impacted on its relationship with US companies. Turkey's introduction of a technology transfer licence in weapons manufacturing had an effect on many US-supported defence industry projects, including assault helicopter projects worth billions of dollars. Accordingly, Turkey's procurement of 20 assault helicopters was not supported by US companies, specifically because of the complications associated with the new specifications.

In 2005, the AKP government relaxed its strict stance against Israel's close cooperation with the Kurds in northern Iraq, as well as their resorting to disproportionate violence in the Palestinian Territories. Following pressure from the strong Jewish lobby in the United States, which signalled the retreat of Turkish support, Prime Minister Erdoğan promptly revived Turkey's commercial, military and political relations with Israel. Prior to his delayed visit to Israel, Erdoğan gave the Unmanned Airplane project to an Israeli company, and thereby soothed Tel Aviv.

An important foreign policy development that made its mark on 2005 was witnessed in Turkey's improved relations with neighbouring Middle Eastern countries generated, in part, by an increase in trade with the region to 16.5 percent over the last five years.

The TSK, Parliament and Government Relations

The government's policy on the military sector and its civilian allies has been focused on maintaining the existing balance. Legal changes are being introduced to comply with the EU's sine qua non criteria, such as the determination of Turkey's domestic and foreign policies by civilian authorities, the restructuring of the MSB along civilian lines, and that the chief of the general staff be placed under the command of the minister of defence. The political will to remove Article 35 from the Internal Service Law, which provides the base for military interventions, has not surfaced.

However, there have been strong reactions to the government's passing of laws which pave the way for the democratic supervision of the TSK. The latest instance of this was witnessed on 7 December 2005, when the AKP Tokat Deputy

instance of this was witnessed on 7 December 2005, when the AKP Tokat Deputy Resul Tosun made a request for the relocation of the TBMM guard and ceremonial battalion out of town, along with other military headquarters. Tosun retreated when the TSK made a statement on 8 December 2005, describing Tosun's call as 'an individual raving.'[25] TBMM Chairman Arınç's statement regarding the battalion, underlined another spoke in the traditional dynamic of military-civilian tensions in Turkey.[26]

The fact that Prime Minister Erdoğan never consults with the General Staff Operations Department Presidency Chairman, Lieutenant General Bekir Kalyoncu, appointed as a consultant to the prime minister, could be indicative of the government's deliberate distancing from the military.[27] Erdoğan's disapproval of the low fly-over of F16 planes, during the funeral of those who died in the bombing of the Şemdinli bookshop, underlined the very real tensions persistent in the civil-military relations.

On the other hand, in order to clarify the military wings reaction, it could be said that the government, which made important reforms on the road to democratisation, also carried out a series of practices that disturbed pro-reform secularist elements. These included the AKP's failed attempt to make adultery illegal in the Turkish penal code in 2004, attempts at alcohol prohibition, Erdoğan's using of the Ulema[**] as a reference against the European Court of Human Rights' stance approving headscarf prohibition and his request for consultation with this religious institution, and finally, the debate Erdoğan entered into with the business world. The AKP's slow progress in the EU harmonisation process, and its attempts to modify the public agenda, are worrying developments and reflective of what former President Süleyman Demirel calls the 'deep state' led by the military and anti-reformists.

Supreme Military Council (YAŞ) Meetings

The TSK's prevention of personnel from returning to the armed forces through judicial means, who have been discharged from the army through YAŞ decisions and on the grounds of fundamentalist activity, continues to be a point of contention between the government and the army. In the YAŞ meetings that are held twice a year and headed by the prime minister, promotions and retirements in the armed forces are determined at the August meeting. The matter of who is to be discharged on the

---

25 As a reaction to this incident, (Anavatan Partisi, ANAP) Istanbul Deputy Emin Şirin claimed in his letter to the chief of general staff on 9 December 2005 that 'an abstruse addressee is targeted' and further stated: 'I invite you to be respectful to and not deprecate members of parliament and to treat those who express their opinions with courtesy.' In the same letter, Şirin said that the location of the battalion should be at the land forces military school, at the same time expressing his reaction to the military's duty of watching over the TBMM, who represent the country's will despite its shortcomings.

26 The parliament's Chairman stated, 'As long as I am in AKP, and as long as my name is Bülent Arınç, I do not have enough power to remove this battalion from here.' ('Meclis'teki taburu kaldırma gücüm yok,' Hürriyet, 7 October 2005).

27 From the writer's interview with well-informed sources.

** The ulema specialises on matters related to Islam.

grounds of fundamentalist activity is discussed at the November or December meetings. In 2005, Prime Minister Erdoğan and Minister of Defence Gönül continued to query the YAŞ decisions on the grounds that they should be subject to judicial oversight. The lowest number of discharges in recent years was decided at the YAŞ meeting of 1 December 2005, and four TSK personnel - three Non-Commissioned Officers (NCO's) and one captain - were discharged at a later date.

The TSK Budget

As other public budgets, the MSB budget is discussed by the TBMM Plan and Budget Committee ((Plan ve Bütçe Komisyonu PBK). Neither the MSB nor the PBK are staffed with military and security experts, so the military budget is discussed as a routine budget matter at the committee meetings. It is therefore accepted without detailed discussions.[28] Budget discussions open to the press precede a five-minute closed session, in which information is presented by the MSB's military personnel to members of parliament. This information is described as secret, even though it can be ascertained in specialised military magazines abroad.

However, as far as we know, not a single parliament member questioned on a public platform has offered any reason for keeping this information secret from the public, despite the fact that it is accessible to everyone.

The resources allocated to defence, including the MSB budget, constituted 10 percent of the total budget in 2006 and 3.2 percent of gross domestic product (GDP). For the first time in Turkey's history, the government announced that the resources allocated to the Ministry of National Education (Milli Eğitim Bakanlığı MEB) exceeded those allocated to the MSB in the budgets of the previous two years. The table detailing the budgets of 2006, 2007 and 2008 confirms this statement (for the Ministry of Finance budget, see Table 1).

However, the impression that the MEB budget exceeds that of the MSB is, in fact, misleading since the table fails to include the extra budgetary resources that have been allocated to the defence sector. In the MSB's White Book 2000 (for the MSB budget, see Table 2), the extra budgetary resources allocated to defence outside the MSB budget read as follows, and the total of these resources attest to the fact that the MEB budget was lower than the MSB budget in 2006:

- Defence Industry Support Fund (Savunma Sanayii Destekleme Fonu, SSDF) (For the resources that constitute the fund income, see Sidebar 5);
- Turkish Armed Forces Strengthening Foundation (Türk Silahlı Kuvvetleri Güçlendirme Vakfı, TSKGV) resources;
- Budget of the General Command of the Gendarmerie;
- Budget of the Coast Guard Command;
- Foreign state and corporation credit which is reimbursed by the Treasury Undersecretariat Budget;
- The income of the Minister of National Defence which is calculated in accordance with special laws.

---

[28] For the minutes of the PBK discussions on 11 November 2005 regarding the MSB budget, see http://www.msb.gov.tr

The aforementioned extra budgetary resources (outside the MSB budget) for 2006 are estimated at YTL 2.6 billion for the General Command of Gendarmerie, YTL 194.4 million for the Coast Guard Command, YTL 2.05 billion (approximately USD 1.5 billion) for the SSDF, and YTL 685 million or more (USD 500 million) for the foreign state or corporation credits supported by the treasury undersecretary every year.

Therefore, when the General Command of the Gendarmerie, the Coast Guard Command, SSDF and treasury aids that constitute the Defence Industry Undersecretariat (Savunma Sanayii Müsteşarlığı, SSM) are added to the MSB budget, which has been stated as a total of YTL 11.8 billion in 2006, then the total resources allocated to the defence sector in fact reached YTL 17.4 billion in 2005. This represents an increase of 7 percent from the previous year (for information concerning SSM's status, see Sidebar 6). Therefore, the total resources allocated to defence exceed the MEB 2006 budget of YTL 16.5 billion.

However, the MSB 2006 budget, which stands at YTL 11.8 billion, constitutes 6.8 percent of the total 2006 budget of YTL 174 billion (USD 127.2 billion) and the greatest resources are allocated to personnel expenditures at YTL 4.3 billion. This is followed by weapons procurement at YTL 3.6 billion. These two resources have increased in comparison to last year by 12.2 percent and 6.2 percent respectively.

The administrative expenditures portion of the SSDF, which is not under parliamentary supervision and which constitutes approximately one percent of the fund, has been included for the first time in the Ministry of Finance's budget. However, the portion allocated to military procurement, which constitutes approximately 90 percent of the SSM budget, has not been declared. Nevertheless, during the TBMM-PBK meeting held on 11 November 2005, Minister of Defence Gönül announced that the SSM budget of 2006 was approximately USD 1.5 billion.

In 2007, the KMYKK – a law which was ratified in 2003 and came into effect in 2005 - will dissolve the SSDF fund which constitutes the source of income for the SSM. The SSM will continue to use the balance for weapons procurement.

The salary information of TSK personnel is not publicly disclosed nor is it provided by the minister of finance's press bureau. However, it is now possible to access this information in an indirect way. For example, if one analyses the tables comparing the salaries of military and civil servants, one finds that a fifth level sergeant earns YTL 938 per month, whereas an assistant medical physician earns YTL 820. A new lieutenant earns YTL 1'038, a chief of police YTL 885, an engineer YTL 846, a doctor YTL 820, and a teacher, YTL 625.[29] (For the salaries of military personnel for 2004, see Sidebar 3). These salary comparisons were published by newspapers upon the complaints of the deputy chief of the general staff, General İlker Başbuğ's, who stated that officers are very poor.

The issues which were covered in the last budget meetings of the MSB that are worthy of attention are as follows: members of parliament allotted only two

---

29 'Silahsız kuvvetlerin maaşı da çok düşük,' Milliyet, 28 January 2005.

hours for debate on the military budget - the largest expenditure by Turkey in the PBK meeting this year - whereas the minister of agriculture's budget meeting took 10 hours on the same day. At the same meeting, two committee members, one from the CHP and another from the AKP, made statements about Turkey's defence expenditure. CHP Trabzon Deputy Akif Hamzaçebi, who took the floor during the meeting, stated that the MSB budget did not reflect the numbers that were transferred from previous to upcoming years and drew attention to the fact that the funds transferred from year to year actually increased. Hamzaçebi pointed out that this number reached YTL 4 billion in 2004, an increase of 30 percent.[30] Minister Gönül's response to Hamzaçebi's statement confirmed that the figures for the MSB 2005 budget was YTL 14 billion, together with the funds transferred from 2004 to 2005.

At the same meeting, AKP Kayseri Deputy Taner Yıldız pointed to the difference between the resources which were known to be allocated to the defence sector in Turkey, and information that was released in international publications on the subject of Turkey's defence expenditure. Yıldız stressed that the amount and proportion allocated to the same items by various countries should be compared in order to understand the size of the education, health and military expenditures in Turkey.[31]

CHP Deputy Onur Öymen stressed that Turkey imports the largest number of weapons, and thus emphasised the necessity of increasing domestic defence manufacturing. Öymen also drew attention to the fact that approximately one fifth of taxable income in Turkey is allocated to defence spending.[32]

Weapons Procurement

According to official figures, Turkey allocates USD 3 to 4 billion for weapons procurement each year. Although countries of the same scale as Turkey, such as Israel and South Korea, also allocate around USD 4 billion for their weapons procurement, unlike Turkey, their dependence on other countries for weapons technology is much lower (for the principal weapons procurements of Turkey, see Sidebar 7). In a paper presented at a meeting organised by the SSM on 10-11 December 2002, SSM expert Alper Köse stated that the total of domestic production, joint venture production and ready made, off the shelf, import models, constituted 73 percent of the total project value. Alper Köse also stressed the fact that in not one of the above mentioned cases

---

30 According to Hamzaçebi's assessment, when the 2006 budget is discussed, the amount that will be transferred over from 2005 is not revealed. Therefore, when evaluating the real size of the MSB budget, this should be taken into consideration.

31 According to Yıldız: 'especially from the point of view of the budget allocated to sectors such as education and health, Turkey is ranked 94th on the human development list (United Nations Human Development Report, 2002). When we compare the education, health and military expenditures of Turkey with those of the first 20 countries, we should say that we are way behind in the fields of education and health, whereas we are ranking second after the United States in the military domain.' See PBK Meeting, 11 November 2005, http://www.tbmm.gov.tr

32 'Savunmada yerli üretim artmalı,' Cumhuriyet, 25 November 2005.

did the design, integration or engineering work fall under the responsibility of local companies. (see Table 4).

99 percent of the USD 1.5 billion SSM budget is allocated to weapons procurement. This constitutes one third of Turkey's total weapons procurement amounting to USD 4 billion. Turkey also has debts exceeding USD 5 billion for weapons purchased from the United States through the US Foreign Military Sales Credit (FMS).

Democratic civilian oversight has not been achieved in the field of the TSK's weapons procurement. A loophole in the Public Bidding Law is used as an obstacle for obstructing transparency in this domain.[33] The lack of supervision in weapons procurement has essentially made the TSK the sole arbiter in this field.

An example of the government's lack of control over weapons procurement was made evident in the purchase of AEW&Cs. The TBMM's investigation committee began a probe with the claim that the state had suffered damages worth USD 180 million during the USD 1.5 billion-worth procurement of planes in 2003, but was eventually forced to terminate the investigation. Minister of Defence Gönül said: 'the TBMM should also be involved in this kind of procurement,' confessing that the government had been left out of the loop in the matter.[34]

Turkey's purchase of AEW&Cs, which are in the inventory of only a handful of countries in the world, is yet another example of how the TSK has based its weapon procurements on the threat perceptions determined by the TSK. The perception of Greece as a threat played an important role in the procurement of these planes, and Greece is competing with Turkey in the purchase of weapons.

The lack of civilian supervision in the area of weapons procurement is an additional burden on Turkish taxpayers. The current level of strain was illustrated most recently by France's arbitration of Turkey's anti-tank missile purchase project. The project of Eryx short-range anti-tank missile procurement was signed in secret by the Ministry of National Defence with the French company MBDA in 1998, at a time when the French parliament was increasing its accusations against Turkey regarding the Armenian genocide. The project, which covered a span of 10 years, and was perceived by the military as an essential addition to Turkish military installations, was brought to a standstill by the TSK in 2004 on the grounds of a technical deficiency. France consequently filed a case against Turkey at Geneva's Interna-

---

33 For article 3/b of Public Bidding Law No. 4734, see Resmi Gazete (Official Gazette) dated 22 January 2002, No. 24648. The article made provisions for an exception in military procurement. Article 3/b of the law gave the Ministry of National Defence the authority to regulate its own rules. For the MSB Military Bidding Decree No. 6392, see Resmi Gazette dated 6 December 2003. With this decree, almost all projects gained secrecy status, whereas there is nothing to stipulate arbitration through an independent body like the public bidding council in cases of disagreement.

34 While Gönül said: 'The most important factor against democracy is the budget committee and parliament not being in the loop. A purchase of USD 1.5 billion takes place. But anywhere else in the world, such procurement should be preceded and followed by parliamentary approval.' He also stated that the project was signed during the previous government's rule, therefore freeing himself of responsibility ('Askerler istemese AWACS'lar alınmazdı,' Milliyet, 9 May 2003).

tional Arbitration Court requesting compensation to the value of USD 489 million, an amount which exceeded the project's worth, which stood at USD 486.5 million.

In a statement made by Erdoğan, he declared that any sizeable procurement of weapons in the future would be decided upon jointly by the military and civilians authorities. The government, if not the TBMM, would henceforth supervise Turkey's weapon procurement proposals in an ever-increasing fashion.[35] In 2005, the government took a positive step to end its dependence on other countries, which stood as high as 80 percent (in terms of the procurement of weapons systems), by allocating a budget of YTL 416 billion to the Turkish Scientific and Technical Research Institution (Türkiye Bilimsel ve Teknik Araştırmalar Kurumu, TÜBİTAK) to be used chiefly in the design of defence projects. The government has stated that its aim is to achieve its target of allocating 2 percent of the total GNP to research and development (R&D) by 2010 and, at the same time, to transfer the authority of R&D projects to civilians, thereby delegating the supervision of such allocations to a civilian authority.

The Fight Against Corruption Within the TSK

In the past, all the claims of TSK corruption were concealed. The most striking example of this was the failure to investigate allegations of fraud by General Tahsin Şahinkaya, the Air Force Commander of the military regime after 12 September 1980.[36] In 2005, the TSK took a historic step in the fight against corruption and fraud within the armed forces and opened the way for a former commanding officer to be tried for allegations of fraud. In the TSK, where the mentality of concealing any fault from the outside world still prevails, the chief of the general staff, General Özkök, defied the taboos in 2004 by initiating the trial of former Naval Force Commander İlhami Erdil for allegations of unjustified benefit, together with his daughter, his spouse, one orderly officer and a friend of his daughter. At the risk of angering any TSK members, Özkök ensured that the trial was open to the public, and thus, a commanding officer was brought before trial for the first time for allegations of fraudulent activity.

A process different to that of former politicians in the Council of State was espoused, and the procedure of scrutinising the property holdings of the defendant was applied. This was an important criterion that would help determine whether the person concerned had obtained unjustified benefit. The court-appointed expert, who

---

35 'AWACS ihalesi sorun oldu,' Radikal, 11 May 2003.

36 The Social Democratic People's Party (SHP) deputy of the period, the late Cüneyt Canver gave a motion of question with 24 other deputies on 24 May 1986, for the investigation of allegations of fraud concerning Şahinkaya, including claims that he obtained unjust personal benefit during F-16 procurements from Lockheed Martin. However, this case was closed. Retired Ambassador Yalım Eralp brought the Şahinkaya incident back into the spotlight with a statement he made in 2001. Working as the Embassy Undersecretary in Washington during the Şahinkaya incident and speaking about the claims of fraud over the F-16 bidding, Eralp discerned: 'The Americans did not name names, but the definition fit Şahinkaya.' Eralp's interview with Yener Süsoy, Hürriyet, 12 November 2001.

scrutinised Erdil's salaries and allowances from the start of his career in 1958, stated that Erdil's two apartments in Istanbul Etiler Alkent 2, which were subject to trial, could not have been bought with his official and recorded savings.[37]

On 7 February 2006, Erdil was sentenced by the military court to 3 years and 1 month in prison for unjustified appropriation and the use of undue influence. The court ruled for the seizure of the apartments. Pending the final sentence, Erdil, who has the right to appeal, will lose his title of Admiral, and will no longer be admitted to officers' clubs.[38]

The Erdil trial demonstrated the willingness of the TSK to investigate allegations of fraud within the armed forces. It also illustrated that the process of military court trials could be shorter than trials conducted by the Council of State.[39] Another case, parallel to the Erdil trial, was filed in relation to allegations of unjust profit worth YTL 150 million in the General Staff Special Forces Command Oğulbey Complex construction, in which contractor Ali Osman Özmen was arrested and detained during trial. The names of the generals who had been bribed by Özmen were obtained from Özmen's appointment book. Also implicated was General Tuncer Kılınç, who was the last MGK general secretary to have a military background and was well-known for his secularist discourse and for frequently speaking about the fundamentalist threat.

Kılınç, who awarded the contract, confirmed that he had 'borrowed' USD 150'000 from Özmen to purchase an apartment while he was undersecretary at the Ministry of National Defence.

Conclusion

It is believed that an accountable, transparent and democratically supervised armed forces makes for a strengthened military sector. Despite the fact that they are often of a smaller size, the armed forces of the United States, Canada and of most EU countries are technologically superior to and stronger than Turkey's, precisely because they are accountable. The modern democratic oversight approach has facilitated endeavours by the media, civil society, politicians, the parliament and citizens, to ask the following questions: as a country which allocates such a large portion of its budget to defence, why has Turkey remained dependent on other countries at rates as high as 80 percent? The undersecretary of the defence industry, Murat Bayar, has regularly questioned how independent will Turkey become in the field of security if it fails to produce its own defence technology to a greater extent. Indeed, when Turkey's technological dependence is taken into consideration, how credible is the argument that its armed forces should be strengthened because of its critical geopolitical position?

The fact that the principle of accountability in the security sector is for the public's good, was elucidated in research carried out by the World Bank in 2002,

[37] 'Evlerin alımı hukuken ve ahlaken mümkün değil,' Hürriyet, 24 November 2005.

[38] 'Evleri, kılıcı ve apoleti gitti,' Hürriyet, 8 February 2006.

[39] The trial of İlhami Erdil lasted less than two years, whereas the trial of former politicians in the Council of State are ongoing.

amongst the countries to which it gave credit. The research illustrated that the inclusion of defence expenditure in public expenses was ultimately a beneficial mechanism, because it provided for a better understanding and acceptance of defence policies by the public, it provided the reasons and justifications for defence expenses, and it facilitated a more efficient and rational use of defence expenses.[40]

[40] Nicole Ball, Malcolm Holmes, 'Integrating Defence into Public Expenditure Work,' Commissioned by the UK Department for International Development (11 January 2002). See http://www.grcexchange.org/docs/SS11.pdf

DIAGRAM I: TURKISH GENERAL STAFF AUG 05

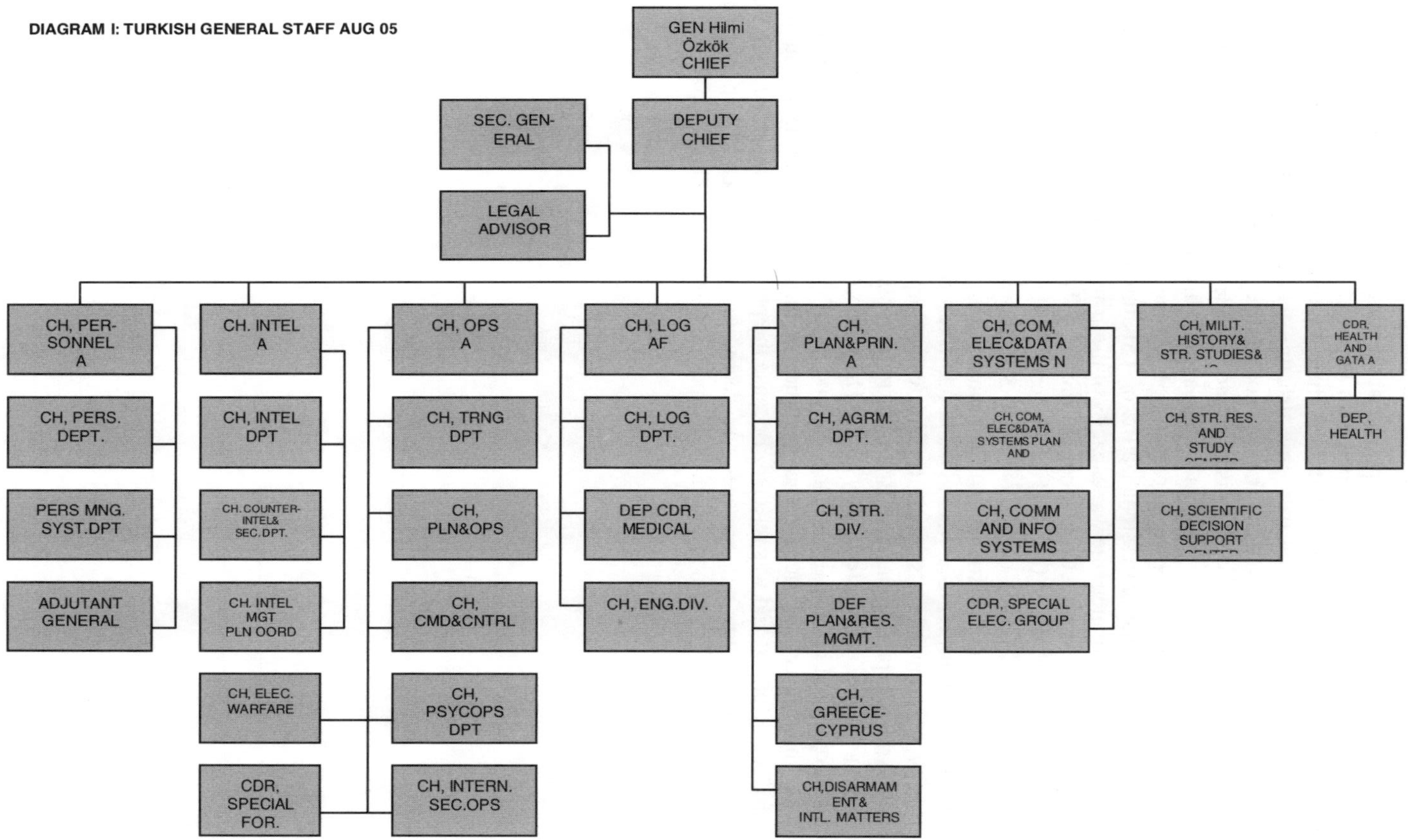

Sidebar 1

TSK is still unable to implement its project of creating an army that is efficient and flexible, small in numbers but equipped with high-tech weapons. For more than 10 years, the Turkish land forces maintained their top-down structure of army-army corps-brigade-battalion. In the past, this structure was in the form of army-army corps-division-regiment-battalion. The division and regiment structures of the past were abolished with the new organisation and brigades were established with two exceptions, namely the army corps in Cyprus and the division in Sarıkamış. It is also known that there is no short-term preparation for the abolishment of compulsory military service and the professionalization of TSK through a meaningful downsizing. In the current situation, the war capacity of the army is kept through compulsory military service and contract personnel are recruited. While he was the commander of the Land Forces under the chief of General Staff of the time, retired General Kıvrıkoğlu, General Özkök carried out a series of projects concerning the reduction of the number of army personnel and the founding of a more flexible army that has faster response. Within this context, Özkök had foreseen the abolishment of the 1st Army Corps Command in Istanbul, the 2nd Army Corps Command in Malatya and the 3rd Army Corps Command in Erzincan, to be replaced by the two army corps, namely the eastern and western army corps. The purpose of the plan was to establish the joint operation capabilities of land, air and naval forces for deterrence way, so that the three forces can act together in times of threat. However, this plan was deemed too reformist and was rejected. Because the plan was aiming at reducing the numbers of army corps and brigades and decreasing the number of Land Forces Command personnel by almost a half, from approximately 402.000 to 280.000.

DIAGRAM 2: TURKISH LAND FORCES COMMAND HQ AUG 05

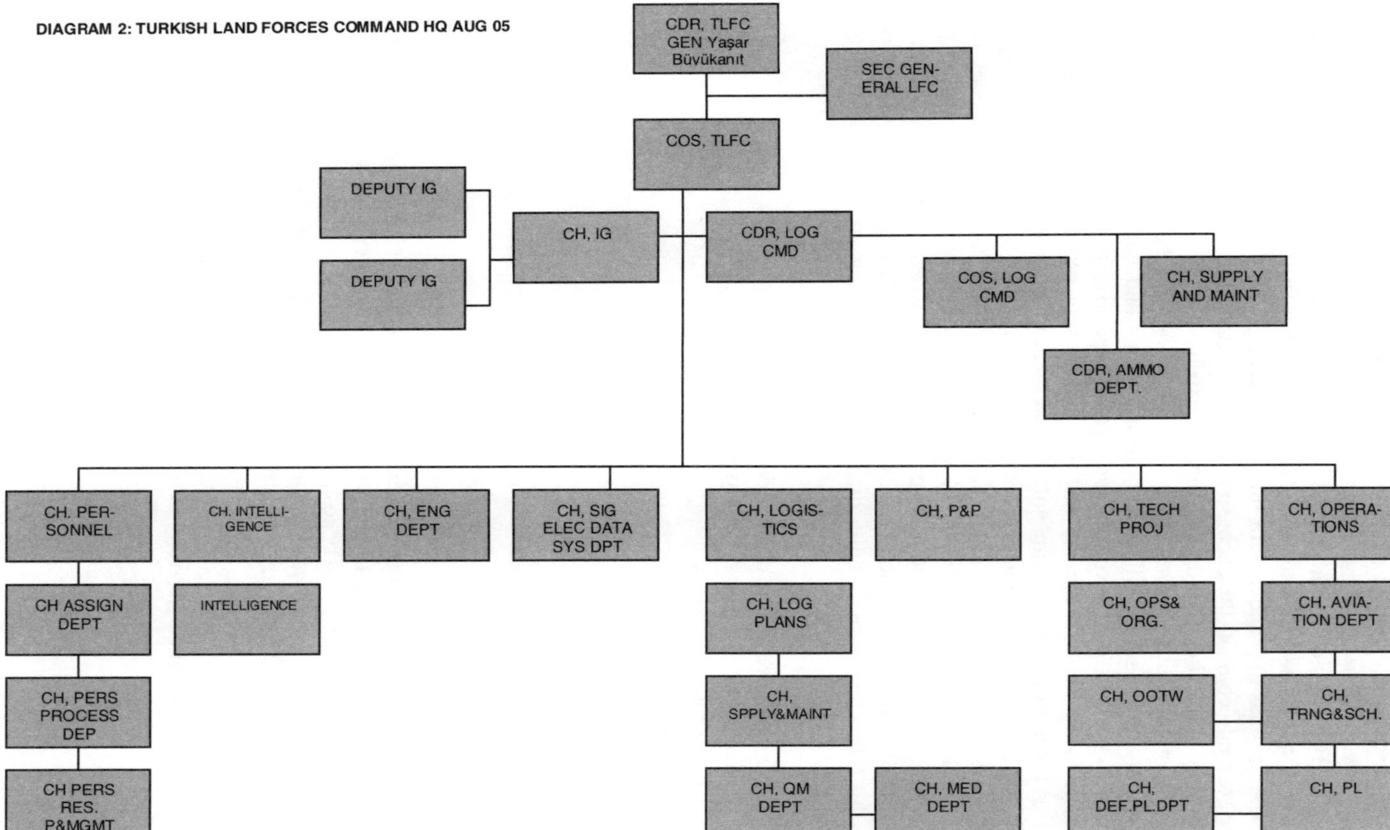

Sidebar 2:

It is clear that the expenses made for a soldier are closely connected to his post. The most varying figure in these expenditure items will be the money spent on target practice. For instance, a soldier who works as a waiter in the officers' clubs will only be doing target practice with an infantry rifle, whereas a soldier using an anti-tank missile also has to practice with this missile along with the infantry rifle. If the soldier goes into combat, the expense related to ammunition consumption will be naturally very high. The clothing and feeding expenses of the soldier will also vary depending on the unit he belongs to, as well as its location. For instance, a soldier who is on duty in the south will wear normal summer and winter uniforms, whereas a soldier in the east will have to wear a more expensive uniform and boots that are suitable to the region's climate and that will prevent perspiration. The feeding expenses for a soldier in a commando unit and that in a normal infantry unit will also vary, since their caloric requirements differ. Also, salary paid to soldiers in southeastern Anatolia -formerly under the jurisdiction of the State of Emergency Region (*Olağanüstü Hal Bölgesi*, OHAL) Governorship- a region that is still sensitive due to terrorism, is higher compared to other regions. Also, when we take into consideration the fact that all of the soldier's needs are met by the state, quantifying the expenses for the following items is quite difficult: The following are costs incurred by the state:

1 Maintenance for the dormitories;
2 Construction of new dormitories when necessary;
3 Costs for washrooms;
4 Laundering;
5 Haircuts;
6 Garment repair;
7 Electricity;
8 Heating;
9 Vehicles, driver's education, gas, maintenance and repairs, depreciation, insurance, etc.);
10 Health-care;
11 Transportation.

Taking into consideration other items that a person might need, this list can be extended. To make a rough estimate, we can say that a soldier's daily costs equal YTL 8-10 million on average; yearly costs are YTL 3-4 billion on average.

When we take into consideration the fact that a soldier's military service normally lasts 15 months, the total costs incurred during this time are approximately YTL 4-5 billion.

Source: Information culled from various military sources (2004)

DIAGRAM 3: ARMY COMMAND AUGUST 05

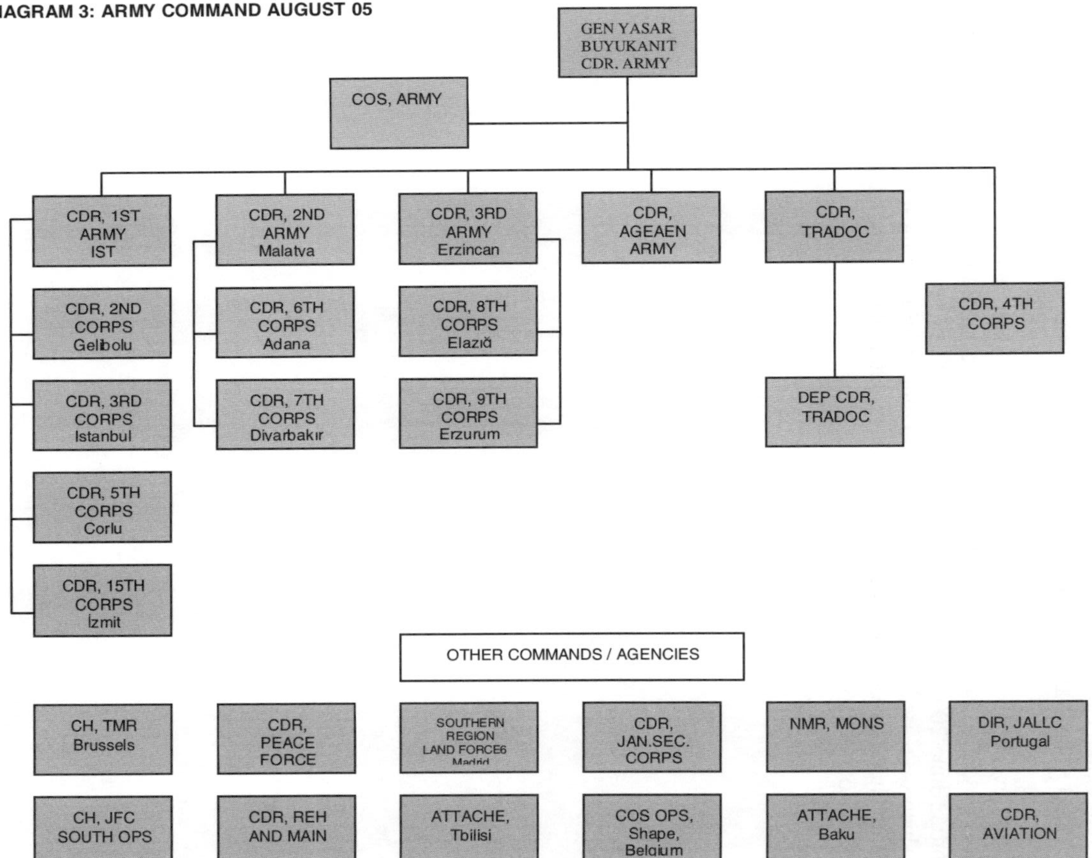

Sidebar 3:
According to the White Book, which was last published in 2000 by the Ministry of National Defence, the number of soldiers per force is as follows:

Land Forces Command: 402.000
Air Forces Command: 63.000
Naval Forces Command: 53.000
General Command of the Gendarmerie: 280.000 (When the fight against the PKK was on the rise, the number of gendarmerie personnel increased considerably)
Coast Guard Command: 2.200
TOTAL: 800.200 (Of which 115.000 are professional soldiers).

This makes the number of soldiers completing their military service 685.200, the majority of whom are privates. The joint staff declared that, with a decision it made on 22 June 2003 it reduced the duration of military service from 18 months to 15, which decreased the number of soldiers completing their military service by 17%. With this decrease, the number of soldiers completing their military service went down to 568.716.

DIAGRAM 4: 1st ARMY COMMAND 2004

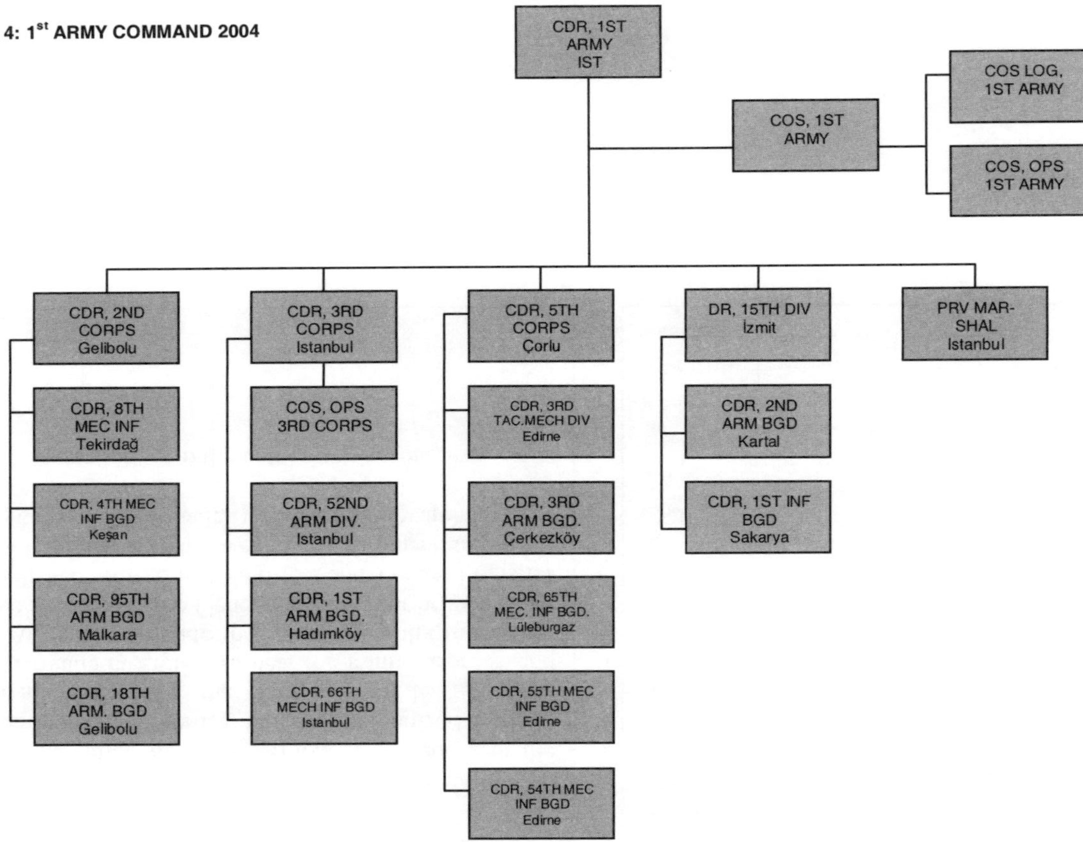

Sidebar 4:

In May 2004, the Turkish armed forces dismantled the 4th Brigade. Thereafter, the 33rd Armoured Brigade near the Bulgarian and Greek border, the 7th Mechanized Brigade in Kağızman-Kars near the Armenian border, the 10th Infantry Brigade in Ercis-Van near the Iranian Border, and the 9th Armoured Brigade in Central Anatolia in Çankırı were also abolished. The Generals of the four brigades that were abolished were transferred to Land Forces Logistics Command, and most of the weapons, equipment and materiel belonging to the brigades were stored in warehouses

Source: Information from the author's own sources.

Sidebar 5:

SSDF's main sources of income are defined in the SSM Establishment Law No. 3238.

Their distribution is as follows:

INCOME	PERCENTAGE	DEFINED IN
1- Income & Corporate Tax	3.5%	Law 2003
2. National Lottery Earnings	95%	Law 1992
3. Book-making proceedings		
a) Horse-race betting	10%	B.K.K. 1986
b) Football betting	3%	B.K.K. 2003
4) Numbers games proceedings (25%)	15%	Law 1985
5) Light frirearms import net proceedings	80%	Decree 1990

Source: SSM

DIAGRAM 5: 2nd ARMY COMMAND 2004

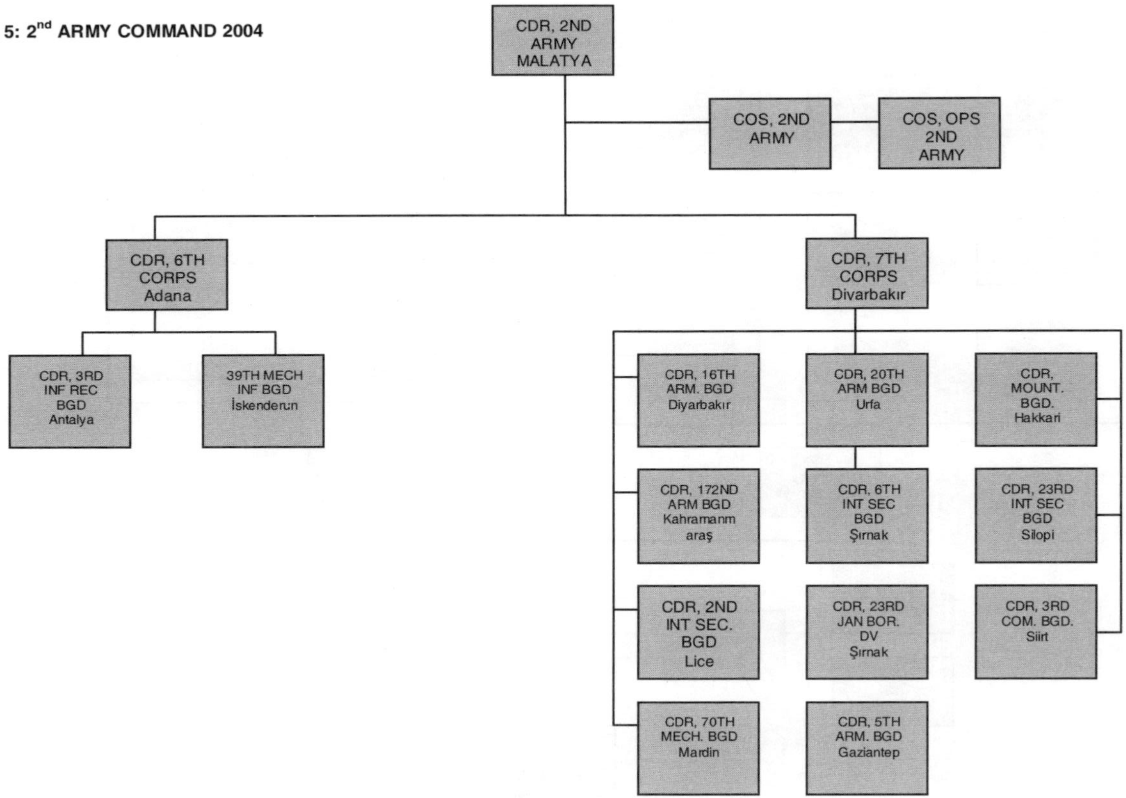

DIAGRAM 6: 3rd ARMY COMMAND 2004

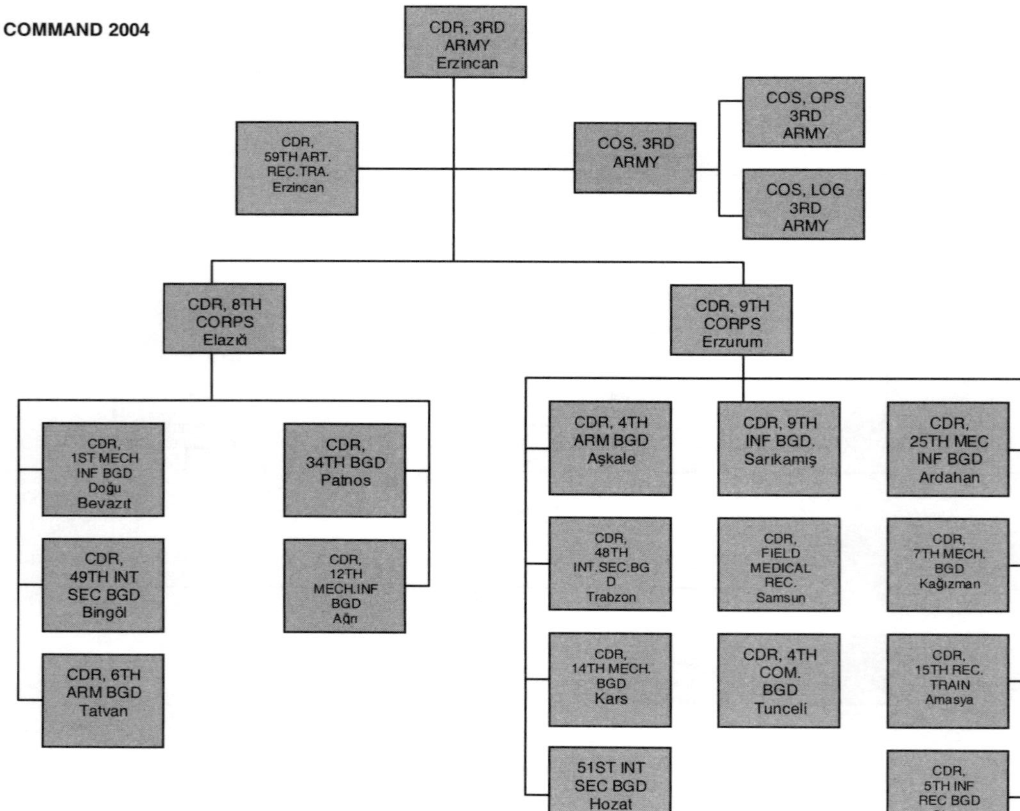

DIAGRAM 7: AGEAEN ARMY COMMAND 2004

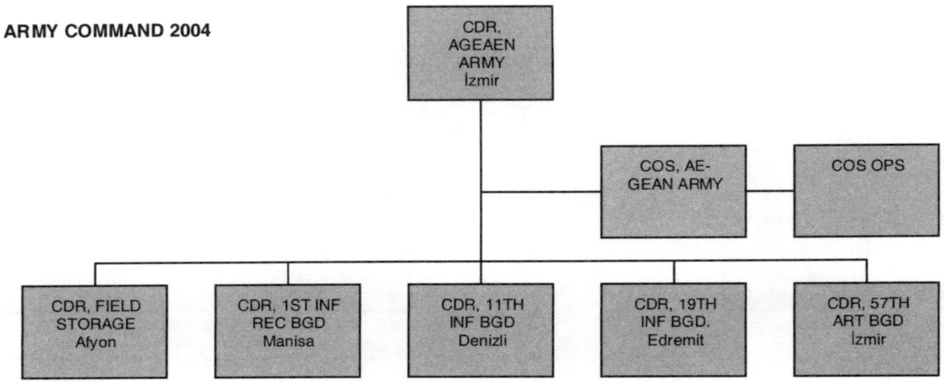

DIAGRAM 8: COMBINED WAR COLLEGES COMMAND 2004

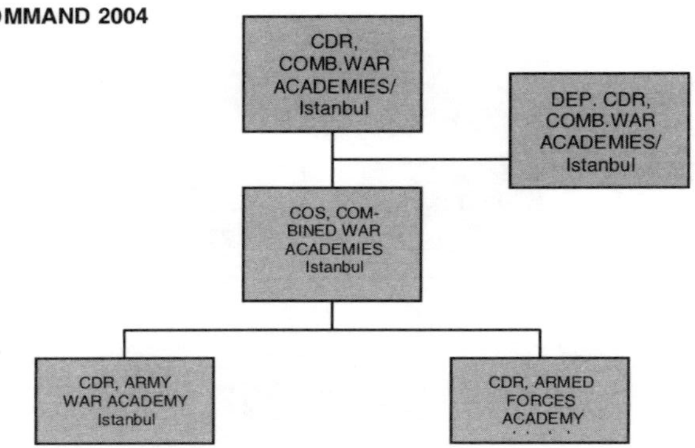

DIAGRAM 9: 4th CORPS COMMAND 2004

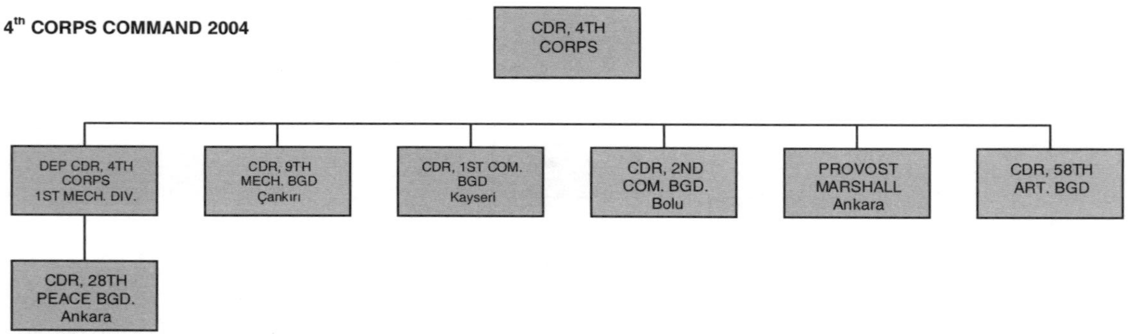

ANKARA GARRISON TGS OTHER SUBORDINATES

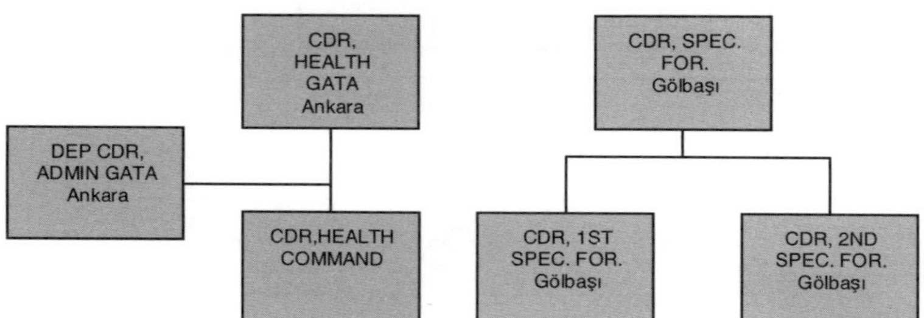

NATIONAL SECURITY COUNCIL 2004

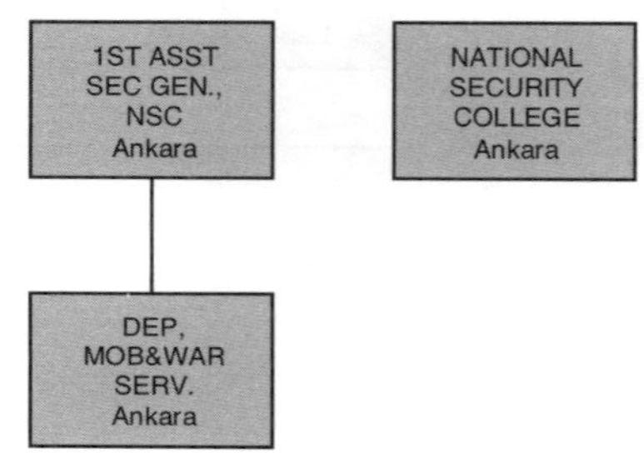

DIAGRAM 10: TRADOC COMMAND 2004

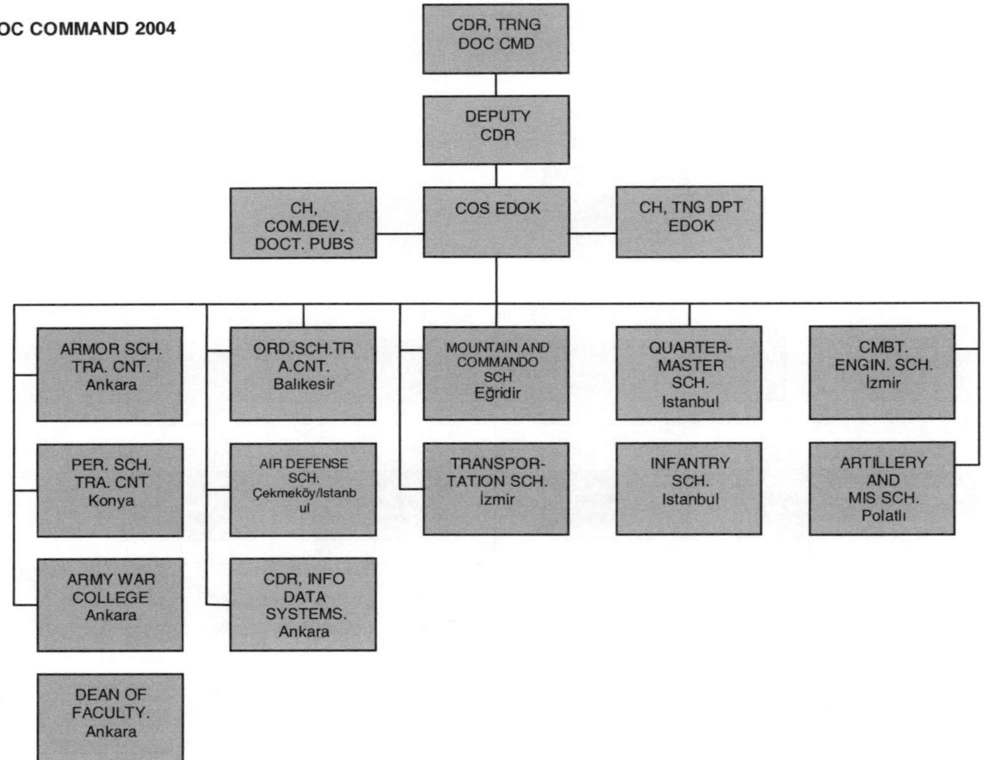

DIAGRAM 11: TURKISH NAVAL FORCES HQ AUGUST 05

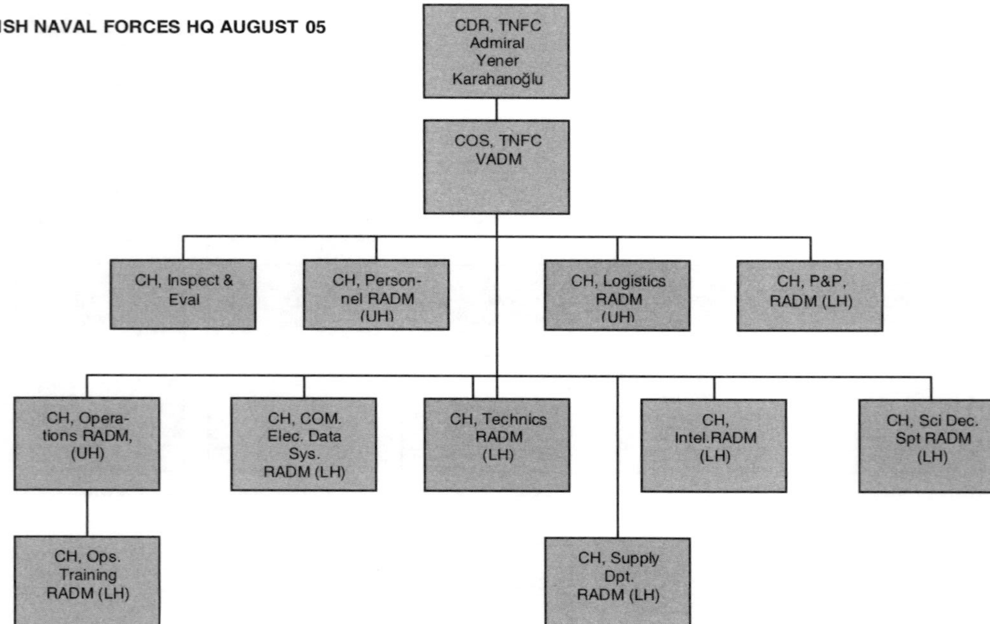

DIAGRAM 12: TURKISH NAVAL FORCES COMMAND AUGUST 05

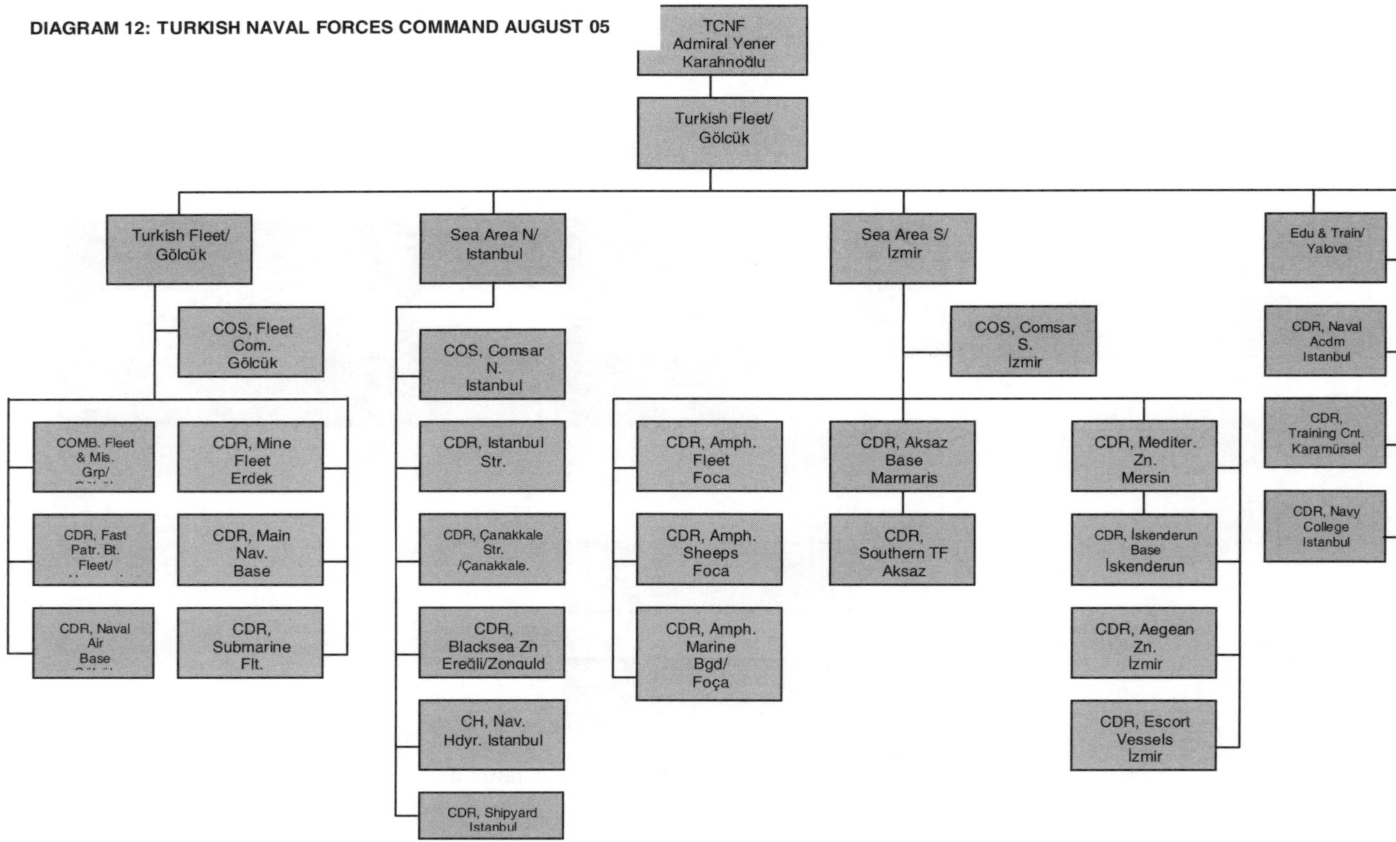

DIAGRAM 13: TURKISH NAVAL FORCES OTHER AGENCIES AUGUST 05

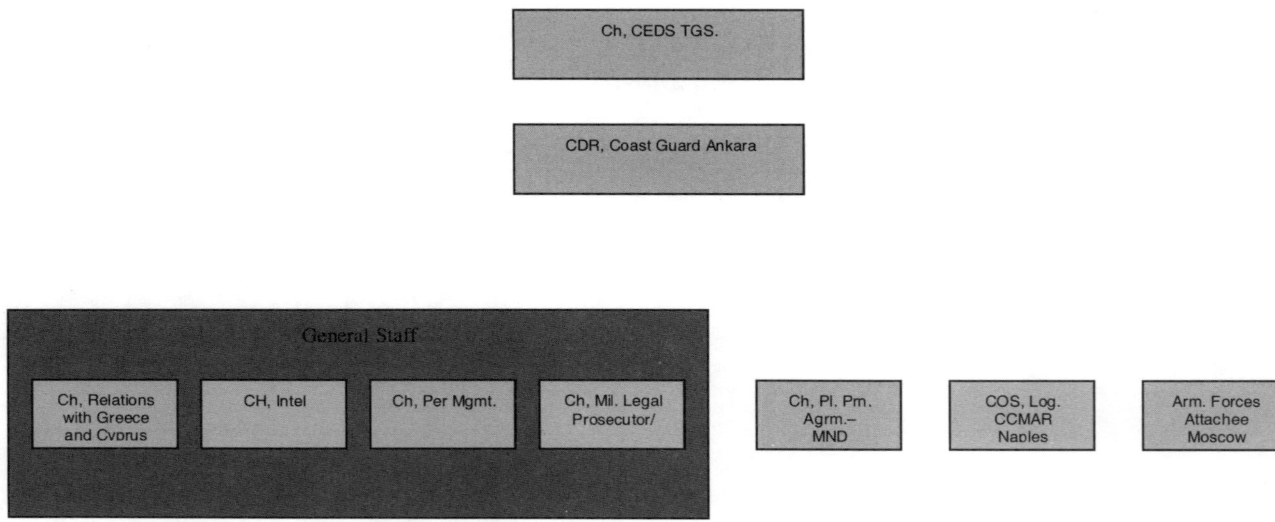

DIAGRAM 14: TURKISH AIR FORCES HQ AUG 05

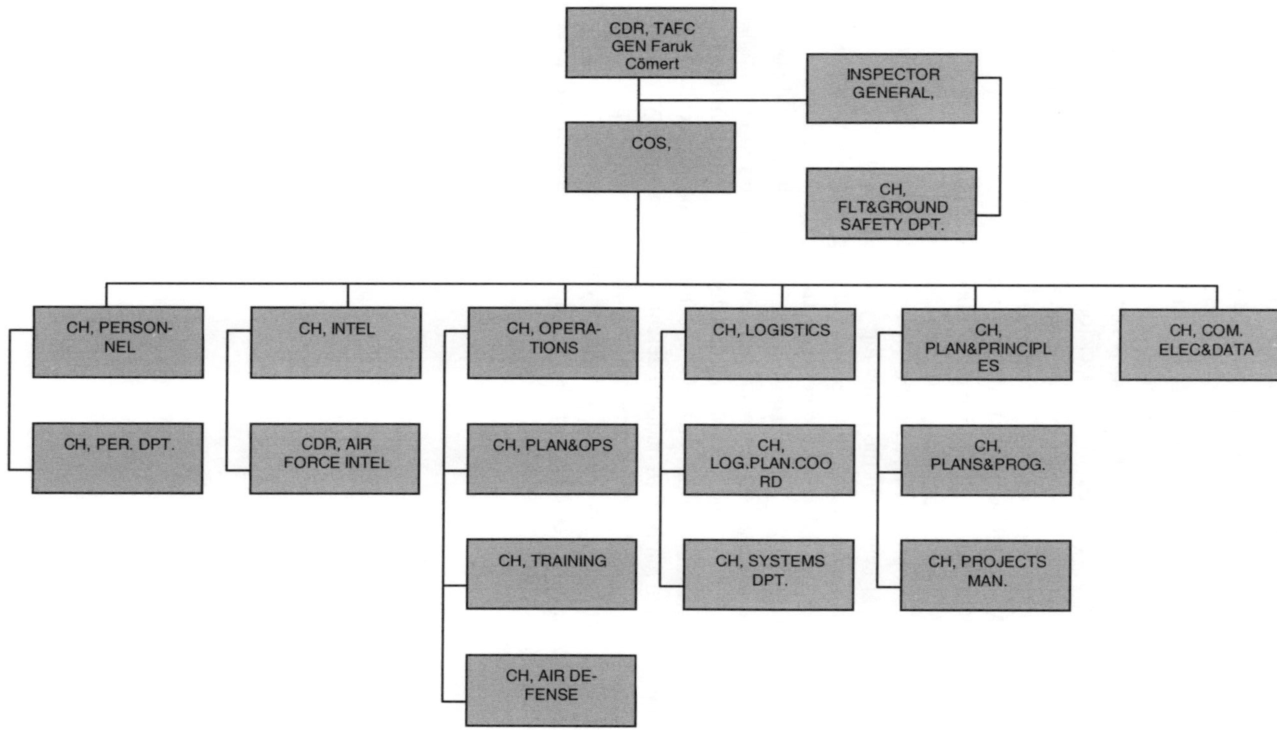

Sidebar 6:
There are two official bodies in Turkey responsible for weapons procurement. One is SSM, founded in 1985; the other is the undersecretary of the Ministry of National Defence, who is a general. The Ministry of National Defence Undersecretariat, which is predominantly involved in readymade weapons procurement, transferred this duty in recent years to SSM. SSM was established in 1985 with Law No. 3238 in order to develop a defence industry infrastructure in Turkey and to decrease dependence on other countries for weapons procurement. SSM is an incorporated public institution with its own budget and is accountable to civilian authority. SSM is charged with the execution of the decisions of the Defence Industry Executive Committee concerning weapons procurement, the committee consisting of the prime minister, the minister of national defence and the chief of general staff. In the 20 years since SSM's establishment, USD16 billion was collected in SSDF and of this amount, 14 billion was used for weapons purchase. Another reason for the establishment of SSM was for civilians to decide matters of weapons procurement like in other democratic countries, and for the TSK to notify this civilian agency of its operational needs. However, in the following years, the SSM was militarized, and the users' (i.e. TSK's) becoming the decision-making body in weapons procurement caused confusion in the relations between the institutions that use and purchase weapons. With the Public Administration Basic Law, which could not be passed for various political reasons and the main purpose of which can be summarized as the transfer of some of the central government's authorities to local administrations for a more efficient administration, one of these two weapons-procurement institutions working under the ministry of national defence, the sole ministry with two undersecretaries, should be abolished. It is planned to abolish SSM and put it under the MSB undersecretariat that works under the military with the passing of this law. If this plan is realized, it will be a backwards step in the transparency and accountability of the weapons-procurement process.

DIAGRAM 15: TURKISH AIR FORCES COMMAND AUG 05

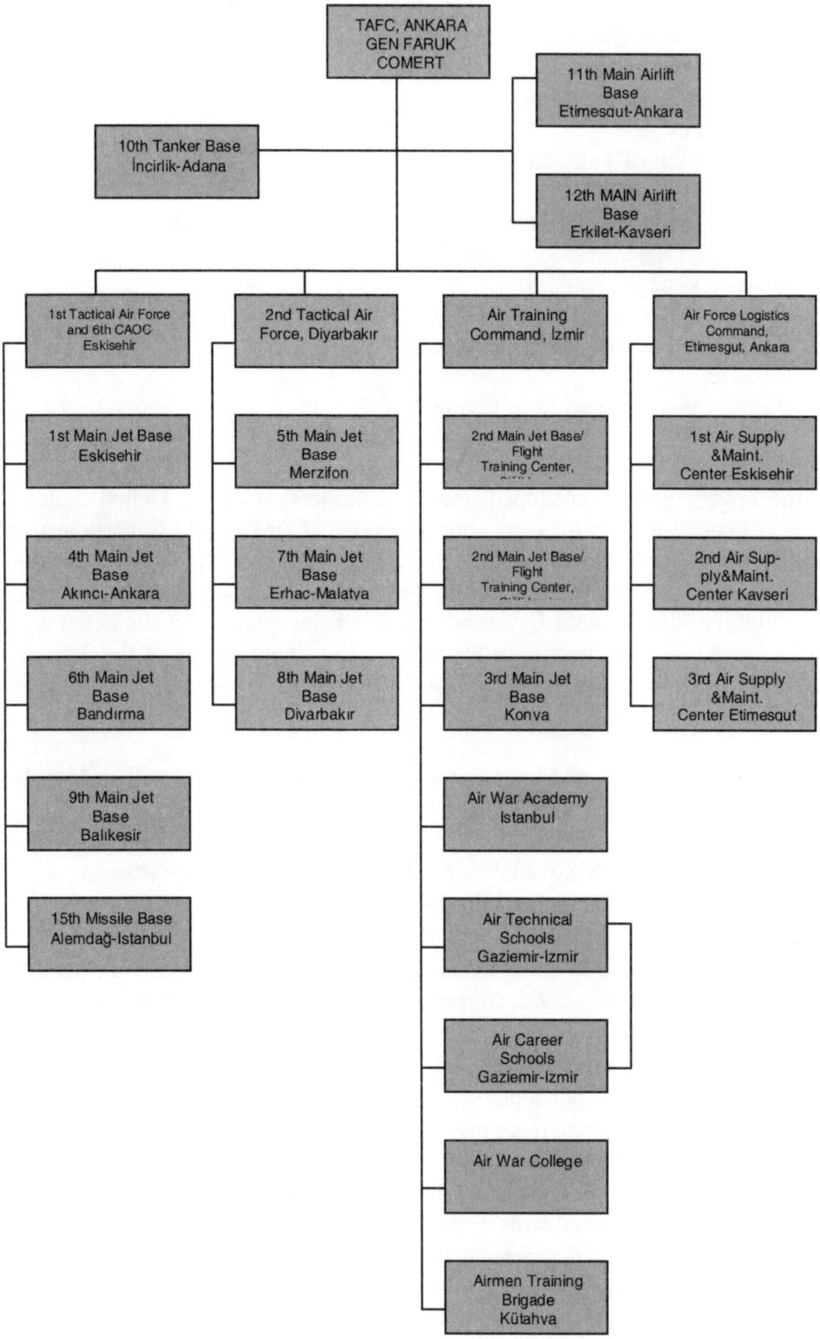

Sidebar 7:
Some of the projects in 2005-2023 that are to be covered by treasury-guaranteed foreign state credit or from the MSB budget are as follows. The total cost of these projects is expected to reach USD 9.8 billion:

1 Modernization of 4 moon-class submarines
2 Construction of 4 submarines of a new type
3 The modernization of the 48 F4 planes in the THKK inventory
4 4 long range regional aerial-defence systems
5 3 Turkish-type frigates (TF-2000)
6 4 advanced aerial/missile defence systems
7 *120 new-generation fighter planes (JSF)

* In the project that is developed under the leadership of the United States, the American Lockheed Martin Corporation proposed to Turkey a local participation of up to USD 5 billion in order to block its European competitors who are pressuring Turkey into buying Eurofighters. During the project that is expected to cost Turkey USD 10 billion, the proposal for spending half of this amount for the strengthening of the domestic industry may pave the way for the strengthening of the defence industry infrastructure and the closing down of some idle companies that do not produce projects.

These fighter planes expected to enter the inventory in 2011-2023 will replace the F-16 fighter planes.

- Projects that will be covered by SSDF in 2005-2014 are as follows:
- Procurement of 50 combat helicopters in the first phase
- The national manufacture of 250 tanks
- Procurement of 298 intermediary generation tanks (through an agreement signed in November 2005, Germany accepted to give used Leopard 2 tanks to Turkey)
- 56 low-altitude aerial defence systems
- 55 general purpose helicopters
- Manufacturing of 7 national patrol ships (Mil Gem – with maximum domestic industry involvement)
- 12 additional naval helicopters (Sea Hawk- American Sikorsky Corporation) that are to be procured with American Eximbank credit
- 16 patrol boats of a new type
- 10 naval patrol planes
- 1 submarine rescue ship
- .1 wet-dock landing ship

- 55 basic training planes
- 1 surveillance satellite
- 2 early-warning satellites
- 3 System+10 unmanned planes

DIAGRAM 16: TURKISH AIR FORCES OTHER AGENCIES AUG 05

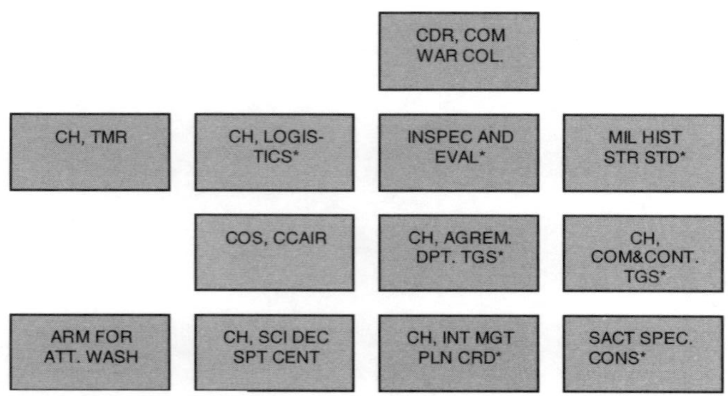

*TGS (Turkish Gernal Staff

DIAGRAM 17: PEACEFORCE COMMAND 2004 (LAND FORCES)

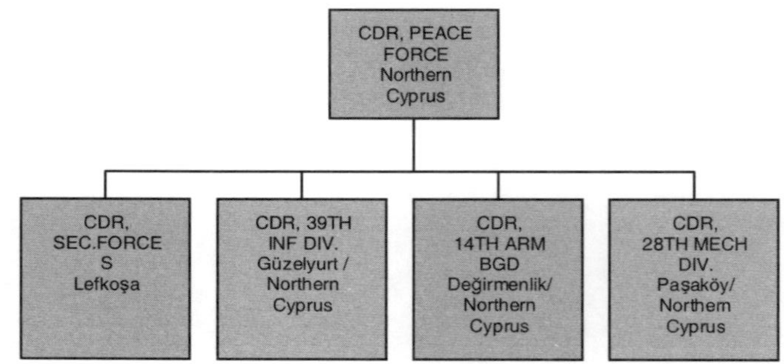

DIAGRAM 18: MINISTRY OF NATIONAL DEFENCE

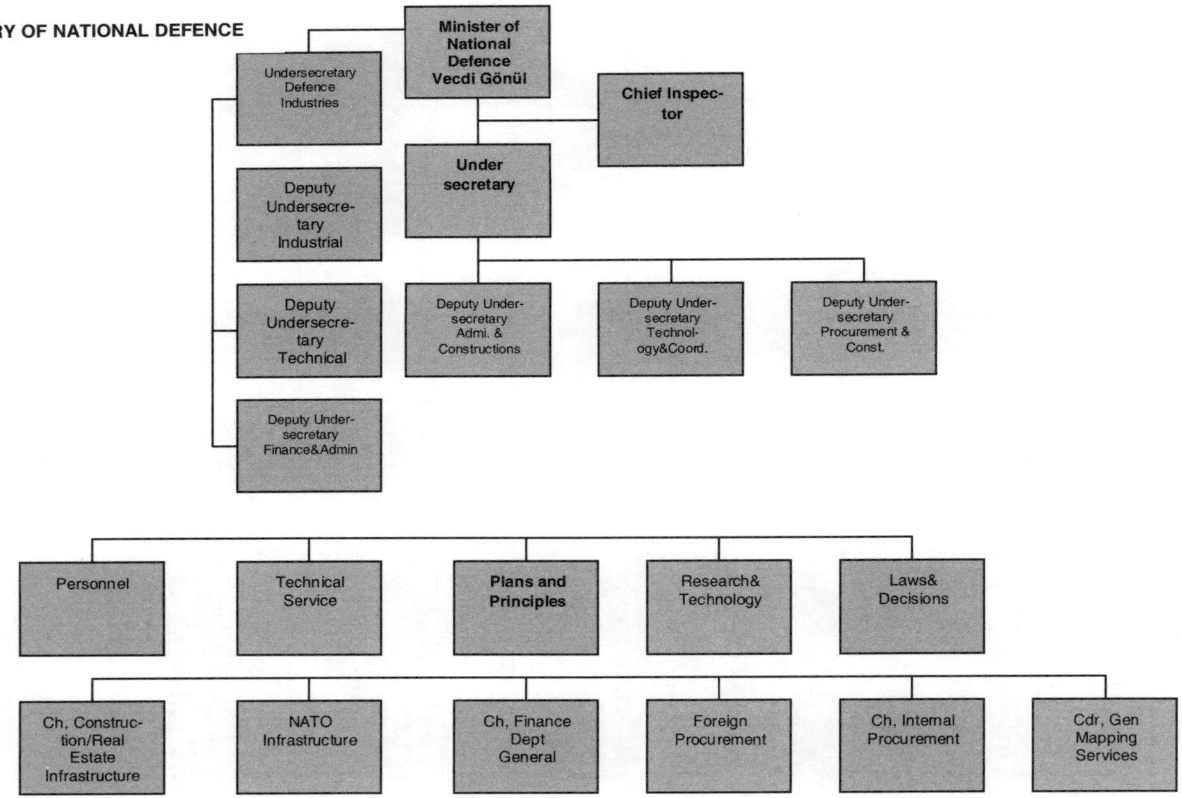

TABLE 1: THE ALLOWANCES OF PUBLIC ADMINISTRATIONS COVERED BY THE GENERAL BUDGET (YTL)

		2005 S.A.	2006 P	2007 P	2008 T
1	Presidency	31,067,570	32,589,000	34,884,000	36,021,000
2	Turkish Grand National Assembly	282,466,549	340,866,000	345,148,475	331,164,356
3	Constitutional Court	8,359,502	19,687,000	24,196,470	24,289,918
4	Supreme Court of Appeals	29,437,958	32,499,000	33,994,903	35,244,689
5	Council of State	19,715,593	21,954,000	23,834,000	24,694,350
6	Court of Accounts	54,231,715	54,431,000	58,151,447	60,318,974
7	Prime Ministry	936,431,161	1,317,236,150	1,418,268,606	1,506,744,460
8	NTNL, Intelligence Org Undersecretariat	296,108,500	352,570,000	395,231,050	409,601,400
9	National Security Council Undersecretariat	11,739,574	10,971,000	12,370,350	12,811,200
10	Press Broadcasting and Information Gen, Dir	41,522,635	43,272,000	45,778,300	47,585,250
11	State Personnel Presidency	10,005,442	8,947,000	9,703,400	9,988,450
12	Prime Ministry Higher Supervision Council	0	9,235,000	9,971,900	10,190,500
13	State Planning Organisation Undersecretariat	117,183,597	264,068,000	282,535,740	291,454,665
14	Treasury Undersecreatriat	61,149,009,043	51,757,408,000	48,520,747,976	43,346,129,306
15	Foreign Trade Undersecretariat	76,729,633	84,646,000	95,320,450	98,701,700
16	Customs Undersecretariat	200,514,878	186,220,000	191,496,700	196,942,600
17	State Statistics Institute Presidency	52,077,764	55,935,00	59,995,992	62,166,560
18	Religious Affairs Presidency	1,125,744,626	1,308,187,000	1,291,005,040	1,340,337,787
19	Administration of the Disabled Presidency	3,616,885	3,507,100	3,684,450	3,817,250
20	Family and Social Studies General Directorate	2,737,819	3,781,000	3,648,150	3,762,200
21	Status of Women General Directorate	959,561	1,606,750	1,482,850	1,534,950
22	Social Assistance and Solidarity Gen, Dir,	0	1,947,000	2,051,700	2,132,400
23	Social Services and S,P,C Gen, Dir,	349,420,756	512,084,000	542,576,300	577,084,200
24	European Union General Secretariat	4,917,228	9,362,000	10,013,150	10,410,660
25	Ministry of Justice	1,600,220,956	1,771,982,000	1,943,735,715	1,924,403,828
26	Milli Savunma Bakanlığı	10,976,455,418	11,877,533,000	12,462,521,205	12,943,620,385
27	Ministry of Internal Affairs	790,717,345	917,872,000	957,127,735	991,356,666
28	General Command of the Gendarmerie	2,371,,673,385	2,571,561,000	2,734,849,940	2,835,080,780
29	Directorate General of Security	4,236,257,718	4,804,713,000	4,894,677,750	5,068,236,720
30	Coast Guard Command	174,658,857	194,459,000	206,070,755	211,996,155
31	Ministry of Foreign Affairs	580,565,420	633,079,000	666,823,800	688,552,150
32	Ministry of Finance	27,489,625,953	33,373,367,352	33,091,138,230	34,624,469,954
33	Income Administration Presidency	0	2,605,564,200	2,736,594,200	2,842,349,850
34	Ministry of National Education	14,835,422,184	16,568,145,500	17,764,811,060	18,551,797,874
35	Ministry of Public Works and Settlement	695,572,988	774,266,000	865,585,900	897,560,750
36	Property and Land Registry Gen, Dir,	286,843,929	356,240,000	344,319,150	311,939,200
37	Public Highways General Directorate	3,482,771,334	3,963,346,000	3,797,800,000	3,789,957,000
38	Ministry of Health	5,447,962,016	7,477,471,000	6,104,957,550	6,410,666,850
39	Ministry of Transporation	670,067,931	989,878,000	1,223,738,850	1,456,390,150
40	Maritime Undersecretariat	44,813,060	49,919,000	53,798,450	55,040,050
41	Ministry of Agriculture and Village Affairs	4,414,428,567	5,156,602,000	5,382,971,010	5,596,158,732
42	Agricultural Reform General Directorate	27,005,014	38,060,000	33,184,430	33,291,900
43	Ministry of Labor and Social Security	65,053,650	76,081,750	19,291,683,850	22,094,185,950
44	Social Security Institution Presidency	12,645,412,898	13,505,231,250	0	
45	Ministry of Industry and Commerce	280,277,654	310,597,000	330,994,600	,340,975,040
46	Ministry of Energy and Natural	248,679,730	280,254,000	263,332,341	275,104,832

	Resources				
47	State Water Works General Direc.	3,634,289,847	3,789,577,000	4,046,371,750	4,164,717,750
48	Petrol Works General Director-ate	3,832,763	3,920,000	3,703,800	3,825,200
49	Ministry of Culture and Tourism	643,190,158	712,381,000	756,570,571	798,148,616
50	Ministry of Environment and Forests	440,427,169	438,502,000	468,181,958	486,292,911
51	State Meteorology Works General Directorate	78,553,384	87,517,000	104,047,450	106,316,300
52	Forests General Directorate	371,659,285	386,977,000	391,491,250	406,013,350
	General Budget	161,340,438,607	170,148,107,058	174,337,176,076	176,351,579,776
	Special Budget Total	9,463,775,026	11,302,981,361	11,768,081,706	12,281,046,248
	Total of Regulating and Super-vising Insitutions	486,124,112	541,141,341	463,880,041	488,212,491
	Total	171,290,337,745	181,992,229,760	186,569,138,453	189,120,838,515,,,
	Treasury Aid	7,341,136,024	7,652,237,552	8,052,458,117	8,479,398,623
	Central Adm, Budget Total	163,949,201,721	174,339,992,208	178,516,680,336	180,641,439,892
	Not: S.A.= Starting Allowance, P=Proposal				
	Source: Ministry of Finance Website				

TABLE 2: MINISTRY OF NATIONAL DEFENCE 2006 BUDGET PROPOSAL, THE DISTRIBUTION OF 2007-2008 BUDGET ESTIMATES BASED ON ECONOMICAL CATEGORISATION AND COMPARISON OF 2006 BUDGET PROPOSAL WITH THE 2005 BUDGET

CODE		EXPLANATION	2005 BUDGET	2006 BUDGET PROPOSAL	DIFFER-ENCE	DIFF. IN %	2007 BUDGET ESTIMATE	2008 BUDGET ESTIMATE
01		PERSONNEL EXPENDITURES	3.849.257.000	4.314.125.000	464.868.000	12.08	4.605.705.300	4.782.942.050
	1	CIVIL SERVANTS	3.061.500.000	3.392.205.000	330.705.000	10.80	3.641.042.100	3.782.678.550
	2	CONTRACT PERSONNEL	4.587.000	2.760.000	-1.827.000	-39.83	2.962.450	3.077.650
	3	WORKERS	689.420.000	790.160.000	100.740.000	14.61	823.238.000	853.337.000
	4	TEMPORARY PERSONNEL	2.000.000	2.000.000	0	0.00	2.146.700	2.230.200
	5	OTHER PERSONNEL	91.750.000	127.000.000	35.250.000	38.42	136.316.050	141.618.650
02		GOVERNMENT PREMIUM EXPENDITURES TO SOCIAL SECURITY INSTITUTIONS	590.475.000	681.104.000	90.629.000	15.35	822.184.100	844.935.300
	1	CIVIL SERVANTS	460.000.000	515.750.000	55.750.000	12.12	649.001.600	674.247.650
	2	CONTRACT PERSONNEL	2.233.000	354.000	-1.879.000	-84.15	588.750	590.850
	3	WORKERS	122.000.000	143.000.000	21.000.000	17.21	149.000.000	155.000.000
	4	TEMPORARY PERSONNEL	42.000	0	-42.000	-100.00	0	0
	5	OTHER PERSONNEL	6.200.000	22.000.000	15.800.000	254.84	23.613.750	15.096.800
03		GOODS AND SERVICE PROCUREMENT EXPENDITURES	6.189.475.000	6.572.475.000	383.000.000	6.19	6.716.700.000	6.985.379.000
	2	CONSUMER GOODS AND MATERIAL PROCUREMENT	5.271.709.760	5.644.973.138	373.263.378	7.08	5.900.420.147	6.137.276.954
	3	TRAVEL ALLOWANCES	144.092.930	149.918.339	5.825.409	4.04	156.422.943	162.679.861
	4	DUTY EXPENSES	17.950.430	17.611.365	-339.065	-1.89	18.403.871	19.140.024
	5	SERVICE PROCUREMENT	300.516.465	309.822.924	9.306.459	3.10	323.724.942	336.715.536
	6	PRESENTATION AND PUBLICITY EXPENDITURES	4.217.580	4.898.826	681.246	16.15	4.976.917	5.175.983
	7	MOVABLE GOODS PROCUREMENT, MAINTENANCE AND REPAIR EXPENDITURES	105.020.310	112.511.157	7.480.847	7.13	117.484.400	122.183.780
	8	IMMOVABLE PROPERTY PROCUREMENT, MAINTENANCE AND REPAIR EXPENDITURES	103.492.525	90.264.251	-13.228.274	-12.78	93.376.780	96.271.850
	9	TREATMENT AND FUNERAL EXPENDITURES	242.475.000	242.475.000	0	0.00	101.850.000	105.935.000
05		CURRENT TRANSFERS	342.360.000	298.929.000	-43.431.000	-12.69	312.380.805	324.876.035

	2	TREASURY AID	267.600.000	224.737.000	-42.863.000	-16.02	234.850.164	244.244.171
	3	TRANSFERS TO NON-PROFIT ORGANISATIONS	50.000	50.000	0	0.00	52.250	54.340
	4	TRANSFERS TO HOUSEHOLDS	10.710.000	10.097.000	-13.000	-0.12	11.178.367	11.625.499
	6	TRANSFERS ABROAD	64.000.000	63.445.000	-555.000	-0.87	66.300.024	68.952.025
06		CAPITAL EXPENDITURES	5.500.000	10.900.000	5.400.000	98.18	5.551.000	5.488.000
	1	PROCUREMENT OF FINISHED GOODS	5.500.000	6.000.000	500.000	9.09	5.261.000	5.270.000
	7	BIG IMMOVABLE PROPERTY REPAIR SPENDINGS	0	4.500.000	4.500.000	100.00	290.000	218.000
	9	OTHER CAPITAL EXPENDITURES	0	400.000	400.000	100.00	0	0
TOTAL			10.977.067.000	11.877.533.000	900.466.000	8.20	12.462.521.205	12.943.620.385

Source: Ministry of National Defence

TABLE 3: 2004 SALARIES FOR MILITARY PERSONNEL

RANK	GRADE	POST	NET SALARY
CHIEF OF GENERAL STAFF	1/4		5.465,95
LAND FORCES COMMANDER	1/4		4.256,22
NAVAL FORCES COMMANDER	1/4		4.256,22
AIR FORCES COMMANDER	1/4		4.611,03
GENERAL	1/4	Land	3.902,79
LIEUTENANT-GENERAL	1/4	Land	3.370,51
LIEUTENANT-GENERAL	1/4	Air	3.971,46
LIEUTENANT-GENERAL	1/4	Navy	3.262,97
MAJOR-GENERAL	1/4	Land	3.123,03
MAJOR-GENERAL	1/4	Air	3.818,63
MAJOR-GENERAL	1/4	Navy	3.110,14
MAJOR-GENERAL	1/4	Medical Doctor	3.096,02
BRIGADIER-GENERAL	1/4	Land	2.924,94
BRIGADIER-GENERAL	1/4	Air	3.696,27
BRIGADIER-GENERAL	1/4	Navy	2.987,79
BRIGADIER-GENERAL	1/4	Judge-President	3.529,14
BRIGADIER-GENERAL	1/4	Medical Doctor	2.892,08
SENIOR COLONEL	1/4	Land	2.554,00
SENIOR COLONEL	1/4	Air	3.363,21
SENIOR COLONEL	1/4	Judge-Member	2.824,80
SENIOR COLONEL	1/4	Medical Doctor	2.459,14
COLONEL	1/4	Land	2.316,69
COLONEL	1/4	Air	3.201,63
COLONEL	1/4	Navy	2.493,14
COLONEL	1/4	Judge	2.806,66
COLONEL	1/4	Medical Doctor	2.213,05
LIEUTENANT-COLONEL	1/1	Land	1.974,97
LIEUTENANT-COLONEL	1/1	Air	2.878,85
LIEUTENANT-COLONEL	1/1	Navy	2.165,06
LIEUTENANT-COLONEL	1/1	Judge-3 years	2.340,30
LIEUTENANT-COLONEL	1/1	Medical Doctor	1.884,36
SENIOR MAJOR	2/1	Land	1.567,48
SENIOR MAJOR	2/1	Air	2.425,92
SENIOR MAJOR	2/1	Navy	1.748,11
SENIOR MAJOR	2/1	Judge	1.892,43
SENIOR MAJOR	2/1	Medical Doctor	1.465,75
MAJOR	3/1	Land	1.492,46
MAJOR	3/1	Air	2.335,75
MAJOR	3/1	Navy	1.677,62
MAJOR	3/1	Judge	1.586,82
MAJOR	3/1	Medical Doctor	1.386,22
SENIOR CAPTAIN	4/1	Land	1.350,47
SENIOR CAPTAIN	4/1	Air	2.178,61
SENIOR CAPTAIN	4/1	Navy	1.555,70
SENIOR CAPTAIN	4/1	Judge	1.509,06

SENIOR CAPTAIN	4/1	Medical Doctor	1.330,11
CAPTAIN	5/1	Land	1.295,37

TABLE 4:
THE DISTRIBUTION OF FOREIGN FINISHED GOODS PROCUREMENT FROM 1985, SSM'S YEAR OF ORGANISATION UNTIL 2001

The distribution of foreign finished goods procurement projects from 1985, SSM's year of organisation until 2001			
Systems	**Units**	**Million USD**	**% (USD)**
Road Vehicle Projects	2	94.4	3%
Air Vehicle Projects	11	2296.4	85%
Electronic Systems Projects	3	18.18	1%
Naval Vessel Projects	3	300.29	11%
Total	**19**	**2709.3**	**100.0**
(Source: Alper Köse – SSM expert. This table is taken from the Papers Compilation of the Strategic Relations in Defence Industry Symposium organized by SSM on 10-11 December 2002 in Ankara			

THE DISTRIBUTION OF SUPPLY MODELS OVER MAIN SYSTEM PROJECTS FROM 1985, SSM'S YEAR OF ORGANISATION UNTIL 2001 (MILLION USD)

The distribution of supply models over main system projects from 1985, SSM's year of organisation until 2001 (million USD)					
Models/Systems	**Air**	**Land**	**Navy**	**Electronics**	**Total**
Domestic Development and Production	63.9	166.76	115.5	72.6	418.76
Joint Development and Production	94.7	603.4	0	190.4	888.5
Consortium	1500	0	0	0	1500
Licensed Production	0	125.8	0	431	556.8
Inland Production	1379.8	1117.1	625	8.2	3130.1
Production in Joint Venture Corporation	530	1670	0	828.5	3028.5
Foreign Finished Goods Procurement	2296.4	94.4	300.29	18.18	2709.3
Total	**5864.8**	**3777.46**	**1040.79**	**1548.88**	**12231.93**
%	47	31	9	13	
(Source: Alper Köse)					

THE DISTRIBUTION OF SUPPLY MODELS OVER MAIN SYSTEM PROJECTS FROM 1985, SSM'S YEAR OF ORGANISATION UNTIL 2001

The distribution of supply models over main system projects from 1985, SSM's year of organisation until 2001					
Models/Systems	**Air**	**Land**	**Sea**	**Elec-tronics**	**Total**
Domestic Development and Production	2	2	4	6	14
Joint Development and Production	1	2	0	1	4
Consortium	1	0	0	0	1
Licensed Production	0	5	0	3	8
Inland Production	7	2	1	1	11
Production in Joint Venture Corporation	1	2	0	3	6
Foreign Finished Goods Procurement	11	2	3	3	19
Total	**23**	**15**	**8**	**17**	**63**
%	37	24	13	27	
Source: Alper Köse, SSM 2002 Paper Compilation					

Police

İbrahim Cerrah[*]

Background

The domestic security sector in Turkey has a dual structure which consists of both public and private security. Public security consists of three main law enforcement institutions: the police, the gendarmerie and the coast guard. The first, i.e. the police force, was established in 1845 during the Ottoman-era, to reflect the modern police organisations of European countries such as Britain and France. These police forces had been founded as a result of the industrial revolution.[1] The gendarmerie and coast guard, however, are military institutions which, on the one hand, are part of the Turkish Armed Forces structure and, on the other hand, are responsible to the Ministry of Internal Affairs as far as their tasks and duties are concerned. The police force, as part of the Directorate General of Security, is also subordinated to the Ministry of Internal Affairs. Besides these three main law enforcement agencies, the establishment of private security organisations has been made possible due to the Law Concerning Private Security Services No. 5188 (Özel Güvenlik Hizmetlerine Dair Kanun, ÖGHDK), that took effect on 10 June 2005.

The Turkish civilian administration system, which includes the police and the gendarmerie as its law enforcement units, is influenced by the French civilian administration system and its approach to domestic security as far as the structure and functions are concerned. According to this model, the residential, urban units fall under police jurisdiction, whereas the rural areas fall under the gendarmerie's jurisdiction. However, the type of structure and distribution of duties that emerged after the Industrial Revolution has evolved in recent years, as a result of the widespread reforms which have taken place throughout Europe. This tendency is reflected particularly in the way in which these institutions are structured today as well as in the quality of service they provide.

Founded in 1829, the London Metropolitan Police, was the first example of a modern police organisation. Although it was established as a domestic security organisation which distanced itself from the military and worked under the supervision of a civilian authority, the modern democratisation of the British police force and its

* Associate Professor. Director of the Institute of Security Sciences, Police Academy.

1 Although some recognise the Constable (Gendarmerie) Marshalry (Zaptiye Müşiriyeti), established on 16 February 1846 - a year later than the police organisation - as the beginning of the gendarmerie organisation; it is widely accepted that the gendarmerie, as a military organisation providing security services, was established in 1839. See Gendarmerie General Command, Jandarma Genet Komutanlığı Tarihi (Ankara: 2002).

embracing of the public service approach transpired only in the 1990s. The situation is similar in other continental European countries. However, the progressive modernisation and practice of civilian control over modern police organisations remains an ongoing process.

Institutional Structure

The Turkish police force belongs to the civilian administration system. However, when compared to Western central administration models, the Turkish structure is over centralised. At first glance, although the Turkish Police is reminiscent of the Federal Security Agencies in the United States, their structure is entirely different from those who come under a centralised federal institutional structure, specifically because of the lack of law enforcement units under the 'national' law enforcement institutions, (i.e. national police, the gendarmerie and the coast guard). The structure of the institution includes two main categories, namely central and provincial police units. The central police force operates under the Ministry of Internal Affairs within the Directorate General of Security, whilst the provincial units operate under the command of governors (vali) and district governors (kaymakam). Civilian administrators (mülki amir) are responsible for the security and well-being of towns and districts. According to legislation and practices, the central and regional structure of the police force is defined as a law enforcement unit that operates within the network of the civilian administration system and carries out its duties under the command and supervision of a civilian authority. Town governors and heads of district administrations supervise the force.

Personnel Structure

The employees of the Turkish Police Force are categorised as part of the Security Services Branch (Emniyet Hizmetleri Sınıfı, EHS), which includes armed, uniformed and civilian personnel.

Total Number of Employees in the Security Services Branch and Civilian Personnel

Security Services Branch:	Civilian Personnel:	Total:
175'058	17'715	192'773

The ratio of the total number of civil personnel (17'715), compared to that of uniformed personnel (175'058) is approximately 11 percent. The civilian personnel are not part of the EHS and consist mainly of assistant and general administrative clerks. Their job descriptions and respective numbers are as follows:

The Job Descriptions of the Security Organisations' Civilian Personnel	
Academic Staff (teachers / instructors)	123
Educational Services	90
Health Services	343
General Administrative Services	3'466
Technical Services	243
Assisting Clerks	12'215
Workers	1'235
Total No. of Civilian Personnel:	17'715

Important criteria for democratic policing include: the ratio of the number of uniformed female to male staff in the security services, their distribution according to ranks, their chances of promotion, and also the ratio of the number of civilian to military personnel and whether they hold influential positions. The figures above can be analysed in light of these criteria.

However, when analysing the ratio of how many domestic security personnel and how many police officers serve how many citizens, then the gendarmerie and coast guard should also be taken into consideration. Even though the gendarmerie and coast guard are military institutions, they provide the same services as the police.

The number of gendarmerie stands at 280'000 personnel approximately, however, according to unofficial figures, the number may exceed 300'000. 80 percent of the existing gendarmerie are not professional soldiers, but consist of conscripts that are fulfilling their military obligation. According to official figures, most of the 2'200-strong coast guard personnel consist of conscripts.

When the number of police force personnel (175'000) alone is taken into account, it is shown that one policeman serves approximately 382 citizens. When the figures from the military institutions carrying out policing duties, i.e. the gendarmerie (280'000) and coast guard (2'200), are added to this total, the average becomes one domestic security personnel per 146 citizens.[2]

2 The calculation of the number of citizens each security personnel serves (police, gendarmerie and coast guard) is based on the 2000 population census result 67,853,315 which was provided by the State Institute of Statistics.

The Total Number of Law Enforcement Personnel and its Ratio to the Population	
Police	175'000
Gendarmerie	280'000
Coast Guard	2'200
Total	457'200
Turkey's Total Population	67'000'000
Number of Citizens per Law Enforcement	146 to 1 (police and military)

The division of the total number of non-military and military law enforcement personnel (457'200) by the total population (67'000'000), results in one law enforcement member for 146 citizens. Although this number seems high in comparison to the averages of European countries, the ratio of police officers working in urban areas (175'000) to the population (44'000'000) is 251 to 1. If one takes into consideration that 44 million people live in urban areas, i.e. 66 percent of the total population, it then becomes clear that the number of police officers working in urban areas is insufficient. This is especially so if compared with the number of gendarmerie operating in rural law enforcement areas. Additionally, if one considers the intensity of the urban population, the high number of crimes committed, the fact that most of the rural population is involved in business within the city and that they spend their leisure time in urban areas, then the workload of the police force and the insufficient numbers of personnel available prove to be a matter of real concern.

The rural population, which is under the jurisdiction of the gendarmerie personnel, stands at 23 million, or 34 percent of the total population. When the total gendarmerie staff number, i.e. 282'200, is divided by the number of the rural population (23'000'000), the ratio is one soldier (gendarme) per 81 citizens.

The Total Number of Law Enforcement Personnel and its Ratio to the Population

Police:	Serving:	Population Ratio:	Citizens per Police Officer:
175'000	44 million	66%	251 citizens per 1 police officer
Gendarmerie:	**Serving:**	**Population Ratio:**	**Citizens per Soldier:**
280'000	23 million	34%	82 citizens per 1 soldier

Gender Distribution of the Turkish Police Force EHS Personnel

EHS (male personnel – all ranks):	EHS (female personnel – all ranks):
165'524	9'534

The police force has a total of 175'500 employees working within the security service branch, of which 9'500 are women. The ratio of women to the number of male personnel is 5.4 percent. Although an increase in female personnel has been observed in recent years, the percentage still remains very low. 9'017 members of the female staff are unranked police officers. There is only one female officer in the highest rank of security director first class. The total number of ranked female staff officers is 518 and this number is distributed amongst the various grades.

However, the lack of women in the organisation should not be seen as that of gender discrimination. The presence of uniformed or civilian female personnel working in police locations has positive effects on both the institution's culture and work environment. To support the employment of female personnel in law enforcement services, a sufficient number of female civilian personnel should also be present in institutions outside law enforcement agencies. This would invariably make the locations where police carry out their duties more welcoming for visiting citizens. When 'male-female' and 'civilian-uniformed' personnel are seen working together in a ratio that reflects the social structure, the locations will become naturally more open and accessible to the public.

The Structure of the Central Organisation of Police (Directorate General of Security)

The Directorate General of Security is hierarchically placed under the Ministry of Internal Affairs. The director general is appointed from amongst the governors who are civilian bureaucrats. In the past, however, the directors post was also occupied by individuals with a military or police background. The director general is appointed by a triple decree, with the proposition of the minister of internal affairs, the recommendation of the prime minister and the approval of the president. The director's term of office is not predefined or limited.

The services in the central structure of the directorate general of security are carried out by the department presidencies. The services carried out by the department presidents are under the supervision of the director general of security, who is supported by his five deputy directors. Each deputy director is responsible for the services carried out by a certain number of department presidencies. The department presidencies in Diagram 1 consist of branches and bureaus (although the branch and bureau names are not displayed in the diagram). The central organisation is constantly expanding, and as a result new departments are established or a number of departments are merged under a single name.

Diagram 1: Organisational Diagram of the Directorate General of Security

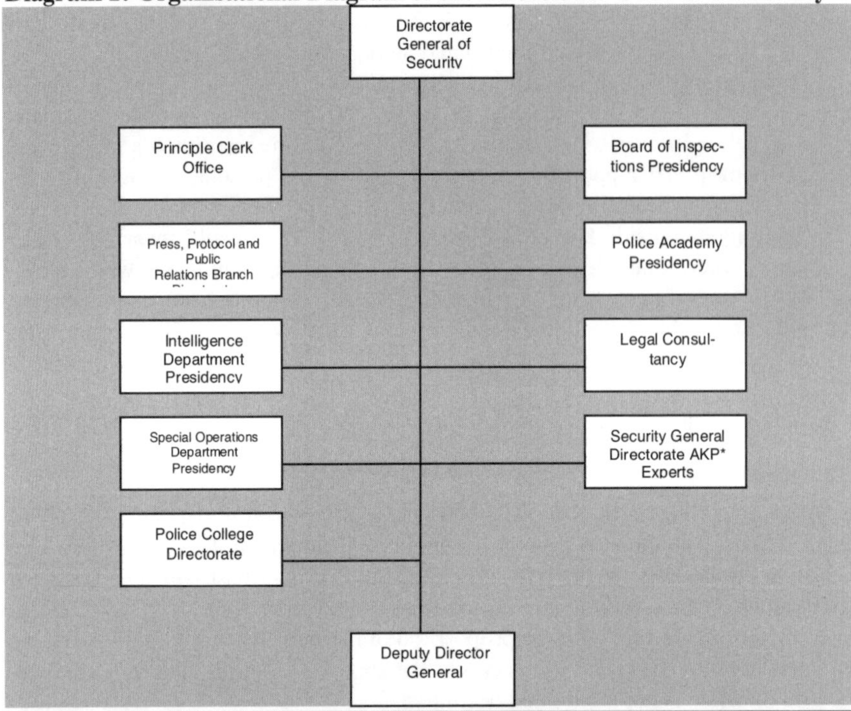

The department presidencies listed below work under the directorate general of security through five deputy director generals.

Department Presidencies within the Directorate General of Security:
Principal Command and Control Department, Archive Documentation Department, Public Order Department, Information Technologies Department, External Relations Department, Educational Department, Security Department, Correspondence Department, Aviation Department, Administrative and Finance Department, Supply and Maintenance Department, Constructions and Real Estate Department, Interpol Department, Fight Against Smuggling and Organised Crime Department, Protection Department, Criminal Police Laboratory Department, Personnel Department, Health Services Department, Civilian Defence Expertise Social Services Department, Strategic Development Department, Anti-Terror Operations Department, Traffic Education and Research Department, Traffic Planning and Support Department, Application and Supervision Department, Foreigners Border Refuge Department and Traffic Research Centre Department.

*APK: Research, Planning and Coordination, Araştırma, Planlama ve Koordinasyon

The Structure of the Provincial Organisations (Provincial Directorates of Security)

Turkey has 81 provinces and each of these are divided into sub-units such as districts, municipalities, villages and neighbourhoods. The central administration's representative of a province is the governor and in the districts this task is carried out by district governors who work under the governors. The governors and district governors are appointed by the central political administration (the government) with the approval of the president. The appointed governors are the representatives of the central administration and responsible for following up and supervising all public service institutions in the provinces and districts under their jurisdiction.

The gendarmerie, which is part of the civilian administration, has the function of a domestic security unit such as the police and also falls under the command and supervision of governors and district governors. However, as documented in the following chapters, the gendarmerie and the coast guard, both of which are military institutions, are not under the full command of a civilian authority. The locally elected administrations (mayors – belediye başkan), which are an important part of democratic administrations, do not have any official authority or influence over the security services in Turkey. This is one of the most distinct differences between the Turkish police organisational structure and the domestic security services of modern administrations.

The extension of the Directorate General of Security's influence in the provincial area (provinces and districts) refers to the provincial and district security directorates. The provincial and district security directorates, such as in Ankara, Istanbul and Izmir, which operate on a special status outside the provinces, have a standard organisational structure (Diagram 2). However, there are slight differences in the number of staff and the institutional structure depending on the size of the population within the provinces and districts. The most important difference between the central and provincial organisations relates to the provincial organisations services that are structured as department presidencies. This is one step down the hierarchical ladder, and takes the form of branch directorates in the provinces and that of supervisory offices in the districts.

Diagram 2: Organisational Diagram of the Provincal Directorate of Security

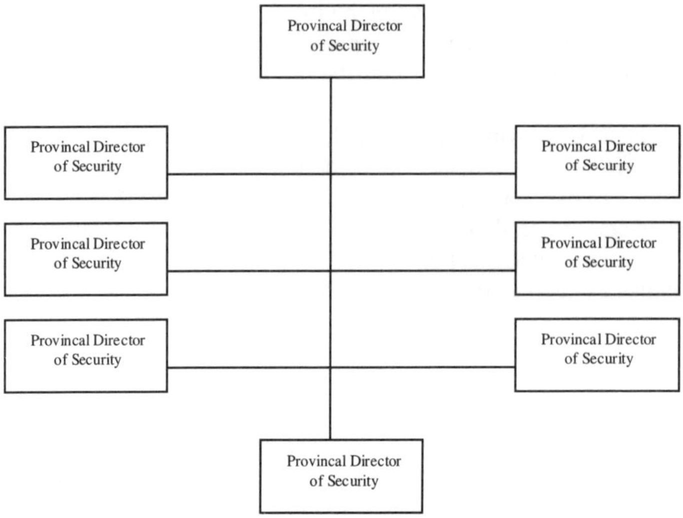

The number of provincial deputy security directors might depend on the size of the population in each province. The branch directorates listed below operate under the provincial director of security through the deputy directors of security.

The Branch Directorates within a Provincial Security Directorate:

General Supervision and Discipline, Intelligence, Interpol, Public Order, Security, Anti- Terror, Fight Against Smuggling and Organised Crime, Special Forces, Crime Scene Investigation and Identification, Supply, Archiving, Correspondence, Electronics, Security Command Control Centre, Protection, Social Services, Traffic Registration, Traffic Supervision, Regional Traffic Supervision, Registration Notification, Tourism, Photo-Film, Passport, Foreigners, Protection of Sensitive Regions, Special Security, Children, Transport, Budget, Legislation Offices and Investigation, Press Protocol and Public Relations, Personnel, Education, Information Technologies, Construction and Real Estate, Esenboğa Airport Protection, Naval Port, Kindergarten and Day Care, Regional Aerial Transport and Regional Police Polyclinic.

Police Education

The Turkish police force has two main categories of training, namely pre-professional and in-house. In-house training is provided by the Presidency of the Department of Education. This department operates directly under the Directorate General of Security and outside the structure of the police academy. In addition, there exist other educational institutions which provide in-house expert training, such as the Turkish International Academy Against Drugs and Organised Crime (TADOC) and the Crime Investigation and Research Education Centre (Suç Araştırma ve Soruşturma Eğitim Merkezi, SASEM).

The pre-professional education that is given to officers, supervisors and executives, operates through three separate institutions which are directed by the police force. These are the two-year professional police vocational schools for officers, the faculty of security sciences for supervisors and the security sciences institute that provides graduate and post-graduate education for executives. With the introduction of Law No. 4652 on 25 April 2001, the Police Academy (Diagram 3), which contains all three of the above-mentioned educational institutions, was granted the standing of an institute of higher education equal to that of a university. The president of the Police Academy is therefore equivalent to a university rector.

Diagram 3: Organisational Diagram of the Police Academy

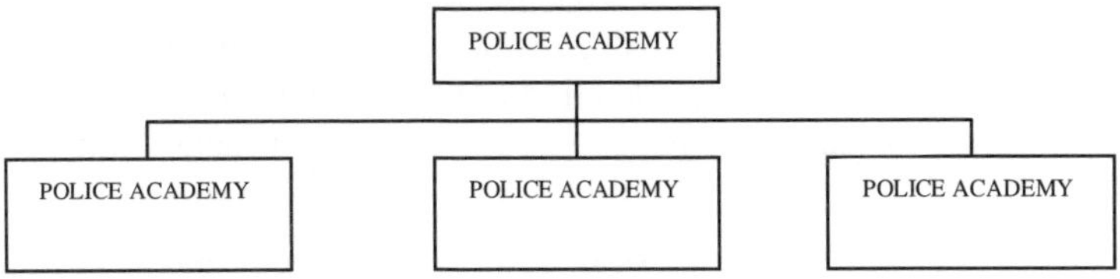

There are currently 24 professional police vocational schools in Turkey. Students are selected from among male and female high school graduate candidates, who are allowed to apply according to the points received in the annual university selection examinations. Currently, there are 13'000 professional police students. These schools provide basic police training for two years. Once they graduate, the students commence work as police officers. The police education consists of the following subjects: law, professional police sciences, police ethics, computer studies, foreign languages, and coursework with social content, such as behavioural sciences and public relations.

The security sciences faculty, which was founded in 2001 under Law No. 2456, is an institution for higher police education that provides four years of undergraduate-level education. As part of the Bologna reform process, the faculty embraced the semester system in the 2005-2006 school year. With the introduction of the new credit system, the faculty became an exact counterpart of the other civilian and police higher education institutions in Europe. After four years of theoretical, practical and internship training, graduates can be appointed as deputy commissioners.

The institute of security sciences which was legally established in 2001, is a higher education institution open to all official and civilian candidates who wish to obtain graduate and post-graduate education in matters of domestic security. The Institute, which runs four different graduate programmes under three different chairs, has a civilian academic serving as director. Besides the graduate programmes, the institute, as part of its promotion process, has provided staff training to middle (security supervisor) and higher (deputy security directors) executive candidates for the past five years.

In-house training of the Turkish Police Force is run by the educational department presidency which operates under the Directorate General of Security. The Presidency of the Educational Department organises in-house training programmes in accordance with demands. Through Law No. 5336, dated 6 May 2005, which was introduced in order to meet the increasing demand for police officers, university graduates were recruited as police officers following pre-professional training of six months. Currently, there are 2'000 students receiving training in five police education centres.

Finally, the police college, which was established in Ankara in 1938, is a high school with boarding facilities. Turkey's two police colleges, which are based in Ankara and Bursa, operate directly under the Directorate General of Security, just as the Police Academy and the Department of Education. The graduates, who receive an education equal to that provided by Anatolian High Schools (Science High Schools), are admitted to the police academy without a prior admissions exam. Graduates who attend civilian universities which belong to the higher system of education, and who receive an education in the subject areas required by the police organisation, are employed by the police force in fields applicable to their areas of education.

Other In-house Training Institutions: TADOC and SASEM

The in-house training provided by the department of education usually aims at meeting general in-house training demands. However, a demand for expert-level skills' training also exists for the personnel of departments such as intelligence, public order and the fight against smuggling and organised crime. The educational institutions established within these departments give training at the national and international level, with an elite educational staff, a scrupulous selection of participants and a superior quality of education.

TADOC, which is part of the Fight Against Smuggling and Organised Crime Department, and SASEM, which is a part of the Department of Public Order, are the most active of these institutions.

Following recent developments in the educational system, the calibre of the police force has in some respects become superior to those of European police systems. The system is set up on the basis of a university structure under the umbrella of the police academy. A faculty that provides undergraduate education (the Faculty of Security Sciences) has been established and the Institute of Security Sciences undertakes scientific research and provides both graduate and post-graduate education. Although the police organisations of some European countries, such as Germany, Spain and Britain, aim to implement a similar educational structure, this has yet to be achieved. The civilian academic staff – many of whom are 1990s graduates and post-graduates from European countries – have made important contributions to the growth of police education in Turkey. The uniformed members of the organisation that are sent abroad for graduate and post-graduate studies have endeavoured similarly to implement the training they have embraced. The idea behind this, is for the level of influence of the many lower and middle-level police personnel on the executive branches of the organisation to be championed in the same way.

Reform of the Police Organisation

The reform/modernisation of the domestic security services involves the incorporation of the concepts of transparency, accountability, civilian control and oversight. Transparency is defined by the opening of public service institutions which are obliged to explain the purpose of their costs and nature of their services. The first point that comes to mind when talking about institutional accountability, is the enactment of legal regulations concerning security services by means of the legislative body of the state. Civilian control, in its broadest sense, is applied on two levels. Firstly, the legislative control that is run by the parliament and the government on a national level and, secondly, civilian and administrative authorities (governors and heads of district) which are appointed by the central government in order to run the public services on a regional level.

The civilian control and oversight mechanisms within the Turkish police organisation can be traced back to the organisation's establishment. With the exception of the president, all remaining six members of the Constable [Gendarmerie] Council (Zaptiye Meclisi), founded in 1846, are civilians.[3] Despite the many years that have passed, the Turkish police organisation has been unable to establish a satisfactory civilian control oversight mechanism. On both, the national and regional level, security policies and practices are run and supervised only by appointed civilian administration authorities and police administrators. The control of the civil administration authorities (governors and heads of districts), which can at best be considered as in-house control, cannot be regarded as proper democratic control. Furthermore, the question should be addressed as to how efficient and productive this in-house control mechanism has become.

3 Ali Birinci, 'Türk Emniyet Teşkilatında İlkler,' Polis Bilimleri Dergisi, 1(3) (1999).

Police Force Transparency

Security units are a part of the service institutions that most vehemently resist transparency. For years, due to the idea that the nature of security services requires secrecy, no systemic information-sharing mechanism was in place. Secrecy is an important and necessary element of security services. It is needed for the operational success of security practices, as well as for the protection of individual rights and freedoms. Secrecy, however, should not be the rule, but the exception. In democratic societies the public is systematically informed about the security services. Annual activity reports include the total cost of the services, their share per citizen and a comparison with prior years. This provides citizens the chance to evaluate the quality of the services that are provided for them and to determine whether there has been a cost increase in comparison with previous years. The implementation of the transparency principle in security services will double the function of healthy supervision. For instance, figures relating to the fight against crime are good indicators of how effectively resources are being used and marks the security services' overall success.

Moreover, the circumstances under which arrested suspects are held, are an important criteria for the determination of the transparency principle. Also, the ratio of suspects who are brought before court from among those arrested and those released, is an important criterion to judge the quality of service provided.

The sharing of accurate information with the public in the areas listed below will not violate the secrecy required by the domestic security services, and it will provide public support and justification to these organisations, thus making them more effective and productive.

- Service policies
- Number of personnel
- Allocation of resources
- Information concerning crime
- Figures concerning crimes committed
- Crimes brought before court
- Investigations that result in imprisonment
- Unsolved cases
- Crime-fighting projects
- Targets
- Yearly success ratios in crime prevention and case-solving
- Public satisfaction with the security service provided by the police
- Types and ratios of crime and their distribution among regions and cities

This and similar information that does not require operational secrecy can be included in national and local annual activity reports, and can be made accessible to citizens on the Internet.

The Press Office, which belongs to the Directorate General of Security, organises a weekly information meeting on a Friday for print and audio-visual media members. These weekly meetings, which have taken place since 2003, inform the public through the media about important incidents, problems, possible crisis, routine/new developments and activities, all of which are related to domestic security. The information provided can be seen as a practice which embraces the principle of transparency.

Problems in Civilian Oversight and Control

TESEV's Security Sector Working and Monitoring Group's activities, as well as the Preparatory Assistance for Civilian Control of Security and Law Enforcement1 project, realised by the Ministry of Internal Affairs and the United Nations Development Programme (UNDP), has unearthed some problems concerning civilian oversight and control at both the national and regional levels.

The control carried out on law enforcement units by the governors and heads of districts appointed by the central government, although of a civilian nature, is clearly not democratic. The security services should be monitored by elected administrators who represent the citizens, i.e. the receivers of this service, or by institutionalised civilian elements, namely the non-governmental organisations (NGOs). Experience in these matters show that the civilian oversight carried out by NGOs in coordination with official civilian control mechanisms provides a much healthier supervision. Although civilian oversight mechanisms appear to be bereft of legal support and a binding force, they are very efficient when it comes to mobilising civilian supervision mechanisms.

In Western European countries such as Britain and France, structures known as the Independent Police Complaints Authority are civilian oversight mechanisms that supervise not only the police, but also the other security units that provide domestic security services such as the gendarmerie. For instance, the National Commission of Deontology and Security (CNDS), established in France in 2000, functions as a civilian control mechanism over all the institutions on French soil that provide security services, beginning with the police and the gendarmerie. As Turkey has an administration and security services structure based on the French model, it is therefore necessary to establish a similar Independent Police Complaints Authority.

Important Developments in 2005

Presented below are some of the important projects in the area of policing, and some of the incidents that can be seen as turning points from the point of view of policing practices. (yes)

As part of the democratisation of the security sector, the two projects mentioned below were carried out in 2005.

- **Security Sector Working and Oversight Group (TESEV):** The activities carried out by the Security Sector Working and Monitoring Group, founded in November 2004 at TESEV, focus mainly on the national (parliamentary) oversight and control of the security services.
- **Ministry of Internal Affairs and the UNDP Project:** Unlike the TESEV project above, the field research entitled Preparatory Assistance for Civilian Control of Security and Law Enforcement, run by the Ministry of Internal Affairs and UNDP, focuses on civilian oversight and control of the security services at the local level.

The Problem of the Superiority of a Civilian Authority: The Incident Concerning the Governor of Diyarbakır and the Director of Security

The problem of the civilian authorities' control over high-ranking domestic security executives came to the forefront in 2005, when the media printed a story regarding difficult working relationships. The incident, which was related to Director of Security Orhan Okur's problems with working under the command of the Diyarbakır governor, Efkan Ala, resulted in the director's removal from office in February 2005. Once again, this incident showed the necessity of reviewing the system of the civilian authorities control over security units within the context of the UNDP recommendations. This incident is important in highlighting the resistance and problems that occur when governors attempt to exert full power over security units, even though the security units are under their command and control of the governors as stipulated by law. Although the exact details of the incident between the Governor of Diyarbakır and the director of security are unknown, it could be defined as a clash of personalities.

The New Code of Criminal Procedure and the Administrative Police vs. Criminal Police Debate

One of the most important debates has been the re-emergence problem between the administrative police (idar polis) and the criminal police (adli polis), as a result of the amendments made to the Code of Criminal Procedure (Ceza Muhakemeleri Kanunu, CMK). The basic functions of the domestic security organisations (the police and the gendarmerie), which fall under the Ministry of Internal Affairs on a national and local level, include two main categories which are classed as administrative and judicial:

- **The administrative function** consists of the security services carried out by security members, under the control of their superiors and civilian authorities, preceding a crime and therefore mainly for the purpose of crime-prevention.

- **The criminal function** consists of the security services carried out by the police, under the control of a district prosecutor, following a crime.

Debates on this matter began with the Ministry of Justice's request for the police officers carrying out criminal duties to work solely and completely under the command of district prosecutors. The Ministry of Internal Affairs and the Directorate General of Security subsequently argued that there should be no institutional distinction between the administrative police and the criminal police, as is the case in western countries. The police services should have a functional distinction but remain under one roof. According to the Ministry of Internal Affairs, both the administrative and criminal functions blend to a certain extent, thus making a definite distinction impossible. For instance, a police squad carrying out the duty of administrative police during a patrol is required to use its criminal police authority when faced with a crime. Therefore, in the event of the establishment of a separate criminal police department, the patrolling squad will have no chance of intervening in judicial matters of this nature. Moreover, practices in Western countries show the fact that the criminal police have refrained from intervening in administrative incidents and the administrative police have refrained from intervening in criminal incidents, has harmed the public's trust in their work.

As a result, the Ministry of Internal Affairs' thesis was accepted in the CMK, and the administrative security distinction remained a functional instead of an institutional one. Accordingly, the police will be known as criminal police when in pursuit of a criminal matter and as administrative police when in pursuit of an administrative matter. In addition, they will receive their orders from the civilian authority or the prosecutor, depending on the nature of the duty. In practice, however, and in order for the prosecutor to know who is under their command, the names of police units and their superiors that are to carry out administrative duties will be given to the district prosecutors in each province and district.

The New Anti-Terror Law

Another issue that was part of the public agenda throughout the second half of 2005 and which remained unresolved legally, involved an (new) Anti-Terror Law (Terörle Mücadele Kanunu, TMK). Although the amendments that came about as a result of the wave created by the 9/11 attacks on the World Trade Centre were still strongly in effect throughout 2005, high-ranking officials of TSK stressed that the existing Anti-Terror Law remained insufficient and that a new regulation was needed. However, the police organisation, which retained jurisdiction in urban residential areas in matters against terrorism, was not as insistent.

The Anti-Terror Law No. 3713, which went into effect in 1991, underwent important changes on 30 July 2003. Within the context of these changes, the amendment made to Article 1 of the TMK stipulated that, in order for an organisation to be considered a terrorist organisation, the use of force can be a part of its mandate. The amendment aimed to expand the limits of freedom of expression as part of the changes made to the constitution, and to create the possibility of expressing and discussing all kinds of ideas, as long as they did not present an immediate or imminent danger to public order.

Once again, and as a result of the same idea, the expression 'propaganda against the indivisibility of the state' was removed from Article 8 of the TMK. This change indicated that the propaganda used by terror organisations was no longer considered a crime, as previously stipulated in Article 7/2, but instead propaganda inciting the use of force and violence was considered a crime.

Nonetheless, these amendments did not imply that all actions involving force and violence would go unpunished under Turkish law. According to the nature of the activity, some activities that were previously within the scope of the TMK could be categorised as crimes against public peace (included in the Turkish Penal Code – Türk Ceza Kanunu, TCK). The new regulations, especially the crimes defined in the TCK Articles 213, 214, 215, 216, 217 and 220 (provoking crime, praising crime and criminals, provoking the public to hatred, (düşmanlık) and insults, provoking lawlessness and founding organisations with criminal intent), were used to fill the gap that emerged after the amendments to the TMK. However, in the new law, the definition of terrorism is being re-evaluated and there exists a desire to remove force and violence as criminal factors, and to perceive all kinds of organisational activity as falling within the scope of terrorism.

Moreover, concerns were expressed about a practice being brought back to the whole of the country, which was similar to the state of emergency that was abolished on 30 July 2002 in south eastern Turkey. In a system where civilian control over the security forces continues to face serious problems, the vast expansion of the authority given to law enforcement agencies is a cause for concern. The fact that the terrorism problem has not only persisted, but has deepened in the region, despite this increase in authority, proves the need for its resolution with methods other than ever-increasing military and police measures.

The Use of Force

One of the most debated issues concerning security services during 2005 was the use of force. The use of force can be analysed in two categories: first, the non-lethal force used by special operations units that operate in mass protest activities as part of the chain of command; second, the lethal force that security forces use in armed conflicts.

The real problem experienced in Turkey concerning meetings and protests is not the permission to exert this right, but the number of incidents that have taken place during the application of this right. The use of force exerted by police against female protestors on 6 March 2005 regarding the 8th of March Women's Day event was widely criticised. Following an internal investigation, the officers involved received disciplinary punishment. The incident was also brought before court and the trial is ongoing. The intensity of criticism may have been linked to the presence of an EU delegation visiting Turkey at the time, and could be seen as critical to Turkish-EU relations. The criticisms, instead of being steadfastly refused by the police force, could be drawn upon as a tool and opportunity to increase the professional standards and level of education within the organisation. Although learning from such incidents and preventing their reoccurrence is a method used in police training, no systematic work has been observed for the development of a complete solution to the problem. In fact, future special operations practices will reveal whether the police have actually learned from this incident.

The Use of Force in Individual Incidents: The Incident of Kızıltepe (Mardin) of 21 November 2004

At times, security units have to carry out terrorist-related operations in urban centres and have to resort to the use of lethal force. Nevertheless, an incident that was widely criticised was the killing of a father and his son, who was officially twelve years old but believed to be older, during an operation in Kızıltepe, Mardin, on 21 November 2004.

The critical media reports did not discuss issues such as the use of force and the sufficiency of police training but the personal mistakes and responsibilities of the individuals involved in the incident. Besides individual mistakes and responsibilities of the security personnel, the question which clearly needs to be addressed is whether sufficient training is provided for such operations.

Police-Gendarmerie Dilemma: Şemdinli (Hakkari) Incident of 9 November 2005

On 9 November 2005, two gendarmerie NCOs were allegedly involved in the bombing of a book shop in the Şemdinli district of Hakkari. The incident reminded many of the government's ties to the mafia, a fact that was publicly disclosed after the Susurluk incident. The Hakkari incident which is still being investigated was significant for several reasons:

The first problem concerns the civilian authority's ability to exert enough control over law enforcement units. The governors of Hakkari and the Şemdinli district, when testifying to the TBMM Şemdinli Investigation Committee, stated that they had not been informed that two gendarmerie NCOs had an intelligence assignment in the district.

The second problem relates to the gendarmerie organisation's right to undertake assignments in urban centres, in spite of the law[4] that defines their sphere of jurisdiction as residential. Although the police and gendarmerie organisations were warned about not complying with the law concerning their spheres of jurisdiction, as explained in the Cooperation and Coordination among Law Enforcement Units memo distributed by the Ministry of Internal Affairs on 13 January 2005, this incident brought the issue of the gendarmerie acting within its legal sphere of jurisdiction back into the spotlight.

---

4 For Article 10 of the Law on the Establishment, Duties and Jurisdiction of Gendarmerie No. 2803 and dated 10 March 1983 see Resmi Gazete (Official Gazette) No. 17985 dated 12 March 1983.

Crime and the Fight against Crime

For over 10 years, the statistics involving public order crimes around the country have been gathered by the Public Order Department's Presidency. The numbers are low in comparison to European countries. This should be viewed positively and as an indication of low crime rates. Ironically, however, this low level is reflective of the fact that crimes remain unreported or unrecorded even if they have been reported. This clearly is cause for serious concern. The difference between the figures of police records and the crimes that were actually committed is called the 'dark figure of crime.'

The Crime Analysis Centre (Suç Analiz Merkezi, SAM) which was established in 2005, should make significant contributions to the strategic development of domestic security policies. Owing to the up-to-date information that is expected to flow to the centre from around the country, the criminal and scientific analyses of these crimes (the social, political, psychological, economic reasons for crimes) will be carried out and an important step will be made towards the fight against crime.

Community Support in the Fight against Crime: Community Policing

As part of the EU's harmonisation process, a project on community policing was initiated in 2005 as a sub-branch of one of strengthening the responsibility, productivity and effectiveness of the Turkish Police's Twinning Projects. The project is coordinated by Spain on behalf of the EU. The project is supposed to last 24 months. The project has provided Turkey with an important opportunity to match the existing structure of its police force with EU standards.

The project has two main purposes: to increase the efficiency and productivity of the administrative and managerial services carried out by the police force through the use of modern managerial tools and, to provide the impetus for necessary change in the areas of service and education, as inspired by the EU's best practices.

In order to improve the nature of services provided to the public, the project aims to improve the police force's cooperation with all levels of the public. The intention is to structure the project based on the police service structures of Britain and Spain, whereby a value is given to the public's (customers) satisfaction. Expanding on the philosophy that, 'in order to satisfy external customers, internal customers should also be satisfied,' important measures for improving police force working hours and conditions and the raising of their standard of living are equally important considerations. Whereas the weekly working hours in most European countries never exceeds 37.5 hours, most security personnel in Turkey work between 12-16 hours per day.

Of great significance is the public's support for the fight against crime, which in developed democratic countries is estimated between 80-90 percent. In Turkey, however, public support is as low as 15-20 percent, clearly indicating the public's sensitivity to the fight against crime. It is also reflective of the lack of dialogue that exists between the Turkish security forces and the public. Finding a resolution to this situation requires security personnel to embrace the fact that the organisation's duty and mission is not one of force but one of providing a service, and this must also be presented to the public as such.

The Istanbul Police Force aims to provide a more rapid, enhanced, efficient and productive service to the community by adopting modern, technological communication systems. This has been made possible through a project developed in 2005, called the Mobile Electronic System Integration (Mobil Elektronik Sistem Entegrasyonu, MOBESE). With the support of an information system, the police will be mobilised more rapidly. The time of arrival at a crime scene/incident should be decreased to a minimum, and especially so in cases involving emergency calls. Even seconds are of essence in emergency situations where the loss of blood, heart attacks, brawls, fires, falling from heights and traffic accidents are involved. For a person who is losing blood, each minute of blood loss increases the risk of death by 35 percent; a delay of even one minute in the case of a heart attack increases the risk of death by 25 percent; and a fire expands by 25 percent per minute. All these examples clearly show the importance of providing a rapid response to emergency calls.

Technology in Crime Fighting: 'Mobile Electronic System Integration' (MOBESE)

Run by the Istanbul police and conceived as one of the largest security projects in the world, the Mobile Electronic System Integration project is expected to contribute greatly to the security and quality of life of the community in Istanbul, including the economic situation of the area.

The prospect of camera surveillance, vehicle tracking through the Global Positioning System – GPS, fast retrieval information, ascertaining difficult addresses through the address query on digital maps of the city, all of which are situated within the scope of the project, provides the possibility for police to ensure speedy arrivals and intervention of emergency calls. This affects the all important time factor.

The project consists of the following main points:

- City watch and observation through camera surveillance units, which is expected to provide two advantages: Firstly, to make the community feel that they live in a secure city and that the security forces work effectively in the fight against crime. This in turn will decrease the fear of crime which has a strong psychological effect. Secondly, to mobilise the nearest squad to a crime scene through observation in areas that are within the camera's range of visibility.
- Determining the positions and mobilisation potential of police squads on digital maps through GPS.
- Mobile communication for police patrol cars.
- Putting the Identification Law No. 1774 into practice through the information systems infrastructure.
- Developing the necessary crime databases for crime fighting and scientific research.

Using the City Geographical Information System.

Conclusion

Despite the accent on service, the Security Services Branch is perceived more as a force. This perception has been expressed time and time again in both oral and written statements made by police force officials.

Democratic societies define domestic security duties as a public service and not as a force practice, and they provide this service within the framework of rules and principles that are also valid for other public services. Defining these functions as a public service brings about internal changes, as well as changes in the relationship with the community that is being served. First and foremost, they consider the internal needs, demands and expectations of the police officers and the external ones of the citizens, and use dialogue and interaction to replace the current chain of command method. In short, democratic principles and values should be the basis for both the internal relationships of personnel, who are the producers of the service, and the citizens, who are the recipients of this service. The relationships that are desired in the public service institutions of modern societies are not an alternative, but a must for democratic governments.

Gendarmerie

*Lale Sarıibrahimoğlu**

The Gendarmerie General Command (Jandarma Genel Komutanlığı, JGK) is a military security force responsible for maintaining security, law and order. In theory, the JCK operates, by all appearances, under the supervision of the Ministry of Internal Affairs in times of peace, and under the command of the land forces as part of the Turkish Armed Forces (Türk Silahlı Kuvvetleri, TSK) in times of war.

In practice, however, the JGK is a TSK component operating under the command of the General Staff, as confirmed by its tasking within the armed forces, organisational precepts, budget, promotion system and the training and education of its personnel.[1]

The fight against domestic threats, as posited by the Constitution, aims to maintain the order of the state, its democratic and secular character and its integrity. Defence against domestic threats fall under the jurisdiction of the Ministry of Internal Affairs, whereas defence against external threats falls under the responsibility of the General Staff and the Ministry of National Defence (Milli Savunma Bakanliği, MSB).[2] However, the TSK also intervenes in matters of domestic security, using the gendarmerie as stipulated by a number of laws and internal memos.

Although reforms that would provide for democratic civilian control of the military have been implemented as part of the EU membership process, the National Security Policy Document (Milli Güvenlik Siyaseti Belgesi, MGSB) on domestic and external threats remains heavily influenced by the military. This, in addition to other factors discussed below, shows that current legislation on domestic threats falling under the jurisdiction of the Ministry of Internal Affairs is not valid in practice.

---

* Journalist, Defence Expert.

1 See http://www.msb.gov.tr, http://www.tsk.mil.tr

2 Mili Savunma Bakanlığı Beyaz Kitap 2000 (Ministry of National Defence White Book 2000), Chapter 4, Section 3, 'Türkiye'nin Milli Güvenlik Güçlerinin İç Güvenlikte Kullanılması,' see http://www.msb.gov.tr. See also Law on the Establishment, Duties and Jurisidction of Gendarmerie No. 2803, ratified by the Turkish Grand National Assembly (Türkiye Büyük Millet Meclisi, TBMM) on 10 March 1983, and the Establishment Law Number 3152, ratified by the Ministry of Internal Affairs on 14 February 1985. This law stipulates that the Ministry of Internal Affairs is responsible for the provision of domestic security, and the term 'internal threat' is not used. However, in Milli Savunma Bakanlığı Beyaz Kitab 2000, the term 'internal threat' is used without reference to any specific article.

In addition to the JCK, the police force is yet another body responsible for the provision of law, order and internal security and is a part of the Ministry of Internal Affairs. Governors have the authority to request military assistance, in accordance with the Article 11 of Provincial Administration Law No. 5442, should these two forces fall short of providing internal security. This law stipulates that military forces are under obligation to meet this request.[3]
However, following a 1996 Constitutional Court decision, an amendment was made in 2003 to clause (d) of the aforementioned article, which eliminated ambiguities concerning the duration of stay of the military forces to the region to which they have been sent.

The amendment authorised the governor to supervise security, law and order, and make decisions on the size of the military force and the duration of its stay,

---

3 Amended Article 11 Clause (d) of the Provincial Administration Law No. 5224 that was ratified in TBMM on 10 June 1949 and published in Resmi Gazete (Official Gazette) on 18 June 1949 is as follows: (Amendment: 29.8.1996 – 4178/1 art.) 'The governors, when they fail or do not deem it possible to prevent incidents that may or do occur in the province with the forces under their command, [or] when they fail or do not deem it possible to implement the measures they have taken with these forces can, in order to use the law enforcement [units] of other provinces or the other forces that are assigned for this job, ask for help from the Ministry of Internal Affairs, and if necessary, from the nearest land, navy or air force command, including the border units of the General Command Gendarmerie or the Land Forces General Command, by sending their request by the fastest means possible. In such cases, the choice of sending the request for the necessary forces to the Ministry of Internal Affairs, to the military units or both is at the requesting governor's discretion. The governor's request for help is to be met without delay. In emergencies, the request can be made verbally, to be put in written form later. If the governor requests for help from military units, the requested unit is stationed at the most convenient location for interception by concurring with the governor in cases where an incident is likely to occur, or in the location of the incident if the incident is already taking place.' (Amended sentence: 17.6.2003–4897/1 art.) 'As the nature of the incident dictates, the requested military force's size is determined by the commander of the military unit in coordination with the governor, and the duration of the duty is determined by the governor in coordination with the commander of the military unit. If the military unit is mobilised independently, the duty is carried out by the military unit under the responsibility of its commander and by his/her commands and instructions, within the framework of the authority stipulated in the Turkish Armed Forces' Internal Service Law and the authority of law enforcement in providing public security. The cooperation and coordination between the security forces and the military forces are defined by the governor, in concurrence with the commander of the military unit. However, if this military unit carries out certain duties together with the gendarmerie or the police, command and administration is assumed by the military commander who has seniority. For incidents that cover multiple provinces, if the governors involved request forces from the same or different military commanders, rules for cooperation between provinces and forces, coordination, mobilisation, chain of command and other related issues are determined by the General Staff and the Ministry of Internal Affairs within the framework of the principles stated above. For the implementation of these rules, the Minister of Internal Affairs assigns one of the governors involved when necessary, in order to provide cooperation and coordination.

based on the nature of the events and in coordination with the garrison commander.[4] In practice, however, this amendment fell short of providing the governor with enough influence to use legal authority in matters of domestic security.

In addition, it is clear that the internal regulations of both the TSK and JGK have an influence over laws. A case in point is the Slander Scandal of 2004, where the TSK gathered information through the gendarmerie, about different segments of society, as authorised by the Provincial Administrative Law mentioned above. (for details, see the section of this chapter entitled the 'Slander' Scandal)

The Function of the Gendarmerie

The JGK was established in 1839 as a military organisation. Its official headcount currently stands at 280'000, and some 80 percent of this number are personnel enlisted through compulsory military service (i.e. conscripts). The unofficial number of personnel is therefore probably closer to 300'000. Currently, 190'000 police officers are responsible for security, law and order in urban areas, whilst the Coast Guard General Command (Sahil Güvenlik Komutanlığı, SGK) is responsible for the protection of naval borders (for detailed information, see the chapter on the Coast Guard General Command).

The JGK's sphere of responsibility differs from that of the police force, and lies in the rural areas outside of urban boundaries, as well as in areas which lack a police organisation. The JGK is responsible for maintaining safety, law and order across 91 percent of Turkey's land surface. This service is provided for one third of the population (27 million), with the exception of the summer months when the number increases to 44 million – i.e. 65 percent of the population - and includes a substantial number of tourists.

The basic law concerning the JGK is the Law on the Establishment, Duties and Jurisdiction of the Gendarmerie No. 2803, which was put into effect by the Turkish Grand National Assembly (Türkiye Büyük Millet Meclisi, TBMM) on 3 October 1983. According to this law, the JGK's functions are listed under four main categories: civil, judicial, military and other.[5] Its main duties involve the provision, protection and maintenance of security and public order; the prohibition, pursuit and investigation of smuggling and initiation of necessary preventive measures; the detection of criminal behaviour; and the apprehension of criminals, coupled with criminal evidence, and their delivery to the appropriate judicial authorities.

The JGK's military responsibilities include the duties assigned by the military laws and regulations to the security forces in general, as well as the duties assigned by the General Staff during martial law, a state of emergency or war.

The JGK also includes the Gendarmerie Air Force Unit, established to support the following domains of security and public order: aerial control of clandestine poppy and hemp fields, the provision of transfers for the sick and wounded as well as search and rescue missions. There are Gendarmerie Group Commands in both Ankara and Diyarbakır and a Helicopter Unit Command in Van.

---

4 Ibid.

5 See http://www.tsk.mil.tr

At any one time, there are around 5'000 gendarmerie conducting special missions in Turkey, such as protecting television transmitters belonging to the Turkish Radio and Television Corporation (Türkiye Radyo Televizyon Kurumu, TRT), securing airports, dams, hydroelectric power stations, refineries, oil production facilities, natural gas and oil pipelines.

11'773 gendarmerie (which includes around 10'000 conscripts) are responsible for providing security along the 397 kilometre Iraqi border, as well as for sections of the Iranian and Syrian borders. There are a total of five regiments, nine battalions and 39 divisions. The remaining land borders are under the responsibility of the Land Forces Command (Kara Kuvvetleri Komutanlığı, KKK), as stipulated by Law No. 3497 introduced in 1988. However, conditions for European Union (EU) accession stipulate the cessation of military border control and the requirement for the formation of a civilian border force to provide land and sea border security (for detailed information see the part on projects concerning the Formation of a Border Police Organisation in this chapter). The JGK also takes part in Peace Protection Force operations abroad (see Sidebar 1).

Personnel and the Hierarchical Structure

The JGK's personnel consist of officers, Non Commissioned Officers (NCOs), specialist or expert gendarmerie, military students, enlisted specialists, privates as well as civilian personnel. The rules concerning the employment, training, promotion, leave, enrolment and promotion of gendarmerie officers and NCOs are established in the Turkish Armed Forces Personnel Law No. 926.

The appointments of third lieutenants, colonels, as well as NCOs and specialist gendarmes are made by the commander of the Gendarmerie General Command. The JGK's generals are appointed upon the recommendation of the general commander of the gendarmerie, the chief of staff, minister of internal affairs, and a resulting joint decree signed by the prime minister and confirmed by the president.

The appointment of the general commander of the gendarmerie is made through a proposal by the chief of staff upon the suggestion of the minister of internal affairs, as a resulting joint decree signed by the prime minister and confirmed by the president. This is stipulated by the Law on the Establishment, Duties and Jurisdiction of Gendarmerie No. 2803. Although this law states that the organisation is under the supervision of governors and official heads of district appointed by the Ministry of Internal Affairs, the TSK website asserts that it is placed under the direct command of JGK headquarters with regard to the maintenance of safety, law and order. According to the JGK website, the JGK headquarters is the uppermost body assisting the general commander of the gendarmerie in the deployment and administration of troops. All cases pertaining to law and order nationwide are monitored by the JGK headquarters and troops are deployed accordingly.[6]

---

6 General Plan and Principles Department Presidency, Milli Savunma Bakanlığı Beyaz Kitap 2000, see http://www.msb.gov.tr; Law on the Establishment, Duties and Jurisdiction of Gendarmerie No. 2803 dated 10 March 1983, see http://www.tsk.mil.tr

In addition, the procedures and principles concerning deployment, administration, and the development and execution of future projects are also the responsibility of the JGK headquarters. Security and the maintenance of law and order are executed by the Gendarmerie Regional Commands. Provincial Gendarmerie Commands are affiliated to the Gendarmerie Regional Commands. (for information about the JGK's structure, see Sidebar 2; for the JGK Organisation, see Sidebar 3). The Provincial Gendarmerie Commands have widespread control in the townships and in villages.

Visitors to the office of the general commander of gendarmerie have an opportunity to view a symbolic example of the JGK's allegiance to the TSK, as they will see that the walls of the commander's room are adorned with pictures of the chiefs of staff, rather than those of the ministers of internal affairs to whom they report in times of peace.

The Education System

The Gendarmerie General Command executes its duties through its officers, NCOs, enlisted gendarmes and specialists, as well as privates, educated and trained at the gendarmerie schools and training units.

The gendarmerie schools train officers who have graduated from the military academy, as well as NCOs who have earned the right to become officers by means of outstanding achievement in the fulfilment of their gendarmerie duties. The existing NCOs and enlisted gendarme are also educated by the Gendarmerie schools.[7]

In accordance with the remaining branches of the TSK, the JGK also employs non-professional soldiers who are performing their compulsory military service (i.e. conscripts). However, this has only served to impede domestic security, law and order, specifically because operations in this domain require specialised training.

There has also been a problem with the lack of a unified education system for the police force and the gendarmerie who, despite their separate areas of responsibility, share the principal duty of providing security, law and order. Domestic security depends on the successful execution of operations by specially-trained professional forces. In rural areas, an NCO is appointed as the head of the security forces responsible for maintaining law and order, whilst the privates under his command (conscripts) receive only basic training for a period of one and a half months. According to police sources, it is arguable, at best, to claim that this training is specifically aimed at maintaining domestic security. In addition, it is also questionable whether the limited weapons training received by the soldiers who are required to carry an automatic rifle is in any way sufficient.

---

7 Milli Savunma Bakanlığı Beyaz Kitap 2000, see http://www.msb.gov.tr; http://www.jandarma.gov.tr; http://www.tsk.mil.tr

EU-JGK- The Border Police Organisation Project

A number of projects have been initiated jointly by the Turkish Ministry of Foreign Affairs and the EU, aimed at ensuring conformity with EU criteria. The projects focus on the government's arrangement of transparent domestic security policies and the formation of a Border Police Organisation consisting of professional civilians in order to replace the separate structures of the JGK, the SGK and the police force.

The Schengen acquis – the roadmap on matters of justice, freedom and security policies established by the EU – stipulates the removal of border control points between EU-member countries. Candidate states are required to adapt their national policies accordingly with integrated and efficient administrative capacity. They are also expected to form a professional, reliable and effective police organisation to provide efficient border control.[8]

As a result, there are three projects currently being implemented by Turkey and the EU. The first proposes a decrease in the number of personnel enlisted through compulsory military service and an increase in the number of professional employees, thereby promoting the transparency of the gendarmerie by means of supervision by the civilian authority. The objectives of this project were accepted by the JGK in 2004, who agreed to work in collaboration with Britain. However, the JGK retracted its involvement in 2005 on the grounds of its relationship with the TSK and, moreover, because of its commitment to the TSK's Personnel Reform 2014 project.[9] The JGK stated that it was expected to follow the TSK's policies on matters of personnel assignment, enrolment and staff matters and, as such, its priority was the Personnel Reform project of 2014. The Personnel Reform Project stipulates a rational policy to fill staffing gaps and to base the promotion of personnel on an individual's record of achievement as opposed to his or her length of service.[10]

The second project initiated by the EU and the Ministry of Internal Affairs involves the establishment of a professional Border Police Force. In order to provide integrated land and sea border security, both parties signed the Integrated Border Security Administration Strategy Document, which stipulated the creation of an action plan.

It is projected that the Border Police Force will be established by the time of Turkey's full membership within the EU. The first phase of preparation is for the gendarmerie and the land forces to terminate their land border protection duties and for the coast guard to terminate its duty of protecting the sea border. The EU does not view the JGK as an active part of any future Border Police Force. However, the integration of the otherwise separate law and order services provided by the police force and the gendarmerie will be observed during the transition period until a Border Police Force is introduced. This project involves ongoing educational cooperation between the JGK and France.

---

8 European Commission, 'Chapter 24: Justice, Freedom and Security,' 2005 Progress Report on Turkey, 9 November 2005 http://www.abgs.gov.tr

9 Taken from an interview between western diplomatic sources and the author in November 2005.

10 Barkın Şık, 'Albaylık zorlaşıyor,' Milliyet, 18 October 2005.

The establishment of a Border Police Force is of vital importance both to Turkey and to the EU's fight against organised crime, illegal immigration, nuclear weapon programmes, drug trafficking and terrorism. However, as stated in the EU Progress Report dated 9 November 2005, progress has yet to be made on the border patrol reform project. According to the report, the main reason is the TSK's – or, more specifically, the JGK and KKK's – reluctance to transfer authority to a professional border guard body consisting of civilian personnel. Progress ultimately depends on the establishment of future amendments to Law No. 3497 which allocates authority for the protection of land borders to the TSK.[11]

However, the Ministry of Internal Affairs did send out a circular in January 2005, stipulating coordination and cooperation among the police force, the gendarmerie and the coast guard in order to provide efficient land and sea border security. In addition, a law was amended to provide for the employment of 10'000 new police officers from amongst university graduates in order to meet this new demand.

The third joint EU and Ministry of Internal Affairs project, which is scheduled for 2007, aims to strengthen the supervisory powers of governors, official heads of districts and prosecutors in order to achieve civilian control over the JGK. The purpose of the project is to enable a civilian authority to define domestic security policies, and to establish the governors, official heads of districts and prosecutors' capacity to supervise the JGK personnel who are responsible for providing law and order. Municipal councils will be given an opportunity to undertake an important role in the project's development.

A serious problem facing both the police and gendarmerie relates to the fact that officers from the security force who have been accused of human rights violations frequently go unpunished. The police are trained in the area of human rights issues and the JGK established the Gendarmerie Human Rights Evaluation Centre (Jandarma İnsan Haklarını Değerlendirme Merkezi, JİHİDEM) on 27 April 2003. However, although 162 complaints have been made to the JİHİDEM to date, mostly concerning mistreatment and wrongful arrest, only three cases of disciplinary action against gendarmerie members have been noted.[12] Authorities claim that the low number of complaints relates to insufficient penal sanctions.

In addition, the content of some of the JGK's staff training not only fails to comply with EU principles, but creates animosity against the EU and resentment toward the government's decision to join the EU. Hürriyet journalist Cüneyt Ülsever reported that the JGK ordered its personnel to read the magazine Yeni Hayat, a publication which contains both anti-US and anti-EU articles.[13]

---

11 European Commission, 'Chapter 24: Justice, Freedom and Security,' 2005 Progress Report on Turkey, http://www.abgs.gov.tr

12 Ibid.

13 'New Gendarmerie Controversy Sparked,' Turkish Daily News, 17 March 2005.

The Gendarmeries Grey Zone and the Problem of Authority-Sharing with the Police

As mentioned above, the basic law concerning the JGK is the Law on the Establishment, Duties and Jurisdiction of the Gendarmerie No. 2803, which was introduced on 3 October 1983 after the 1980 military coup. This law left the gendarmerie in a semi-military grey zone between the General Staff and the Ministry of Internal Affairs. Although Article 10 defines the JGK's zone of duty as being outside urban boundaries, the fact that the JGK sometimes operates within the police force's area of jurisdiction only highlights the need for democratic supervision. While investigating the Şemdinli incident, which is discussed below, the TBMM ad-hoc Şemdinli Committee launched an enquiry into why two NCOs were located in the police forces's area of jurisdiction.[*] Similarly, one of the 13 questions which the opposition party (Cumhuriyet Halk Partisi, CHP) member and Hakkâri Deputy Esat Canan asked, concerning the incident, was why the NCOs in question were gathering intelligence outside their area of jurisdiction without informing the local police. The Committee's report states that the conflict and lack of cooperation between the gendarmerie and the security forces hindered the investigation of the incident.[14]

Another example of the confusion regarding the gendarmerie and the police's areas of jurisdiction is the fact that some universities which fall under police jurisdiction are being protected by the gendarmerie. For instance, when the Middle East Technical University (Ortadoğu Teknik Üniversitesi, ODTÜ) was established, it was situated far from the city centre, thus placing it in an area under the protection of the gendarmerie. However, the population increase has extended the city limits towards the campus, and the 50km periphery surrounding the province has subsequently been considered to be within city limits. As a result of this enlargement, the ODTÜ´s jurisdiction is now within these limits. The municipality and the government claim to be responsible for ODTÜ, while de facto the situation is just the opposite. Whilst the Gendarmerie Provincial Administrative Law bestows the authority upon the governors and the heads of district to decide which regions belong to which internal security forces – the gendarme or police - additional permission is required from the general commander of gendarmerie for this decision to become effective.[15] Thus, the ODTÜ remains to fall under the responsibility of the gendarme because the commander of the Gendarmerie Forces has not given permission for this university to be under the police control.

---

* Editor's Note: in November 2005, a renegade member of the PKK currently employed as an 'informant' by the security forces, two officers of the local Gendarmerie and possibly higher level officers were involved in the bombing of a local bookstore and forming illegal networks that targeted suspect militants of the PKK and 'sympathising' citizens. For further details, see, 'Security Developments and Press Reflections: A Overview of 2005,' in this volume.

14 'Suçlamada geri adım,' Hürriyet, 26 January 2006.

15 Taken from an interview between Ministry of Internal Affairs officials and the author of this chapter in November 2005.

The JGK justified this practice by effectively by-passing the law and simply issuing an internal memo.[16] In addition to Law No 2803, approximately 500 laws and regulations define the gendarmeries responsibilities and duties.

The Conflict of the Division of Authority between the Police and the Gendarmerie in Gathering Intelligence

The ongoing dispute between the JGK and the police force, concerning the maintenance of law and order, has been compounded by a lack of relevant information and intelligence sharing. According to information provided by an undisclosed police force executive, the gendarmerie does not share statistical data obtained after the confiscation of narcotics in its rural area operations. Another example can be found in the completely different area of football. An important tool for easing tensions and increasing a sense of affiliation between two countries is through football games, and as such a number of friendly matches are organised. However, in Turkey, the conflict between the gendarmerie and the police carrying out similar duties has reached such a level that such games are not even considered. The most striking example of this clash of wills came from an intelligence note contained in the TBMM ad-hoc Şemdinli Commission's minutes. A diary said to have belonged to one of the arrested NCOs, Özcan İldeniz, has an entry containing intelligence information about the JGK's working principles in which the JGK has been warned against contacting or giving information to the police about the bomb assault, and which states that they should not even 'play football' with police officers.[17]

As opposed to countries in the West, Turkey has a serious weakness in its intelligence gathering capacities. In EU-member countries, all intelligence concerning domestic and external security is gathered by an institution, which is managed by the civilian sector and which reports to the prime minister. In Turkey, however, the gendarmerie and the TSK act in isolation and exert power over the civilian authority, specifically in relation to intelligence gathering, maintaining control over security policies and the assessment of domestic threats.

Minister of Justice Cemil Çiçek has underlined the problems associated with multiple agencies and the lack of coordination between them as follows: 'there are many intelligence units. But the question is, are they successful? There is domestic and foreign intelligence in other countries. The intelligence agencies share the same resources. We cannot make legal regulations by thinking that everybody considers themselves in a different galaxy.'[18]

To avoid the arbitrary tapping of phones and to gather intelligence centrally, the TBMM introduced Law No. 5397 on 3 July 2005, through a series of amend-

---

[16] Taken from an interview between an AKP deputy who wishes to remain anonymous and the author of this chapter in November 2005.

[17] Gökçer Tahincioğlu, 'Yemin gibi İlkeler,' Milliyet, 20 December 2005.

[18] ''Adli kolluk' resmi görüşe rağmen geçti,' Sabah, 28 November 2004; 'Adli kolluk komisyondan geçti,' Zaman, 28 November 2004.

ments in the annexed Article 7 of the Law on Police Duties and Powers No 5397.[19] The aim is to gather all the intelligence obtained by the JGK, police and the National Intelligence Agency (Milli İstihbarat Teşkilatı, MİT) by tapping from a single, central unit. This unit is the Board of Telecommunications which is part of Turkish Telecom and reports directly to the head of Telecom.

According to information provided by officials, the Gendarmerie Intelligence and Anti-Terror Organisation (Jandarma İstihbarat ve Terörle Mücadele, JİTEM), was legalised under Law No 5397, under the name of the Gendarmerie Intelligence Organisation (Jandarma İstihbarat Teşkilatı, JİT), and obtained the right to tap telephones in its area of jurisdiction.[20] However, the actual existence of this organisation is not clearly determined, even by prime ministers, and it has also reportedly been involved in a number of illicit activities.

The civilian authorities under the Ministry of Internal Affairs, such as governors and heads of districts, employ a two-tiered structure to maintain law and order, namely the gendarmerie and the police. This approach is similar to the methods developed by EU countries, such as Spain, France and Italy. In Turkey, however, the lack of integration between these forces leads to serious breaches in the maintenance of peace and order. The main reason for this is that in EU countries, the armed forces answer directly to a civilian authority, as opposed to Turkey where this system of dependency has not yet been established.

---

19 According to Article 2 of Law Number 5397, the following article was annexed to the Law on the Establishment, Duties and Jurisdiction of Gendarmerie No. 2803, dated 1983: Annexed Article 5 – (Ek: 3.7.2005 – 5397/2 md.) 'When carrying out the duties stipulated in Article 7 of this law, in order to take preventive and precautionary measures and in order to prevent the crimes named in the Code of Criminal Procedure No. 5271, dated 12 December, 2004, Article 250, Clause 1, subparagraphs (a), (b) and (c), with the exception of espionnage crimes, the gendarmerie can, in its own area of jurisdiction, determine and monitor telecommunications, assess and register signal information through court order, or in cases where a delay is disadvantageous, by the written order of the director general of security or chief of the intelligence department. In cases where a delay is disadvantageous, the written order that was given is presented to the authorised judge for approval. The judge decides on the matter in maximum 24 hours. In the case this term is exceeded, or in case the judge decides against the order, the measure is removed immediately. In such a case, the recordings of the monitoring are destroyed in 10 days at the latest, the situation is noted in an official report and this report is kept, to be reproduced in cases of inspection. These procedures are carried out by the center that is established in reference to annexed Aarticle 7, Clause 10 of the Law on Police Duties and Powers No. 2559, dated 4 July 1934. The eavesdropping covered by Article 135 of Law No. 5271 ia also carried out through this centre.

20 Ibid. Subsequently, JİTEM gained legal status with an article annexed to the Telephone Eavesdropping Law in July and was named Gendarmerie Intelligence Organisation (Jandarma İsthbarat Teşkilatı, JİT). With this article, the term 'Intelligence Presidency' entered the Law on the Establishment, Duties and Jurisdiction of Gendarmerie, 'Şemdinli patlamalarına JİT ve MİT savunması,' Sabah, 27 December 2005.

Democratic Oversight and Control of the Gendarmerie

In parallel to its umbrella organisation the TSK, the JGK is not supervised by the elected government. Despite the many legal changes that have been initiated in Turkey as part of its efforts for increased transparency and visibility, one of the most significant setbacks lies in its struggle to redefine the concept of the 'state secret'. Just who conceives and determines this concept and how it should be applied, remains open to debate. Illicit activities carried out under the cover of the state secret concept has naturally tarnished society's trust in its government (see the sections entitled 'The 'Slander' Scandal' and 'From Susurluk to Şemdinli' below).

The TBMM ad hoc Şemdinli Commission confronted the state secret concept while investigating the Şemdinli incident. CHP Hakkâri Deputy Canan said in his statement, that the incident could not be resolved as long as new regulations concerning the concept of a state secret were not introduced, thus preventing many institutions from providing information.[21]

In the name of responsible and transparent use of public resources, it is of vital importance that parliament – an institution which is accountable to the public – controls the budgets of security organisations. However, the gendarmerie and the SGK budgets, in parallel to that of the TSK, have not yet been put under the reach of parliamentary control. Despite the fact that the JGK and SGK budgets are part of the Ministry of Internal Affairs' budget, they remain under the TSK's management and are represented as defence resources in addition to the TSK's budget.[22]

Moreover, the JGK members have never been accountable to parliament. This was highlighted when a crisis erupted during a meeting between the Gendarmerie General Chief of Intelligence, Brigadier General Mehmet Çörten and the Head of the ad-hoc Şemdinli Investigation Commission, Musa Sıvacıoğlu, which took place without the knowledge of the Committee members.[23]

One of the most pressing problems associated with the issue of oversight is the fact that, although the gendarmerie is accountable in theory to the governors and heads of district while performing public-order duties, it remains, in practice, under JGK command. The TBMM Interior Affairs Commission has yet to actively supervise the JGK. Some parliamentary members have pushed for an end to the existing duality and argue that the JGK, as an internal security force, should be accountable to the Ministry of Internal Affairs not only in theory but also in practice.

An AKP deputy spoke of the following incident which he experienced while he was deputy of a certain province, which clearly illustrates the gendarmerie's

---

21 'Commission Deliberated Axing State Secret Shield,' Turkish Daily News, 28 December 2005.

22 General Plan and Principles Department Presidency, 'Mali Kaynaklar ve Savunnma Harcamalari,' Milli Savunma Bakanlığı Beyaz Kitap 2000, Chapter 9. See http://www.msb.gov.tr

23 Members from CHP insisted that Çörten be invited to a committee hearing, 'Şemdinli komisyonunda Tuğgeneral gerginliği,' Milliyet, 29 December 2005. Indeed, as a response to these reactions, Çörten later informed the committee members.

allegiance to the TSK in its performance of maintaining law and order: 'During a ceremony in honour of the president visiting the province where I was deputy, I ordered the Provincial Gendarmerie Commander to take up his post in the dam of the province. However, I noticed that he had ignored me and was waiting for the president at the airport. When I tried to intervene, he replied by saying 'You cannot give me orders' and I said, 'You are no different to the Chief of Police.' In the end, the Provincial Gendarmerie Commander went to the dam, just as I had instructed him to. But why should I, as a deputy, be exposed to a scolding from this commander along the lines of 'You cannot give me orders?' The provincial authorities are disturbed by the fact that the gendarmerie takes orders from the military while performing law enforcement duties.' The same deputy complained about the fact that gendarmerie members cannot be reviewed or appointed by civilian authorities.

According to this deputy, the gendarmerie takes orders from the general commander of gendarmerie, and the governor and district governors are merely informed after the fact. The deputy also pointed out that, although the gendarmerie takes orders from the military while performing law enforcement duties, it is the Ministry of Internal Affairs, a civilian institution, which is assigned the blame when security problems arise.

The TBMM ad-hoc Şemdinli Commission's investigation showed how inadequately the local government representatives' supervision of the gendarmerie was executed. On 28 December 2005, statements were taken from former Hakkâri Governor Erdoğan Gürbüz, former Head of Şemdinli District Mustafa Cihan Feslihan and the Head of the Directorate General of Security's Anti-Terror Bureau, Selim Akyıldız. In these statements Gürbüz and Feslihan said they were unaware of the fact that the NCOs who were arrested were conducting intelligence work on the day of the incident. When the officials in question said 'The gendarmerie takes care of this process internally, there is no mechanism in place that would make them inform us,' it led AKP Adıyaman Deputy Hüsrev Kutlu to reprimand the men, saying: 'Even the Land Forces Commander, General Yaşar Büyükanıt knows these NCOs personally.[24] How is it that you, as local authorities, do not know them?'[25]

Finally, a comment made by columnist Ali Bayramoğlu should be mentioned: 'Following 28 February [1997], the military took over the posts traditionally controlled by the police and the governors. The gendarmerie moved from the rural area to the urban area. Security and Public Order Assistance Squads (Emniyet, Asayiş Yardımlaşma Birlikleri, EMASYA) obtained authority above that of the governor. A domestic security structure has been established that posits society itself as being the greatest threat. This structure goes against democracy. Governors and heads of districts simply cannot transfer their authority to military squads. More-

---

[24] General Büyükanıt, in a statement he made immediately after the Şemdinli incident, said that he knows one of the petty officers in question and that he knows him to be a decent person. This led to Büyükanıt being accused of trying to influence the legal process. The statement was also a kind of admission of the official connection that exists between the Gendarmerie officer in question and TSK.

[25] 'Hakkari ve Şemdinli'nin mülki amirleri komisyonda dinlendi: Astsubayları tanımıyorum,' Milliyet, 29 December 2005.

over, the power to gather intelligence in a country should not rest in the hands of the military. Today, it is the military that defines threats, it is the military that gathers intelligence, assesses social incidents and bases all of its findings on internal security documents rather than legal criteria.'[26]

Important Developments in 2005

The 'Slander' Scandal

Although the incident known as the Slander Scandal took place in 2004, when evaluated together with the Şemdinli incident of 2005, it reinforces the theory that the mechanisms of the 'state within the state' are still very much in place. When the intelligence-gathering known to the public as 'high society slander' was recently unearthed, evidence of the ways in which the intelligence was gathered led to very important discussions concerning the issue of how some security organisations have positioned themselves above the constitution. According to a Hürriyet newspaper headline of 10 March 2004, the Second Armoured Brigade Command sent a memo to military squads and heads of districts, requesting that information be gathered about people and institutions involved in 'separatist and subversive' activities. Among these people and institutions were EU and US sympathisers, members of high-society, Satanists, freemasons, minorities, internet newsgroups and, strangely, Ku Klux Klan members. It was later discovered that the question concerning the Ku Klux Klan had been directly translated from field manuals prepared by the US Army.

After the incident was exposed by the media, Prime Minister Erdoğan stated that information gathering was not a TSK duty, and stressed that the act of 'slander' is a crime.[27] The General Staff acknowledged the slander incident and released the following statement on 10 March 2004: 'In accordance with the Provincial Administrative Law No. 5442, the local civilian authorities can, if they deem it necessary, request assistance from the closest land, air or naval squad commands for the prevention of incidents. For effective precautions to be taken, pre-planning is a necessity. The activity of intelligence gathering reported in the news article in question, about the high society slander, has to be evaluated with this in mind.' The statement also mentioned that 'necessary investigations are being carried out in order to correct some aspects of intelligence gathering,' hinting at a potential 'narrowing' of the criteria used for slander.

It was later claimed that the organisation behind the slander incident was EMASYA, an institution which has existed since the 1960s but whose structure has changed. According to Bayramoğlu, 'after 28 February, the armed forces determined that there is a fundamentalist threat in the country, and due to their possible mistrust

---

[26] Ali Bayramoğlu's interview with Neşe Düzel, Radikal, 12 April 2004.

[27] Constitutional Law Professor Zafer Üskül stressed that the 2nd Armored Brigade Command has no authority for requesting information from provincial administration offices. 'Üskül: 'Yetkisi yok', Milliyet, 11 March 2004; 'Erdoğan: TSK'nin görevi değil,' Cumhuriyet, 15 March 2004.

of the police, wanted total control of the domestic security domain. As soon as the Refahyol* cabinet was toppled in 1997, the structure of the EMASYA squads changed. A protocol was signed between Sadettin Tantan, the minister of internal affairs at the time, and the General Staff. The squads were assigned the authority to intervene in social incidents whenever the military deemed it necessary, without having to wait for a request from the governor's office. As a result, these squads became regular squads on duty 24 hours a day and seven days a week.'[28]

Bayramoğlu connected the EMASYA squads to the slander incident in the following way: 'This protocol actually provided the legal ground for these slanders. The EMASYA squads under the command of the land forces became intelligence-gathering units, requested information from deputies' offices, and almost manipulated deputies' offices, all thanks to the authority bestowed upon them by this protocol. The last slander was based on this, because with this protocol, the sphere of authority of the governor, the head of the district and the police was taken over by the 'soldiers.' EMASYA squads are not just any squad. These are organisations that exist in every garrison in every city in Turkey. They have the authority to stake out all of society. Such authority is inconceivable; it is a mad, terrible thing, an uncontrolled activity. Justice and law are not in effect.'[29]

Stressing that the protocol itself is illegal, Bayramoğlu discerns that the Ministry of Internal Affairs is unfortunately not the only ministry to have such protocols: 'For instance, the Forest Ministry also signed a protocol after 28 February, which gave the authority to the gendarmerie to inspect factory waste and the condition of workers in factories'. The forest minister abolished this protocol with a unilateral memo, stating that 'such authority of a civil nature cannot be given to the gendarmerie. The Ministry of Internal Affairs must do the same. Of course, courage, competence and timing are of the essence in such delicate matters. If the government is really democratic and in favour of the empowerment of the civilian authority, then it will abolish the protocol at a time when the risk of conflict is low.'[30]

From Susurluk to Şemdinli

Despite Bayramoğlu's warning about the gendarmerie's expanding sphere of jurisdiction, the gendarmerie still retains the right to withhold information from the public prosecutor. This was witnessed in the Şemdinli incident in 2005, where findings alluded to an illegal structuring of power.

Twenty days after a grenade assault on Seferi Yılmaz's Umut Bookshop in Şemdinli on 9 November, gendarmerie intelligence NCOs Özcan İldeniz and Ali Kaya were arrested on charges of disrupting the unity of the State. Two people died and many were injured in the incident. A notebook found on the officers showed that they failed to turn in the file they had prepared on Yılmaz to the public prosecu-

---

* Editor's Note: A compound title used to refer to the coalition government between the Virtue Party (Refah Partisi – RP) and the True Path Party (Doğru Yol Partisi – DYP).

28 Journalist Ali Bayramoğlu's interview with Neşe Düzel, Radikal, April 12, 2004.

29 Ibid.

30 Ibid.

tor's office.[31] Also stated in the Şemdinli Report ordered by former Prime Minister and Leader of the Democratic Left Party Bülent Ecevit was the suspicion that the JİTEM was a key player in this incident, even though the existence of such an institution has been adamantly denied by official authorities.[32]

The slander scandal and the Şemdinli bookshop bombing demonstrate the extent to which the TSK and the JGK have expanded their spheres of influence against domestic threats, through institutions such as JITEM and by activities independent of any civilian authority. The Susurluk incident exposed the civilian offsets of these illicit formations.[33] CHP Deputy Canan defined the Şemdinli incident as even graver than the Susurluk affair.[34]

It is clear that positive developments have been made to date, and these can be seen through the efforts made by the parliament in illuminating the Şemdinli incident, as well as the steps taken to focus on the state secret concept that some officials use as a cover. However, the attempts of the TBMM Commission to omit important information in the Şemdinli Report have undoubtedly shattered the expectations of uncovering some illegal activities.[35]

---

31 'Yemin gibi ilkeler,' Milliyet, 20 December 2005.

32 'Ecevit: Türkiye'de derin devlet hep var,' Ajanslar, 21 November 2005.

33 The Susurluk incident occurred on 3 November 1996, as a result of a car crash between a Mercedes and a truck. Abdullah Çatlı, who was a convicted killer in the incident known as the Bahçelievler Massacre (involving the killing of seven Turkish Labor Party (Türkiye İşçi Partisi, TİP) members in 1978). Çatlı's girlfriend, former beauty queen Gonca Us, and former Deputy Police Commissioner Hüseyin Kocadağ, who were in the Mercedes, all died. Then DYP Deputy Sedat Bucak was also in the car and was seriously injured. In the 10 years following this incident the dirty ties within the mafia-politics-state triangle were revealed. However, the mystery remains unsolved. The core of this incident is the intricate web of relations and cooperation between state security officials and crime organisations involved in a series of murders. Only a few people, including former MİT member, retired Marshall Korkut Eken, were prosecuted in relation to the Susurluk Scandal, for founding and heading crime organisations. When Bucak presented some secret documents and photographs to the court years later, under the cover of 'state secret,' the scandal gained a new, military aspect. One of the generals next to Çatlı in the photographs was identified as the Gendarmerie Public Order Commander of the period, Hasan Kundakçı. Kundakçı said: 'I could be the one in the picture, I wish I knew Çatlı.' Korkut Eken was supported by almost all of the high-ranking commanders immediately after his prosecution by statements along the lines of 'Eken did everything within our knowledge; his services to the country are of great value.' 'Bucak gizliliğe sığınıyor' Cumhuriyet, 1 October 2004.

34 'Canan: Susurluk'tan beter,' Milliyet, 11 November 2005.

35 Upon insistence from members of the CHP, the Commission removed the accusatory statements concerning General Yaşar Büyükanıt from the report. It was reported in the draft that Büyükanıt's words to the effect of: 'I know him, he is a good soldier' about the petty officer involved in the incident could influence the court process, 'Suçlamada geri adım,' Hürriyet, 26 January 2006. The following segment was also reportedly omitted from the first report: 'The relevant institutions must make the necessary explanations as to whether units like JİTEM and JİT exist. Illegal formations should be eliminated, and those involved, whether voluntarily or through negligence, should be punished. The public felt that the low flight of fighter planes during the funeral in Yüksekova was a form of intimi-

SIDEBAR 1

Turkish Gendarmerie Units work within Peace Force Troops in

- West European Squad (BAB) Multinational Police Consultation Unit (MAPE), deployed in Tirana/Albania,
- Albania Humanitarian Aid Force (AFOR),
- SFOR Headquarters deployed in Sarajevo/Bosnia-Herzegovina,
- International Temporary Existence (TPIH) deployed in Al-Khalil-Israel
- NATO Kosovo Peace Force deployed in Pristina/Kosovo (KFOR),
- Kosovo Turkish Task Force deployed in Pristina/Kosovo that were put together by UN Decisions.

Source: http://www.tsk.mil.tr

dation (...)'. When AKP Adıyaman Deputy Faruk Ünsal, who objected to the removal of these segments, refused to approve the report, the document was shelved. 'Şemdinli raporu sonunda rafa kalktı,' Sabah, 31 January 2006.

SIDEBAR 2
Gendarmerie General Command (JGK)
Commander: General Fevzi Türkeri
LIEUTENANT GENERALS
Staff Chairman/Ankara
Supervision Chairman/Ankara
Training Chairman/Ankara
A varying number of Provincial Gendarmerie Regiment Commands work under the following Gendarmerie Regional Commands. Provincial Gendarmerie Regiment Commanders have the rank of Colonel, whereas Regional Commanders have various general ranks.
MAJOR GENERALS
Adana Regional Commander/Adana
Gendarmerie Schools Commander/Ankara
Chairman of Operations/Ankara
Gendarmerie Regional Commander/Tunceli
Gendarmerie Regional Commander/Erzurum
Gendarmerie Regional Commander/İstanbul
Gendarmerie Regional Commander/Ankara
BRIGADIER GENERALS
Gendarmerie Regional Commander/Aydın
4th Commando Training Brigade Commander/Foça-İzmir
JGK Chairman of Logistics/Ankara
JGK Chairman of General Planning & Principles/Ankara
21st Gendarmerie Border Brigade Commander/Yüksekove-Hakkari
Gendarmerie Regional Commander/Giresun
Gendarmerie Regional Commander/Bursa
JGK Chairman of Personnel Department/Ankara
Gendarmerie Chairman of Logistics/Ankara
3rd Gendarmerie Traning Brigade Commander/Zonguldak
1st Gendarmerie Commando Brigade Commander/Şırnak
Gendarmerie Regional Commander/Diyarbakır
Gendarmerie Training Command Staff Chairman/Ankara
Gendarmerie Regional Commander/Tokat
JGK Chairman of Intelligence/Ankara
Gendarmerie Regional Commander/Kayseri
Gendarmerie Regional Commander/Konya
2nd Gendarmerie Training Brigade Commander/Bilecik
Gendarmerie Regional Commander/Batman

Source: Information gathered from various sources by the author

SIDEBAR 3

The Organisation of the General Command of Gendarmerie;

1. Headquarters and its Troops
2. Domestic Security Troops

a Gendarmerie Troops that are not part of the district administration organisation

(1) Gendarmerie Commando Troops,
(2) Gendarmerie Aviation Troops,

b Gendarmerie Troops that are part of the district administration organisation

(1) Gendarmerie Regional Commands
(2) Provincial Gendarmerie Commands (regiment level)
(3) Provincial Centre and District Gendarmerie Commands
(4) Gendarmerie Station Commands
(5) Gendarmerie Protection Troops,
(6) Gendarmerie Public Order Commando Troops,

3. Border Troops,
4. Training Troops,
5. Gendarmerie Schools,
6. Administrative and Logistic Support Troops and,

other departments that will be established in accordance with the nature of the duty.

Source: http://www.tsk.mil.tr, http://www.Jandarma.gov.tr

Coast Guard

*Lale Sarıibrahimoğlu**

Background

The Turkish Coast Guard Command (Sahil Güvenlik Komutanlığı, SGK) was established by Law No. 2692 and was accepted by the Turkish Grand National Assembly (Türkiye Büyük Millet Meclisi, TBMM) on 9 July 1982, as an armed security force, distinct from the Turkish Naval Forces[1] (Deniz Kuvvetleri Komutanlığı, DKK).

Turkey's coastal security services were formerly performed by the Customs Guard General Command which was formed in 1932 by Law No. 1917, and was affiliated with the General Staff. This institution was charged with preventing naval smuggling and maintaining the security of Turkish territorial waters. The Customs Guard General Command, which remained active until 1956, reported to the Ministry of Customs and Monopoly as far as its functions were concerned, and was part of the General Staff with regard to security of the sea border and personnel training. In 1956, the coast guard services were transferred to the General Command of the Gendarmerie (Jandarma Genel Komutanlığı, JGK).

The SGK, as stipulated by Law No. 2692, continued to operate under the JGK from 1982 to 1985, until the infrastructure for its own establishment was complete. As of 1 January 1985, it has operated under the Ministry of Internal Affairs in times of peace and matters of domestic security, and under the Turkish Armed Forces (Türk Silahlı Kuvvetleri, TSK) in times of war (For the SGK organisational chart see Table 1).

The SGK works in coordination with the Ministry of Internal Affairs in matters of crimes committed within the continental shelf, such as poaching and the trafficking of drugs and fuel. Until 1985, the registries of the SGK were under the jurisdiction of the general commander of gendarmerie, and its budget was regulated by the JGK, whereas today, the registries are under the jurisdiction of the chief of the general staff. The general commander of gendarmerie is answerable to the minister of internal affairs in matters of law and order, whereas the coast guard commander has no such affiliation with the minister of internal affairs.

During the establishment of the SGK, and in order to fulfil the duties stipulated by Law No. 2692, the necessary personnel, armaments, ammunition and tools

---

* Journalist, Defence Expert.

1 For Law No. 2692 on the Turkish Coast Guard Command dated 9 July 1982 see Official Gazette (Resmi Gazete) No. 17753 dated 13 July 1982, http://www.basbakanlik.gov.tr, Legislation Information System.

were defined by the DKK and JGK, and were provided according to a plan advised by the General Staff and approved by the Ministries of National Defence and Internal Affairs.

With an amendment made to the aforementioned law on 18 June 2003, the SGK was no longer affiliated to the Turkish Naval Forces in relation to personnel matters, and similar to the JGK eventually became autonomous. As a result of this, the SGK was allocated its own budget which it used to expand its weapons inventory significantly. The SGK, which has started to acquire its own staff, is aiming to increase its control over the seas surrounding Turkey from five percent to more than 50 percent. This area includes the Black Sea, the Mediterranean and the Aegean Sea, and is currently being fulfilled by the air and naval forces.

In 2003, with an amendment made in Law No. 2692, the status of the SGK's personnel was also elevated and regional commanders holding the rank of colonel were promoted to admiral. One of the main purposes in making the SGK autonomous, was to decrease its burden on the relatively limited DKK budget, which according to unofficial figures constitutes 14-16 percent of the Ministry of National Defence's (Milli Savunma Bakanlığı, MSB) budget.

The SGK's method of performing its activities can be summarised in the following way: SGK personnel carry out their duties in accordance with the TSK Internal Service Law No. 211, within their own chain of command. The SGK performs the duties laid out by this law through cooperation, mutual assistance and coordination with relevant ministries, civil and judicial bodies, as well as other security forces and related institutions when necessary. In addition, the SGK takes part in training and manoeuvres organised by the DKK. Attention is paid, however, to avoid disrupting the SGK from carrying out its principal duty of providing naval security.

The SGK's Duties and Sphere of Jurisdiction

The sea borders of Turkey are approximately three times larger than its land borders. The length of Turkey's land borders is 2'573 kilometres, whereas the sea borders, including the islands, are 8'333 kilometres long.

The SGK's coastal security duties cover the supervision and control activities in accordance with the related laws, statutes and regulations, under the Ministry of Internal Affairs and as stipulated by its establishment law and related statutes. These duties are carried out along the 8'333 kilometre long coastal line, in an area of jurisdiction consisting of territorial waters, the exclusive economic zone and search and rescue territory. This area begins from the Georgian sea border Sarp and extends to the Bulgarian sea border İğneada in the Black Sea; from the Greek sea border Enez in the Aegean Sea to the Syrian sea border Samandağ in the East Mediterranean.[2] The SGK's duties fall outside the scope of responsibility of the DKK.

---

2 For Law No. 2692 on Turkish Coast Guard Command dated 9 July 1982 see Resmi Gazete (Official Gazette) No. 17753 dated July 13 1982, http://www.basbakanlik.gov.tr, Legislation Information System; General Plan and Principles Department, Milli Savunma Bakanlığı Beyaz Kitap 2000, <http://www.msb.gov.tr

Other SGK duties include: the protection and enhancement of the security of Turkish coasts, territorial waters, internal ports and gulfs; performing duties which fall outside the scope of responsibility of the DKK, in the waters under Turkish jurisdiction, as defined by national and international law; defining the principles and methods concerning the prevention and surveillance of all kinds of naval smuggling and related criminal proceedings; prevention and surveillance of smuggling in general, protection of forbidden military and security zones, territorial waters, historical artefacts, cultural and natural objects; prevention, surveillance and apprehension of criminals involved in sabotage, activities harmful to the life and property on the sea and violations of fishery, trade, customs, wireless communication, the Turkish flag, passports, promotion of tourism, health and environmental regulations. The coast guard is also required to follow the necessary proceedings and deliver apprehended persons and confiscated vessels to the judicial authorities.

The SGK are also expected to take the necessary measures to clear the area of stray mines, explosives and suspicious objects. They are also required to confiscate weapons and ammunition found on refugees that enter Turkish territorial waters and hand them over to the relevant authorities. Additionally, the SGK is tasked with protecting strategically important industrial complexes against naval threats, such as pipelines for example; to participate in training and manoeuvres organised by the DKK; to provide security during land and air force firing practices on the water; to perform search and rescue missions during air force missions over the sea and, to escort national/international yacht races organised by Turkish yacht clubs.

SGK Budget

In parallel to the JCK, the SGK operates under the Ministry of Internal Affairs in times of peace, its budget is allocated from the Ministry's budget, and it is also under the supervision of the TSK.[3] However, the SGK's weapons, ammunition and tools are provided independently from the SGK's budget, in compliance with DKK standards and according to a plan that is prepared together with the DKK and approved by the Ministry of Internal Affairs.

As is the case with the JGK, all exceptions and exemptions concerning customs and all kinds of taxes, imposts, fees and storage dues apply to the SGK, as stipulated by budget and other relevant laws.

Despite the legal changes which were introduced as part of Turkey's bid for full membership within the EU, it was observed that the TBMM and the relevant committees were not yet fully able to establish control mechanisms over the SGK's budget. This is also the case with the budgets of the Turkish Armed Forces and the JGK. The minutes of the TBMM Plan and Budget Committee's meetings on the budget of the Ministry of Internal Affairs are open to the public. However, when

---

3 For detailed information, see General Plan and Principles Department Presidency, Milli Savunma Bakanlığı Beyaz Kitap 2000, http://www.msb.gov.tr. SGK 2006 budget draft was defined as 194.4 million YTL and this meant an increase of 11,34 % compared to 2005. For the SGK budget details, see the table of Ministry of Economics budget in the chapter on 'Turkish Armed Forces' in this Almanac.

they were analysed, it was apparent that the members of the Turkish Grand National Assembly had neglected to question the budgets and the justification of weapons purchases by these three security organisations for the sake of accountability, transparency and the appropriate use of public resources. Therefore, it is not clear whether or not the SGK's weapon procurements reflect genuine demand, and whether taxpayers receive information, through their elected representatives, about how their taxes are spent.

As decreed by Article 32 of the Rules of Procedure, a brief confidential meeting follows the TBMM Plan and Budget Committee meetings to discuss those parts of the JGK and the SGK's 2006 central administration budget that involves deliberations on secret de facto employment policies.[4]

The SGK's Hierarchical Structure

The Ministry of Internal Affairs is in charge of domestic security and law and order. The Ministry is also responsible, through the heads of the civil service (governors and heads of districts), for the services provided by the police force, and the paramilitary forces of the JGK and the SGK which are both affiliated to the military. The SGK also works in cooperation with a number of government bodies to provide naval security.

However, although the SGK theoretically works under the Ministry of Internal Affairs in times of peace, in reality it actually operates under the directives of the General Staff. For instance, despite the protocol that stipulates the coordination of cooperation between the SGK personnel and the naval police for maintaining law and order, there are problems concerning multiple superiors and the overlapping of duties. Legally, the Boat and Squadron Commands outside Ankara and therefore considered to be in a rural area, can only be inspected by the governor, and not by the heads of districts who are responsible for the region. The SGK, which is in effect under the supervision of the TSK in times of peace, can be placed in part or completely under the command of the DKK Operational Command in extraordinary situations, upon the request of the chief of general staff. In times of war, the SGK is completely under the DKK's command.

The SGK's area of activities, its bases and its areas of deployment are defined by the Ministry of Internal Affairs, in consultation with the General Staff, and its affiliated institutions and staff are regulated by the Ministry, again in consultation with the General Staff.

SGK personnel consist of officers, NCOs, enlisted specialists, military students and privates as well as civil servants and civilian employees. According to official figures, the SGK has a total of 2'200 personnel, which consists mainly of conscripts, and includes 460 civilians.

The officers and NCOs required by the SGK are trained in the DKK or other TSK training institutions and expenses are overseen by the SGK's budget. Education, promotion, leave, registration, punishment and award processes are carried out

---

4 The Plan and Budget Committee meetings on the budget for the fiscal year on November 24, 2005. See http://www.tbmm.gov.tr

in accordance with TSK Personnel Code No. 926. The admirals, officers, NCOs and civilian personnel of the SGK are subject to specific laws as far as employee rights are concerned. Therefore, despite the fact that SGK personnel have been fulfilling the same duties as the police, i.e. internal security, the former are paid higher salaries in comparison to their civilian counterparts, since they are subject to TSK laws. The payments in cash and in kind, that the personnel of the JGK and other institutions receive, are also given to SGK personnel under the same provisions. SGK registry procedures for its personnel comply with TSK principles.

The educational expenses of the officers, NCOs, enlisted specialists and privates who are trained to work for the SGK are overseen by the SGK budget. As mentioned above, their training is conducted within the DKK or other TSK training institutions, and the specific training required for services performed by either military or civilian personnel are structured in accordance with the principles laid out by the Ministry of Internal Affairs.

The demand for officers and NCOs that cannot be met by the SGK's resources are covered by other branches of the armed forces and the JGK, upon the SGK's request and the general staff's approval. However, these personnel remain bound to their respective branches of command.

The selection of a coast guard commander is made by appointment of the naval forces commander, a proposal by the chief of general staff, with a letter of promotion by the minister of internal affairs and a joint decree which is signed by the prime minister and approved by the president. Except for some rare instances, decrees of appointment are signed routinely by the civilian authorities cited above, without any interference in the promotional structure. The appointment of officers between the ranks of third lieutenant up to colonel, as well as NCOs, civil servants and the enlisted specialists, are done by the SGK. The allocation of enlisted specialists and the privates to their various posts are realised by the SGK.

In the case of a crime that begins at sea and continues on land, the SGK personnel continue to exert their authority on land until an authorised security force intervenes. This is in order to prevent evidence from being lost or those responsible from fleeing. The local civilian authority is notified of the situation by the quickest means available.

The SGK's Structural Problem: The Sharing of Military and Civilian Authority

In a similar vein to the JGK, there is a duality inherent in the way in which civilian and military forces provide security for Turkish waters. For instance, the General Directorate of Coastal Safety and Salvage Administrations[5] operates under both the SGK and the Prime Minister's Maritime Under-secretariat, precisely because of the similarity of duties exercised by the two organisations. This duality has continued despite the fact that a modified regulation has been issued.

---

5 Established as stipulated by the Decision No. 9466 of the Council of Ministers dated 12 May 1997.

The duality can be explained by the fact that basic instructions concerning naval security are given to the SGK by the TSK, as opposed to the government, regardless of the fact that the coast guard operates under the Ministry of Internal Affairs in times of peace. As a means of resolving this issue, the Council of Ministers issued the Turkish Search and Rescue Regulation No. 3275 on 20 September 2001, to regulate civilian naval search and rescue missions. It took effect following its publication on 12 December 2001 in the Official Gazette (Resmi Gazette) No. 24611.

With Regulation No. 3275, the responsibility and coordination of civilian naval search and rescue activities was handed over to the SGK. Additionally, and in compliance with the National Search and Rescue Plan, search and rescue duties on the sea were entrusted to the SGK, whilst the Directorate General of Civil Aviation was entrusted with search and rescue duties in the air. This Plan was published on 11 July 2002 in the Official Gazette No. 24812 with Communiqué No. 2002/4. The administration of both was entrusted to the Principal Search and Rescue Coordination Centre of the Directorate General of Sea Transport in the Maritime Under-secretariat.

The SGK is responsible for maintaining national security against domestic and foreign threats, together with the police, which is a civilian security force. However, one of the main reasons for the confusion of authority between the SJK and other civilian institutions which carry out the same duty, is the ongoing organic relationship which the SGK has with the TSK in practice, even though the SGK is only a semi-military security force, similar to that of the JGK. However, in order to provide the security of the country, in accordance with the principles of efficiency, transparency and accountability, then both civilian and military security forces should be under the direction and management of the government.

This structure that exists in Turkey differs from the functions executed in the EU countries concerning the enhancement of security at seas. Coast guard duties in EU countries are administered by institutions such as the Maritime or Environment Under-secretariat's, or are shared between various ministries. The common principles among these countries convene that the protection of territorial waters is a duty that is performed by professionally trained, civilian institutions which operate within the government. Coordination is shared between all the security forces that are responsible for maintaining law and order. This policy is based on the idea that the institutions responsible for national security can only succeed in the face of threats such as organised crime, nuclear weapons trafficking, terrorism and the spreading of weapons of mass destruction, by maintaining professional, well organised security forces.

Given the fact that Turkey faces both domestic and foreign threats, then co-operation between institutions should be paramount and power struggles should naturally be avoided. These threats include: illegal immigration from both sea and land, weapons of mass destruction, drug trafficking, infiltration by international terrorists, and fuel smuggling, which is seriously harmful to the national economy. In the European Commission's Progress Report which was released on 9 November 2005, it was argued that coordination between the police, the gendarmerie and the SGK is essential, within the framework of the quest for solving the structural problems that lead to a multiplicity of authority and a lack of service efficiency. These three institutions should be part of a single body which receive their directives from civilians, and the enforcement of establishing such a structure was deemed essential. In addition, Turkey is required, according to the EU's criteria, to establish a non-military border police force, consisting of civilian professionals, in order to protect the sea and land borders efficiently.

In view of the above, Turkey planned to implement an integrated border management arrangement in 2003 and the subsequent Action Plan is being administered by the Ministry of Internal Affairs. However, as stated in the EU Progress Report dated 9 November 2005, there has been no progress made as yet in the development of this plan. The main reason for this has been the combined reluctance by the TSK, the JGK and the SGK to transfer the authority for protecting Turkey's borders to civilian professionals. Indeed, a related project, which was initiated by the EU in 2004, came to a standstill precisely because of the JGK and the SGK's reluctance to transfer authority to civilians.

On a more positive note however, in January 2005, the Ministry of Internal Affairs released a circular which reiterated its mission to protect land and sea borders, provide efficient security and increase cooperation and coordination between the police, the gendarmerie and the coastal security forces. For such a course of action to be applied, however, significant structural changes are required. This changes will entail the JGK and SGK to become professionally staffed forces, and the placement of both under a civilian authority. To date, the government has been unable to make the necessary legal changes which would allow the JGK and the SGK to provide public order under the elected government. The inability to initiate such basic changes is reflective of the strength of the military over the civilian sector. The prevailing view is that such actions aim to undermine the military sector at large.

Table 1: SGK Organisational Chart

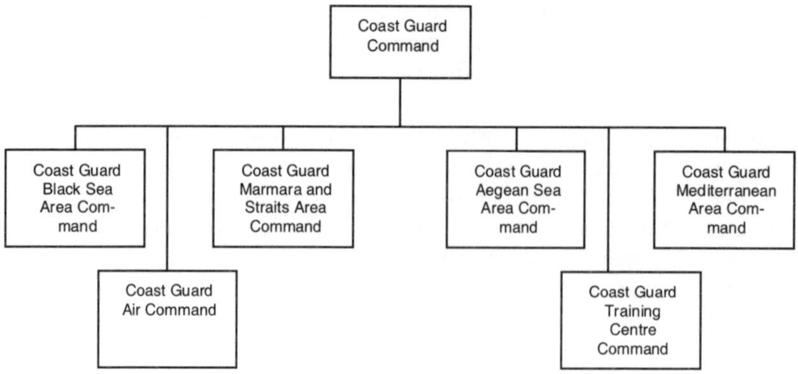

Source: Ministry of National Defence White Book 2000

There are also three Group Commands and Repair Support and Supply Support Commands per Regional Command. The Repair Support and Supply Support Commands provide logistical and technical support to ships in the inventory. The SGK established an air squadron for coastal security duties consisting of helicopters and airplanes.

Special Operations Unit

Ertan Beşe

Background: The Appearance of Special Anti-Terrorist Teams

On 5 September 1972 during the Munich Olympic Games, 11 Israeli athletes were kidnapped by eight Palestinian guerrillas from the 'Black September' Organisation, which was established by the Al-Fatah Group.[1] A hostage rescue operation was organised by police units belonging to the German Federal State of Bavaria. During the ensuing confrontation, the guerrillas killed all 11 hostages, five of the guerrillas were killed and another three were captured. It could be argued, therefore, that this failed rescue attempt gave rise to the creation of modern anti-terrorist units.

The events in Munich brought to light the inadequacies of the German police in such circumstances, and as a result, European countries subsequently determined the need to establish specially trained security personnel for rapid intervention in the event of future hostage crises. Special police units were therefore formed, provided with superior firepower, and trained in high risk operations, special communications, armed and unarmed conflict, prompt intervention procedures, secret access, hostage rescue, negotiation and persuasion techniques.

The first special anti-terrorist units were selected from existing special forces, and therefore assumed a paramilitary character. However, these units proved to be reasonably costly as they required a continuous supply of personnel and equipment as well as intensive training.[2] These special anti-terrorist units were designed to operate as hostage rescue teams, and these types of missions were undoubtedly the toughest assignments for any unit to undertake. Concurrently, given the nature of their training, equipment and skills, these teams were highly suited to the execution of other kinds of operations, such as proactive measures against imminent terrorist attacks, performing sensitive guard/escort jobs, avoiding attacks and performing high risk operations. When assigned to anti-terrorist missions, these units were regarded as 'paramilitary police.'[3]

Anti-terrorist units in Western Europe are often established within the police, and the best examples of those are found in Germany, France, Belgium, Italy, the

---

1 The military wing of the Palestine Liberation Organisation (PLO).

2 For example, following the Achille Lauro hijacking incident in 1985, Germany decided to form a special team for marine operations within the GSG-9, which cost them over DM 3 million just for the provision of initial equipment requirements.

3 Here, paramilitary stands for training, equipment, philosophy and organisation of a semi-military nature.

Netherlands and Spain. One exception, however, is Britain's Special Air Service Regiment (SAS), which is the principal special forces unit of the British Army, and is used in anti-terrorist operations and other specialised missions.

The Establishment and Functions of Turkish Special Operations Police Teams

Special Operations Police Teams (Polis Özel Harekât Timleri, PÖHT), were organised in 1983 in the cities of Ankara, Istanbul and Izmir, within the Presidency of the Department of Public Order (Asayiş Dairesi Başkanlığı), under a central Special Operations Branch Directorate (Özel Harekât Şube Müdürlüğü) and a Special Operations Group Authority (Özel Harekât Grup Amirliği). The teams were specially trained to carry out sensitive operations which required special skills. These included interpreting the armed actions of terrorist organisations in inhabited or rural areas, overpowering or capturing the perpetrators of terrorist actions and rescuing hostages in enclosed areas such as planes, vehicles and buildings.

As a result of the changing style and quantity of terrorist events, the PÖHT moved from the Department of Public Order in 1987, to the Anti-Terror and Operations Office (Terörle Mücadele ve Harekât Dairesi Başkanlığı), where it remained until 1993, under the name of Special Operations Branch Directorate (Özel Harekât Şube Müdürlüğü). Due to a rise in separatist terrorist acts, the Special Operations Department was transformed into the Special Operations Office (Özel Harekât Dairesi Başkanlığı, ÖHDB) in 1993, by means of a Council of Ministers' decree dated 26 July 1993. This development was not published in the Official Gazette (Resmi Gazete).

The decree published on 12 August 1993, authorised the establishment of a Special Operations Police Academy (Özel Harekât Polis Okulu) and specialist training of personnel. The regulation concerning the activities of the office was qualified as 'top secret' and the office was directly attached to the director general in accordance with this regulation.

At its centre, and in the Branch Directorates of Special Operations in 48 cities, the contemporary ÖHDB incorporates the Departments of Education/Training, Personnel, Support, and Operations, Planning and Evaluation. The ÖHDB reports directly to the director general of security, whereas the Branch Directorates of Special Operations report directly to the branch director of security.

Special operations personnel are selected from amongst volunteers and employees of the general directorate of security, who possess the skills required for police duty combined with the following qualities: physical strength, athleticism, composure, discipline, determination and stamina, as well as an ability to perform effectively and successfully during training and in the use of small arms. Training is conducted for at least three months, during which time the recruits practice firing a variety of weapons used by special operations units, as well as sniper/sharp shooting, weapon techniques, trekking and mountaineering, sports, close combat defence and hostage rescue in confined areas. They are also taught the principles and reforms of Atatürk as well as human rights. Those who successfully complete basic training are appointed to the Branch Directorate of Special Operations.

Since its inception, the ÖHDB has conducted 29 rounds of special operations courses, where it has trained 8'928 staff and officers, as well as five persons from the Uzbeki domestic safety units and 44 persons from the domestic safety units of the Turkish Republic of Northern Cyprus (Kuzey Kıbrıs Türk Cumhuriyeti, KKTC). While some personnel have retired, other officers, who are over 35 years of age and staff who are over 40, have been appointed to various other units in accordance with the regulations. The reduction in ÖHDB numbers has been attributed to the relative decrease of terrorist activities in Turkey.

The ÖHDB also organises training courses on demand for other Turkish security units and for the domestic safety units of Turkmenistan, the Palestinian territories and Macedonia. These courses focus on intervention techniques in the event of hostage taking.

Special Operations Teams (ÖHT) in Light of the Susurluk Report

During the second half of the 1980s and the first half of the 1990s, where the Kurdistan Workers' Party (Partiya Karkerên Kurdistan, PKK) terrorism was felt most strongly in Turkey, the Special Operations Teams (Özel Harekat Timleri, ÖHT), otherwise known as Special Teams, were frequently the focus of attention and criticism. This was, on the whole, due to the attire, attitude and behaviour of some team members, as well as the specific 'formations' which evolved as a result of the particular conditions of the period.

The ÖHT received notable attention because of the successful operations they conducted against terrorist organisations, and in particular against the PKK. This led to a number of claims being voiced that the special teams had a Turkish nationalist agenda. It was claimed that they used symbols representative of specific political parties, played Janissary Band marches from armed personnel carriers, and greeted one other by a special hand signal ('grey wolf' symbolism, associated with extreme right-wing formations). In addition, most team members wore their moustaches in a crescent-style (also associated with the extreme right-wing).

However, the ÖHT's public image was most seriously damaged by the Susurluk accident which occurred on 3 November 1996. One of the victims of this accident was Hüseyin Kocadağ, an ex-ÖHT member and director of security. For the government, Kocadağ's presence at the scene was a symbol in the triangle that also included 'mafia' and 'politics.' Yet the real problem emerged with the investigation and reports, which proposed to unravel the Susurluk event after broad media coverage.

An investigative report (known in brief by the public as the 'Susurluk Report')[4] was prepared by the chief of the Prime Minister's Inspection Committee, Kutlu Savaş, upon the order of Prime Minister Mesut Yılmaz. According to this report, the Susurluk controversy could be traced back to the time when former Prime Minister Tansu Çiller stated that the government had 'on hand the list of those businessmen who aid the PKK.' Summary executions of numerous businessmen fol-

---

4 Kutlu Savaş, 'Susurluk Raporu', m.0001 (10 January 1997).

lowed this statement and the question centred on who gave the orders for these executions? The report assumes the Susurluk event to be 'the replacement of national and patriotic considerations with personal interest.'[5]

The report included striking arguments and information about the ÖHDB— otherwise known as 'the Special Team' — under the heading of the Directorate General of Security (Emniyet Genel Müdürlüğü, EGM). One of these statements concerned the decisive influence of politics on the fight against the PKK and on the functioning of the ÖHT. The report asserted that there was no difference between the 1980s and 1990s, in terms of the government's militarisation of the issue. It also affirmed that a sea of change towards civilianisation began with Mehmet Ağar's appointment to the post of director general of security, whereby the ÖHT appeared to be an indicator of this change:

> '...The fight against the PKK was left to the armed forces during the 1980s. It has been criticised, even in political discussions, that the successive governments have taken no precautions against terrorism and entrust this issue to the military. Subsequently with the governmental change at the end of 1991, it cannot be claimed that a meritorious alteration in the fight against terrorism has hit the agenda. At least, no substantial difference in practice and outlook has become apparent (...). Finally, in 1993, radical change was targeted and the period of the 'war hawks' began. The prime minister presented the prevention of terrorism as the priority activity on the agenda. Mehmet Ağar took office in the Directorate General of Security and a serious decision was made: the police (force) was promoted to a position where it would be more active in the fight against terrorism and the 'Special Operations Teams' have gained more importance.'[6]

The report states that the provincial governors demand that the ÖHT direct (or at least take part in) every important event that requires special security.[7] The report also provides detailed information concerning the structuring of special operations. It stipulates that teams consist of, at least, 20 personnel and that they perform outside police regions, in provinces or in rural areas, upon the demand of military units and under the responsibility of military authorities.

The report further asserts that the examination of existing documents and correspondence show that the ÖHDB occupies a privileged status and position. This creates serious problems, the most important of which is the deployment of forces to a variety of areas, instead of a consolidation where the need is most pressing. The report reiterates the problems identified in the ÖHDB's information file of 30 June 1997, the most significant of which is the increase in the number of personnel in the provinces and regions devoid of terrorist activities:

---

5 Ibid., p. 10.
6 Ibid., p. 11.
7 Ibid., p. 12.

> 'The total number of personnel trained is 8'443, of which 2'043 have left for various reasons. The work, vacation and annual leave conditions of the teams are generally heavy and arduous, for which compensatory payments must be made (...) Serious problems have occurred over a short period of time in the distribution of the special operations personnel. In 1998, 5'000 personnel members were assembled in Turkey at large and outside of the Martial Law Region, due to the appointment of personnel to other places after completion of their tour of duty. This left only 1'600 personnel in the region. Also, personnel have marked preferences in (terms of) location and they focus on five cities in the west of the country. This situation reveals that, over a short period of time, the Office of Special Operations has deviated from its expected function.'[8]

The briefing report clearly expresses that an unbalanced provincial distribution will lead to a substantial vacuum in the eastern and south-eastern provinces, which are the principal areas of duty for the ÖHT, and to a simultaneous increase in the number of special operations personnel in the western provinces, which will create further problems. Furthermore, although it seems possible to overcome the first problem by arranging new courses, it will prove impossible to avoid the accumulation of personnel in the western provinces, In addition, the financial burden that will be imposed by the new courses is also considerable.[9]

Savaş states in the Susurluk report that the influence of Korkut Eken[10] over the ÖHDB substantially increased, following the appointment of İbrahim Şahin to the position of the chief of the Special Operations Office (ÖHDB), by proxy in

---

8 Ibid., p. 13.

9 In recent years, this problem has been solved with the appointment of special operations police officers considered below-standard or extraneous, to posts in different branches.

10 Korkut Eken was born in Ankara in 1945. He graduated from the Turkish Military Academy in 1965. Eken officiated as team or company commander in various units such as the Commando Brigade, Air-Landed Operations Brigade, Turkish Forces Regiment of Cyprus and the like. He took part in the Cyprus Peace Operations and was awarded the Ribbon Badge Certificate (Şerit Rozet Beratı). In 1978, he was appointed to the Special Unit Commandership of the Special War Office (Özel Harp Dairesi Özel Birlik Komutanlığı, a unit composed of officers and non-commissioned officers with superior education) where he participated in various courses abroad. In 1982, he took charge of the establishment of Special Operations Police Teams (PÖHT). In 1987, he retired voluntarily from the Turkish Armed Forces as lieutenant colonel and took office at the National Intelligence Organisation as vice-president of the Office of Security. In 1988, he quit the National Intelligence Organisation voluntarily. In 1993, he took charge of the organisation of the activities of re-equipment and training of the Special Operations Teams (ÖHT) within the Directorate General of Security upon the invitation of the Director General of Security Ağar. Subsequent to the Susurluk accident in 1996, he was given a six-year jail term on the charge of 'forming an organisation for criminal purposes and leading it.' He began to serve his sentence on 1 March 2002 and was released on 28 July 2004. For further information, see http://www.korkuteken.com/kimdir.htm

1993. The office was strengthened during this period, the number of personnel increased, and the success and effectiveness of Special Teams in the east and southeast reached its prime. The director general of security, Mehmet Ağar, became somewhat influential owing to the support provided by Prime Minister Çiller and the widespread activity of the police throughout the country.[11]

Following the accident in Susurluk, and once the relationships between the victims and the evidence had been obtained, allegations made by the Istanbul State Security Court and the Chief Public Prosecutor's Office (Devlet Güvenlik Mahkemesi Cumhuriyet Başsavcılığı) were examined during the cross-examination summary (Susurluk Fezlekesi)[12] dated 30 January 1997.

The summary stated that 'It was not convincing to define an event as 'a simple holiday or condolence call', when the following took place: an armed activist wanted in Turkey on charges of murder, was found together with a high-ranking member of the police in charge of capturing him, as well as some police officers and members of parliament, who not only had their licensed guns with them, but also assault weapons and ammunition used for assassinations and manslaughter.'

The turning-point came when the state began to use Special Operations Police Teams (PÖHT) against the PKK — which uses guerrilla tactics — in addition to military units, who until that time did not possess adequate tactical or strategic experience for such a war. This enabled the state to gain military control in the region. At the same time, these developments allowed for the introduction of tools, suited to the character of the threat, into the environment of low-intensity conflict which prevailed in the region.

The concept of resorting to a specialised force, specially trained and equipped to combat guerrilla fighting methods was eventually adopted by security units other than the police. The Turkish Armed Forces (Türk Silahlı Kuvvetleri, TSK), reviewed and reorganised its existing units of special forces in order to combat this threat, and formed new units accordingly.

Subsequent to the wide establishment of state authority in the region, and to the incrimination of members of special operations in some important aspects of the Susurluk event, special operations units tried to redress the issues that drew criticism. These efforts yielded fairly positive results and, for a long period, the force gained attention for its successes rather than its failures. The special operations teams that were accused of wrongdoings, began a campaign of renewal to reform their image by avoiding the sporting of symbols with political and ideological associations and by shaving off their moustaches.

The Office of Special Operations (ÖHDB) and the Developments of 2005

The ÖHDB drew recent attention through a tragic event in an ambush near Mosul, Iraq on 17 December 2004, where five personnel lost their lives. At the end of 2004 and the start of 2005, the ÖHT was questioned, once again, about the killing of Ah-

11 Savaş, Susurluk Raporu, p. 16 – 17.

12 Preparation No: 1997/221; Cross-examination Summary No: 1997/1, (30.01.1997).

met Kaymaz and his son Uğur, during the course of an operation carried out in the quarter of Turgut Özal in the Kızıltepe district of Mardin on 21 November 2004.

According to a report detailing the last two years' activities of the ÖHDB teams headquartered in Gölbaşı, Ankara, the organisation had suffered six losses as of March 2005, including the five as mentioned above (Chief Superintendent Officer Nihat Akbaş, Police Chief Bilal Ürgen and police officers Süleyman Karahasanoğlu, Âdem Çiçek and Bülent Kıranşan). These personnel were killed when the team was heading to Baghdad on a mission to defend the Turkish Embassy and this constituted the greatest loss suffered at any one time by the special operations unit.

The Directorate General of Security has reportedly intensified its educational programmes, in an effort to prevent members of special operations teams from drawing the public's attention with extrajudicial killings and violations of human rights. In an attempt to substantially improve their image, the teams are changing their methods of operation and establishing seminars on human rights. Upon the instructions of the director general of security, Gökhan Aydıner, 4'920 special operations team members have been given information on the new Turkish Criminal Code (Türk Ceza Kanunu, TCK) and the Code of Criminal Procedure (Ceza Muhakemeleri Kanunu, CMK), which came into effect on 1 June 2005. According to an ÖHDB report, 677 suspected terrorists were apprehended and 29 were killed in the past two years. In 2003, the teams apprehended 357 suspected terrorists and killed ten. In 2004, 318 suspected terrorists were apprehended, 19 were killed and two were wounded.[13]

The ÖHT has undertaken significant operations against terrorist organisations in the past two years such as Hizbullah,* Al-Qaeda, DHKP-C, TKP-ML/TİKKO, MKP and MLKP and, in particular, PKK/KADEK/Kongra-Gel∞. Ammunition stores of separatist and radical Islamist organisations have been discovered, and 49 rifles, 82 guns, 76 hand grenades, three rocket launchers and two missiles belonging to terrorist organisations have been seized. Furthermore, in searches carried out in rural areas, terrorist cells and caves, a substantial amount of diverse ammunitions, medical material, organisational documents, bomb-making material, foodstuffs, communication devices such as radios and satellite phones, and other equipment have also been found.[14]

---

[13] 'Özel timciler genel müdürlükten olumlu not aldı,' Zaman, 27 March 2005.

* Editor's Note: Hizbullah, or the Party of God, is a militant Islamist Sunni group unrelated to the Lebanon-based Shi'ite Hezbollah.

∞ Editor's Note: DHKP-C, the Revolutionary People's Liberation Party – Front; TKP-ML/TİKKO, the Communist Party of Turkey-Marxist Leninist/Turkish Workers' and Peasants' Liberation Army; MKP, the Maoist Communist Party; MLKP, the Marxist Leninist Communist Party; PKK/KADEK/Kongra-Gel, Kurdistan Workers' Party/Kurdistan Freedom and Democracy Congress/Peoples' Congress of Kurdistan.

[14] Ibid.

The Kızıltepe Event

On 21 November 2004, in an operation carried out by PÖHT in the Kızıltepe district of Mardin, a truck driver named Ahmet Kaymaz and his 12-year-old son Uğur, were shot dead in front of their house. The Kaymaz family claimed these were extrajudicial killings, asserting that Ahmet and his son were killed gratuitously, whereas the Mardin Provincial Governorship and the security authorities argued that 'the father and son were terrorist-organisation members and were killed as a result of a clash.' Discussions began after the event as to whether these deaths were a case of an 'extrajudicial killing', a 'wrongful death' or an 'unlawful use of force.'

The indictment drawn up by the Mardin Chief Public Prosecutor's Office on 27 December 2004, states that 'the Kızıltepe operation was organised with the purpose of capturing the PKK member Nusret Bali, code-named 'Kabat', and Ahmet Kaymaz who helped the PKK at the district centre as a militiaman. According to the information and documents included in the file, Ahmet Kaymaz realised that his house was under police observation and came out of the house with his son Uğur, in order to allow Nusret Bali, who was in the house, to escape from the back. Ahmet took measures to ensure that his son Uğur was mistaken for Nusret Bali, and as such, Uğur Kaymaz was not identified as Ahmet Kaymaz's son, due to the fact that he was armed (...)' In brief, the indictment claimed that Uğur Kaymaz had been killed by the ÖHT in error, because he was mistaken for Nusret Bali.

Various claims were made in relation to this event by political parties and different groups. These generally focused on whether the event was an extrajudicial killing or one that resulted from the unlawful and unauthorised use of arms. Consequently, the event drew allegations that the attitude and behaviour of the security forces had still not reached the standards appropriate for a state governed by the rule of law, and that the police unnecessarily resorted to an excessive use of force. Approximately 14 bullets were found in the body of Uğur Kaymaz, all of which were fired at short-range. According to some claims, there was no sign of a clash in the area and the arms seized on these persons were, in fact, planted subsequent to their deaths. However, the authorities claim that both persons were PKK members and that they had opened fire on the police.

Following the event, 5'000 people held demonstrations in Kızıltepe to protest against the security forces, which, together with all the other developments, naturally made the question of what was happening in Mardin a pressing one.* This was the first large-scale demonstration held against state authorities in the region in recent memory.

The Directorate General of Security declared that the two kalashnikovs seized at the scene in the deaths of Ahmet Kaymaz and his son Uğur, were proven by laboratory examination to have been used in the clash. Furthermore, it was also ascertained that one of these arms had been used in the raid of the Yenişehir Police Station on 7 August 2004, where two police chiefs and two police officers were wounded.

---

* Editor's Note: Kızıltepe is a district of Mardin.

According to one of the allegations that appeared in the press — attributed to different witnesses or anonymous public servants — 'the father and son were shot during a shift away from the real target, when the PKK member who was in the house escaped (…) There was actually a PKK member in that house, but it was neither Ahmet Kaymaz nor his 12-year-old son. The special operations police had gone there as part of a planned mission and they had taken up their position around the house beforehand. The reason that the father and son were shot at such close-range, was the fact that the police had gone to the vicinity of the house in advance and taken precautionary measures. Yet in the course of the operation, the PKK member in the house escaped from the opposite side, so both father and son were shot. During the operation, a shift in target had occurred and the wrong targets were hit. The fact that the bullets found in the two bodies were from pistols, shows that a serious operational mistake had occurred and that there had been a significant problem with tactical planning and implementation.'[15]

Examinations were carried out in Mardin and Kızıltepe, by a delegation which consisted of two members of parliament who had been assigned to the Kızıltepe case by the Turkish Grand National Assembly Human Rights Committee. These parliamentarians were: sub-committee member and Mersin deputy of the Republican People's Party (Cumhuriyet Halk Partisi, CHP) Hüseyin Güler, and Batman Deputy of the Justice and Development Party (Adalet ve Kalkınma Partisi, AKP) Nezir Nasıroğlu. According to Nasıroğlu's statement, which appeared in the press following the examination, 'some indications pertaining to the allegations of extrajudicial killing were found.' 'It is certain that a mistake was made in this event, in that a 12-year old child can neither use a gun nor be a terrorist. We think the public servants made a mistake here. On the other hand, even if the allegation that these people were 'terrorists' was true, it seems that it was within the realm of possibility for them to be captured alive. The event occurred in an open area near the main road. We do not believe that these people were 'terrorists' as alleged by the public authorities. A father will protect his son in such an event even if he is taking part in terrorist activities.'[16]

Furthermore, the delegation of the Human Rights Association (İnsan Hakları Derneği, İHD), Mardin Branch,[17] which carried out an investigation at the crime

---

15 Fuat Akyol ''Mardin'de şehven infaz,' ('Erroneous Extrajudicial Killing in Mardin'), Aksiyon, 13 December 2004. According to the report of the Institution of Forensic Medicine (Forensic Medicine 1st Specialised Department), Uğur Kaymaz was shot in the back by 11 bullet shells and 13 foreign bodies. The report also states that the bullets found in the back of Uğur hit the body one after the other and very close to one another and that the person could not have continued to shoot after having incurred these wounds which damaged the heart. ''Kaymaz'ın sırtındaki 9 kurşun da ölümcül,' Milliyet, 18 December 2005; 'Kaymaz'ın çatışmaya girmesi imkânsız,' CNN Türk, 19 December 2005.

16 'Terörist değillerdi' Radikal, 1 December 2004.

17 The delegation consisted of the east-southeast Regional Representative of İHD Mihdi Perinçek, İHD Mardin Branch President Attorney Hüseyin Cangir, İHD Diyarbakır Branch President Attorney Selahattin Demirtaş, İHD Diyarbakır Branch Managing Committee Member Attorney İrfan Eser and İHD Mardin Branch Secretary Attorney Erdal

scene, stated that 'the scene where the event occurred is an open area' and that 'it is highly probable that these people could have been captured alive and not hurt at all.'[18]

In the conclusion of the aforementioned report, the delegation 'surmised from the interviews they had with eyewitnesses, relatives of the victims and official authorities, and from the examination of the crime scene, that both victims were civilians and that one was a child; that the probability of them having fired weapons is extremely low; that the event in question may in fact be an example of extrajudicial killing; that these civilians may have been killed by the security forces either by mistake or intentionally.'

On the other hand, the report prepared by the Turkish Bar Association (Türkiye Barolar Birliği, TBB), states that the father was a PKK militiaman. Furthermore, in their conclusion to the investigation they made in Kızıltepe, the TBB delegation proposed an explanation that legitimised the use of arms in the event.[19]

The four special operations policemen that participated in the operation were prosecuted on charges of 'homicide exceeding the limits of self-defence' and, in November 2004, an administrative investigation into the actions of their supervisors was launched. A report was submitted subsequently to the Supervisory Board by the two chief inspectors, who went to Mardin by order of Minister of Internal Affairs Abdülkadir Aksu. This report stated that the four policemen might be 'at fault and responsible,' and as a result of this the policemen were temporarily removed from office for the sake of a sound investigation. Mardin's Assistant Director of Security, Kemal Dönmez, and three special operations policemen were removed temporarily from office.

The policemen were returned to their posts before the case was heard. In the administrative investigation, it was suggested that the policemen be fined, and that their place of work (Kızıltepe) be changed. The policemen, who had not attended the first hearing of the case in Mardin's 2nd High Criminal Court on 21 February 2005 on the grounds that the they did not have life insurance, were appointed to different provinces. The subsequent claim that they be arrested because of the probability of obstructing the gathering of evidence, was rejected.

The court ruled that the statement of the policemen be received from their place of work. The court also rejected the appeal by Reşat Kaymaz, the brother of Ahmet, to take part in the case as the intervening party. The court in Mardin decided

---

Kuzu. The delegation went to Kızıltepe district and carried out investigations and interviews on 23 November, 2004.

18 'Mardin İli Kızıltepe İlçesinde Ahmet Kaymaz ve 12 Yaşındaki Oğlu Uğur Kaymaz'ın Yaşam Hakkının İhlal Edildiği İddialarını Araştırma-İnceleme Raporu,' 25 November 2004. See, http://ihd.org.tr/rapozel/kiziltepekaymaz.html

19 'The fact that security forces used 9 mm MP5 and uzi machine guns in this event where they generally use rifles in operations or clashes can be seen as an indication of extrajudicial killing. However, 9 mm MP5 and uzi machine guns are arms suited to close combat and the location of this operation was a street where it would not be possible to use rifles.' 'Kızıltepe Olayı'nda Baro Raporu: Baba Kaymaz PKK Milisi,' Milliyet, 22 May 2005.

the case should be heard at the Eskişehir High Criminal Court on grounds of security.

The hearing in Eskişehir, which took place on 18 December 2005, was conducted under extraordinary security measures. The four indicted policemen asserted that the father and son shot at them first and that the clash lasted for a period of ten minutes. One of the attorneys of the accused, Veysel Güler, argued that the confrontation occurred in an 'L shape', so that the victims had to turn their backs. Güler stated that the terrorist organisation (PKK) had been playing on people's emotions through the use of children and stressed that 'the use of the dead boy's (Uğur Kaymaz) photograph in demonstrations from when he was a second year primary-school student, was aimed at creating supporters/sympathisers for the organisation'. He also stated that 'children were being used in such a way in various other parts of Turkey.'

Güler also noted that photographs presented to the press of Uğur, who was allegedly 12 years of age at the time of death, dated from when he was younger. In addition, Uğur, who measured 165 cm (5 ft. 5) and weighed 45 kg (99 lbs) was, in fact, estimated to have been approximately 15 or 16 years of age in the post-mortem examination.

Güler asserted that Ahmet Kaymaz and his son Uğur were PKK members, and that Nusret Bali, code-named 'Kabat', who had escaped from Kaymaz's house where the events took place, was killed in March 2005 in a clash with security forces.

Güler presented ten photographs to the court depicting 14 and 15-year-old children receiving PKK military training in the mountains, as well as images of children burning the Turkish flag in Mersin.[20]

After the indicted policemen answered the judge's questions pertaining to the guns that were used in the operation, the hearing was postponed until 22 February 2006. The postponement was intended to allow sufficient time for the statements of witnesses in Kızıltepe to be obtained and the issue of missing documents to be resolved. The attorney's request that the accused be arrested was rejected.

Conclusion

From the outset, governments faced with the threat of terrorism generally elect to implement anti-terrorist strategies, increase their intelligence capacity and activities and form anti-terrorist commando or police units to be used in rescue or raid operations. The next step involves the imposition of new legal statutes which provide the concerned state units with the required authority necessitated by anti-terrorist policies.

The defining of the domain of responsibility of such special units and the control of the units is of great importance, especially when an armed action plan (war model) is adopted and specially trained anti-terrorist teams are employed. When signs come to light indicating that special units have committed certain acts

---

20 'Uğur Kaymaz davasinda avukat protestosu,' Hürriyet, 24 October 2005.

with complete disregard for the ascendancy of the law or rule of law, at least some of the public, depending on the prevailing political ambience, will perceive that the state has not followed a balanced anti-terrorism policy aimed at the preservation of individual rights and liberties.

The most severe and dangerous consequence of the failure of adequate control of the special police (paramilitary) or military anti-terrorist units, is the development of what is known as a dirty war encountered in certain countries. The concept of a dirty war became widely known in the 1980s (especially after 1982), when Britain resorted to using the SAS (Special Air Service) Regiment against the PIRA (Provisional Irish Republican Army).[21] The SAS possess superior fire-power and are considered to be the most elite soldiers in the world, The concept of dirty war was cultivated particularly by the Special Support Unit (SSU), trained by the SAS and situated within the Royal Ulster Constabulary of Northern Ireland, which adopted the policy of deliberately killing suspected PIRA terrorists instead of capturing them alive and charging them. This policy, and in particular the reaction of Amnesty International which demanded an independent judicial investigation, elicited an internal investigation undertaken by Deputy Chief Constable John Stalker, a high-ranking officer of the Manchester police force. The SSU was found to have killed five people illegitimately. However, the investigation could not discern whether high-ranking police authorities were involved in this shoot-to-kill policy and John Stalker was mysteriously removed from office before the investigation was completed.[22] Moreover, the British Secret Services, MI5 and MI6, were accused of involvement in the murder of Belfast attorney Paul Finucane, who was representing the families of three PIRA militants shot dead by the SAS in Gibraltar in March 1988.[23]

In liberal democracies and states governed by rule of law, the effectiveness of the fight against terrorism depends on the legitimacy of this fight with respect to the criteria of democracy and the rule of law. The long-term results and effects of certain policies and practices resorted to in the fight against terrorism, must be carefully calculated. The solutions proposed against terrorism must not interfere with democratic governance in the long-run.[24]

The following can be observed concerning the PÖHT: these teams have proven to be extremely effective in the fight against terrorism and they have made great sacrifices. In recent years, society has witnessed their sincere efforts to put an end to the adversities of the past and to keep them from recurring. However, certain unfortunate events, such as the Kızıltepe incident, sadly still take place. The investi-

---

21 'Dirty War' is also used to refer to the kidnapping of thousands of people by the security units and their subsequent 'disappearance' particularly in the course of the military dictatorship in Argentina between 1976 and 1983.

22 John Stalker, Shoot to Kill and the Affair, (Ireland: Harmondsworth, Penguin, 1988); Leslie MacFarlane, 'Human Rights and the Fight Against Terrorism in Northern Ireland,' Terrorism and Political Violence 4/1 (April, 1992), p. 93- 94.

23 Ertan Beşe, Terörizm, Avrupa Birliği ve İnsan Hakları (Terrorism, European Union, and Human Rights), (İstanbul: Seçkin Yayıncılık, 2001).

24 Ibid.

gation of this matter is ongoing, and the real dimensions of the event will only become evident once the investigation has been completed. The security units must learn from this catastrophe and try to determine the weak points of the system, in order to prevent similar events or mishaps from occurring and in order to allow for these well-intentioned units to thrive.

The fact that these teams are located within the Directorate General of Security, and are therefore attached to the Ministry of Internal Affairs, makes their administrative, legal and even political supervision and control, apposite to democratic criteria. In fact, in cases of allegations of illegitimate practices, as mentioned in the above event, the necessary judicial process must be instigated. Public satisfaction over the issue depends on the adequacy of the information provided to it. It is for this reason, that in parliamentary democracies the commissioning of security units involved in the fight against terrorism under civilian scrutiny in the fight against terrorism, proves to be more suitable to the mindset required for the conditions of democracy and a state governed by rule of law.

Due to an increase in the presence of land mines especially and to a decrease in a great number of security personnel midway through 2005, the military in particular began to voice its concerns that laws passed in the process of accession to the European Union (EU), the new Turkish Criminal Code (TCK) and the Code of Criminal Procedure (CMK), restrict the authority required by the security forces to fight effectively against terrorism and, therefore, impede the course of this fight. These concerns elicited a review of the Anti-Terror Law No. 3713 and considerations to increase the authority of security forces with regard specifically to the fight against terrorism.

Contrary to these considerations, however, there is also the growing perception that terrorism is an internal security matter and therefore falls within the province of the police. The foremost argument cited on this point is the fact that it costs the lives of dozens of inadequately trained and equipped soldiers to confront the PKK.[25] Moreover, the use of military forces against the PKK, legitimises the latter on the international plane and contributes to an erosion of the armed forces.[26]

To conclude, special operations teams are specialised units trained to undertake high risk operations. Their establishment attest to this country's attempts to 'catch up' with European states in particular, and to arrive at a corresponding level of security both in theory and in practice. However, to remedy the structural behavioural weaknesses that have been explored herein, the necessary political will must be sustained. Ensuring that such forces remain subject to democratic, civilian oversight will ultimately render them stronger and able to function more effectively.

---

25 Thus, the Turkish Armed Forces introduced the special units which were suited to the conditions of the eastern and south-eastern regions and the character of existing terrorist activity into the fight against terror along with the standard military units.

26 To read a striking evaluation on this issue, see Kemal Ulusoy, 'Askerin Yetkisi Az Değil Fazla Bile!' Aktif Haber, 12 August 2005, see http://www.aktifhaber.com

Private Security

Mesut Bedri Eryılmaz[*]

The Concept of Private Security

Ensuring public security is the raison d'être of virtually every state, in view of the fact that political, economic and social activities and individual rights and freedoms can only be fulfilled if the public enjoys a secure and peaceful environment in which to live.

It is the legitimate responsibility of the state to provide security for its citizens, however, the sovereignty of today's free market makes it more difficult for states to meet these security requirements. Individuals, and firms, that were accustomed to performing their economic and social activities under the protection of the state, are facing unprecedented economic and social upheaval under free market conditions. In addition, with increasing crime rates and the rising cost of injury to the lives and property of citizens, the need for security has become even more pressing.

Conversely, however, funding for security services has decreased, and with the advent of a free market and the demise of the state, the void in security services performed by the public domain has become more evident. When it became apparent that the state was unable to fulfil all the necessary security requirements, the private sector was encouraged to provide security services, in the same way that the education and health sectors were encouraged to privatise. Paving the way for a rise in private security outfits, the state delegated personal security to its citizens, whilst it assumed responsibility for broader public security. The state has also embraced the demands of citizens who request the right and freedom to protect their lives and property against unfair assault.

Security is now provided by both the private and the public sector, as is the case with education, health and transportation. From a liberal point of view, the state enables the public sector to train private security personnel.

For instance, in Turkey only 14–15 percent of police staff are assigned to the security of individuals. After the initiation of private security services, the political parties, trade unions, international organisations and embassies were all advised to acquire private security services.

Therefore, private security is defined as those security service units that are empowered to perform duties on behalf of the public such as searching, confiscating,

---

* Associate Professor, Police Academy, Faculty of Security Sciences, Professor of the Department of Law of Criminal Procedure.

capturing and using force, in areas owned by private organisations or institutions, provided that the personnel employed by these units are subject to the control of the state.

The History of Private Security

Even though the idea of private security is a relatively new one, the concept of the state allowing private security organisations to operate in the public domain by means of special laws, has a long history. In 1930, with Municipality Law No. 1580, a municipal police force was established to bolster local security with respect to the local government's field of operation. It was decided that those who resisted the municipal policemen should be punished in the same way as those who resisted public law enforcement forces. Village guards and officers, district guards, forest security officers and customs monopoly guards were the main examples of this concept.

There was an attempt to settle private security matters on a legal basis by means of Law No. 2495, on the Protection and Security Services for Public Institutions and Organizations, dated 22 July 1981. In order to fulfil the requirements of the private security sector, which made significant progress in the 1990s, the Private Security Services (Özel Güvenlik Hizmetlerine Dair Kanun, ÖGHDK) Law No. 5188 was introduced in June 2004.[1]

Concurrent with the private security service attaining legal status, international corporations entered the Turkish market. This became an increasingly attractive career move for retired army and police personnel, and many of then entered the sector, including: the former Undersecretary of the National Intelligence Organisation (Milli İstihbarat Teşkilatı, MİT), Sönmez Köksal; the former chief of MİT in the Istanbul region, Nuri Gündeş; Brigadier Veli Küçük, the former Governor of Istanbul Erol Çakır, and the former Head of the Bureau of Narcotics, Ferruh Tankuş.

In the Private Security Services (Özel Güvenlik Hizmetlerine Dair Kanun, ÖGHDK) Law No. 5188, the following issues were clarified:

(1) All security companies in the private sector were registered and authorised to provide private security services exclusively. This entailed security for buildings, utilities and individuals. It also made provisions for the secure transfer of money and high value goods, while allowing for alarm systems, video surveillance, CCTV (closed-circuit television) and similar advanced electronic and technologic devices to be used by private security companies. These combined factors have contributed to the transformation of the private security sphere into a profession.

(2) Cooperation and task-sharing between the public and private security sectors has evolved, whereby public forces have been authorised to regulate and control private security. It was decreed that companies and private training institutions

[1] The law was passed on 10.06.2004 and went into effect when it was published in the Official Gazette (Resmi Gazete) No. 25504 dated 26 June 2004. The executive regulation implementing Law No. 5188 also went into effect when it was published in the Official Gazette No. 25606 dated 07 October 2004.

which operated outside their fields of operation and conducted criminal activities should be abolished. In addition, the founders and managing personnel of these companies should lose their appointments, and associated entitlements, in any of the private security companies or training institutions across the board.

(3) Local Province Security Commissions consist of members from the public and private security sectors as well as the Chamber of Commerce and Industry. This diversity has allowed for the development of a more democratic and participatory decision-making mechanism, particularly with respect to the commissions' role in evaluating and developing private security.

(4) Provisions dealing with questions of financial responsibility for private security, stipulated the compensation for third parties for losses caused by private security personnel. The establishment of private security services and training outfits in the field of private security are subject to the approval of the Ministry of Internal Affairs.

(5) As a rule, it has also been determined that private security outfits should be unarmed, except in cases that require such protection.

(6) The vested rights of private security organisations and that of their personnel, established according to Law No. 2495, are protected for a period of five years commencing with the implementation of Law No. 5188. At the end of this five-year period, the approval of such organisations shall be renewed and the identity cards of personnel shall also be renewed following the completion of their training.

(7) Companies that are not subject to Law No. 2495, but are established in accordance with commercial law to conduct private security services, are permitted to carry out their activities provided that the conditions set forth by the law are fulfilled within six-months of the regulation coming into effect.

Substance of the Private Security Service

How are Private Security Approvals Granted?

Individuals can receive private security services by employing private security officers, establishing private security units under the auspices of an institution or organisation or by hiring personnel from private security companies.

Individuals or organisations must apply to the office of the governor in their own province in order to procure private security permits.

The private security commission under the office of the governor is responsible for reviewing requests for private security permits, determining the method of service, the maximum number of personnel and the maximum number of arms to be kept or carried.

The Private Security Permission Certificate is bestowed to individuals/enterprises who/which have been granted a private security permit.

A list of the private security officers who are employed by private security units and a copy of the firm's insurance policy, must be submitted to the office of the governor within 15 days following the first working day of personnel.

Private security units and private security companies must submit a sample of their security and protection plans related to the location of their services to the governorship within 30 days. The office of the governor can request amendments to security and protection plans or request correction of any deficiences in those plans to be completed within 30 days.

The activities of a company and the private security services provided to third parties are subject to the approval of the Ministry of the Interior. In order to obtain this permission, the company's field of activity should fall exclusively under the province of 'protection and security services.'

The founders and managing personnel of private security companies:

(1) Shall be citizens of the Republic of Turkey;

(2) Shall not have been sentenced to any of the following (with the exception of crimes of negligence): 'heavy imprisonement,' imprisonment for more than six months; crimes against the 'personality' of the state even if pardoned; misappropriation of funds; malversation, bribery, theft, fradulent deal-making, breach of trust, forgery, fradulent bankruptcy or employment, smuggling (except consumer goods), rigging a competitive bidding process, disclosing state secrets, verbal harassment, sexual assault, rape, abduction of a girl, woman or child, incitement to prostitution; pandering; using or smuggling narcotics.

Managers should have a four-year degree, should not be prohibited from public service and should have successfully completed basic training.

The office of the governor conducts background checks on private security officers and managers to be employed in private security companies and in private security training institutions. Those whose background check proves acceptable and who successfully complete basic training are awarded a five-year work permit by the governorship.

As of 31 October 2005, 572 private security companies applied for a work permit of which 464 were granted the Private Security Company Permission Certificate.

The Relationship Between Public and Private Law Enforcement Forces and the Sphere of Duties of Private Security Officers

Public law enforcement forces operate throughout the country alongside the police, gendarmerie and the coast guard. Private security forces, which have been established by a special law, consist of law enforcement units that are entitled to work in a limited arena only, and with restricted authority.

When the authority of the police, gendarmerie and coast guard was examined, it was noted that neither the content nor the scope of their authority differed from one another. Essentially, it is inconceivable to conclude that the authority of law enforcement forces, which perform equivalent duties in different regions, might differ.

However, some special law enforcement forces, which fall outside public law enforcement, such as forest security guards, customs officers and private security officers, are prohibited from fully exercising the powers of the police and gendarmerie. The authority of private law enforcement forces are essentially of a judicial nature and include search, arrest and the use of force necessary for these purposes. Officers are not granted with any special authority such as those of judicial survey, secret monitoring, tapping phone lines and recording testimonies, since having such jurisdiction requires technical structuring and close relationships with judges, public prosecutors and lawyers. According to Article 77 of the Village Law, village guards are entitled to use arms but only to protect the purity (ırz), life and property of people within the bounds of the village.

Similarly, in accordance with Articles 77, 78 and 79 of the Forest Law, forest guards are authorised to search, arrest, confiscate and use arms in order to protect the forests. By the same token, according to Article 3 of the Law on Marketplace and Neighbourhood Guards, guards are empowered to gather evidence and use arms under the conditions determined by Article 16 of the Law on Police Duties and Powers (Polis Vazife ve Selahiyet Kanunu, PVSK).

The duties and responsibilities of private law enforcement officers have been delineated in law. In accordance with the respective laws, forest security guards are authorised to perform their duties within the borders determined by the law; marketplace and neighbourhood guards within a specific area inside the municipal borders; private security forces officers within the borders of the related establishment, and village guards within the bounds of the village. Private security officers are permitted to use their authority during their tours of duty and within their specified fields of operation. The period of time and nature of these operations are determined in terms of the working hours of the security personnel, their tour of duty or contract of employment.

Private security officers can only attempt to arrest a suspect within the limits of their field of duty. If the suspect escapes from the range of their authority, officers are only permitted to pursue and arrest the suspect in their capacity as private citizens.

In accordance with Supplementary Article 4 of the PVSK, public law enforcement officers (police and gendarmerie) can always intervene in a judicial incident with the aim of prevention within the borders of their field of duty. Officers are also authorised and assigned to uncover criminal evidence and to protect and deliver evidence to the authorised police force. At this point, the service department, the location and time of the incident in relation to the intervention of a public security officer are all inconsequential.

Therefore, a security officer assigned to the Keçiören police station in Ankara can intervene in an incident in Dikmen — which is also in Ankara — if that officer is off-duty and returning home. However, when on holiday in Fethiye — which is in Muğla — for example, the officer can only intervene in the capacity of a private citizen.

As members of the public security forces, coast guard officers are authorised to exercise their authority along the entire coast of the Republic of Turkey, in the internal waters of the Marmara Sea, the Bosphorus and the Dardanelles, its ports and bays, its territorial waters and other waters under Turkey's control and sovereignty.

The distribution of tasks and responsibilities between the police and the gendarmerie, which are the other two units of public security, are determined in Article 10 of Law No. 2803 on the Establishment, Duties and Jurisdiction of Gendarmerie. According to this article, the gendarmerie's arena of duties and responsibilities generally falls outside that of the police, which, in turn, falls outside municipal areas and/or districts without an organised police force.

In other words, the gendarmerie cannot work within municipalities. The exception to this rule, however, is when a police force is lacking within the municipality. If a police force has not been established in the municipality for any reason, an outfit from the gendarmerie may be established in its place. Similarly, the implementation of gendarmerie outside municipal borders depends on the presence or absence of a police force.

The Training of Private Security

Basic training for private security and refresher training courses are held in the special training institutions certified by the Ministry of Interior. An application is required for those wishing to obtain a permit to conduct private security training. Upon receiving the necessary information, an inspection commission determines whether the applicant has the necessary qualifications to operate a training centre.

The selected candidates chosen are subject to a minimum of 120 hours of basic training. 30 hours are dedicated to artillery and shooting practice. Private security officers who are not licensed to carry firearms are not obligated to take these courses. The training program of these officers is to be not less than 90 hours.

The managers of private security companies and private training institutions must attend refresher training courses every five years and present the resulting certificates to the ministry.

Refresher training programs consist of 60 hours coursework. Theoretical and practical courses are offered by the related training institution with a selection of lessons from the basic training program. The lessons cover recent developments in education and jurisprudence. 20 of those hours are spent in shooting practice.

Individuals who pass the written and practical examinations receive a refresher training certificate. Applicants for the exams are asked for proof of their attendance.

Individuals take written and practical examinations following the completion of basic training. Written examinations are held in the provinces and include questions prepared by the Central Examination Commission.

Certificates of basic training and refresher training for private security are valid for five years.

Those officers who retired or resigned from public law enforcement forces (after working for at least five years) are not required to complete basic training for the private sector. Their exemption expires after five years.

As of 31 October 2005, 338 training institutions for private security submitted an application of which 312 were granted the Private Security Training Institution Permission Certificate.

To provide certificates for trainees who are given basic training in training institutions:

1522 candidates took the first private security examination on 7 January 2005, 1253 of whom passed,

29,533 candidates took the second private security examination on 14 May 2005, 18,793 of whom passed,

38,601 candidates took the third private security examination on 15 July 2005, 28,840 of whom passed.

54,000 candidates took the fourth private security examination on 12 November 2005, and the results are pending.

The number of active private security personnel – in accordance with Law No. 2495 which was abolished on 26 June 2004 –reached 57,855. In accordance with provisional Article 1 of Law No. 5188, personnel were not required to have a private security training certificate. These former private security officers combined with a total of 48,886 candidates obtained the right to acquire the certificate and become officers. By passing the first three examinations, the total number of private security officers employed in the sector reached 106,741. The expected growth rate of the private security sector in 2006 stands at 15%.

This number is nearly half the total number of police in Turkey. This indicates that private security has contributed considerably to the maintenance of general security and the fight against escalating incidents of theft, crimes related to sniffing glue and snatch-and-run theft.

In European countries, the numbers of police and private security officers are proportional to one another. In the United States, the number of private security officers is triple that of the public police force, which numbers at 600,000.

The Authority of Private Security Officers

In contrast to private security officers, the duties of public law enforcement officers fall under the scope of both crime-prevention and investigation. This authority was granted in the PVSK No. 2559, dated 1934.

The following activities underscore the pre-emptive power of public security personnel: patrol duty, gathering intelligence, and search and capture. Law No. 5188 permits private security officers to conduct 'search and arrest' for the prevention of crime. To exercise this authority, a crime should not yet have been committed and the law enforcement units use this authority to prevent offences from occurring.

On the other hand, the authority of security officers after a crime has been committed, is rather comprehensive. This authority is defined as judicial and, in legal terms, is expressed as 'protective measures.' These measures consist of judicial review, intelligence-gathering, identification, phone tapping, secret monitoring, searching, confiscating, banning trips abroad, capturing, using force and recording testimonies.
The Code of Criminal Procedure (Ceza Muhakemeleri Kanunu) No. 5271 of 2004, defines the jurisdiction of security officers. Law No. 5188 grants private security officers some of the judicial powers of a security force, including the protection of evidence and its provenance, identification, confiscation, search and arrest, as well as the use of arms.
In the security service arena, private security officers are expected to safeguard the security demands of every segment of society, which is clearly increasing. However, private security is a complementary element of the states' own security forces, whereby private security personnel are permitted to use only part of the powers assigned to public law enforcement forces to justify their raison d'être. The authority granted to private security officers is, thus, rather limited.
The powers of private security officers were classified in Article 7 of the ÖGHDK. According to the law, private security officers have been granted the following authority:

a) Performing access control at building entrances by means of security doors, frisking by detector, inspection of personal belongings through an x-ray machine or similar devices;
b) Identification, performing access control by means of sensitive doors, frisking by detector and inspection of personal belongings through x-ray or similar devices at meetings, concerts, sporting events, stage shows and similar events, as well as funeral and wedding ceremonies;
c) Conducting search and capture missions within reason, according to Article 127 (Article No. 1412 of the new CMK);
d) Capturing and arresting persons within their area of jurisdiction;
e) Assisting in serious emergencies and entering homes or workplaces within their area of jurisdiction, when natural disasters such as fires or earthquakes occur;
f) Identifying, performing access control by means of security doors, frisking by detector and inspection of personal belongings through x-ray or similar devices in facilities providing public transportation such as airports, ports, train stations and terminals.
g) Provided that public law enforcement forces are immediately informed, safeguarding criminal, threatening or other related evidence found during a search;
h) Keeping lost or found belongings;
i) Taking a person(s) into custody with the aim of protecting his/her well-being or life;
j) Protecting evidence and its origin and taking a person(s) into custody with these aims in mind, in accordance with Article 157 of CMK (according to the new CMK, Article 168, prohibition by force);

k) Using force in accordance with Article 981 of the Turkish Civil Code, Article 52 of Law on Debts and subclauses 1 and 2 of clause 1 of Article 49 of the Turkish Penal Code (Türk Ceza Kanunu, TCK) (Articles 24 and 25 of the new TCK);

In addition, Article 8 of the same law authorises private security officers to keep and carry weapons;

In brief, the realm of authority of private security officers can be defined as follows;
(1) To protect evidence and its origin;
(2) To intercept, identify and search;
(3) To keep in safe custody;
(4) To capture;
(5) To use force and prohibit;
(6) To assist in case of emergency;

Punishment of Private Security Personnel
Private security personnel are considered officers in accordance with the TCK. Therefore, as stated in Supplementary Article 4 of PVSK, crimes committed against private security officers on duty (who use their authority) are considered on par with crimes committed against public officers on duty. Crimes committed by private security personnel are considered on par with crimes committed by an (assigned) officer on duty.

Thus, a private security officer on duty can be either the perpetrator of a crime or the victim of a crime as stated in the TCK.

In addition to the TCK, some administrative crimes concerning punishment of private security officers are also laid out in the ÖGHDK.

a. Crimes Defined in the Turkish Penal Code
According to TCK, potential crimes by private security officers are defined as follows:
Restriction of freedom (TCK Article181);
Unjustified bodily search (TCK Article183);
Invasion of privacy (TCK Article194);
Misappropriation of funds (TCK Article.202);
Malversation (TCK Article 209);
Bribery (TCK Article 212, 213);
Arbitrary acts and harsh treatment (TCK Article228);
Breach of duty (TCK Article 230);
Failing to report a crime to authorities (TCK Article 235);
Abuse of authority (TCK Article 240);
Torture and mistreatment (TCK Article 243);
Mistreatment and excessive use of force (TCK Article 245);
Conduct unbecoming an officer (TCK Article 252).

The following are defined as crimes committed against private security officers:
The use of force, violence or restraint against an officer (TCK Article 254);
Resisting an officer (TCK Article 258);
Insulting, cursing and assaulting an officer (TCK Article 266);
Assault and battery of the officer (TCK Article 271).

b) Crimes Defined by the Law on Private Security Services
The ÖGHDK defines three types of crime committed by private security officers, all of which have an administrative character:
(1) Breaching the ban against effectuating a strike;
(2) The use of firearms against ÖGHDK regulations and allowing third-party use outside the area of jurisdiction;
(3) Allowing another person to use his/her ID badge.

The penalty for these crimes is YTL 1,000. This punishment is given by the highest-ranking civilian authority. Objections can be raised through an authorized administrative court within seven days following the notice of punishment. The decision of the administrative court can be appealed in a regional administrative court. However, decisions of regional administrative courts are absolute.

Moreover, the work permit of the private security officer is abrogated and the officer can no longer be employed as a private security officer.

The Rights of Private Security Officers

As per the order listed by the ÖGHDK, private security officers have the following rights and obligations:
(1) Private security officers must obtain identity cards, which are given by the governors of the cities. The identity card bears the name and surname of the officer and discloses whether the officer is armed or not. This identity card is displayed on the officer's uniform so as to be clearly visible during working hours and in the line of duty. An officer without an identity card is not authorised perform his/her duties. (ÖGHDK Article 12);
(2) A private security officer must take a refresher training course of not less than 60 hours to renew his/her knowledge following the basic training of 120 hours;
(3) In the event that a private security officer is wounded, becomes disabled or dies in the line of duty, he/she or their inheritors are entitled to compensation within the framework of conditions determined by the employment contract and the collective bargaining agreement;
If a private security officer serves a public institution or organisation, compensation is determined in accordance with the collective bargaining agreement and the Law on Cash Compensations and Salary. The highest amount, as determined in the contract or by law, is consequently awarded. This com-

pensation does not affect payment of other compensations according to the Labour Law No. 4857;
Moreover, the right of an injured private security officer or his/her legal inheritors to request further compensation is reserved by general provision (ÖGHDK Article 15);

(4) Private security officers cannot be recruited for any duty other than protection and security as determined by law;

(5) Private security officers cannot be dismissed during a lockout. However, they do not have the right to strike;

(6) Private security officers have the right to ask for private financial insurance to protect against any possible third-party harm they may be responsible for, and their employer is obliged to provide this insurance.

Improvements in 2005 and Expectations for the Future

The ÖGHDK is a relatively new law. In 2005 this law was criticised and amendments were therefore made to correct these flaws. However, it has been difficult to adapt the current Law No. 5188 to the former Law No. 2495, which was in force for approximately 24 years, and the issue of partially regulated private security outfits has yet to be adequately addressed.
In order to overcome some of the difficulties associated with Law No. 5188, the following measures were taken:

(1) A rather comprehensive circular of eight pages, concerning the implementation of the law and related regulations, was published by the Ministry of Internal Affairs on 19 April 2005. In this circular, many questions were answered with respect to the law and some supplementary regulations were made regarding implementation;

(2) Some amendments were made on 21 April 2005. However, the implementation of Articles 19 and 20, including the punishments foreseen for those who fail to fulfil their responsibilities, were postponed until 31 December 2005 to grant time to those implementing the changes;

(3) To create greater employment opportunities, secondary school graduates were given permission to work as unarmed private security officers;

(4) Those organisations employing a specific number of security officers and which had the necessary space for training, were permitted to give 'on the job training.'

(5) The implementation of Article 5 of Law No. 5149, on the Prevention of Violence and Disorderly Conduct at Sporting Events, was postponed for four years by means of Article 23 of Law No. 5340. This law was approved on 28 April 2005 by the Turkish Grand National Assembly (Türkiye Büyük Millet Meclisi, TBMM), and came into effect with its publication in the Official Gazette (Resmi Gazete) No. 25806 on 5 May 2005. Law No. 5149 grants entities with the power to buy private security services for the purpose of security maintenance at sporting events and on the playing fields. The aim is to allow sporting clubs to fulfil their responsibilities of providing security on the field.

The initial optimism resulting from the creation of the new law was somewhat mitigated however, due to the ambiguity of some aspects regarding its execution, the delay in offering qualifying examinations, the problem of achieving a standard implementation throughout the country, and the bureaucracy which resulted in particular from the aforementioned circulars.

Nonetheless, private security sector actors have initiated a number of measures to protect the 'sector' against these hurdles. The Association of Security Systems and Oversight Organisations (Güvenlik Sistemleri ve Gözetim Organizasyonları Derneği, GUSOD), which has been in existence since 1994, endeavours to restructure, organise and increase its members in Ankara and Izmir. It continues to establish new branches throughout the country. The Private Security Sector Businessman's Association (Özel Güvenlik Sektörü İş Adamları Derneği, ÖGSİAD) was established in Istanbul and a similar association is projected for Ankara. The Private Security Social Assistance and Solidarity Association (Özel Güvenlik Sosyal Yardımlaşma ve Dayanışma Derneği, ÖZGÜVDER) was founded in Ankara. Employees have also been given the opportunity to participate in the activities of employer associations.

To ensure stability of the private security sector, which is a matter of public concern and covers a wide range of fields, efforts should be made to enhance information systems, experience and overall tenacity. Non-Governmental Organisations (NGOs), whose roles are expanding in the current world climate, also have the potential to assist in the stabilisation of the private security sector. By means of healthy dialogue with official authorities, within the framework of a liberal approach, the reputation of this sector can be improved as a valid professional choice, and basic and effective methods for operations can be provided as a substitute for bureaucratic formalities. These can only be beneficial to the field in every respect.

Within this context, the government's expectations can be summarised as follows:

(1) Primarily, the revision of laws, regulations and circulars, considering the protection of private security as a sector and its development in accordance with the law; the elimination of incongruous, contradictory regulations and bureaucratic tax formalities coupled with the maintenance of standardised, fair and objective implementation;

(2) The prevention of the growth of 'parallel formations,' i.e. obscure structures devoid of any legal basis which are potentially damaging for this otherwise legitimate sector;

(3) Avoiding extra financial burdens on the sector and its employees, especially considering that the total fees paid by companies receiving permission to carry out private security activities has reached YTL 6'216'000. Fees collected from security officers who have completed their training as of June 2005 stands at YTL 56'000. The state has the financial resources required to maintain officers, equipment, examinations, monitoring and other expenses. Considering that there is no provision regarding fees for examinations, then ammunition required for shooting exams, for example, should be provided by training institutions. Institutions should not demand any additional payment from the private sector or its employees.

(4) The decrease of VAT on education by the Ministry of Finance from 18 percent to eight percent, should also be applied to private security training courses.

(5) For the healthy development of the private security sector, dialogue between it and the government must be maintained in relation to both the formulation and implementation of legislation;
Moreover, it is essential that conformity with the universal principles of ethics is realised and implemented. The survival and dignity of the private security sector depends on this.

Conclusion

Implementing the ÖGHDK has been difficult due to the lack of agreement with regard to the private protection of individuals. Law No. 2945 regulates several important elements of private security services: the unfeasibility of establishing private security organisations for companies not provided for in the law; the obligation of enterprises and institutions to establish private security organisations and the sanctions for those who engage in non-compliance. Many institutions and organisations, despite the fact that they are not covered by Law No. 2495, provide their own security in various ways, according to their own requirements. Many companies have begun to conduct private security services without permission and devoid of any monitoring, in order to meet market demands.

Furthermore, the protection of the public and property in meetings, concerts and ceremonies, as well as during the transfer of money and valuable goods, are some of the most essential duties of the state. Equally, individuals also have the right to protect their life and property against assault. This is turn means, that along with the public security provided by the state, individuals should also have the opportunity to protect their life and property. With this aim in mind, Law No. 5188 superseded Law No. 2495. By means of this law, a new service sector was created under the name of 'private security', with the aim of providing security services both effectively and democratically and in line with contemporary requirements and developments, under the approval and control of the state.

This new law enforcement unit and its officers were created to operate within the private sector. Accordingly, detailed regulations on mandatory liability insurance and compensation for damages sustained by third parties, punishment of officers in the event that offences are committed, and the training, rights and authority of officers have been established. Law No. 5188 provided the appropriate conditions for the private security sector to be legitimised as a profession. It established a legal basis for private security and contributed to the development of its liberal, participatory and democratic structure. Private security officers have, to a large extent, relieved the burden of the public law enforcement forces, i.e. the police and gendarmerie. Nonetheless, Law No. 5188 and its related regulations have failed to satisfy all the expectations and needs of the concerned parties. Therefore, it is anticipated that positive changes, even though small, will continue to be introduced into this field in the future.

Temporary Village Guards

Ertan Beşe[*]

The Emergence, Functions and Legal Basis for the Temporary Village Guard System

Article 68 of Village Law No. 442, dated 1924, stipulates that 'Within village limits, village guards are present for protecting citizen's purity (ırz), life and property.'[1] Article 74 of the same law stipulates that, 'If thieves should emerge during harvest time, then the village headman and the elderly council should make a list of potential guards, from among the villagers who can use weapons, and hand it to the head of the district. If the head of the district allows, then these voluntary guards will protect the village and the villagers from pillagers and bandits.' However, the roots of the guardianship system go beyond these considerations, and the current Temporary Village Guard System can, in fact, be seen as the extension of the 'Hamidiye regiments' that were established in 1891 during the Ottoman Empire. Hamidiye regiments were military units, formed by the Empire that was ruled from İstanbul, in order to maintain public order in the eastern provinces. They consisted of members of the local populace and were used against the Armenians in particular.

Some of the views concerning the historical role and influence of the Hamidiye Regiments have been maintained by the Temporary Village Guard System (Geçici Köy Koruculuğu, GKK).[2] For instance, it has been argued that the Hamidiye Regiments, just as the village guards, have strengthened the bonds between Kurdish clans.[3]

The story of the Temporary Village Guard System dates back to 1985, when the Kurdistan Worker's Party (Partiya Karkerên Kurdistan, PKK) was establishing itself and intensifying its attacks. In response to the massacres which targeted populations in scattered villages in rough terrain and in regions that were difficult to access, the GKK system was established with the amendment of the Village Law No 442, Article 74 through to Law No 3175, dated March 1985. The law helped the

* Assistant Professor, Police Academy, Faculty of Security Sciences.

1 The first Temporary Village Guardianship was formed with this law, in order for the villagers to protect themselves against bandits who took advantage of the state's weak presence in those regions in the 1920s during the Liberation War.

2 On Hamidiye Regiments, see Osman Aytar, Hamidiye Alaylarından Köy Koruculuğuna (İstanbul: Medya Güneşi Yayınları, 1992).

3 Mete Tuncay, Türkiye Cumhuriyeti'nde Tek-Parti Yönetiminin Kurulması (1923–1931) (İstanbul: Cem Yayınevi, 1992), p. 132.

security forces to protect citizens in the more remote residential areas and offered the villagers some form of self-protection.[4]

The system continues to serve an important role in the provinces, as determined by the Council of Ministers, in cases where the declaration of a state of emergency might be necessary, where serious signs of violent acts have been observed in or around a village, or where violations of the lives and properties of villagers have increased. The guards are appointed upon the proposal of the governor and the approval of the minister of internal affairs, which as part of the Ministry of Finance and Customs (Annex: 26.3.1985 – 3175/1) covers the salary, severance pay and clothing expenses of the guards. In case of injury, disability or death of voluntary village guards or temporary village guards, the rules of the Law Concerning the Cash Compensation and Monthly Salary No. 2330 are applied.

Therefore, the establishment of the Temporary Village Guard System was based on securing a regional domination against the PKK and the concept of 'stamping out the PKK's existence in the region.' Their appointment was linked to specific, extraordinary conditions, and the fact that the GKK system would cease to exist once these had disappeared, i.e. when normality had returned and law and order had been re-established.

The current working procedures of the village guards are regulated by the 'Village Guards Regulation' which was published in the Official Gazette (Resmi Gazette) No. 24096 on 1 July 2000. The regulation was based on the Village Law and was prepared by the Ministry of Internal Affairs, in order to regulate the rules and procedures defining the recruitment, sphere of jurisdiction, duties, responsibilities, training, dismissals and other personal employee rights of the village guards.'

According to Article 11 of the regulation, village guards at the administrative level are placed under the control and supervision of the village headman. At the professional level, guards are placed under the command of the Gendarmerie commander in the village in which they work. The Provincial Gendarmerie commander ensures that the personal rights of the village guards organisation are respected. In the name of the civilian authority, the commander is responsible for both the training and supervision of village guards.

As legally armed units, the guards' duties and responsibilities are defined by law,[5] and the fact that they are armed and granted a certain authority makes their

---

4 Annex: 26.03.1985 – art. 3175/1; Amendment: 07.02.1990 – art. 3612/2

5 For Article 9 of the Village Guards Regulation, see Resmi Gazete (Official Gazette) dated January 7 2000, No. 24096. 'The duties of the village guards are as follows: a) Determining those who violate the lives, chastity, property and security of their possessions, following them, to notify the village headman and the nearest gendarmerie unit as soon as possible, to prevent them from running and hiding, to apprehend them with the help of the villagers and the village's municipal police; b) Apprehend perpetrators during or after the crime, before their tracks are covered; c) In incidents involving judicial law enforcement, taking necessary measures for preventing loss of evidence; d) When informed about disasters such as fire, flood, earthquake, landslide or avalanche, notifying the village headman and the nearest gendarmerie unit; e) Investigating the business and relations of ex-convicts or suspects who are in the village, following up on draft evaders, handing over the information obtained to the village headman or the gendarmerie; f) Taking necessary

training and supervision even more important. Village guards are subject to training at the nearest military unit prior to undertaking active duty, and in the course of their duty if necessary - as stipulated by the rules and methods defined by the General Command of Gendarmerie. Training and its duration are continuously reviewed and continue after the start of active duty.

Besides providing for the security of villages and fields in the region, the temporary village guards that are employed within the framework of the regulation in question carry out duties involving operations against terrorist organisations. They also protect industrial complexes and establish road security measures. Various government offices have noted that due to their extensive knowledge of the area and the region, the village guards have in fact made important contributions to the fight against terrorism and the operations run by security forces. They have conducted dangerous missions and led operations specifically because of their familiarity with the region. Approximately 1'400 guards have lost their lives, and guards' families have been targeted due to their involvement in the fight against the PKK.

The Current Status of the Temporary Village Guard System

The Temporary Village Guard System was initially implemented in the following 22 provinces: Diyarbakır, Hakkâri, Şırnak, Tunceli, Batman, Bingöl, Bitlis, Mardin, Muş, Siirt, Van, Adıyaman, Ağrı, Ardahan, Elazığ, Gaziantep, Iğdır, K.Maraş, Kars, Kilis, Malatya and Şanlı Urfa. As stipulated by law, the Council of Ministers has the authority to decide which provinces will be subject to the GKK system and the Council of Ministers Decision No. 9632 was the first ruling ever to be made in that respect on 27 June 1985.

When the system was first implemented in 1985, the practice started in 22 provinces, as listed above. Together with the Voluntary Village Guard System, that was practiced in 13 additional provinces and began in 1993, the total number of provinces increased to 35. There are currently 58'000[6] temporary village guards on active duty, however, the state has a total staff of 66'000 employed within the Temporary Village Guard System.[7]

---

precautions for all kinds of violations against vineyards, gardens and their roads, drinking water complexes, transformer stations and common village property, water wells, retaining walls and canals and similar village structures, and helping the general or specific law enforcement in their protection.'

6 This number changes almost daily. The numbers usually given are 57,453, 57,500. Therefore, the number 58,000 has been given as an approximation.

7 According to Article 5 of the Village Guards Regulation, these are the requirements for becoming a village guard: '1) Being a Citizen of the Republic of Turkey, 2) Being literate in Turkish, 3) Having completed his military service, 4) Being older than 22 and younger than 60 years of age, 5) Not being deprived from public rights, 6) Not having been convicted of a crime, 7) Not being involved in separatist, subversive or fundamentalist activities, 8) To have a reputation of being good natured and not having habits of fighting and drunkenness, 9) To be a resident of the village where the duty will be carried out, 10) To prove with a medical certificate that no physical or mental illnesses or handicaps exist that

In September 2005, in a statement answering a parliamentary question, Minister of Internal Affairs Abdülkadir Aksu stated that there were 57'757 active duty guards in 22 provinces. The province with the most significant number of temporary village guards was Hakkâri. The numbers of village guards were documented as follows: 5'187 in Diyarbakır, 6'756 in Şırnak, 2'887 in Batman, 2'511 in Bingöl, 3'730 in Bitlis, 3'323 in Mardin, 1'860 in Muş, 4'661 in Siirt, 7'320 in Van, 7'614 in Hakkâri, 368 in Tunceli, 1'485 in Adıyaman, 1'838 in Ağrı, 91 in Ardahan, 2'083 in Elazığ, 555 in Gaziantep, 362 in Iğdır, 33 in Kilis, 2'236 in Kahramanmaraş, 558 in Kars, 1'365 in Malatya, and 934 in Şanlıurfa.[8]

For guards in full employment, the average salary as of December 2005 was YTL 390 per month;[9] and clothing, shoe and food allowances are provided by the state. Therefore, in 2005, the annual cost to the state for this system stood at around YTL 300 million.

Approximately, 22'000 temporary village guards have resigned since 1985 and a significant number have had their employment terminated for various reasons. 1'400 have been killed on duty, 2'000 have died of natural causes and approximately 900 have been imprisoned for various crimes.

In addition to the temporary village guards currently in full employment, there are 25'000 voluntary village guards. The voluntary system is regulated by Chapter 8 of the Village Law No. 442, Article 74, entitled 'Village Guards and their Duties.'[10] Since it is based on a system in which villagers protect themselves against the PKK, it consists entirely of civilians. The guards are appointed by the head of the district, based on the decisions and proposals of the village headman and the council of elders. Pending approval from the head of the district, the voluntary guards protect the village against thieves in conjunction with the legitimate temporary village guards.

In contrast to the temporary guards, voluntary guards are unpaid, although their weapons and equipment are supplied by the state. They are not authorised to take part in precision operations targeting terrorists and, therefore, their duties and

---

would prevent him from carrying out his duty.' See http://www.mevzuat.adalet.gov.tr/html/20524.html

8 '5 bin köy korucusu suç işledi,' NTV-MSNBC, 28 September 2005.

9 Article 6 of the Village Guards Regulation regulates the selection and recruitment of village guard candidates. The Article states that 'The names of the guards that are determined by the council of elders are given to the head of the district by the village headman. A copy of the birth certificate, a document showing the educational status, a medical certificate and four snapshots are added to file to assist the council of elders in their decision'.
The head of district evaluates the matter and should he or she see fit, approves and finishes the recruitment process. The village headman is notified of the result.
See http://www.mevzuat.adalet.gov.tr/html/20524.html

10 Village Law Number 442, dated 18 March 1924, Article 74: 'If looters emerged during harvest time, the village headman and the elderly council make a list of potential guards from among villagers who can use weapons and hands it to the head of district. If the head of district allows, these voluntary guards, together with the actual guards, protect the village and the villagers from looters.'

authority are limited to passive defence, that is to 'protecting the village and themselves.'

The Main Problems Involving the Temporary Village Guard System in Relation to Economic and Social Security

Problems concerning the employee rights of the temporary village guards, who were recruited following the rise of terrorist incidents, have not been resolved in a manner that meets expectations and demands. Guards have not been provided with the health and social security mechanisms that would normally generate a regular income and insurance, and their family members lack sufficient health support. Although their work puts them in constant danger, the fact that guards are not provided with reliable social security leaves many in a difficult situation. This is especially true for those who have to support large families.

In cases of sickness or injury, medical expenses are met by social assistance and support foundations, and in the case of injury, death or disability on duty, the Law Concerning Cash Compensation and Monthly Payments No. 2330 applies. If a village guard is shot during an armed conflict, compensation is awarded and his family receives a sum of money every three months. Although the same applies for injuries causing permanent damage, if a guard is killed as a result of an accident, then his rights are greatly diminished or even waived. In short, the limited allowance and support fails to meet the needs of the village guards.

In the years when terrorism was at its peak, 58'993 temporary village guards were recruited and together with the 30'300 voluntary village guards, the total number of village guards reached 89'293. In order to provide social security rights for the temporary guards, who did not have any form of social security besides the monthly payment, a paragraph was added to Article 74 of Village Law No. 442 in the Draft Concerning an Amendment to Village Law, dated 4 October 2005, prepared by the Ministry of Internal Affairs. The aim was to provide health services to village guards as well as their dependants, who were not covered by any social security institution,[11] by issuing them with a Green Card. At the same time this Law also aimed to exempt them from the requirements set forth by the 'Law Concerning the State Coverage of Treatment Expenses of Citizens who lack the Ability to Pay by Issuing a Green Card' No. 3816.

For several years, the Ministry of Internal Affairs has been planning to introduce legal regulations aimed at improving the guards' socio-economic circumstances. In 2004, the Ministry prepared the GKK Draft which contained the following rights:

---

[11] The following paragraph was added to Village Law No. 442, dated 18 March 1924, Article 74: 'Village guards, who are not covered by any social security institution, as well as their dependents, will be issued a Green Card while, at the same time, exempting them from the requirements set forth by the 'Law Concerning the State Coverage of Treatment Expenses of Citizens who lack the Ability to Pay by Issuing a Green Card' No. 3816. In the determination of the dependants, the rules of the Civil Servant Law No 657 apply.'

Article 209 of the Public Servants Law No. 657 refers to the health assistance given to the temporary village guards and their dependants. Guards under the age of 45, or over the age of 45 but with less than 10 years of service, will receive double their normal salary multiplied by the amount of years in service as severance pay, regardless of the duration of their service. The family members of those guards killed in action will receive a compensation equivalent to double the normal salary.

Temporary Village Guards over the age of 45 years and with a minimum of 10 years of service are expected to retire and will receive a monthly salary equivalent to a public servant's salary multiplied by a specially calculated indicator. Those who receive this salary will benefit from health assistance as stipulated by the provisional Article 139 of the Retirement Fund Law No. 5434, along with their dependants. Those who receive the salary will be issued with an identity card, as stipulated by Article 127 of the same law.[12]

The Effects of the Temporary Village Guard System on the Clan Structure in the Region

Over time, differences between the clans developed in relation to their acceptance or refusal over who could become a guard. These differences resulted in the emergence of the concepts of a 'state-friendly clan' and an 'anti state–friendly clan'. Such arguments have emphasised the likelihood of an escalation of conflict between village guard clans and non village guard clans. Bearing this in mind, it can be said that within the GKK system, there is a high risk of serious conflict and dissension among Kurdish clans, particularly in the long-term. This threat should be taken seriously, and the means for its peaceful resolution need to be identified.

The Investigation Report (dated 1 January 1997, No. M.001), also known to the public as the Susurluk Report, prepared upon the request of the prime minister by the Chief of the Prime Minister's Inspection Committee Kutlu Savaş, stresses that 'since those public servants with a tendency to commit crime, and the central [administration] share a mutual interest in these crimes, these corrupt alliances known as 'gangs' have emerged.' This development is associated with the clan structure in the region.

The existence of the feudal structure in the east and southeast, the conflicts between clans, the fact that the GKK system is based on the feudal structure, the extensions of the clans in Iran and Northern Iraq, the regional economy's links to smuggling and above all, drug trafficking, have also been significant in creating resources for illegal activities.[13]

The Problem of Expropriation of Evacuated Villages

Another severe accusation made against the temporary village guards is the claim that guards personnel have appropriated the property in some evacuated villages.

[12] Enis Tayman, 'Korucular için 'çıkış yolu' aranıyor,' Tempo, 30 August 2004.

[13] Kutlu Savaş, Susurluk Raporu, p. 83. (Here, the page numbers of the Susurluk Report booklet published as a supplement to Aktüel Magazine on 5 February 1998 were used).

One example is the Assynan/Synai Orthodox (Süranyi) 'Sare (aka Sarı) Village, in the İdil Province of Şırnak, which was abandoned by the villagers who migrated to Europe in 1994 as a result of the terrorist activity within the region. The guards settled in Sare in order to be more effective in the fight against terrorism and refused to leave despite the Süryanis express wish to return.

The Süryanis, who are the lawful inhabitants of Sare, submitted formal written requests to the president, the prime minister, the general staff, the Ministry of Internal Affairs, the Şırnak governor's office and the İdil district administration. The Şırnak governor's office gave notice to the guards instructing them to evacuate the village by 15 June 2004. Those who continued to reside in a total of 28 houses were forcibly removed from the village by the İdil gendarmerie command teams in September 2004. The officials said that they had evacuated the guards in order to guarantee the return of the Süryanis who were the lawful residents of the village.[14]

This situation, however, turned into a grievance for both villager and guard alike. The guards claimed that they had settled in this village upon the request of the administration, who had then summoned them to the station one night under the pretext of an upcoming mission. They were then kept waiting there all night, while gendarmerie teams went to the village and subsequently evacuated their families. A total of 300 guards claimed that they were not even permitted to pick up their belongings and that they had no other option but to go and live with relatives. The guards made a request for houses to be built for them in order to solve their problem.[15]

It was claimed that the village guards were originally involved in forced migration practices and were, therefore, involved in murders and kidnappings. It was frequently reported in the press that the guards appropriated the property of villagers of Kurdish origin, used the fields that were left behind, and attacked those who returned.[16]

---

14 Hüseyin Kaçar, 'Süryani köyündeki korucular jandarma tehdidiyle çıkarıldı,' Sabah, 13 September 2004; 'Jandarma, Süryanilerin boşalttığı köydeki korucuları zorla çıkarttı,' Zaman, 13 September 2004.

15 'Korucular yakalandı,' Radikal, 29 September 2002.

16 For news reports on this matter, see Radikal, 29 September 2002. In 1997, in Beytüşşebap Province, Mayor Hüsnü Timur raided the courthouse with 300 guards after his brother was taken into custody, and forced his release. On 11 September 1997, a hand grenade belonging to a guard accidentally went off in a wedding in Cizre. In the ensuing random fire, which was started by the guards who panicked, 9 people lost their lives and 57 were injured. On 2 April 2001, in Malagir Village, guards opened fire on villagers who were disemnarking from their pickups trucks. One died, the remaining three fled. On 17 November 2001, in Silvan, Diyarbakır, a 12 year old girl named 'Necla Tünle' was kidnapped by the relatives of head guard Abdulsamet Sümbül. Tünle was detained for 40 days and was eventually freed by the military. On 3 June 2002, agian in the Beytüşşebap province, guard Mehmet Yüce was caught red-handed while trying to sell heroine to the police. Based on information provided by Yüce, 5 kg of heroine were seized in the homes of two guards. On 9 July 2002, in Nureddin Village in Malazgirt, Muş, three people died as a result of gun fire started by the guards against the villagers who wanted to reap hay. On 29 July 2002, the guards who opened fire on the house of the Elhan Family who re-

On July 31, temporary village guards allegedly organised a raid in the Kankalesi Plateau near the Akpazar Village of Diyadin–Ağrı, killing the villagers Şemsettin Sarıhan, Şamil Sarıhan, Remzi Sarıhan, Mustafa Sarıhan and Ali Sarıhan, and injuring Kemal Sarıhan. It was argued that the Akpazar Village Guards organised the raid because the Sarıhan family's cattle trespassed on [Gündoğdu] property.[17] The guards involved were: Mustafa Gündoğdu, Mahmut Gündoğdu, Ahmet Gündoğdu, Ercan Gündoğdu and Kıyas.

Ongoing Problems and Debates in 2005

The 'Secrecy' Debate

An incident related to the temporary village guards that sparked ongoing debate and remained an important part of the agenda in 2005, concerned the existence of a secret regulation concerning guards employed in the east and southeast.

The CHP Diyarbakır Deputy Mesut Değer put forward a parliamentary question to the Turkish Grand National Assembly (Türkiye Büyük Millet Meclisi, TBMM) about whether the government had issued a secret regulation. In a written response, the Minister of Justice, Cemil Çiçek, stated that publication of the regulation which controls the village guards' appointments, determination of sphere of jurisdiction, duties and responsibilities in the Official Gazette (Resmi Gazette) would create problems,[18] and it therefore remained unpublished.

In his response, Minister Çiçek stressed that the regulations to be published in the Official Gazette are defined in Article 124 of the Constitution, and referred to in Article 1, Clause 2 of the Law Concerning Regulations that are to be Published in the Official Gazette No. 3011, where it is written that ' regulations concerning national security and national safety, and that are classified as secret are not published.'[19] Çiçek explained that this practice was compliant with the law by referring to a State Council's decision in a case involving the abolishment of the GKK regulation.[20]

Undoubtedly, the Temporary Village Guard System was established to prevent separatist terrorism which has been at the forefront of Turkey's agenda for almost 12 years. However, there is little doubt that the publication of the Temporary Village Guards regulation, which governs staff appointments, spheres of jurisdiction, duties, responsibilities and dismissals, would lead to problems.

---

turned to their village Suluca, Muş from İzmir, injured Netice Elhan, aged 15. On 21 August 2002, three shepherds in Maraş were killed by a guard named 'Hasan Dağlan.'

17 The Human Rights Foundation of Turkey, 'Ağustos 2004 Raporu,' see http://www.tihv.org.tr/rapor/2004_08/agukurtsorunu.html, [Access Date: 08 August 2006].

18 'Gizli yönetmelik, soru önergesiyle ortaya çıktı,' Zaman, 25 July 2005; 'Koruculara 'gizli' yönetmelik,' Yeni Şafak, 14 August 2005.

19 'Gizli yönetmelik, soru önergesiyle ortaya çıktı,' Zaman, 25 July 2005.

20 'Koruculara 'gizli' yönetmelik,' Yeni Şafak, 14 August 2005.

Obviously, this situation conflicts with the established practices of transparency and the rule of law, which are basic principles of a democratic approach to public administration. If the authorities, recruitment processes, training regimes of the police, the gendarmerie and similar organisations responsible for maintaining security in a country are public knowledge, then the same information a propos the guards should be available as well. This is reminiscent of the official secret concept which Max Weber describes as the 'specific invention of the bureaucracy.' In other words, secrecy can lead to a series of problems stemming from the fact that government does not adequately share information with the citizenry.

According to the World Trade Organisation (WTO), transparency in public administration has three main conditions: the proclamation of laws, regulations and other policy documents related to public administration, the promulgation of all legal regulations to related parties, and the constant, objective and rationalistic use of legal regulations.[21]

Involvement in Criminal Activities[22]

Notwithstanding the important contributions that the temporary village guards have made in the fight against terrorism, the most significant problem has been their involvement (forcible at times) in 'dirty dealings' and illegal activities. Their low level of education, coupled with the financial problems experienced by the guards, has facilitated their abuse by illegal organisations and organised crime groups.

Evidence has linked the guards working in the east and southeast to illegal activities such as racketeering, smuggling, blackmail and murder. In 2005, several guards were named in incidents attributed to JİTEM. In his answer to CHP İzmir Senator Türkan Miçooğulları's question in September 2005, the Minister of Internal Affairs, Abdülkadir Aksu, declared that since the beginning of the Temporary Village Guard System on 26 March 1985, 4'972 guards had committed crimes and of these, 853 had been arrested.[23] According to Aksu's statement, 2'384 crimes involved terrorism, 934 crimes involved property, 1'234 crimes were against individuals and 420 crimes involved smuggling.

According to the latest information, 4'938 guards have committed crimes in the past 18 years: 928 crimes involving property crime, 1'215 crimes against individuals, 411 crimes involving smuggling, and 2'384 crimes of various other types.

21 World Trade Organisation, Working Group on the Relationship between Trade and Investment, 'Transparency,' WT/WGTI/W/109, (02-1561), 27 March 2002, p.1. See http://www.dfait-maeci.gc.ca/tna-nac/documents/W109-e.pdf, [Access Date: April 30, 2006].

22 Village Guard Resolution Article 16 (Deeds Forbidden to Guards): 'The deeds that are forbidden to guards are as follows: 1) To run a business other than being a guard, e.g. opening a store, coffee house, inn, or being a partner in these; 2) To abandon his duty in order to work for himself or in another villager's service; 3) To unlawfully benefit from the vineyards, fields and produce he protects; 4) To put out to graze his own animals or to become a shepherd for the village; 5) Failing to carry his sign, identity, uniform or weapon, or changing these.' See http://www.mevzuat.adalet.gov.tr/html/20524.html.

23 '5 bin köy korucusu suç işledi,' NTV-MSNBC, 28 September 2005.

The ratio of those who had committed a crime in relation to the total number of guards was 8.5 percent. Depending on the nature of the crime, a guard's employment can be terminated based on Article 17 of the Village Guards Resolution.[24]

In the past two years, there has been an increase in crimes involving temporary village guards. In Aksu's answer to the question asked by the CHP Deputy, Mesut Değer, on 20 June 2003, it was stated that 4'804 guards had been prosecuted for crimes. Of these crimes, 2'275 were for aiding and abetting the PKK and 2'376 were of various other types. The types of the crimes committed were reported in Tempo magazine.[25] Some of the offences have been listed as follows: extortion, robbery, murder, mutilation, armed conflict with municipal police, aggression against municipal police, armed attacks on property and vehicles, kidnapping, use of explosives, arson, aiding and abetting terrorism, drug trafficking, weapons and ammunitions trafficking, trafficking of goods subject to regulations, livestock trafficking, historical artefact smuggling, rape, armed struggle among villages and clans, armed kidnapping of women, carrying a gun without a licence, swindling, house break-ins, livestock theft and grand auto theft.

In another statement released on 16 September 2003, Aksu stated that the total number of temporary village guards in the 22 provinces (whose combined monthly salaries, including compensation, is 253 million) had exceeded 58'000, costing the government YTL 15 million per month. At that time, 2'376 village guards had been prosecuted for allegations of crime.[26]

The Report of the Parliamentary Investigation Commission (10/90) for Politically Motivated Unsolved Murders in Various Regions of Our Country,[27] dated October 12, 1995, underlined that the Temporary Village Guard System had deviated from its original purpose, just like the shriver system, and had become a source of illicit income by some. Reference was also made to the guard's involvement in illegal activities.[28]

Many citizens, fearful of retribution and aware of the government's weakness in the region, have stopped informing the state of the alleged criminal activities being committed by temporary village guards. Government officials have found it very difficult to resolve this issue. It has been argued that some guards work with the

---

[24] Village Guards Regulation Article 17 (Termination of the Village Guard Duty): 'Those guards who show negligence or laziness, or those who carry out the forbidden deeds stated in Article 16 receive first a warning, and the second time, a reprobation, both of which are registered in their record. On the third time, they are discharged. Those who fail to turn up for their duty station for two consecutive days, or abandon it without permission or valid excuse are discharged. Also, a guard who loses his weapons and ammunition through negligence or deliberately is immediately discharged, the head of district is notified for penal action and the guard repays the cost of the weapon and ammunition.'

[25] Enis Tayman, 'Korucular için 'çıkış yolu' aranıyor,' Tempo, 30 August 2004.

[26] 'Bölgenin ve Devletin Sırtındaki Kambur Koruculuk,' Göç-Der News Bulletin, No. 26, 2003, p. 11. Quoted in Füsun Üstel, 'Zorunlu İç Göç Sonrası Köye Dönüş (ön) Raporu,' TESEV (2004), p. 44.

[27] No: 10/90, Issue No: A.01.1.GEÇ/300–554, Decision No: 10 (12.10.1995).

[28] Fedai Erdoğ, TBMM Faili Meçhul Siyasi Cinayetleri Araştırma Komisyon Raporu (İstanbul: Gizli Saklı Yayınevi, 2005), p. 99.

illegal organisations out of fear, while still receiving their salaries from the state, whilst others use their positions to smuggle weapons and drugs. As a consequence, regional drug and weapons trafficking has remained in the hands of the guards. Influential members of the community have also used the guard system to maintain their influence. The clan chiefs, who were formally guard leaders, have oppressed their opponents in a lawless and merciless fashion often naming the latter as PKK members. Some guards have murdered villagers against whom they had a vendetta and then claimed that they had been members of the PKK, whilst others have exploited and forced their opposition out of their villages.[29]

Research carried out in 2001 by Yüzüncü Yıl University and the Gendarmerie Public Order Command in 19 villages, showed that the guards' loyalties lie, to a greater extent, with the clan leaders, rather than with the state. In addition, as the guards became accustomed to receiving salaries from the state, their [agricultural] productivity declined, and their involvement in illegal activities, such as drug and weapons trafficking, increased.[30]

Conclusion and Evaluation

The Temporary Village Guard System returned to the spotlight during the decline in PKK terrorism at the end of the 1990s. Discussions at the time centred on whether or not the system should continue to exist. Some circles began to talk seriously about its abolishment and news about its future existence was published in July 2003 as part of the European Union's (EU) compatibility process.

Rumours about the abolishment of the Temporary Village Guard System have caused unrest and, taking into account its cost to the state, any outcome of the proposed abolishment must be favourable to both the state and the guards. The system's abolishment, however, could threaten those who have taken part in the fight against the PKK, making them open targets. Moreover, it might place a greater financial burden on guards who have abandoned their previous professions and whose sole income comes from this type of work.

As the guard system has become a way of life for those involved in agriculture and farming, it has effectively transformed producers into consumers. With the stabilisation of security and the future existence of the system in question, any return of the guards to their former positions in society presents a serious problem. Consequently, governments have been generally reluctant to make decisions that might destabilise the system. Furthermore, the fact remains that guard duty is usually carried out by clans. These clans and their guard force, whose members number in the thousands, are very influential, at least as far as their voting potential is concerned. These factors play a significant role in the continuing existence of the guard system which has remarkable power, both politically and as a militia unit.

---

29 Ibid., p. 101.

30 'Bölgenin ve Devletin Sırtındaki Kambur Koruculuk', Göç-Der News Bulletin, No. 26, 2003, p. 10. Quoted in Füsun Üstel, 'Zorunlu İç Göç Sonrası Köye Dönüş (ön) Raporu,' TESEV (2004), p. 35–36.

The following assessment from the suggestions chapter of the Susurluk Report by Kutlu Savaş is still pertinent: 'the dissolution of the clan structure in the region stopped, and the structure became even stronger due to the clan-based GKK system which strengthened the semi-feudal structure that exists in the region. Clan leaders and family heads became stronger with the income provided and other crime and terrorist organisations emerged. Removing the influence of certain family and clan leaders in the region is a necessity.'[31]

Once any decision to abolish the GKK system has been made, all possible economic and social problems should be considered beforehand and the necessary measures should be taken. If it is decided that the GKK system should continue, then social security for the 1'400 guards who have lost their lives in the fight against terror should be provided. For the remainder, involvement in crime should be prevented, all kinds of negativity should be stopped and the expectations of those who have carried out their duties in a fashion that respects the law should be met. To this end, the regulations that have been initiated by the government in order to resolve problems involving the GKK system, to increase the social security of the guards and improve their financial situation should be implemented. This should begin with the Draft Concerning Amendments to the Village Law.

Some NGOs are of the opinion that the Village Guard System should be abolished, and that those who were made guards by force should be provided with improved possibilities for returning to civilian life.[32] In the research conducted by the Yüzüncü Yıl University and the Gendarmerie Public Order Command mentioned above, three suggestions were made: the first is to use the guards in the barren hills and mountains, and the long-term employment of others to maintain natural and sustainable resources. The second suggestion is to meet the public institutions' demand for unskilled labour in other regions of Turkey. The third involves the return of arms and voluntary resignation, since employment in residential areas might worsen the living conditions of former village guards.[33]

Additionally, TESEV's 2005 report entitled, 'The Problem of Internal Displacement in Turkey: Assessment and Policy Proposals,' reaches the following conclusions on the Temporary Village Guard System: 'In order to facilitate peace and security, both PKK militants and village guards must be reintegrated into society. A central policy needs to be outlined to guarantee their disarmament and, unless they have a criminal record, to remove policies that restrict their employment. However, neither the PKK militants nor the village guards should be employed in fields such as education and security. Leaving the initiative concerning village guards to local institutions, as well as developing faulty employment policies, increases social tensions and leads to new problems. In addition, conflicts between village guards and

31 Proposal No. 13, p. 92–93.

32 Turkish Human Rights Movement Conference, November 25–26 November 2000. For the Final Report and the Conclusion Statement see http://www.turkeiforum.net/konf/conf3-tr.html

33 'Bölgenin ve Devletin Sırtındaki Kambur Koruculuk', Göç-Der News Bulletin, No. 26 2003, p. 10. Quoted in Füsun Üstel, 'Zorunlu İç Göç Sonrası Köye Dönüş (ön) Raporu,' TESEV (2004), p. 37.

villagers, village guards and combatants, and combatants and villagers need to be resolved. Village guards must also be provided with social security coverage, in order to prevent them from becoming re-involved in armed clashes and from abusing the power that stems from their positions for corrupt or violent purposes. In addition to centralised policies on these matters, NGOs should also play an important role in facilitating reconciliation.'[34]

It is clear that the guard system retains important functions in the east and southeast; firstly, by the contribution of the guards to the provision of security in the region, through their role in the fight against terrorism and, secondly, in terms of the economic contribution of the system as a source of employment. The system has been the sole source of income for approximately 60'000 families in the region and some have argued that the system has become an institution in the region. Even if the need for the guards diminishes, the abolishment of this system has the potential to create substantial problems, unless alternative institutions are established.

The guards receive orders from the Provincial Gendarmerie Commander, as stipulated by the regulations. The relevant gendarmerie units, therefore, serve an important function in the prevention of problems related to the guards. As such, incidents that put the gendarmerie under suspicion should not be permitted, especially given the fact that some activities involving guards and shrivers appear to be organised.

In conclusion, the GKK system has evolved as a result of the socio-economic circumstances in East and Southeast Anatolia, where Turkey has battled against terrorism for years. In this sense, any abolishment of the system seems unfavourable unless its security and law and order functions, and the financial support it provides to an important number of local citizens, can be replaced with an alternative. Therefore, even if a security system is established where there is no need for the village guard practice, economic and social alternatives should be in place, since the matter is not merely a security problem.

---

[34] Tamer Aker, A. Betül Çelik, Dilek Kurban, Turgay Ünalan and Deniz Yükseker, 'Türkiye'de Ülke İçinde Yerinden Edilme Sorunu: Tespitler ve Çözüm Önerileri,' TESEV (2005), p. 10. See http://www.tesev.org.tr/eng/events/TESEV_IDP_Report.pdf

Police Intelligence

Mesut Bedri Eryılmaz[*]

Introduction

The essence of policing is to create a secure and stable environment for citizens to live in by maintaining order, preventing and detecting crimes and apprehending criminals. However, a decrease in crime, or an increase in the number of criminals apprehended as a result of effective policing practices, are not the only criteria for measuring success. The core of the security services mandate is to build trust in the community, provide peace and welfare, increase citizens' well-being and thus their quality of life. If policing is to be conceived as a social service meant to provide peace and harmony, and not as a harsh and authoritarian legal force disconnected from the public and dealing purely with solving crimes, then police intelligence needs to provide active crime-fighting units with accurate and sufficient information in order to assist in the formulation of improved crime-fighting strategies.

In democratic societies, the intelligence branch of the police is the primary part of the domestic security service. Although the apprehension of persons involved in a bombing is qualified as a policing success in the short-term, it does not negate the damage caused by the bombing (such as the killing or wounding of citizens, economic loss, and an environment of panic, mistrust and fear). What is imperative is the prevention of such incidents before they occur by making use of intelligence activities. Indeed, the security debates triggered by the 9/11 attacks, exposed the weaknesses of intelligence organisations and thus highlighted the need for more effective intelligence gathering.

The Turkish police force work to prevent crime, with the help of intelligence, as stipulated in Article 2 of the Law on Police Duties and Powers (Polis Vazife ve Selahiyetleri Kanunu, PVSK). As stipulated in PVSK Article 1, the police fulfil the responsibilities of 'protecting public order, providing security for the public, individuals and property, and the privacy of the home' as well as 'protecting the life, property and purity (ırz) of the public, and securing peace in the community.' In order to achieve this, the police organisation is comprised of three main departments, namely the administrative, judicial and political. Intelligence is classified under the political department, as stipulated by the Police Force Law (Emniyet Teşkilatı Kanunu). With this function, the police force not only protects the lives and property of citizens, but also helps prevent the potentially negative economic

---

* Associate Professor, Police Academy, Faculty of Security Sciences, Department of Law of Criminal Procedure.

and psychological effects of crime on society. A successful intelligence infrastructure will have a deterrent effect on those contemplating crime, by increasing their perception of the difficulties inherent in crime.[1]

The best known characteristic of intelligence units is their ability to collect secret data. This is directly related however, to individual rights and freedoms and the confidentiality of private life, and these are principles which are protected by the constitution. In this context, intelligence units, which are seen as the guarantors of national security, should be institutions that are effective, politically neutral and sensitive to the code of professional ethics. They also need to be democratically controlled and should only be operating within their legal sphere of jurisdiction. Thus, the importance a country gives to the principles of accountability, and those of rights and freedoms in its administrative approach, should be proportional to the workings and implementation of intelligence organisations.

The European Parliament noted in its report (2001/2098 I INI): 'For the purposes of guaranteeing national security and order, the state's right to obtain information is extended beyond the scope of individual investigations, prompted by firm evidence that a crime has been committed. National law authorises the state to carry out additional measures to secure information about specific persons or groups, with a view to the early detection of extremist or subversive movements, terrorism and organised crime. The relevant data is collected and analysed by specific domestic intelligence services.' This demonstrates that intelligence activities are a necessity and should always be carried out within a legal framework.[2]

The Concept of Intelligence

The concept of intelligence, known as information gathering in Turkey, is technically described as the gathering of information through all available means, concerning the aims, plans and capacities of enemy or potential enemy states and groups or individuals with criminal intent. However, the US Department of Defence defines intelligence as 'information and data gathered about an opponent through observation, research, analysis and comprehension.' The concept of 'opponent' in this definition can include all manner of individuals, groups or states that pose a threat to the system and society. Given the various definitions of intelligence in the literature, it can also be described as information which is perceived as meaningful by the existing public administration philosophy. This information is gathered, verified, interpreted for specific purposes, analysed, categorised and distributed to policy-makers who use it for the continuity (bekâ) and welfare of the state.[3]

---

1 Aytekin Geleri, Hakan İleri, Organise Suçlarla Mücadelede Gizli ve Örtülü Yaklaşımlar (Ankara: Seçkin Yayınları, 2003), p. 44.

2 For Şükrü Önder, Bazı Kanunlarda Değişiklik Yapılmasına Dair Kanun Teklifi ve İçişleri Komisyonu Raporu, 2005, see http://www.tbmm.gov.tr/sirasayi/donem22/yili101/ss962m.htm, [Access Date: 09.12.2005].

3 H. Uçak, 11 Eylül Sonrası ABD İç Güvenlik ve İstihbarat Çalışmaları No. 89 (Ankara: EGM İDB Yayınları, 2005), p. 13.

Strictly functional descriptions of intelligence also exist in the literature, in addition to those of a theoretical nature. The functioning mechanism of intelligence is commonly known as the 'wheel of intelligence' and it is widely regarded as a circular process. The wheel of intelligence points to the transformation process of raw information/data into intelligence. The wheel of intelligence is defined by the criminal intelligence unit as planning and directing, information gathering, processing and production, analysis, distribution, information verification, comparison and analysis, distribution of intelligence, its application and assessment.[4] The wheel of intelligence has also been defined as the receptor of raw information or news, its categorisation, assessment, interpretation and distribution. Both of these basic approaches show that the main factors in intelligence activities are the gathering of raw data, its exposure to scientific analysis, and its presentation to the policy-maker. The information thus gathered and assessed, points out the sensitive targets and weak points of enemy states and individuals, as well as the physical and moral resources available to them.

The concept of secrecy is also an inherent part of intelligence. From the most liberal countries to the most severe dictatorships, intelligence activities are carried out in secrecy. News that is known or accessible to the public has no intelligence value.[5]

The Historical Background of the Police Intelligence Unit and its Current Activities

In order to understand the modern day police intelligence unit, which is responsible for domestic security together with the gendarmerie intelligence, one must understand the historical background of the institution. The foundation of the intelligence department is based on the Important Issues Directorate (Önemli İşler Müdürlüğü, IID) which is contained in Police Force Law No. 3201 of 1937, Article 16, Paragraph (a), Clause 5. In 1951, the Special Bureau was established directly under the Directorate General of Security (Emniyet Genel Müdürlüğü, EGM), in order to gather information about ideological trends, counter-espionage, and various smuggling-related activities. Following the training of Intelligence agents for mobilisation and operations, 'Small Group Units' were established in Hatay, Ankara, Istanbul and Izmir, and intelligence units were formed. Of these, Hatay was mainly active in undercover foreign intelligence gathering, whereas the other units focused on counter-espionage and terrorist activities.

On 27 May 1960, the Special Bureau was abolished along with the Small Group Units, and an attempt was made to create the Important Issues Directorate, which was established in accordance with Police Force Law and in compliance with its founding principles. In 1963, a memo was sent out to 10 provinces requesting the recruitment of intelligence personnel who fulfilled the necessary requirements set by the IID, and training was organised in order to establish intelligence groups in these

---

4 Ibid, p. 25.

5 M. Şenel, A. Turhan Şenel, İstihbarat ve Genel Güvenlik Konularımız No. 56 (Ankara: EGM İDB Yayınları, 1997), p. 27.

provinces. This type of 'basic training' facilitated the establishment of intelligence groups in the provinces and ensured that an educational cohesion was achieved within these groups. The IID rapidly took on the characteristics of an intelligence organisation, and following a rise in ideologically motivated incidents in the 1970s, the Important Issues Directorate became the Important Issues Department Presidency (Önemli İşler Daire Başkanlığı). In 1975, it was renamed the Intelligence Presidency (İstihbarat Başkanlığı) and, in 1983 it became the Intelligence Department Presidency (İstihbarat Daire Başkanlığı, İDB).[6]

Today, the İDB consists of central and district units, and provides intelligence services in the provinces, through intelligence units within the provincial security directorates. The İDB, working directly under the Director General of Security, is structured as stipulated by the decree dated 13 February 1989, which is compliant with the Police Force Law No. 3201.

To date, 7'138 police officers have served the department. 4'262 people are currently employed in the service, of which 783 are executives, 3'457 are officers, five are general administrative clerks and 17 are assistant technicians. In addition, 21.8 percent of the personnel (999 people) are university graduates, 76.9 percent (3,207 people) hold associate or high school degrees and the remaining 1.3 percent (59 people) completed junior high school.

As stipulated in Article 7, Clause 1 annexed to the PVSK No. 2559 in 1985, the central and provincial units of the department perform the following duties:

> The police carries out intelligence activities at a national level in order to take the necessary precautionary and protective measures related to the indivisible integrity of the State and Nation, its constitutional order, and its general security; and to this end gathers, assesses and transfers information to the authorities or to those state institutions for whom the information would be of use. It also cooperates with the other state intelligence institutions.

However, the authority to conduct information gathering, as defined by law, lacks the criterion of 'providing a clear and concise definition,' which is imperative for the rule of law. Accordingly, the Annexed Article 7 does not clarify who is responsible for gathering and storing information about suspects and under what circumstances. Additionally, the article does not contain any regulation about the control of such an important authority. In its current state, the manner in which the article has been formulated has left it wide open for abuse, allowing for the arbitrary infringement of individual rights and freedoms.

This gap was addressed with the amendment made to the PVSK's Annexed Article 7 in Law No. 5397 on 3 July 2005, in compliance with constitutional Article 13, which states that the infringement of basic rights and freedoms should be regulated by law without exception, and as a result of the need for clarity and conciseness. A decree which provided for more detailed regulations on the use of intelli-

---

6 Directorate General of Security Intelligence Department Presidency, https://www.egmidb.gov.tr, [Access Date: 09.12.2005].

gence took effect on 10 November 2005, following its publication in the Official Gazette (Resmi Gazete) No. 25989.

Conditions of the Use of the Intelligence Authority

In order to carry out the duties stipulated in Paragraph 1 for prevention of the crimes listed in the Code of Criminal Procedure No. 5271, dated 12 December 2004, Article 250, Clause 1, Paragraphs (a), (b) and (c),1 with the exception of crimes of espionage, telecommunications can be intercepted and monitored, information signals can be assessed and registered by a court order, or in cases where delay might be disadvantageous, through the written order of the director general of security or chief of the intelligence department. In cases where delay would be disadvantageous, the written order is presented to the authorised judge for approval. The judge then renders a decision within a maximum period of 24 hours. In the event that this time-frame is exceeded, or if the judge decides against the order, the measure is to be immediately removed. In such a case, recordings made of the monitoring process are destroyed within 10 days at the latest, the situation is noted in an official report, and the report is kept on file to be produced in case of inspection.

The security unit must seek approval from a judge who carries the authority within his/her area of jurisdiction and who is a member of the High Criminal Court established by Law No. 5271, Article 250, Clause 1.

Included in the decision and the written order are: the identity of the person subject to the measures taken, the type of communication device, the phone numbers used, or whatever can be determined from the area code, as well as the nature of the measure taken, its period of coverage and the reasons for the request. Decisions can be made for a maximum of three months; these may be extended in the same way for a further three-month period and for a maximum of three times. However, for ongoing danger stemming from a terrorist organisation's activities, the judge might see fit to extend the duration for longer than this maximum time limit, if deemed necessary.

In cases where the monitoring period expires, the recordings of the monitoring are destroyed within 10 days at the latest, the situation is noted in an official report and this report is kept on file to be produced in case of inspection.

In order to prevent the crimes listed in this article, technical monitoring can be carried out in intelligence activities, provided a court order is in place. Moreover, a written request can be made to public organisations and institutions in order to benefit from the necessary documents and information they possess. In cases where these institutions and organisations withhold information on legal grounds, or because the information contains trade secrets, this information and these documents can only be used by court order.

The records obtained as a result of activities carried out in compliance with this article cannot be used for purposes other than those stated in Clause 1. The principle of secrecy applies to preservation of the information and records obtained. Those who act in violation of this article's provisions are subject to investigation by a public prosecutor, even if the violation takes place during or due to the assignment.

Court orders and written orders are carried out by members of the İDB. The start and finish time and date are recorded, as well as the identity of the member conducting the process.

Supervision of the activities stipulated in this article is carried out by the institution's superiors, inspectors of the EGM and the related ministry, as well as a person or commission specially designated by the prime minister.

The activities stipulated in this article and the monitoring to be carried out in accordance with Law No. 5271, Article 135, are administered through a single centre named the Presidency of Telecommunications (Telekomünikasyon İletişim Başkanlığı) working within the Institution of Telecommunications (Telekomünikasyon Kurumu) and acting directly under its president. This board consists of one president and three experts, namely, technical, legal and administrative. The board also has one representative from the National Intelligence Organisation, the Directorate General of Security and the General Command of Gendarmerie. Sufficient personnel are employed to carry out the duties. The President of Telecommunications is appointed by the prime minister upon the proposal of the president of the institution. The president has the same employee rights as members of the institution. The minister of transport has the duty of preparing the necessary infrastructure for this centre. The funding expenses of this centre are met by the budget of the institution. A variety of goods and services procurement pertaining to the establishment of the centre, as well as construction work, is exempt from Public Bid Law No. 4734 and Public Bidding Agreements Law No. 4735, except in cases of wrongdoing or of bidding bans.

Monitoring carried out in violation of the procedures and principles laid out in this article is legally invalid and those who undertake such actions are subject to the rulings of Turkish Penal Law No. 5237, dated 26 July 2004.

The procedures and principles concerning the application of this article are to be regulated with a by-law to be published by the prime minister's office within a period of three months, in consultation with the Ministries of Justice, Internal Affairs and Transport.

In order to eliminate potential future dangers for the state or society and to increase awareness of any anomalies, the government should be authorised to use public information and to monitor specific personnel, in addition to carrying out the activities of information gathering, assessment and communication intervention. The law meets such needs, defining the realm of intelligence not only as eavesdropping, but also as a way of gaining access to public records that might contain important information about targeted persons, and the secret monitoring and recording of their activities.

Intelligence information is described by law solely as information gained as the result of eavesdropping, analysis of public records and information, and evaluation of information gathered. However, in practice, law enforcement agencies also collect important information through the interrogation and interview of terrorist organisation members, apprehended persons, agents within an organisation, and informants from the media and from the local intelligence community.

With the 2005 amendment of the PVSK, a central structure was formed and all information collected as a result of intelligence gathering was recorded and properly filed. Concurrently, supervision of the process was delegated to an individual civilian authority outside the intelligence units. This authority lies with the Presidency of Telecommunications, working within the Institution of Telecommunications, who by its own initiative conducts a wide variety of communication interventions with the use of superior technology.

In order to protect individual rights and freedoms from excessive intervention by the state, as well as to ensure the efficient elimination of threats and dangers against the state and society, it is important that there is a limitation of the intelligence sector to monitor certain types of organised crime. There is also a need to recognise potential future dangers, and for the establishment of an efficient judicial and civilian supervision mechanism along with a custody and control procedure over the aforementioned records.

Moreover, owing to this central structure, the monitoring of persons by all three intelligence units (i.e. the National Security Organisation (Milli İstihbarat Teşkilatı, MİT), police intelligence and gendarmerie intelligence), at the same time or at different times, will be prevented, thereby eliminating the possibility of long-term interference in the private lives of citizens.

Although the placement of monitoring/eavesdropping activities under one administrative body represents an important step, there is wide public belief that devotion to the rule of law is the only means of preventing the police and the gendarmerie from undertaking independent, illegal monitoring of individuals and institutions without permission from the central authorities. There is, therefore, a clear need to ensure our citizens that the state does not monitor anyone illegally. Accordingly, in an effort to provide the greatest guarantee for society, the activities of intelligence units, as for the other units of the security sector, will be placed under democratic control and oversight by the parliament, the media and non-governmental organisations (NGOs).

These changes notwithstanding, it should also be noted that an ideal intelligence infrastructure does not merely entail the separation of monitoring/eavesdropping from other spheres in the sector. In light of the fact that the single-handed gathering of information facilitates the single-handed harnessing of power, then the units which analyse information and those which act on this analysis to organise operations should also be separated. Information should be divided so as to make the fragmented pieces of the information meaningless, thus eliminating the capacity of one body to gain total control of the information. In other words, those who gather the information should not know the content of it while those who receive and analyse the content should not be able to carry out an operation by making use of its content. From this point of view, the new PVSK Annexed Article 7 is incomplete because, according to the article, although communications are recorded at another centre, the police and the gendarmerie are authorised to analyse the information and carry out an operation accordingly.

Besides the authority to carry out intelligence activities, the amendment of 2005 gave additional powers to police intelligence. In accordance with the prime minister's office circular bearing a 'top secret' seal, the İDB has the authority to form a special unit to carry out witness protection, undercover infiltration, the issue of passports/identity cards, to pay for plastic surgery, and even to establish dummy corporations when deemed necessary. The budget for this unit will come directly from the prime minister's resources. Although it is acceptable to have a certain extent of secrecy surrounding intelligence activities, a question which needs to be answered is how this authority came to be granted by mere decree, when it should normally be granted by law and known publicly by everyone. Other important questions to be asked are why, as a general rule, are these and other similar authorities, which are granted to intelligence organisations around the world, established in 'secret', and why are their expenses not met by the general budget?

Developments in 2005

Thanks to information gathered through intelligence activities, important successes have been achieved in the fight against common crimes such as murder, theft, fraud, rigging of a competitive bidding process, as well as in the fight against terrorism and organised crime. However, although the information and evidence are transferred to the units which investigate these crimes, the intelligence units do not conduct a follow-up on the results. This in fact means that the intelligence department does not keep a record of operations which are carried out as a result of information provided to the department about common crimes. As a result of this practice, the following information regarding developments only relates to student protests, terrorism and organised crime, which are believed to be the motivators behind the establishment of intelligence-gathering facilities.

Developments about Student Protests and Incidents

Although some provocation was witnessed in student protests and incidents, it bore no results on account of the measures which were previously undertaken by the security forces. Just as in previous years, there was no incident involving widespread violence in 2005. A total of 63 incidents were recorded involving minor scuffles and fights, 272 people were taken into custody of which 33 were charged, and 74 people were wounded as a result of these incidents.

Developments Concerning Organised Crime

Organised crime continued to be an important topic in 2005. Throughout this period, 1'403 people were apprehended during 252 operations, of whom 766 were charged. Seven rifles, 780 pistols, 237 kg of cocaine, 551 kg of marijuana and 1'799'529 synthetic drugs (pills) were seized. Customs and fuel trafficking rings worth YTL 8 million were also uncovered.

Developments Concerning Terrorist Organisations

The armed actions of terrorist organisations significantly decreased in 2005, in comparison with previous years. However, it is believed that terrorist groups have retained the potential to commit armed actions, with the exception of groups with a religious agenda which were severely dealt with in the past. It is thought that the supranational determination to fight terrorism, which emerged in the aftermath of violent acts linked to Al-Qaeda in various countries, has hastened this development.

However, in 2005, 544 bomb assaults, two deaths from hunger strikes, 6'442 illegal demonstrations (without prior approval and outside areas defined by the governor's office), the placing of placard's, protests and the distribution of handouts, were carried out by terrorist organisations. As a result of these acts, 99 law enforcement members and 30 citizens lost their lives. Of the terrorist organisation members, 48 were killed, and 5'784 were apprehended. The following information involves terrorist organisations:

The PKK/KONGRA-GEL

PKK/KONGRA-GEL is still the most significant terrorist organisation in Turkey with approximately 1'600 members within the country and 3'550 members across the border. In 2005, through 192 planned intelligence operations in 27 provinces, 19 suspected members were killed and 572 suspected members were apprehended. After being brought before the court, 326 of the organisation's members were charged.

After apprehending the personnel, 121 kg of A/4-C/4 plastic explosives, 160 detonators, 30 rifles, 93 pistols, 2'151 cartridges, 69 hand grenades, six mines and 40 fake identity cards were seized.

Again, due to these operations, 26 new potential members from urban areas were prevented from joining the rural part of the organisation. In the same period, 115 suspected members fled the organisation and surrendered to the law enforcement authorities.

Owing to this organisation's operational work, attempts to spread violence in metropolitan areas and tourist regions in 2005 were significantly hindered. As a result of operations which were carried out in five cities (namely, Ankara, Istanbul, Izmir, Mersin and Muğla), 157 people were taken into custody, of whom 102 were charged. Together with the apprehended organisation members, 63 kg of plastic explosives, 55 detonators, two rifles, 11 pistols, five hand grenades, 250 cartridges and 22 fake identity cards were seized.

In order not to substantiate the West's view of PKK/KONGRA-GEL being a terrorist organisation, the organisation carries out its activities in tourist regions under the cover of a mock organisation called the Kurdistan Freedom Falcons (Teyrebazen Azadiye Kürdistan, TAK). However, it should be noted that sources within the PKK deny any relation to the TAK.

DHKP /C (Revolutionary People's Liberation Party/Front)

As a result of the operations which were carried out in 2005, many of the militants involved in armed activities were apprehended, activities in rural areas were terminated, and finally, thanks to an operation run in five countries simultaneously from 1 April 2005, numerous illicit activities were uncovered. The organisation thus decided to move into the field of democratic activities, such as protesting against the municipal dismantling of squatter dwellings.

As a consequence of the operations that were carried out in several cities, internal documents, bombs, bomb-making materials and devices, and weapons were seized. Following an operation in Adana, an individual who was thought to be a member of the organisation was taken into custody and charged; following an operation in Istanbul which was conducted between 5 – 24 July 2005, 21 people were taken into custody, seven of whom were charged; following an operation in Diyarbakır on 27 April 2005, 11 people were taken into custody; following an operation in Ankara conducted between 17 November – 2 December 2005, two people were taken into custody; following an operation in Edirne on 29 April 2005, two people were taken into custody and one was charged; following a demonstration for DHKP/C held in Ankara Kızılay Square on 17 January 2005, 198 people suspected of participating in the demonstration were taken into custody, six of whom were charged; following an operation in Istanbul on 7 January 2005, three people were taken into custody and one was charged, and following an operation in Erzincan on 4 December 2005, one person was taken into custody, however, no arrests were made. An attempted suicide attack was made by the organisation on 1 July 2005, targeting the Ministry of Justice. The intelligence units had failed to detect the plan beforehand.

MKLP (Marxist - Leninist Communist Party)

This organisation carried out 28 bomb assaults in 2005, and following the operation in Istanbul on 1 January 2005, three people were taken into custody, of whom one was charged; following the operations in Sivas on 12 and 26 May 2005, 10 suspected members were taken into custody; following an operation in Izmir on 7 April 2005, one suspected member was taken into custody; following an operation in Adana on 28 April 2005, five suspected members were taken into custody and two were charged; following an operation in Mersin on 17 August 2005, three suspected members were taken into custody; following an operation in Malatya on 29 April 2005, four suspected members were taken into custody; and finally, following operations in Ankara on 22 September 2005 and 16 November 2005, two suspected members were taken into custody and later charged.

MKP (Maoist Communist Party)
The intelligence operations that took place in 2005 led to the collapse of this organisation. Thirty members were killed in these operations.

Following operations in Ankara between 3 – 10 October 2005, four suspected members were taken into custody and later charged; following the operations in Tunceli on 15 September and 8 – 9 October 2005, four suspected members were taken into custody of whom two were charged; following two separate operations in Tunceli on 14 January and 17 June 2005, 22 suspected members were apprehended, and pursuits made as a result of these operations led to the apprehension of another 12 suspected members, five of whom were released pending trial, while the remainder were released. Finally, in two separate operations in Niğde carried out from 29 – 30 September 2005, two suspected members were taken into custody and charged.

TKP/ML (Turkey Communist Party/Marxist-Leninist) Conference
Following an operation in Mersin on 21 September 2005, one suspected member was taken into custody and later charged; following an operation in Bursa on 31 May 2005, 14 people were taken into custody and eight were charged; following an operation in Ankara on 7 November 2005, seven suspected members were taken into custody, two of whom were charged whilst three were released pending trial. Finally, following an operation in Tokat on 15 September 2005 three suspected members were taken into custody and later charged.

Hizbullah*-İlim Group
This organisation has sustained considerable damage as a result of successful intelligence work and operations and has 500 of its members imprisoned. The organisation has somewhat languished and is now attempting to revive its existence through legal 'front' agencies, such as publications, youth groups, etc. However, in 2005, following operations carried out in 22 provinces, 142 suspected members, 77 of whom were later charged, were taken into custody, along with weapons, ammunition and internal organisational documents.

İBDA-C (Great Eastern Islamic Raiders-Front)
This organisation, which has recently come into the spotlight through its acts of violence, currently conducts work through various publications. In 2005, four suspected members were taken into custody as part of operations carried out in Istanbul and Muğla, of whom only one was charged.

* Editor's Note: Hizbullah, or the Party of God is a militant Islamist Sunni group unrelated to the Lebanon-based Shi'ite Hezbollah.

Caliphate State (İCCB-AFİD)
This organisation was founded by the late Cemalettin Kaplan in Germany. The jihad which Kaplan declared against Turkey, the plane assault on Anıtkabir and the occupation of Fatih Mosque were prevented by good intelligence work. The leader, Metin Kaplan, was returned to Turkey in 2004. In operations involving the organisation in five provinces in 2005, 17 people were taken into custody together with weapons, ammunition and internal documents, of whom three were charged.

Al-Qaeda Organisation
Al-Qaeda's recent involvement in Turkey commenced with simultaneous suicide bombings in Istanbul on 15 and 20 November 2003, which resulted in 59 dead and 700 wounded. 40 people remain under arrest in connection with these events, 31 have been released and a total of 71 people have been tried.

Al-Qaeda's organisation of destructive activities has nonetheless continued, and Louai Sakka and his courier, Hamed Obysi were apprehended on 6 August 2005 in Antalya as they prepared to bomb Israeli cruise ships. 6 kg of C4 plastic explosives and 864 kg of hydrogen peroxide, 105 kg of acetone, one yacht and one zodiac boat were seized during the operation.

Following an operation in Balıkesir on 28 April 2005, a person known to have sent a significant number of people to training camps was charged. Additionally, 15 people were taken into custody as part of operations carried out in six provinces, three of whom were charged.

After an attack on the newspaper Hürriyet on 2 August 2005, eight suspected members were taken into custody and six were charged.

Hizb-ut Tahrir
Before 2005, approximately 800 suspected members of this group had been apprehended on account of their distribution of pamphlets, including three people who claimed to be Hizb-ut Tahrir leaders. They were handed over to the court. In 2005, 317 people were taken into custody as a result of operations carried out in 15 provinces, 128 of whom were charged.

The Evaluation of Activities and Conclusion

The police intelligence/İDB, which was established in 1937 and began serving nationwide in 1983, seems to have achieved considerable success in the fight against organised crime. The most pressing necessity was the authority to carry out intelligence activities, and this was granted to the law enforcement agencies, albeit rather late, in 2005. The coverage and conditions for this authority were also defined by law. What is of importance now, is to adapt the practice to legal regulations and to create an environment of 'human security' where people are not stalked, where their communications are not monitored and where information about them is not gathered arbitrarily.

Intelligence remained an important weapon in the fight against crime in 2005. Although terrorist organisations maintained their potential for activity, this period saw a considerable decrease in armed acts due to specific intelligence operations. Of the 983 intelligence operations which were carried out in 2005, 4'113 people were taken into custody, of whom 1'480 were charged and 48 were killed. A considerable quantity of drugs, contraband gasoline, 62 rifles and 883 pistols were seized.

The police intelligence's success in crime prevention is undoubtedly linked to past experience and trial and error. Indeed, Turkey has suffered from terrorism for years, and has sustained considerable economic and physical loss, whilst also creating a second group of victims through the violation of innocent people's rights and freedoms. Given the current world climate, where the effects of global terror are felt in many countries irrespective of their size, and where there are intensive ongoing debates concerning the clash and accord of civilisations, the positive and negative results of Turkey's fight against terror certainly has the potential to set an example for other countries.

However, the intelligence sector cannot measure its success by its capacity to unveil plots and abolish organisations alone. Equally important factors are how intelligence activities have been carried out, whether individual rights and freedoms have been respected, and how much importance has been granted to the contemporary security approach which prioritises 'human security' over the security of the state.

A relative decrease in the number of terrorist organisation members killed (approximately one percent) is evidence of an increase in the understanding by the police of the right to life (i.e. refraining from extrajudicial killings). This development also results from careful planning and the adoption of precautions to prevent damage to apprehended persons and third parties.

However, the fact that the majority of those who are apprehended are released without trial (approximately two-thirds), shows that many people are unjustly taken into custody and that their freedoms are arbitrarily restricted. Law enforcement explains this state of affairs by emphasising its need to utilise the intelligence that has been gathered and to organise operations before any criminal activity takes place. In other words, people are apprehended in the preparation phase of an operation. Since those who contemplate a crime have not actually committed one, it is difficult to prove individual intent and/or whether such a crime would have actually taken place.

Another factor which explains why so many people are released after their apprehension, relates to the lack of trust between the law enforcement agencies and the judiciary. The judiciary does not perceive that information gathered about those apprehended has necessarily been collected in a reliable manner. In fact, in cases where supplementary material evidence is lacking, a judge has no way of verifying the intelligence information presented. Intelligence circles believe that the amendments that were made to the PSVK in 2005, which define clear procedures for intelligence activities in accordance with the principles of transparency, precision and democratic control, will reduce and eventually eliminate this distrust.

Arguments concerning the lack of coordination and multipolarity in the Turkish intelligence sector, which usually came to light in the aftermath of terrorist attacks, continued unabated in 2005. Since knowledge means power, the National Intelligence Organisation, the Directorate General of Security and the General

Command of the Gendarmerie abstain from sharing information which is collected as a result of intelligence activities, thus abstaining from power-sharing. Each institution therefore has a piece of the puzzle and it is virtually impossible to see the bigger picture without assembling every piece. This leads to the question of why two separate institutions, carrying out the same duty, do not work together under one roof.[7]

In conclusion, the net result of activities carried out by intelligence units in the police force in 2005 was better than imagined. This was true particularly in terms of providing 'human' security, not endangering unprotected people, remaining open to democratic legal control, informing the public while maintaining a healthy level of secrecy, cooperation and the division of labour with other security institutions, as well as making use of other countries' best practices.

---

7 Former Intelligence Department President Sabri Uzun claims that Turkey would save USD 3 billion if security services were carried out by a single agency. See his communiqué entitled, 'İç Güvenlik Hizmetlerinin İdeal Yapılanması,' presented at the International Domestic Security Conference, 22-24 January 2004, Police Academy, Ankara. An example which illustrates the lack of cooperation between various agencies, surfaced when the Gendarmerie General Command carried out an operation in Syria in 2003, apprehending 22 suspects and bringing them to Turkey. However, the police intelligence/İDB stated that they were trailing Hilmi Tuğluoğlu, who was among those taken into custody by the gendarmerie, waiting for him to meet with Azad Ekinci and Gürcan Baç, [the 'bigger fish' who allegedly gave the orders for the terrorist bombings in Istanbul] and claimed that 'the gendarmerie acted too fast, ruining the operation.' See, 'Polisten jandarmaya sitem,' Hürriyet, 3 December 2003.

National Intelligence Organisation

Ferhat Ünlü[*]

The History: Secret Organisations during the Ottoman Empire

The modern intelligence activities of the Turks were, to a great extent, shaped by the concept of 'Westernisation'. As the decline and demise of the Ottoman Empire was blamed on the lack of intelligence, the first modern intelligence agency was subsequently formed, based on the example of the French Secret Police.[1] According to a book attributed to Mavroyani Paşa (who was of Greek origin), the first intelligence organisation in the modern sense was built in the middle of the 19th century, when the activities of foreign agents increased, in order to monitor possible riots in the Balkans. Paşa was the court doctor of Sultan Abdülhamid II (1876-1909), an emperor who was known to attach great importance to intelligence. It is interesting to note that first Ottoman intelligence organisation appointed Cinivis Efendi as the chairman, who was also of Greek origin. However, when the organisation failed to meet expectations, Sultan Abdülaziz (1861-1876) formed another one in 1863. The appointed chairman, Baron C. was said to have been removed from office due to his activities against the country.[2]

The most important of the secret organisations in the Ottoman Empire was the 'Yıldız' (Star) intelligence organisation which was founded by Abdülhamid II in 1880. This organisation continued to exist until 1908, when the 2nd Constitutional Monarchy was declared.[3] The organisation later played an important role in the founding of the Special Organisation (Teşkilat-ı Mahsusa), which was the intelligence organisation of the Union and Progress Party (Ittihat ve Terakki), and set an

---

* Journalist specialising in matters of security, intelligence and terrorism

1 Although it is said that the first modern intelligence organisation of the Ottoman Empire was under French influence, there are also claims that the organisation was established with the instigation of the British. According to these claims, the British Ambassador Startford Canning's suggestions played a role in the founding of the organisation. There are other claims stating that Cinivis, who was the first chief of the organisation, was a double agent. The reference for all the information about the period in question is the booklet attributed to Mavroyani Pasha. There are also claims that Mavroyani was a double agent who worked as a doctor in the imperial palace. In the times that followed, German influence was greater on Ottoman intelligence.

2 Erdal İlter, Milli İstihbarat Teşkilatı Tarihçesi: Milli Emniyet Hizmetleri Riyaseti (M.E.H/MAH) (1927/1965) (Ankara, 2002). see http://www.mit.gov.tr/tarihce/giris_1.html.

3 Ibid, see http://www.mit.gov.tr/tarihce/birinci_bolum_B.html

important precedent in the Turkish intelligence tradition. It embraced a more domestic approach to intelligence, partly due to its limited means, and partly due to the chaos caused by the internal struggles of the time. The Republic of Turkey's National Security Service (Milli Emniyet Hizmeti, MEH) and, later, the National Intelligence Organization (Milli İstihbarat Teşkilatı, MİT) practiced this concept of work, which occasionally generated criticism.

Teşkilat-ı Mahsusa – Special Organisation

It would not be wrong to say that the groundwork for Turkish national intelligence was laid by the Special Organisation. Unlike other secret organisations of the Ottoman Empire, an empire that based its existence on the bonding concept of religious unity (ümmetçilik) until its demise, the Special Organisation resembled the national intelligence agency of a nation state. Although the organisation's main purpose was to unite the world of Islam around the idea of being Ottoman, it was formed by Minister of Defence Enver Paşa in the aftermath of the riots that were inspired by nationalism and the Balkan Wars. Its activities, which consisted principally of espionage, played an important role in shaping the idea of national intelligence.

The Special Organisation, which became an official and international organisation after the Union and Progress Party came to power, was active from the Indian sub-continent to Africa, from the Middle East to the Balkans and from the Arab Peninsula to Mid-Asia. Mustafa Kemal Atatürk took part in some of the organisation's activities.

According to research based on the archives of the Military History and Strategic Studies Board (Askeri Tarih ve Stratejik Etüt Başkanlığı, ATASE), the Special Organisation was established on 17 November 1913.[4] Its first chairman was Staff Major Süleyman Askeri Bey, its second was Ali Bey Başhampa and Hüsamettin Ertürk was the last.

The Special Organisation was a modern organisation that embraced an operational working style. It was structured around small military squads that conducted guerrilla activities, specifically in the Caucasus and the Middle East. Kuşçubaşı Eşref was one of the organisation's most renowned leaders at a time when the organisation had 30'000 members. He later became the head of the region of Arabia and was involved in fighting tactical battles against the British agent Lawrence of Arabia.

The Special Organisation was later abolished by Hüsamettin Ertürk, after Enver Paşa and his associates fled abroad in a German submarine.

The National Security Service (MEH/MAH)

The National Security Service (Milli Emniyet Hizmeti Riyaseti, MEH/MAH), the precursor of the MİT, was established at the direct request of Atatürk immediately following the founding of the Republic, to meet Turkey's need for a modern intelli-

---

4 Ibid, see http://www.mit.gov.tr/tarihce/birinci_bolum_B.html

gence organisation. The organisation was founded on 16 December 1926 by a Council of Ministers decision under President Mustafa Kemal Atatürk, and for ease of pronunciation it also used the initials MAH. The acronym MAH was later interpreted inaccurately as the Service to the National Deed (Milli Amele Hizmet), Service to the National Deeds (Milli Âmâle Hizmet) and the National Public Order Service (Millî Âsâyiş Hizmeti).[5]

The MAH has been one of the most misinterpreted acronyms in the history of the Republic, so much so that it has been cited as the Service to the National Deed (Milli Amele Hizmet) even by experts and authors of the MİT's unofficial history.[6] In addition, even Mehmet Eymür, a former member of the MİT used this explanation in his book Analysis (Analiz).[7]

The MEH, the first secret service of the newborn Republic, faced numerous hardships whilst conducting its espionage and counter-espionage activities in a period that also covered WWII. During this time, its activities mostly focused on espionage attempts against the young Republic, the activities of the Ottoman dynasty and their supporters, and preventive measures against activities which were considered subversive and separatist according to official ideology. This included Armenianism, Hellenism, Kurdism, communism and opposition to the regime. The organisation aimed to facilitate society's acceptance of reforms based on the modernisation principle, whilst eliminating a fundamentalist approach.[8]

The military undoubtedly exercised a strong influence on the intelligence sector, and prior to the founding of MİT in 1965, seven out of the eleven MEH chiefs had a military background and had been in the Turkish Armed Forces prior to assuming the role of Secret Service Chief. These seven were: Şükrü Ali Ögel (1886-1973), Mehmet Naci Perkel (1889-1969), Behçet Türkmen (1899-1972), Emin Çobanoğlu (1901-1983), Ziya Selışık (1900-1966), Naci Aşkun (1906-1982), Mehmet Fuat Doğu (1914-2004). However, the remaining four, Hüseyin Avni Göktürk (1901-1983), Ahmet Salih Korur (1905-1982) and Ahmet Celâlettin Karasapan (1899-1974), were civil servants who were appointed to lead the intelligence agency after working in various civil service posts.

17 years after its establishment, the MEH set secrecy aside, the presidency was attached to the prime minister by means of a law implemented on 29 June 1943, and the National Security Service became the National Security Services in 1954.[9]

In Dr. Erdal İlter's book of the MİT's History, the MEH's activities were briefly listed as follows:[10]

---

5 Ibid, see http://www.mit.gov.tr/tarihce/ikinci_bolum_D4.html#D4

6 Tuncay Özkan, Bir Gizli Servisin Tarihi: MİT (İstanbul: Milliyet Yayınları, 1996), p. 99.

7 'Analiz 06:MAHT'tan MİT'e,' Anadolu Türk İnterneti (ATİN), 1 August 1991. See http://www.atin.org/detail.asp?cmd=articledetail&articleid=115

8 İlter, Milli İstihbarat Teşkilatı Tarihçesi: Milli Emniyet Hizmetleri Riyaseti (M.E.H/MAH) (1927/1965). See http://www.mit.gov.tr/tarihce/ikinci_bolum_E2.html#E2a

9 Ibid, <see http://www.mit.gov.tr/tarihce/ikinci_bolum_D4.html#D5>

10 Ibid, <see http://www.mit.gov.tr/tarihce/ikinci_bolum_E2_1.html>

a. Confront Armenians, 'Kurdists,' those inclined to establish Red Lazistan in the Black Sea region, Mussolini's Italy, which is believed to have ambitions for an assault in the Mediterranean, and the activities of the Greek Patriarchate.
b. Contribute to the nationalisation of commercial enterprises owned by foreigners.
c. Play a key role in the definition of borders and the annexation of Hatay to Turkey.
d. Fight against foreign secret services during and after WWII.

The Establishment and Development of the National Intelligence Organization (MİT)

The MİT, which is the current intelligence organisation of the Republic of Turkey, was established when the National Intelligence Organisation Law Number 644 took effect on 22 July 1965. With this law, the organisation known as MEH or MAH became the MİT. The National Intelligence Coordination Committee (Milli İstihbarat Koordinasyon Kurulu, MİKK) was also established as part of this law, under the MİT Undersecretary, to coordinate with the National Security Committee (Milli Güvenlik Kurulu, MGK) and the Turkish Armed Forces (Türk Silahlı Kuvvetleri, TSK).

The economic, social, political and military changes brought about by both the Second World War and the Cold War had a notable influence on the establishment and development of the MİT. From 1965 to the collapse of the Soviet Union in 1990, many of the MİT's activities exhibited traces of secret US policies involving its war against communism and the Soviet Union.

The MİT was a powerful and modern organisation, as far as its working style and the resources available to it were concerned, and particularly when compared to the National Security Services. The MAH retained its name and became the intelligence gathering unit within the MİT. With the implementation of the Governmental Intelligence Services and National Intelligence Organisation Code Number 2937 on 1 January 1984, the MİT's main duties were established and the organisation became directly responsible to the prime minister. In 1984, the sub-unit of the MAH was abolished and its duties were transferred to Internal and External Intelligence Presidencies.[11]

On 2 March 1966, retired Lieutenant General Fuat Doğu was appointed as the MİT's Undersecretary. Doğu had a great influence on both the organisation and on the many young intelligence members who were recruited during his time and subsequently become directors in the 1980s, 1990s and 2000. The current undersecretary, Emre Taner, his predecessor Şenkal Atasagun, and the deputy undersecretary during the Özal era, Hiram Abas,[12] were all recruited during Fuat Doğu's time. Also greatly influenced by him was Mehmet Eymür, who wrote the first MİT report while

[11] Ibid, see http://www.mit.gov.tr/tarihce/ikinci_bolum_F.html#F
[12] Abas was killed on 26 September 1990. The Revolutionary Left (Devrimci Sol), an illegal organisation claimed responsibility.

he was the Head of Security Board and was recruited a few months prior to Doğu's appointment as undersecretary. In his book of memoirs Analysis (Analiz), Eymür mentions Doğu's influence on Abas.

Historically Controversial Points about the MİT

In its 41 year history, the focus of controversy has centred on the armed forces' influence on the MİT. The very first undersecretary, Avni Kantan (1910-1966) graduated from a military academy and his successor, Fuat Doğu (1914-2004) was made undersecretary prior to his retirement from the army. Nurettin Ersin (1918-2005), undersecretary from 1971-73, also performed various duties in the TSK, and Bülent Türker (1926 -), who acted as deputy undersecretary from 1973-74 and undersecretary from 1980-81, was also a soldier. The following were also all members of the military: Bahattin Özülker (1914-1974), who was appointed in the same year, Hamza Gürgüç (1913-1988) the undersecretary from 1974-78, Adnan Ersöz (1917-1991),[13] who was Gürgüç's successor for a year, Burhanettin Bigalı (1927-), who was on duty from 1981-86, Hayri Ündül (1929-), who was the undersecretary from 1986-89 and Teoman Koman, who was in charge from 1986-89. Most were appointed before their retirement from the TSK and in short, not a single civilian was appointed undersecretary until 1992.

Only three civilian undersecretaries were appointed during the MEH period, which highlighted the military heritage that was implicit in the development of the Turkish security sector and especially in the MİT. In 1992, during Tansu Çiller's tenure as prime minister, a former foreign ministry official named Sönmez Köksal, was appointed undersecretary as a result of the government's attempts to gain greater control over the organisation. Şenkal Atasagun, who was appointed in 1998, was the first civilian undersecretary to come from the MİT ranks.

Hiram Abas, who was appointed deputy undersecretary during Turgut Özal's presidency, as a result of government attempts to purge the military's influence on the MİT, stressed the influence of the armed forces and made the following suggestions in a letter to Özal:

> 'In democracies, since the duty of protecting the regime against the population is not performed by the [secret] services, then the military and the intelligence service need not be too close. In democracies, because the mission of intelligence is mainly focused on other countries, and because intelligence is considered as a specialisation, it is preferable that the senior ranks of the [intelligence] organisations are filled by intelligence officers who have had on-the-job training and hands-on experience. In our state, it is not yet clear which office the MİT is attached to.'[14]

---

13 Ersöz died as a result of an armed assault.

14 'Analiz 07: Gehlen ve İstihbarat,' Anadolu Türk İnterneti (ATİH), 1 Ağustos]. See http://www.atin.org/detail.asp?cmd=articledetail&articleid=116

Abas stated that the MİT did not even notify prime ministers of the military's plans for coups. Indeed, several authors have written interesting articles on the fact that the MİT did not communicate the coup plans of the TSK's higher command to the prime ministers in 1971 and 1980.[15]

It was during the 12 March 1971 era (marked by the military's ultimatum against the government) that rumours of the fact that the MİT used torture reached their peak. It was known that people interrogated at the Ziverbey Villa were subjected to physiological and psychological coercion. Amongst those subjected to torture at Ziverbey were retired officers Talat Turhan and Numan Esin, who were involved in the 27 May coup, as well as journalists and writers such as Doğan Avcıoğlu, İlhan Selçuk and İlhami Soysal.

The introverted structure of the intelligence organisation was another controversial point. It was claimed that the organisation gave priority to internal enemies in its categorisation of internal and external enemy concepts, which led to practices which harmed the democracy. It was also understood that the organisation tapped the phones of politicians, assembled reports about senior personnel in the government (known to the public as 'profiling') and that these reports influenced appointments within the government. According to Faruk Bildirici's book the Land of Secret Ears (Gizli Kulaklar Ülkesi), Turgut Özal found numerous electronic bugs around the building when the family moved to the prime minister's residence, and because of his distrust of the MİT, Özal personally supervised the electronic counter-measures.[16]

After the strengthening of the police force's intelligence unit in the 1990s, and as part of the fight against the PKK, phones were tapped intensively. From 1985 to 1996, both the police and the MİT performed frequent joint technical stakeouts. The Susurluk Report by the former director of the Prime Minister's Inspection Committee highlights the struggle that ensued between Mehmet Ağar, the Director General of Security and subsequent Minister of Internal Affairs, and Mehmet Eymür, who was the director of the MİT Anti-Terror Centre.[17]

The conflict, widely known as the Ağar-Eymür struggle, was the central point of the debates involving murders committed by the Gendarmerie Intelligence and Anti-Terror Organisation (Jandarma İstihbarat ve Terörle Mücadele Teşkilati, JİTEM) in Eastern and South Eastern Turkey, as well as the Susurluk incident which involved the police force, the JİTEM and the MİT. It is understood that the National Intelligence Organisation made two secret assassination attempts on Abdullah Öca-

---

15 In 1971, when the Minister of Foreign Affairs of the time, İhsan Sabri Çağlayangil was invited to Iran by Shah, the Shah said to Çağlayangil during the meetings: 'In a few months, the army will make a coup in Turkey.' See Cüneyt Arcayürek, Darbeler ve Gizli Servisler (Bilgi Yayınevi, 1989), p. 61

16 It is significant that bugging equipment was found in the prime minister's residence after the first democratic election following the coup of 12 September.

17 Kutlu Savaş, Susurluk Report (online version). See http://siyaset.bilkent.edu.tr/susurluk/kutlu/p3.html

lan,[18] and Mahmut Yıldırım, known as 'Yeşil,' served in both of the Öcalan operations. During that time, the top executives of the security sector were so relaxed, that they did not refrain from involving the Viranşehir Mayor, Halil Keleşabdioğlu, in the attempt to assassinate Öcalan in Damascus by detonating a minibus loaded with a ton of C-4 explosives. However, Öcalan survived the attack and another assassination attempt in Beirut also missed its target. The police team led by Mehmet Ağar, also planned assassination assaults against Öcalan during that period.[19]

The examples of Abdullah Çatlı[20] and Yıldırım (Yeşil), the MİT's staff policies and the use of civilian operatives both abroad and within the country led to justified criticism. According to Kutlu Savaşlı's Susurluk Report, the MİT undersecretary of the time, Sönmez Köksal, answered questions on this subject as follows, 'Do you think that the MİT always works with respectable people?'[21]

One of the points of reference on this subject is Tuncay Özkan's book 'The History of a Secret Service – MİT' (Bir Gizli Servisin Tarihi – MİT), which contains important information regarding the problems associated with the MİT's working conditions, its limited budget and, most importantly, insufficient personnel numbers.[22] Özkan states that priority should have been given to the problem associated with the managerial structure which was inherited from the military.[23]

As the only representative of the national intelligence network from 1965 to the 1990s, the MİT was therefore required to 'share its power' in the 1990s, with the police force and the JİTEM, an organisation which was better known for its kidnappings and assassinations. One should also bear in mind that until the 1990s, the MİT was under the influence of the military.

In developed countries, there is often more than one intelligence organisation. For instance, in the United States, the Central Intelligence Agency (CIA) is responsible for foreign intelligence, whereas the Federal Bureau of Investigation (FBI) is responsible for domestic intelligence. Similarly, in Great Britain, MI6 covers foreign intelligence and MI5 looks into domestic intelligence. In recent years, the suggestion has frequently arisen that the MİT should focus on foreign intelligence whilst the police force investigates domestic intelligence affairs. However, the MİT does not favour these suggestions, and as stated in its official website in 2005, it supports the idea that domestic and foreign intelligence is run by the MİT in an integrated fashion.[24]

The purging of the MİT's military heritage, and its transformation into a more civilian and transparent institution, started in the 1990s and accelerated in the new millennium. As a result of this, the organisation is now run by civilians and the

---

18 MİT memo dated 1 December 1996. See Ferhat Ünlü, Eymür'ün Aynası: Eski MİT Yöneticisi Anlatıyor (İstanbul: Metis Yayınları, 2001), p. 66, p. 74.

19 Savaş, Susurluk Report. See http://siyaset.bilkent.edu.tr/susurluk/kutlu/p3.html

20 Far-right militant used by the MİT in the 1980s. Died in the Susurluk accident on 3 November 1996.

21 Savaş, Susurluk Report. See http://siyaset.bilkent.edu.tr/susurluk/kutlu/p4.html

22 Özkan, Bir Gizli Servisin Tarihi: MİT, p. 332.

23 Ibid p. 310.

24 See http://www.mit.gov.tr/merak-Cevap17.html

last three undersecretaries, Sönmez Köksal, Şenkal Atasagun and Taner were originally from the Ministry of Foreign Affairs. As part of the movement towards greater transparency, the MİT has been releasing information about the organisation on its website for the last five years, albeit in a limited fashion.

The MIT Developments in 2005

The Impact of Democratic Advances and New Laws on MİT's Working System and Transparency, as Part of the EU Membership Process

It is widely believed that the democratisation efforts that are part of the European Union's (EU) membership process have had an impact on the MİT and partially damaged the working system of the organisation. The efforts accelerated particularly during the Justice and Development Party's (Adalet ve Kalkınma Partisi, AKP) rule and the fight against terrorism.

The MİT argued that the Turkish Penal Code (Türk Ceza Kanun, TCK) No. 5237, brought limitations on electronic eavesdropping which could cause problems in the fight against terrorism. The TCK made it onto the public agenda following intensive debate at the beginning of 2005 and went into effect on 1 June 2005 instead of the planned date of 1 April 2005. MİT Undersecretary Şenkal Atasagun presented a special MIT draft to Prime Minister Recep Tayyip Erdoğan in a meeting where the Minister of Internal Affairs, Abdülkadir Aksu, Minister of National Defence, Vecdi Gönül, Minister of Justice, Cemil Çiçek, Gendarmerie Commander General Fevzi Türkeri and Director General of Police, Gökhan Aydıner, were also present.[25] The draft in question gave the MİT the authority to tap phones in urgent situations with the permission of the undersecretary.[26] However, it is not known whether the MİT received the authority for eavesdropping as a result of this.

The new Anti-Terror Law, which is another draft closely related to MİT's working system, has not been introduced because of the controversy surrounding it. The document, which was prepared by the Ministry of Justice, is of a draft bill nature and contains articles that would enhance the work of all security units, and especially that of the intelligence organisation. There is a widespread belief that the bill contains anti-democratic elements, and these concerns have been expressed by members of parliament. It has been argued that the bill paves the way for the mischaracterisation of people who have no insurgent affiliations as 'terrorists' and that the draft should be revised for compliance with EU criteria. As of February 2006, the draft had not been given to the Turkish Grand National Assembly (Türkiye Büyük Millet Meclisi, TBMM) Justice Commission and rumours suggest that it has been shelved.

Although the MİT made important progress in matters of transparency, the fact that some of its members have been involved in scandals invariably tarnishes its image. In 2005, the MİT investigated External Operations Director Kaşif Kozinoğlu's alleged connections to the organised crime leader Alaattin Çakıcı, following

[25] 'MİT telefonunu istiyor,' Milliyet, 10 March 2005.

[26] 'MİT' ten dinleme ısrarı,' Milliyet, 31 March 2005.

accusations that Kozinoğlu 'assisted a criminal organisation.'[27] In the conclusion and comments section of a three-page report, it was concluded that 'in the carrying out of the duties he was given, Kozinoğlu has acted in compliance with the organisation's working principles.'[28] Kozinoğlu's subsequent acquittal, however, damaged the principle of transparency that the MIT had formally embraced.

Although the problem of transparency is related to the staff structure and the organisation's traditional working style, the real problem centres on the fact that the universal working style of the secret services is not exactly compatible with democratisation. Intelligence organisations use conspiracies, coups, assassinations, psychological warfare, and act in total secrecy. In an environment where a lack of supervision prevails, opportunities arise for secret service members such as Kozinoğlu to become involved in corrupt relations.

Repercussions of the Early Retirement of Şenkal Atasagun, the First Civilian Undersecretary promoted from the Ranks of MİT

Şenkal Atasagun was appointed as MİT Undersecretary in February 1998, while Mesut Yılmaz was prime minister. He performed this duty for approximately seven years, during a time when important developments were taking place in Turkish politics and the security sector. Atasagun was the longest serving undersecretary and the first to come from the organisation's own ranks. Born in 1941, Atasagun was a graduate of Galatasaray High School and the Faculty of Political Science at Grenoble University in France, and entered the MİT in 1967.

It was believed that Atasagun would resign after the AKP came to power and several newspapers named the retired General, Edip Başer, as his likely successor. However, the appointment never took place and Atasagun remained in post until May 2005, before retiring of his own accord on 11 June 2005.

Atasagun's early retirement caused widespread media speculation that internal conflict within the government was behind this move.[29] One article claimed that

---

27 The former Head of the Supreme Court of Appeals, Eraslan Özkaya was also said to be involved in the scandal in question.

28 'Tek soruda aklandı,' Milliyet, 17 May 2005.

29 The following was reported in a news article in Milliyet Newspaper,: 'It was claimed that Atasagun's mysterious retirement decision had to do mainly with the debates concerning MİT Head of the External Operations Kaşif Kozinoğlu, and that Atasagun and the government had disagreements over working principles, especially in the last four months. It was recorded that the first crisis between MİT and the government broke out when a passport for former MİT member Faik Meral was found on Alaattin Çakıcı, who was apprehended in Austria, and that the scandal involving former Head of the Supreme Court of Appeals Eraslan Özkaya, Çakıcı and Kozinoğlu put a further strain on the relations.' In another article in Hürriyet Newspaper, the following has been said about the early retirement decision: 'According to insider information, Atasagun who had problems in his relation with Prime Minister Erdoğan, had been considering early retirement for some time, and reached a decision in order to 'prevent harm to the organisation.' Atasagun, whose term of office would normally have ended in 2006, presumably told his close colleagues about his problems in his relations with the government and said, 'We have to save the

the MİT had failed in its intelligence forecasting concerning the January elections in Iraq, which caused an air of unease in the government.[30] It was also argued that a report was presented to the Prime Minister's Office, containing intelligence about the Turkmen parties gaining 30 seats in the Iraqi Parliament. However, at the end of the election they had won only three seats.

This news was not officially denied on the MİT official website even though the MİT, on occasion, does formally deny articles in the press. It is therefore not difficult to assume that the denials were based on the content of the news, as well as its repercussions. As the MİT does not openly or regularly inform the media of their activities, news concerning the organisation is typically based on information received from confidential sources, which can lead to speculative and manipulative reporting. It should also be kept in mind that speculations concerning the MİT are usually released by the media first, and often before they have actually occurred. Atasagun's retirement was a case in point.

Debates Concerning MİT's Gaining of Authority gained by a Court Decision to Tap Phones and E-Mails in Turkey

In 2005, the issues of electronic surveillance and eavesdropping, one of the most controversial subjects in the dilemma concerning the fight against terrorism versus democracy debate, was unearthed by the press. When a court order gave the MİT the authority to tap all phones in Turkey, intensive public debate ensued.

For years, electronic eavesdropping has dominated debates about the Turkish intelligence units and in the past, information about the MİT tapping phones without court orders was published both in the press and in books about the subject. Unlike the police force, the MİT did not require a court order to tap phones, until a short while ago.

The electronic surveillance incident of 2005 brought the subject back into the spotlight. Before elaborating on the events, the difference between surveillance and eavesdropping should be explained. Electronic surveillance refers to the technical surveillance of a communications device in order to determine who has been contacted. It is not possible, therefore, to find out about the nature of a phone call through mere technical surveillance. Electronic eavesdropping, on the other hand, is the recording of all the conversations that take place over a communications device.

On 1 June 2005, the newspaper Vatan hit the news stands with the headline 'The document that will shake Turkey'. It revealed that the MİT had the authority to undertake surveillance of all communications in Turkey, thanks to a decision by the Sixth High Criminal Court of Diyarbakır. A brief summary of the article is as follows:

'The National Intelligence Organisation has put all kinds of communications in Turkey under surveillance in the last two months. All landline phone calls, includ-

---

organisation. In order to prevent further harm to the organisation, my early retirement would be well-advised.'

30 'MİT Müsteşarı Şenkal Atasagun' un neden emekliliğini istediğini açıklıyoruz;' Haftalık, 29 June – 5 July 2005.

ing overseas calls, all calls on Turkcell, Telsim, Avea mobile phones, all e-mail correspondence, the most detailed information about fax and SMS transmissions were handed over to the MİT by court order.'[31]

On the same day the news was published, and on the basis of the court's decision, the Turkish Penal Code (Türk Ceza Kanunu, TCK), Article 22 of the Constitution and Articles 2, 4, 11, 16 of Code Number 4422 ceased to be effective. In other words, the MİT had the authority to put all phones in Turkey under surveillance just before the new TCK took effect.

The surveillance news even caused reactions amongst the Council of Ministers, and Deputy Prime Minister Mehmet Ali Şahin commented that 'This can never be approved.' It was also discovered that the MİT's initial application for the same decision to be taken to the Eleventh High Criminal Court of Ankara had been refuted, and therefore they subsequently applied to the Sixth High Criminal Court of Diyarbakır.[32]

MİT was swift in making a statement:

> 'It is observed that the media published news about the National Intelligence Organization on the 1st and 2nd of June 2005, which creates the impression that communication devices belonging to all people and institutions are under illegal surveillance. The National Intelligence Organisation takes pains over performing all its activities in accordance with a legal basis and within the law that defines its foundation and its duties. The latest surveillance and detection work that was requested by our organisation and that raised great interest in the media was realised in order to provide national security intelligence for the public good, within the mainframe of the court's decision, and only within the scope of the mission, akin to its precursors.'[33]

After the news was published, many people and institutions filed criminal complaints against the MİT. However, the public prosecutor of Ankara decided not to process the complaints, and the Office of the Prosecutor deemed the surveillance incident as 'due and proper.'[34]

Another important decision concerning stakeouts and eavesdropping was taken in July 2005. The bill which had given authority to the MİT, the police and the gendarmerie to carry out eavesdropping via telephones was accepted by the TBMM General Council. It stipulated that eavesdropping was to be made from a single centre that was part of Turkish Telecom.[35]

---

31 'Türkiye'yi sarsacak belge;' Vatan, 1 June 2005.

32 'MİT izlemesi Bakanlar Kurulu'nda; Milliyet, 2 June 2005.

33 MİT Press Release, 2 June 2005. See http://www.mit.gov.tr/basin23.html

34 'Savcı: Dinleme Yasal;' Milliyet, 25 June 2005.

35 'Telefon dinleme yetkisinde son nokta:' CNN Türk; 4 July 2005. See http://www.cnnturk.com/HABER/haber_detay.asp?PID=318&HID=1&haberID=108432

Emre Taner's Appointment as MİT Undersecretary and the Kurdish Problem

Emre Taner entered the MİT in 1967, just like his predecessor Şenkal Atasagun. A political science graduate from Ankara University, Taner worked in different levels of the organisation and influential journalists described Taner as an expert on the Kurdish problem. During his time as Deputy Undersecretary, Taner was authorised by the government to meet the PKK's Leader Abdullah Öcalan in İmralı prison.[36] He as also known to be in the intelligence team that interrogated Öcalan during a meeting where such a methodology should not have been practiced.

After Taner's appointment as the MİT undersecretary in June 2005, the government took revolutionary steps to address the Kurdish problem. Certainly, the government's decisions and conjecture played a larger role than Taner's expertise on the 'Kurdish problem ' in this. In recent times, however, the view that terrorism and the Kurdish problem could be eliminated through economic, social and political measures, found support in the security sector. This view has also been expressed by military officials on a number of different occasions.

Taner visited the city of Selahaddin in October 2005, specifically to discuss the Kurdish problem, the PKK and issues in northern Iraq with Massoud Barzani, the leader of the Kurdish Democratic Party's (Partiya Demokrata Kurdistanê, KDP). This visit was a first from the viewpoint of the Turkish government which had a short-term diplomatic crises with the US, based on the reason that Kurdish authority in northern Iraq was becoming stronger every day after the Second Gulf War. Although MİT officials might have met with Massoud Barzani or Celal Talabani in the past, such meetings probably took place when Barzani or Talabani visited Ankara, as there is no information regarding a former MİT undersecretary's visit to Barzani or Talabani in northern Iraq.

The meeting was brought into the spotlight by Hürriyet Editor-in-Chief, Ertuğrul Özkök, when he was quoted in the English-language newspaper The New Anatolian published in Ankara.[37] The story was broken first by the newspapers owner, İlnur Çevik, who is a journalist known to have good relations with the northern Iraqi leaders.

---

[36] Ertuğrul Özkök, 'The first extraordinary visit in İmralı;' Hürriyet, 6 December 2005. ['(...) I believe this visit made by Emre Taner to İmralı, is much more important than his meeting with Barzani. Taner is an interesting MİT member. He built almost his whole career on the 'Kurdish problem.' For instance, he knows Barzani, with whom he met in the recent past, since his [Barzani's] childhood. Because when he was meeting with Barzani Senior in northern Iraq 40 years ago, the son was also present. That child has now grown up and became the head of the Iraqi Kurdish movement. In other words, he and Emre Taner have a past. Taner always says to people close to him, 'I learned the Kurdish problem from Musa Anter.' Because he was one of the MİT Members who followed Anter. He took an active role in his four arrests, and he interrogated him. 'He is one of the MİT Members who find it utterly wrong that Anter was killed.' He looks at the Kurdish problem from a realistic perspective (...)'].

[37] Ertuğrul Özkök, 'MİT Müsteşarı gölgeden çıktı,' Hürriyet, 24 November 2005.

In a news article on the subject, it was said that Taner asked for Barzani's help to eliminate the PKK from northern Iraq. Barzani's answers to the requests made by the Turkish side were listed as follows:

> 'Alternatives other than [military] operations should be taken into account for the elimination of the organisation. These operations yield no results.'
> 'If the PKK militants are to come to Turkey, shouldn't the Law of 'Reintegrating Citizens to Society' be used more efficiently?'[38]

Another article stated that 'the Kurdish authority in northern Iraq is set to take action in cooperation with Turkey, in order to eradicate the PKK. Barzani will declare the anti-PKK cooperation to last until the PKK lays down arms and is completely eradicated.This declaration targets the international community and Barzani favours Turkey's request on this matter.'[39]

On 2 December 2005, the MİT officially denied the statements: 'In the articles in question, some of the claims are false and do not reflect reality.'[40] It is interesting to note, however, that the MİT chose not to deny Hürriyet Editor-in-Chief Ertuğrul Özkök's articles about Taner's meeting with Öcalan in İmralı and his visit to Barzani, deciding instead to release a formal denial of two articles which appeared in weekly magazines on the same day.

Despite the denial, it was later repeated in news articles that the Kurdish authority in northern Iraq, under the leadership of Barzani, did not favour a military operation against the PKK. In another article, it was alleged that during a conversation between Barzani and Taner, the former asserted: 'Do not expect me to take armed action against the PKK. The times of Kurds killing Kurds, and using Kurds to eliminate Kurds is over. Forget it.'[41] The emerging picture revealed that the Kurdish Leader Barzani had refrained from taking military action against the PKK 'only because Ankara requested it.'

Taner's visit to Barzani could be seen essentially as a manifestation of Turkey's desire to regain the initiative that it lost in northern Iraq after the bill of 1 March was refuted, and to solve the PKK problem, if not the Kurdish problem, by using Barzani's influence.

The MİT's Budget - Publicly Declared For the First Time in Its History

One of the important developments that reflected the MİT's principle of transparency in 2005, was the public declaration of its projected 2006 budget for the first time in national intelligence history. As part of the new budget policy, the MİT's

38 'MİT Müsteşarı ile Barzani ne konuştu?,' Haftalık, 2-8 December 2005.
39 'Welcome to Kürdistan,' Tempo, 2 December 2005.
40 MİT Press Release, 2 December 2005. <See http://www.mit.gov.tr/basin24.html
41 'Kritik diyalog,' Bugün, 23 January 2006.

resources were stated as a total of YTL 352.5 million by the Turkish Grand National Assembly.[42]

This figure was the largest budget ever reserved for the MİT. Of this, YTL 255 million were allocated for the MİT's personnel which included the security expenses of YTL 74.5 million. A total of YTL 44.5 million was reserved for the procurement of goods and services, YTL 31 million for capital expenditures, and YTL 30 million was reserved for investments. The organisation had an allowance of YTL 126.5 million in 2000, 117.5 YTL million in 2001, YTL 172.09 million in 2002, YTL 262 million in 2003 (in compliance with the instructions to economise, YTL 13 million and YTL 113 million was saved from the 2003 budget) and YTL 301 million in 2004.[43] The budget allocated for 2005 was YTL 296.1.[44]

The FBI and CIA Chiefs' Visits to Turkey

Of great importance to the security policies of Turkey were the individual visits made by FBI Chief Robert Mueller and CIA Chief Porter Goss to Turkey in December 2005. As part of their visits, the FBI and CIA Chiefs met with MİT Undersecretary Taner.

Turkish-US relations were altered after the rejection of the 1 March bill that would have allowed the American soldiers to enter Turkish soil before the Second Gulf War. The refusal to pass the bill damaged cooperation on matters of both security and intelligence. In spite of this, however, the high level CIA and FBI visits emphasised the desire for intensive cooperation from both sides, particularly concerning terrorism.

After Al-Qaida's attacks on 11 September 2001, the United States repeatedly stressed that Turkey was experienced in fighting terrorism and as such, the United States were looking for ways of cooperation. In the same vein, it became clear that Turkey needed full US support and cooperation in its fight against the PKK. Ankara claimed that the PKK's existence in northern Iraq was condoned by the United States and the Kurdish authority in the region, and frequently called for sincere cooperation with the United States. It is therefore, not hard to assume that the possibilities for cooperation in the fight against terror were sought during the CIA and FBI Chiefs' visits.

Although the purpose of the meetings was clear, news in the Turkish press about the CIA and FBI Chiefs' visits to Turkey was contradictory. It would not be inaccurate to suggest that news about US willingness to provide full support to Turkey on the PKK issue and its eradication from northern Iraq was somewhat exaggerated. The United States had not undertaken any military preparations to eradicate the PKK from the region and, even if that had been the case, it was also known to the Turkish side that eradication by the use of arms would never be straightforward.

In conclusion, reliable and detailed information about the subjects that have been discussed on the CIA and FBI Chiefs' visits to Turkey was hard to find. How-

42 'MİT bütçesi sessiz geçti,' Milliyet, 11 November 2005.

43 For the MİT budget, see http://www.mit.gov.tr/stat_butce.html

44 The chart concerning the MİT budget can be found in Appendix 1.

ever, as previously mentioned, it is most probable that the general tenor of the meetings was to discuss ways in which the intelligence agencies could cooperate in the fight against terrorism. Indeed, in a press conference organised prior to his return to the United States, Mueller stated that the meetings focused on regional issues and joint intelligence efforts. Mueller concluded that 'With the improvement of relations, strengthening of personal connections and advanced intelligence sharing, we will achieve results together.[45]

The Reaction of Former MİT Deputy Undersecretary Cevat Öneş to the Kurdish Problem

Several months after retiring from his position as Deputy Undersecretary, and much to the surprise of the intelligence community, Cevat Öneş wrote an article about the Kurdish problem, security and democracy for the Newspaper Radikal on 7 December 2005. Due to the nature of their work, and even after their retirement, MİT members by and large refrain from expressing their views on the organisation or security policies in general as part of a tradition as well as the law. In Law No. 2937, which defines the MİT's duties and responsibilities, it is deemed essential that all information pertaining to its duties and activities are kept secret. As stipulated by Article 27 of the aforementioned law, the MİT has the right to sue its former employees who make statements or publish articles after their retirement, should it wish to do so. As a result of this, relations between the MİT administration and some of its former members who violated this rule have been damaged.

The article in question argued that the Kurdish problem could be solved through democracy, under the headline, 'Taboos are being broken.' In his article Öneş wrote:

> 'Turkey can solve its Kurdish problem, and other national issues, by strengthening its democratic secular institutions and at once fulfil EU conditionality criteria. This is certainly preferable to other regional alternatives and the risks that an Iraq-Syria-Iran triangle could pose. Such a development can create new horizons and new opportunities for Turkey in the region and in the global balance of power.'[46]

Öneş's article sparked debate and comments. The same newspaper published a second article by Öneş on 28 December, in which he claimed that he had not written the previous article to explain MİT's, the government's or the state's approaches and quests.[47]

It is interesting to note that Öneş wrote the articles following MİT Undersecretary Taner's October meeting with Barzani in the northern Iraqi town of Selahaddin, which was known as the KDP's capital.

---

45 'FBI Başkanı MİT' e de gitti,' Radikal, 10 December 2005.

46 Cevat Öneş, 'Terör-kimlik-türban...Güvenlikte yeni arayışlar,' Radikal, 7 December 2005.

47 Cevat Öneş, 'Güvenlik ve Demokrasi,' Radikal, 28 December 2005.

2005 can be seen generally as the year when not only the government's political arguments, but also its intelligence policies underwent a significant change, as far as its Kurdish policy is concerned. Prime Minister Erdoğan's statements on the 'Kurdish problem' and sub-identity and main identity arguments, were combined with political determination and – probably with the support of the bureaucracy - radical changes in security policies.[48]

Despite the fact that Öneş's articles cannot be considered as representive of MİT's approach, they are nevertheless important, as they reflect similar approaches adopted by the security sector with regards to the Kurdish problem.

[48] It should also be considered that the government also took the military's opinion on matters of the Kurdish problem and the PKK, which are directly linked to the 25-year security concept of the state.

The Organisational Chart of MİT

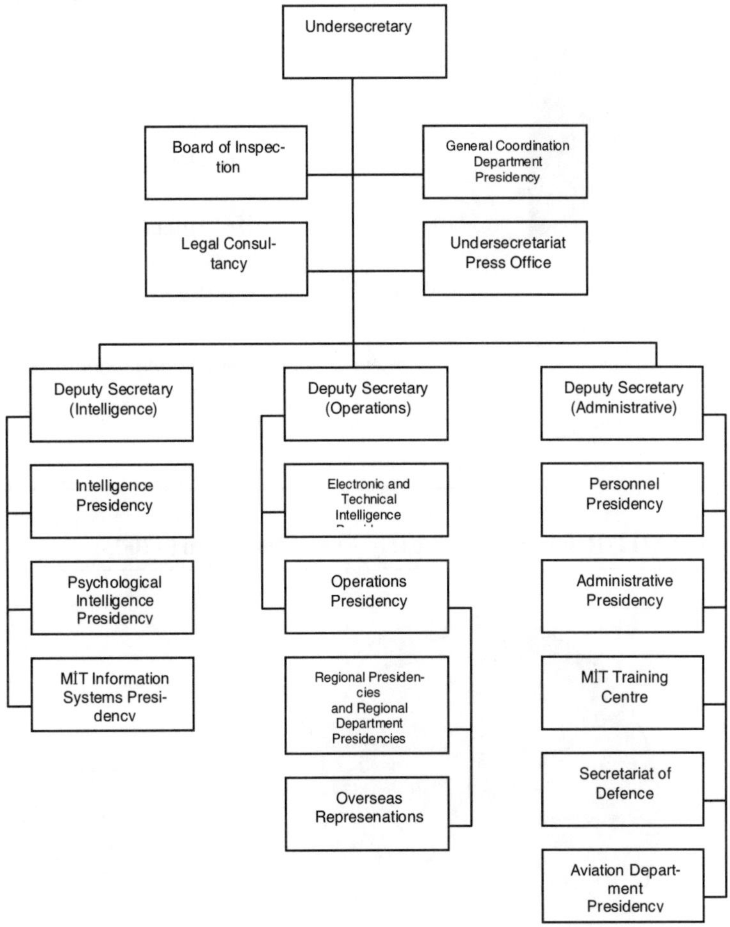

Showing MİT Website Transactions

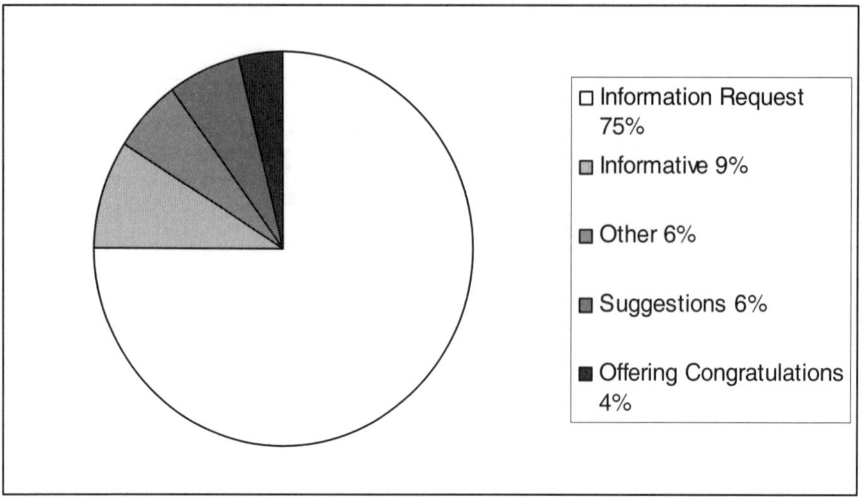

Evaluation of MİT-Related News, Yearly Evaluation Chart (2005)

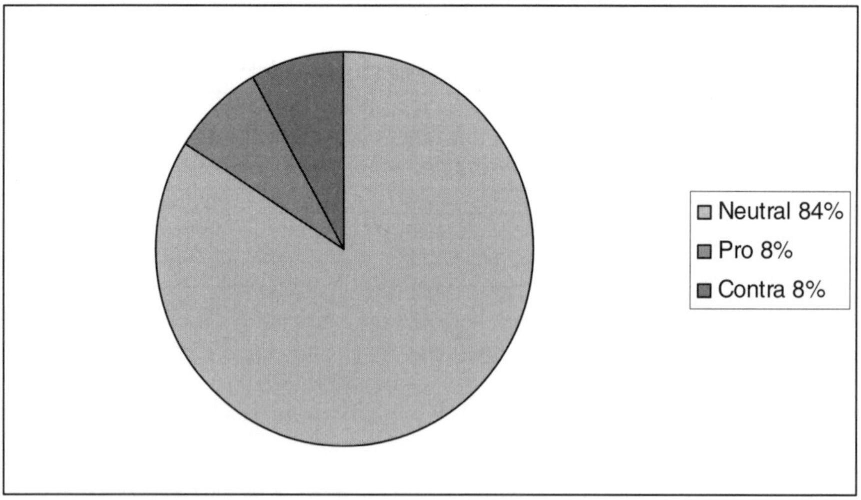

Chart Outlining MİT Web Transactions

Visits to the Website	801,669
Incoming E-mails	27,910
Outgoing Replies	8,979
Informative	2,545
Information Request	20,867
Congratulating	1,016
Suggestions	1,704
Other	1,778

MİT Undersecretariat Budget in 2000-2004 (as compared to 2005)

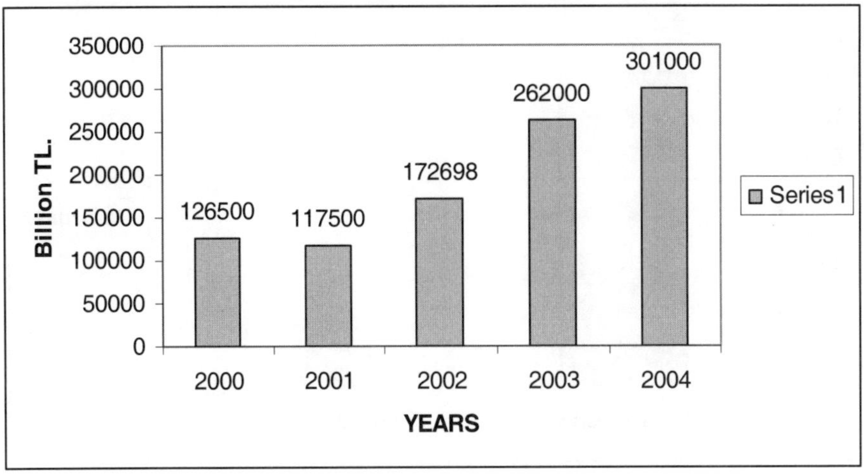

Chart Outlining MİT Personnel's Educational Status

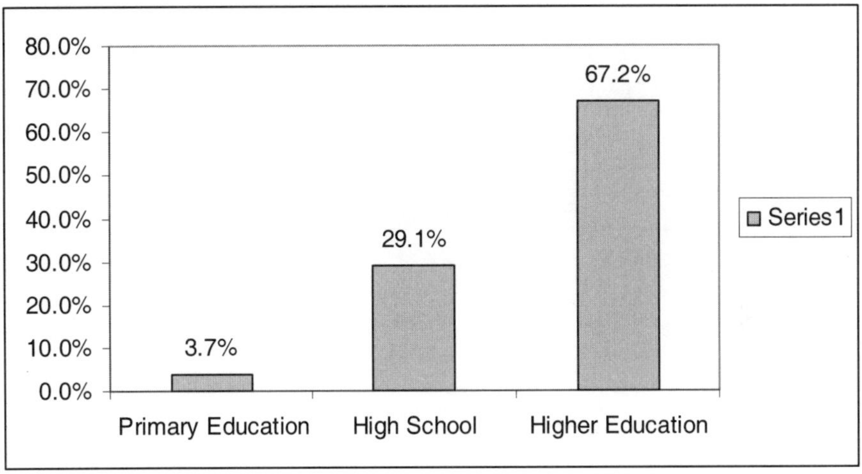

MİT Personnel Gender Percentage Chart

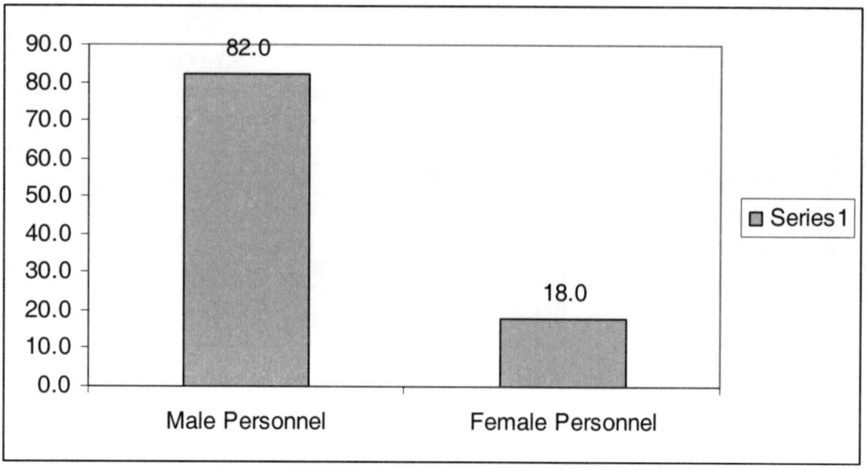

Gendarmerie Intelligence (JİTEM & JIT)

Ertan Beşe[*]

The JİTEM Story told through Documents and Publications

Throughout the 1990's, the Gendarmerie Intelligence and the Anti-Terror Organisation (Jandarma İstihbarat ve Terörle Mücadele Reşkilatı, JİTEM) was very much in the public eye, as it was during this time that the fight against the PKK terrorist organisation had reached its peak. However, very little was actually known about the institution of JİTEM itself. At the start of the new millennium, it seemed that JİTEM had faded from the public's interest, but the echoes of the bomb that exploded in the Umut Bookshop in Şemdinli in November 2005 brought the institution back to the centre of attention once again.

What made JİTEM a part of the public agenda in the 1990s, and such an important subject for conspiracy theorists, was Gendarmerie Major Ahmet Cem Ersever. Ersever was identified as one of the founders of JİTEM and attained fame due his enigmatic lifestyle, which looked as if it had come straight out of an adventure novel and which was punctuated by the mysteries of the realm of intelligence. As in every adventure novel, this story also had its 'winners' and 'losers.' Yet it seemed as though the winners in the story were not as apparent to the eye as the losers. Moreover, among the losers were not only the victims of the many unsolved murders attributed to JİTEM, but also one of the key figures of the game, Ahmet Cem Ersever himself.

Ersever's adventure ended in November 1993, when it was announced that the body of a male, which was found bound and gagged in the lime quarry near Ankara Elmadağ with two shots to the head, was that of 'Retired Gendarmerie Major Cem Ersever.' Two of the people closest to Ersever, namely Mahsune Dguebe and Mustafa Deniz also shared the same fate. Mahsune, who was a woman in her thirties, had been found dead a week earlier in a forest near Kızılcahamam, and the bound body of Mustafa Deniz, who was a PKK shriver.[1] Ersever's assistant, was

* Assistant Professor, Police Academy, Faculty of Security Sciences.

1 Article 1 of the 'Law Concerning Sentences for Some Criminals' No. 3419 defines shrivers as 'those who are members of organisations that were established for political and ideological reasons in order to commit crimes defined in Turkish Penal Code [Türk Ceza Kanunu, TCK] Articles 125, 131, 146 and 162, but who did not take part in committing the [aforesaid] crimes; those who did take part in a crime but are not investigated. If shrivers provide information to help disperse the organisation or prevent crimes that the

found in Polatlı, killed by a single shot to the head. The manner in which the story evolved was also significant as the bodies were left in three different locations in Ankara, a symbol reminiscent of Ahmet Cem Ersever's Book, The Conspiracy of the Triangle (Üçgendeki Tezgab).

As the Ersever murder hit the headlines, the name JİTEM began to be discussed openly throughout the country. Before this event, JİTEM had hitherto only been cited in east and southeast Anatolia, but as a result of it, the names of Ahmet Cem Ersever and JİTEM became practically interchangeable. Ersever had also coined a slogan using his own initials: 'ACE, the best detergent for cleaning terrorism!'

In November 2005, the man who was captured while allegedly trying to flee the scene after executing the bombing in Şemdinli, turned out to be another shriver. In addition, the two people waiting for this man in a nearby vehicle were later identified as gendarmerie intelligence members and these incidents revived the JİTEM puzzle.

Most of the information about JİTEM, an organisation which is either praised as a legendary force in the fight against terror, or blamed for gruesome murders worthy of a horror film, came from the accounts and depositions of PKK shrivers who were generally employed by JİTEM.

One of the most famous PKK shrivers is Abdülkadir Aygan. In addition to the claims made about him in the Susurluk Report[2], produced by Kutlu Savaş, Head of the Prime Minister's Inspection Board, a book with his memoirs has also been published[3] entitled 'The Shriver: A JITEM Member is Talking' (İtirfaçi: Bir JİTEM' ci Anlatti).[4] In this book, Aygan details the events he witnessed. Aygan's account made it possible to find the bodily remains of Murat Aslan, who disappeared under arrest 12 years previously. This led the Diyarbakır District Prosecutor's Office to bring five shrivers to trial as they were thought to be JİTEM members. They included one retired army officer and one active surrogate officer, all of whom were suspected of involvement in eight murders between 1992 and 1994.

The book also contained documents, showing Aygan being made an official government worker under the name of Aziz Turan on 1 September 1991, as well as

---

organisation intends to commit, or if they lay down arms and surrender, they will be exempt from criminal prosecution.' The law's second article regulates the protection of the shriver and his/her family.

2 Kutlu Savaş, Susurluk Report, m.0001 (10.01.1997).

3 Abdülkadir Aygan, who was a PKK militant, surrendered in 1985 to become a shriver and put in the 'Shriver Ward' in Diyarbakır Prison. He was released in 1990 thanks to the Repentance Law and was enlisted. During his time in the military, he was recruited as part of the first staff of JİTEM, consisting of seven people. He used the shrivers' right to become a 'civil servant' and became a government worker. His codename was changed from 'Şerif Aslan' to 'Aziz Turan' and had an official birth certificate under this name. Abdülkadir Aygan, who worked for JİTEM for 10 years, left the country after his confessions were published in Özgür Gündem Newspaper. Aygan, father of five, is still known to live in Sweden.

4 Timur Şahan, Uğur Balık, İtirafcçi: Bir JİEM'ci Anlattı (İstanbul: Aram Yayıncılık, 2004).

JİTEM's salary roll entries under this name. The gendarmerie salary cheque among these documents shows that Aygan is appointed to JİTEM. These documents are the most solid, official proof of JİTEM's existence, showing that the institution was engaged in official correspondence, and was employing people with the status of government workers, even though its existence was adamantly denied by the authorities,. In other words, JİTEM existed officially, at least for some time. Moreover, while stationed in Burdur, Abdülkadir Aygan, alias Aziz Turan, applied for membership and was admitted to the Army Solidarity Institution. (Ordu Yardımlaşma Kurumu, OYAK)

On 20 September 1992, the writer and poet Musa Anter was killed in Diyarbakır, whilst attending a culture and arts festival. His daughter, Rahşan Anter Yorozlu, subsequently had a meeting with Abdülkadir Aygan on 12 January 2006, together with journalist Ersin Kalkan from Hürriyet. Aygan was part of the team whose mission it was to kill Musa Anter and details of the meeting were published by Ersin Kalkan in Hürriyet on 22 January 2006. Kalkan and Yorozlu later answered questions about the meeting live on the CNN-Türk show 'Tarafsız Bölge,' hosted by Ahmet Hakan Coşkun.[5]

Two of the two most thorough official research documents on this matter are the Susurluk Report[6] produced by Kutlu Savaş, the chief of the prime minister's inspection committee, who was commissioned to investigate the Susurluk incident, and the 'Susurluk Investigation Commission Report and Minutes,'[7] written by the committee responsible for unveiling the Susurluk incident. The Susurluk incident was triggered by a car in Various Regions of Our Country' (10/90) dated 12 October

---

5 In Abdülkadir Aygan's confessions, the 29 people who were said to have been killed by JİTEM are the following: Musa Anter, Vedat Aydın, Musa Toprak, Mehmet Şen, Talat Akyıldız, Zahit Turan, Necati Aydın, Ramazan Keskin, Mehmet Ay, Murat Aslan, İdris Yıldırım, Servet Aslan, Sıddık Yetmez, Edip Aksoy, Ahmet Ceylan, Şahabettin Latifeci, Abdülkadir Çelikbilek, Mehmet Salih Dönen and his uncle whose name could not be ascertained, İhsan Haran, Fethi Yıldırım, Abdülkerim Zoğurlu, Zana Zoğurlu, Melle İzzettin and his driver whose name could not be ascertained, Hakkı Kaya, Harbi Arman, Fikri Özgen and Muhsin Göl.

6 Savaş, Susurluk Report.

7 TBMM ad-hoc Susurluk Investigation Commission was established on 26 November 1996, based on the TBMM General Board Decision No. 472, dated 12 November 1996, in order to 'uncover the ties between the state and illicit organisations, and the accident in Susurluk and the relations behind it.' The Commission, consisting of nine members, finished work on 3 April 1997. The Commission consisted of Fikri Sağlar (CHP İçel Deputy), Hayrettin Dilekcan (RP Karabük Deputy), Mahmut Yılbaş (DYP Van Deputy), Mehmet Bedri İncetahtacı (RP Gaziantep Deputy), Mehmet Elkatmış (RP Nevşehir Deputy), Metin Öney (ANAP İzmir Deputy), Nihan İlgün (DYP Tekirdağ Deputy), Sema Pişkinsüt (DSP Aydın Deputy), Yaşar Topçu (ANAP Sinop Deputy). During the six months that it was active, the Commission held 41 meetings, 10 special assessment meetings, went through 50'000 documents and interviewed 57 people. However, Mustafa Bayram, Teoman Koman and Necdet Ürüğ did not visit the Commission, although it was required of them to do so.

1995 and the summary by Istanbul National Security Court General Attorney dated 30 January 1997[8] (the Susurluk Summary).[9]

The Susurluk Report by Savas and the TBMM Ad-hoc Susurluk Committee Reports and Minutes, shed some light on the relationship between illegal organisations and government institutions, as well as the accident in Susurluk and the ties behind it. When the assessments in these reports were taken into consideration, the following conclusions were reached: Firstly, racketeer influenced organised crime formed ties to some government institutions and their members, and more importantly, this led to the creation of illicit organisations within the government that rapidly spiralled out of control. These ties took the form of 'turning a blind eye' to illegal activities, as well as taking an active part in them. They emerged as a consequence of the disregard for the legal principals of government. This resulted in a multi-faceted, dark web of ties, which involved both government bodies and high-level bureaucrats, either deliberately or unintentionally.

Secondly, these reports unearthed some structural problems within the security units, and the intelligence organisations, responsible for fighting serious crimes such as terrorism and organised crime. It was discovered that the existence of multiple intelligence organisations and units with similar duties and spheres of authority led to conflict and lack of coordination between the aforementioned institutions. This was yet further solid proof of JİTEM's existence and of its activities.

These findings also revealed how some of the government workers serving in these organisations became involved in activities and relationships for their own personal gain, as a result of the opportunities created by terrorism. In addition, the public were made aware of the fact that some intelligence officials, such as Gendarmerie Major Ersever, were involved of their own volition in covert operations, which were outside the supervision of the hierarchy and the chain of command.

The reports in question brought to light the structural problems stemming from the socio-economic and political constitution of South-eastern Turkey during the fight against terrorism in the 1990s, as well as the key players of this formation. This led to the emergence of the concept of terror profit. The reports pointed the finger at people who benefited and profited from their various involvements in this way. It was stated that the terror profit, brought about by the socio-economic structure of the region, was intrinsically linked to the feudal structure in Eastern and South-eastern Turkey, the status of tribal chiefs, conflicts between tribes, and the tribes' physical extension into Iran and Northern Iraq. This led to the questioning of the Village Guard System, which was modelled on the feudal structure of the region, and the PKK shrivers. The reports also contained numerous references to tribe involvement in drug trafficking and weapons smuggling, and to hundreds of unsolved murders. For example, it was stated that locals and the PKK shrivers employed by JİTEM had been left to their own devices over time, and that this had now became a significant problem due to the lack of control and authority over them. It was also pointed out that the PKK shrivers, and other people stationed in the southeast, were

---

8 Susurluk Digest, Prep. No. 1997/221, Digest No. 1997/1 (30.01.1997).

9 Keynote No: 10/90, Issue No: A.01.1.GEÇ/300–554, Decision No: 10 (12.10.1995).

later transferred to larger urban centres, and these transfers were specifically related to their pursuit of personal profit and involvement in corruption.

Findings regarding JİTEM and Ahmet Cem Ersever were also published by researchers and journalists. One of the first and most detailed of these was by Soner Yalçın, who, at the time, was a journalist working for 2000'e Doğru, and who later became known for his articles on the 'deep state' and related issues. Yalçın's articles and research on these subjects after 1991, made him a leading figure in the field and the foremost concept supervisor for television series and movie scripts on related themes. Yalçın even managed to interview Ersever, and subsequently published the interviews in 'Marshall Ahmet Cem Ersever's Confessions (Binbaşi Ersever'in İtiraflari).'[10]

Seven months after the release of the Susurluk Report, a book was published entitled 'Cem Ersever and the JITEM Reality (Cem Eserver ve JİTEM Gerçeği).' The book was written by a journalist and friend of the Ersever family called Çetin Ağaşe. According to Ağaşe, Ahmet Cem Ersever was like a son to General Eşref Bitlis, the general commander of the gendarmerie, and reported directly to him. Ersever resigned from the army a month after Bitlis' death. The appendix of the book contained two important documents: the first was a certificate of appreciation dated 30 November 1990 in which JİTEM Group Commander Major Ersever was commended on his 'success as a commander in the planning and execution of single strike operations.' This certificate was signed by Lieutenant General Hikmet Köksal, the gendarmerie public order commander at that time. Moreover, Ağaşe also published the 1994 telephone directory of the General Command of Gendarmerie, which contained the numbers of the JİTEM Group Commander and the JİTEM units in each city. This, once again, provided further proof of the official existence of JİTEM and of Ersever's position within the chain of command.

After the Şemdinli incident in November 2005, TBMM President Bülent Arınç addressed the government, and asked if an institution or organisation called JİTEM really existed, requesting a clear explanation as to how it worked and what kind of duties it carried out. Arınç assigned the task of investigating the matter to the Chair of the TBMM Human Rights Commission, Mehmet Elkatmış.

According to officials - JİTEM does not exist?

Whilst the existence of the JİTEM has been established in various documents, reports, media reports and in books, its existence has been continuously denied by government authorities. Doğan Güreş during his time as chief at the general staff, and a previous general commander of the gendarmerie, Teoman Koman, both stated that the JİTEM never existed, and Güreş even stated that the JİTEM was a work of fiction.

In his letter to the TBMM Susurluk Committee, former undersecretary of the National Intelligence Agency (Milli İtihbarat Teşkilatı, MIT) (1988-1992) and General Commander of Gendermerie Koman stated, 'There is no legal or illegal entity

---

10 Soner Yalçın, Binbaşı Ersever'in İtirafları (İstanbul: Kaynak Yayınları, 1994).

within the gendarmerie called JİTEM, but there is a group outside the gendarmerie, performing illegal activities under this name.' Again, during his tenure as gendarmerie commander general, General Teoman took part in the NTV show 'Enine Boyuna,' hosted by Nuri Çolakoğlu, in February 1998. During the show, Teoman stated that the name JİTEM was used as a fantasy. There is no legal entity called JİTEM and therefore, how can something that does not exist have a name? A group of people came together and invented an impressive name, the JİTEM, and because the name was used so many times, some authorities started to think it was an official institution.'

This denial reached such levels that the Vice-President of the Security Intelligence Agency Hanefi Avcı, made the following statement to the TGNA Susurluk Investigation Committee in his deposition dated 4 February 1997, 'Following the PKK's serious activities, some government officials started believing that the government had shortcomings in dealing with PKK members and PKK supporters through legal means. In order to overcome these weaknesses it was felt that an illegal approach had to be adopted, and as a result the JİTEM official Cem Ersever started operating in this manner.' The Committee subsequently sent a written enquiry to the General Command of the Gendarmerie, only to be rebutted: 'We have no such organisation!' Journalist Ali Bayramoğlu claims that during a conversation he personally witnessed the following warning made by Erol Özkasnak, who was the general secretary of the joint staff in the post during 28 February period, 'Those who mention Susurluk and the Turkish Armed Forces in the same sentence and those who talk about JİTEM are traitors.'[11]

Although the official existence of the JİTEM has been so vehemently denied, its actual existence has been indisputably proven by the above mentioned certificates of appreciation, governmental salary rolls, Investigation Committee reports, depositions and confessions of the people who worked for the organisation.

Seven months prior to assuming the role of prime minister, following the Refahyol Cabinet's dissolution after 28 February, Mesut Ylmaz was assaulted and had his nose broken in Budapest. This was done by a group of people who were allegedly organised by Mahmut Yıldırım, dubbed 'Yeşil,' who was an infamous PKK shriver heavily involved with the JİTEM.[12] Although the assailants were arrested, returned to Turkey and brought before the State Security Court, Yılmaz did not press charges and the assailants were never tried. Nonetheless, during his period as prime minister, he assigned the then Chief of the Prime Minister's Inspection Committee Savaş with the task of investigating all activities involving money, power and benefits, and operating under the guise of 'national interests' and the 'fight against terror.' Savas produced a report on his findings.

In a way, it was clear that the developments leading to the Susurluk Report started with a conflict between the key players of the Susurluk incident and the prime minister of the time. This report, known as the 'Susurluk Report,' was made public in January 1998 by Prime Minister Yılmaz. It consisted of approximately 120

---

11 Ali Bayramoğlu, 'Şu JİTEM dedikleri ve Şemdinli,' Yeni Şafak, 15 December 2005.

12 For this claim, see Necdet Açan, Serhan Yedig, 'Yumrukta 'Yeşil' Damgası,' Derin Devletin Peşinde (İstanbul: Karakutu Yayınları, 2005), p. 82-86.

pages, 11 of which were classified as 'national secrets,' and therefore not available to the public. The most striking information about JİTEM came from the PKK shriver, İbrahim Babat. A significant section of Babat's deposition was shielded from the public view for reasons of national secrecy. However, while he was serving time, this important witness talked with journalist Necdet Açan from Aktüel. Açan published the full transcript of his interview with Babat in prison.

Açan reported that Babat was a PKK shriver dubbed 'Mete,' and the second in command of a JİTEM group led by Ersever which consisted solely of PKK shrivers with the metaphoric 'license to kill', reminiscent of the movie hero 007 James Bond. Babat could not recall how many people he had killed for the government or for personal gain. When he was arrested in an armed conflict in Kadıköy, Istanbul, he was originally given seven years in prison, but after being sentenced to 17 years and six months, he applied to present a deposition to the Istanbul State Security Court and the Prime Minister's Investigation Committee.

In light of his poor command of Turkish, Babat's 11 pages of hand-written confession was dictated to a fellow inmate in Kırklareli Prison, and part of it found its way onto page 75 of the Susurluk Report. The full confession was handed to Prime Minister Yılmaz as Appendix 10 of the report.[13]

In his confessions, Babat claimed that besides its success in fighting terrorism, JİTEM conducted some arbitrary and illegal activities that placed the government in a compromising position. However, his most shocking declaration concerned the number of people he claimed to have killed in the name of JİTEM.

Babat also mentioned that 1990 saw important changes in JİTEM, and explained that some of the shrivers who were captured and released during that year, were enlisted by the JİTEM Group Command, in order to assemble all soldier shrivers under one roof. During this period, an illegal group was formed under JİTEM and Babat became one of their members. Babat claimed that they were ordered to kill anybody suspected of involvement with the PKK in Diyarbakır and its surroundings. He said that they killed these people and covered their tracks, instead of capturing them and bringing them to justice, because this is what they had been ordered to do. The JİTEM group was also involved in bombings during 1991.

In conclusion, Babat claimed that the JİTEM squads which had been formed for the purpose of fighting terror, deviated from the lawful paths and became illegal entities. Instead of fighting terror, the squads became involved in organised crime, unlawful activity and profiteering, which effectively undermined the government and Babat maintained that this was the reason why he had chosen to talk. The 'fight against terror' had become a 'fight for profit,' and members of the government became involved in politically motivated and unsolved murders. Babat wrote his deposition, apparently of his own volition and under no outside pressure, in order to ease his conscience and clear the government's name,.

After reading the report in 1998, Yılmaz was convinced of JİTEM's existence. However, after consulting with officials, he publicly declared that JİTEM does not exist anymore, because it has been cleaned out. In other words, Yılmaz

[13] Ibid, p. 15.

recognised the existence of JİTEM from the report but believed in what he was told about its dissolution. On the TV programme Arena, on Channel D on 22 January 1998, Yilmaz reaffirmed what he had been told:

> First of all, as you said, the Armed Forces were never involved. It wasn't the Gendarmerie; this was all about this institution formed within the Gendarmerie under the name of JİTEM, the Gendarmerie Intelligence and Anti-terrorism organisation. It was later dissolved. JİTEM does not exist anymore. In other words, they took the first radical step. As you said, they cleaned out the people involved in this through their internal disciplinary mechanism. The chief of the general staff has very clearly said to me: 'If there are people whom we overlooked after these investigations, we will find them and clean them out as well[14]

When İsmail Hakkı Karadayı assumed the role of the chief of the general staff, (30 August 1994 – 30 August 1998), news regarding JİTEM's dissolution was leaked to the press.[15]

The last declaration about JİTEM's dissolution came from the former commander of the gendarmerie in the State of Emergency Region (Olağanüstü Hal, OHAL), retired Lieutenant General Altay Tokat. Tokat was also known as the commander of 'Operation Hammer' in 1997, which was one of the most extensive operations against the PKK in Northern Iraq. He stated in his interview with the newspaper Zaman that JİTEM was 'an intelligence unit that fought against the PKK in the OHAL region' and that it had 'fulfilled its role and was dissolved. Its units were transferred from a central structure to a regional structure and they now report to their local gendarmerie command posts.'[16]

Tokat was asked about the indictment issued by the Diyarbakır Public Prosecutor's Office, in relation to the extra-judiciary killings carried out with the knowledge of some JİTEM commanders. In his reply Tokat said that, 'It is wrong to mention JİTEM in an indictment prepared by a prosecutor who is not an intelligence expert, an indictment based on depositions of people who have no idea about how intelligence works.' According to Tokat, the Gendarmerie Intelligence Agency (Jandarma İstihbarat Teşkilıı, JIT) did indeed exist and that there may have been some individual illegal incidents, but to imagine a unit that reverted to aggression and was involved in covert operations and illicit activities was out of the question.[17]

All of these are important in officially ascertaining the existence of JİTEM, even though there were some conflicting statements. This means that there was an institution that was not openly defined by the relevant laws and regulations, whose

---

14 See http://www.anap.org.tr/anap/genelbaskanlar/YILMAZ/konusmalar/1998/ocak98/22ocak98.htm, 22 January 1998.

15 Serhan Yedig, 'Bir var bir yok! Hem var hem yok JİTEM,' Hürriyet, 21 November 2005.

16 'Tokat Paşa: Suçlular cezalandırılsın, ordu yıpratılmasın,' Zaman, 29 December 2004.

17 Ibid

activities and staff were kept secret, and to which organisation they were accountable was not known.

This is how JİTEM was mentioned in the TBMM ad-hoc Unsolved Murders Committee Report:

> We fail to understand the nature of JİTEM's activities in the region. When invited for a deposition, Captain Ş. Dönmez mentioned that the Gendarmerie intelligence units are not a separate entity, they do not have a separate administrative body and that they are parts of regular squadrons. They are not subject to separate laws, their units belong to the Gendarmerie Public Security Command and are employed for the purpose of intelligence gathering as a part of the Gendarmerie Intelligence Teams founded in the OHAL Region, as stipulated in the Law on the Establishment, Duties and Jurisdiction of Gendarmerie, Articles 5, 44, 46, 42, 84 and Code No: 6815, Article 5. They mainly gathered intelligence about separatist terrorists and secondly about drug trafficking and weapon smuggling, and they followed the procedures in submitting the information to the executive bodies fighting terror, namely the OHAL Governor's Office, regional governor's offices and security units. Even this information shows that some governmental bodies moved outside the legal limits, abused their authority, and formed new structures using legal loopholes. Moreover, the fact that so many units operate in the same area leads to a confusion of authority and prevents clear-cut task definitions. Those who benefit most from this confusion are provocateurs and terrorist organisations who act against the government and the republic. In an environment where some governmental bodies act outside their scope of duty, terrorist organisations spread rumours, causing agitation among the citizens. The fact that JİTEM is staging operations in a precinct, without informing the police, makes the citizens question authority. It would be a positive step for our government, that holds the law above everything, to stop the activities of this institution with no legal basis, an institution that has deviated from the path and is involved in illicit activities.[18]

In Kutlu Savaş's Susurluk Report, the following points about JİTEM were made:[19]

1. JİTEM existed: 'Although denied by the General Command of Gendarmerie, the existence of JİTEM is not a fact that can be ignored. JİTEM might have been abolished, its staff relocated, its documents sent to archives, but many people who worked for JİTEM are still alive.'[20]

---

18 Fedai Erdoğ, Türkiye Büyük Millet Meclisi (TBMM) Faili Meçhul Siyasi Cinayetleri Araştırma Komisyon Raporu (İstanbul: Gizli Saklı Yayınevi, 2005), p. 124–126.

19 Savaş, Susurluk Report, (in the references made to the report, the page numbers of the Susurluk Report booklet published as a supplement to Aktüel Magazine on 5 February 1998 were used).

20 Ibid, p. 26.

2. The report assesses the existence of JİTEM as a normal occurrence, stating that it was formed due to a necessity to manage and dispatch the special teams in the region.[21]
3. It is said that JİTEM performed very efficiently in the region, and even the local gendarmerie squads were not aware of its presence.'[22]
4. It is also said that the high number of village guards and shrivers working for JİTEM led to a rise in the individual crime rate.[23]
5. The report explains the founding and development of JİTEM.[24]
6. One of the most significant aspects of the report is the way in which it points out how some JİTEM members, including officers, became corrupt and started acting outside of the governmental hierarchy.[25]

Along with these points, the legal characteristics of the report are highlighted in the preface, which states that it is not an executive summary, investigation report, or an inspection report. This sets it apart from the 'Susurluk Investigation Committee Report', the General Assembly Investigation Report on Unsolved Politically Motivated Murders and the Susurluk Summary. These documents have a legal basis, whereas the Susurluk Report was conceived to inform the prime minister and to provide suggestions. In the introduction, it was stated that one of the main purposes of the report was to 'shed light into the intricate and mostly illegal web of ties and to present them in a holistic manner before they loose their significance in a police investigation.' At this point, the Prime Ministerial Supervision Committee was careful not to move into the sphere of justice, aiming instead to assist the judiciary wher-

21 This was expressed in the report in the following way: '(…) Also, JİTEM's existence does not constitute negligence. Actually, JİTEM came into being due to a necessity. (…) It was seen that in order to coordinate the administration of special teams, the group called JİTEM was activated (…),'p. 26-27.

22 '(...) JİTEM performed efficiently in the region. Many of its activities were unknown to local Gendarmerie squads (…)', p. 27.

23 '(…) In time, the activities of civilian and military JİTEM members started to draw attention in the region. Because it had many village guards and shrivers as members, individual crime rates increased. These people left the region over time and continued their activities in other, feasible environments (…),' p. 27.

24 '(…) In the past, Gendarmerie Intelligence was very small and weak, almost level with urban public order intelligence. During General Hulusi Sayın's term of office as Chief of General Staff, JİTEM was improved. It was reinforced with people who spoke the local languages and it was slowly strengthened. But it never became as powerful as MİT or the Military Intelligence. This was not necessary either. The armed conflict environment of the 1980s created by PKK was the source for Gendarmerie Intelligence. Therefore, JİTEM had a development parallel to the southeast problem, which was more or less its raison d'être (…),' p. 81.

25 '(…) But the shrivers and locals who were employed by JİTEM became the source of a separate and significant problem, when they were left to their own devices. Not only the locals, but also the regular intelligence employees were left out of the military hierarchy. Major Cem Ersever was able to act individually in an environment where higher ranked officers were present (…),' p. 81.

ever possible. This approach was beneficial in the production of a report that maintains this integrity.

Another interesting argument in the introduction, was the fact that the Susurluk incident was divided into segments instead of being treated as a whole, hence the essence and the basis of the incident were overlooked, particularly during the judicial process.

Additionally, the difficulties encountered during the preparation of the report were also mentioned, and it was concluded that 'it was no longer possible to investigate every aspect' of the Susurluk incident, because of the various governmental mechanisms and the processes of the investigation committees. What caused the Prime Minister's Investigation Committee to arrive at this conclusion was the fact that some points fell under police jurisdiction and it was therefore very difficult for investigators to tap into these resources.

While the authenticity of JİTEM's existence was still under discussion, the denial of its 'official' existence by government officials, made its way into an indictment prepared by Diyarbakır Public Prosecutor Mithat Özcan, dated 29 March 2005, at the 2nd Diyarbakır Criminal Court, for the trial of eight PKK shrivers.[26] These men were suspected of being JİTEM members, and were charged with eight separate unsolved murders[27] between 1992-1994. The suit was filed following an application by the Diyarbakır Bar, after PKK shriver Aygan's allegations were published in Ülkede Özgür Gündem. The trial was hence known as the 'JİTEM Case' and the 'Unsolved Murders Case.'

The 3-page indictment prepared by the office of the prosecutor, stated that the eight murders were committed in the name of the 'so-called government' organisation JİTEM, but through illegal means.[28] Because the defendants were ex-military personnel, the Diyarbakır 2nd High Criminal Court transferred the file to the 7th Army Corps Military Court, on the grounds of lack of jurisdiction, and denied requests for their arrest.

The defendants were accused of 'forming an organisation with criminal intent, engaging in torture to obtain confessions for crimes, and premeditated murder.' Their trial started at the 7th Army Corps Military Court, and the first hearing commenced on 27 January 2006 with none of the defendants in attendance. As a result of this hearing, the court decided to arrest Aygan, however there were no further arrests for the remaining seven defendants. It was also discovered that Saniye Emlük, a civil servant in the Diyarbakır Military Office, had previously had his Turkish citizenship revoked. The trial was postponed.

---

26 These people are: Mahmut Yıldırım (aka Yeşil), Abdülkadir Aygan, Muhsin Gül, Fethi Çetin, Kemal Emlük, Saniye Emlük, Yüksel Uğur and Abdülkerim Kırca.

27 The defendants are accused of the unsolved murders of Harbi Arman, Lokman Zuğurli, Zana Zuğurli, Servet Aslan, Şahabettin Latifeci, Ahmet Ceylan, Mehmet Sıddık Etyemez and Abdülkadir Çelikbilek and are tried for three consquitve life sentences.

28 'Yeşil'in yargılandığı JİTEM davası başlıyor,' Zaman Newspaper, 24 January 2006.

Intelligence Activities of the Gendarmerie and the Most Realistic Account of JİTEM

The PKK raids of Eruh and Şemdinli took place on 15 August 1984, only four years after the 12 September 1980 coup which aimed to prevent anarchy and terrorism. This raid represented the beginning of something very different from the pre-1980 terrorism and anarchy, and something that would cost tens of thousands of lives.

This new wave of terrorism and its accompanying guerrilla tactics turned into a long-term civil conflict, and it was a situation that the officers and non-commissioned officers (NCOs) of the gendarmerie were not adequately trained or equipped for. These personnel were trained for conventional warfare by the Turkish Army Land Forces, and were educated in judicial matters and the maintenance of law and order. Their weapons and equipment were, as such, selected with these elements in mind. In contrast, the training and skills of the PKK members, and the weapons and equipment used by the organisation, were specifically designed for guerrilla tactics and were based on a hit and run strategy.

The same might be said of the intelligence organisations. Intelligence units did not have the mechanisms in place to fight against the PKK in the open ground. The level of inefficiency in the intelligence network made it impossible for land forces to perform specific operations, to prevent terror raids and to develop a strategy against the PKK's front activities. This increased the PKK's success on the political activities' front, and strengthened public support for the organisation.

Under these circumstances, the only source of information for the security units came from militants who had been apprehended, as well as from confiscated PKK documents and diaries. In other words, intelligence units could only familiarise themselves with the PKK's tactics and targets from the testimonies of militants who were apprehended or who surrendered.

In 1984, the year in which PKK terrorism took hold in Turkey, the intelligence units of the gendarmerie consisted largely of intelligence branches in the urban regiments and regional commands. The intelligence staff operated in uniform with limited resources, and were stationed mainly at intelligence headquarters'. After becoming the Diyarbakır Public Order Army Corps Commander in 1987, Lieutenant General Hulusi Sayın aimed to increase the efficiency of the intelligence sector, and as such he established units similar to those in the Directorate General of Security, who specialised in intelligence and reported directly to the general command.[29]

JİTEM was made a legal entity by Article 5 of the 'Law on the Establishment, Duties and Jurisdiction of Gendarmerie'[30] No. 2803, and Article 4 of the Law

---

29 Saygı Öztürk, 'Komutan 'JİTEM' Gerçeğini Açıklıyor!,' Medya24, 14 November 2005.

30 For Article 5 of the Law on the Establishment, Duties and Jurisdiction of Gendarmerie No. 2803 see Resmi Gazete (Official Gazette) No. 17985, dated 12 March 1983. 'The Gendarmerie General Command Organisation is stated in its own establishment and staff decrees, in accordance with the nature of its duties and the principles of the Turkish Armed Forces. The Gendarmerie General Command's establishment, staff and duty stations are regulated by the Ministry of Internal Affairs, in consultation with the General

Concerning the Transfer of Our Borders, Coasts and Territorial Waters' Protection and Anti-Smuggling Activities to the Ministry of Internal Affairs Number 6815.[31]

From their inception, the teams were involved in intelligence activities, as well as counter-terrorist tasks, and this was the reason why the name 'JİTEM' was devised. However, this was not in keeping with later practices and since the teams were specialising in 'intelligence,' they were not supposed to be involved in actual operations. This principal is in keeping with the structure of similar units in the police force. For example, there is an 'Intelligence Presidency' and 'Intelligence Branch Offices,' and there is also a 'Fight against Terror and Operations Board' and its branch offices, which carry out the operations based on intelligence provided by the former. This structure is based on the principle of separating intelligence gathering from operations.

From what is understood about JİTEM to date, these teams carried out their activities using the 'staff system' [eleman sistemi][32] and 'technical stakeout' procedures. The information gathered was analysed, it then became 'intelligence' and was

---

Staff. During times of mobilisation and war, squads under the command of military departments are organised with the approval of the General Staff. The organisation and mobilising of gendarmerie squads that are charged with security and public order duties, are based on civilian divisions except in inevitable situations. To provide productivity and efficiency of service, organisations that cover more than one province are also considered'.

31 For the Law Concerning the Transfer of Duties of Elimination and Pursuit of Smuggling to the Ministry of Internal Affairs for the Provision of Border, Coastal and Territorial Waters, see Resmi Gazete (Official Gazette) No. 9363 dated 24 July 1956. 'Article 4: For the Prohibition and Pursuit of Smuggling, an intelligence agency is established by the Ministry of Internal Affairs and is allocated a budget each year.' With the Law Concerning the Protection and Security of Territorial Waters No. 3497, new regulations were made. See the Resmi Gazete (Official Gazette) No. 1997, dated 22 November 1988. 'Article 5: As this Law goes into effect, the articles of the Law Concerning the Transfer of Duties of Elimination and Pursuit of Smuggling to the Ministry of Internal Affairs for the Provision of Border, Coastal and Territorial Waters No. 6815, date 16 July 1956, of the Gendarmerie Organisation's Tasks and Authority Resolution No. 2803, dated 10 March 1983 and of other laws that contradict this law cannot be put into force (...)' Provisional Article 1: 'Until the duty of the protection of eastern and southeastern borders is actively taken over by the Land Forces Command, the duties arising from Law No. 6815 are to be carried out by the Gendarmerie General Command'.

32 The 'Worker System' (eleman sistemi) is the intelligence method used for gathering intelligence information about activities and people by infiltrating people into the targeted activities and organisations, or by converting existing members of these organisations. The people used to this end are defined as 'workers' (eleman) by the security forces; whereas the terror and organised crime organisations call them 'agents'. These people differ from the official employees of an intelligence organisation. The official employees are government clerks on a government payroll, who have qualifications defined in relevant laws, who are usually part of the permanent staff and their promotion and whose working conditions are regulated. Whereas the 'workers' are temporarily employed either voluntarily, or in exchange for benefits, in order to provide specific services. For instance, a 'MİT member' refers to permanent National Intelligence Organisation (MİT) staff, and 'MİT Worker (eleman)' means a temporary employee who provides previously-defined services for the organisation as part of a mutual agreement.

subsequently handed to the Intelligence Group Command. Every report was assembled by the Intelligence Group Command and operation teams were dispatched accordingly.

Despite the very significant problems that occurred at a later date, the JİTEM appears to have used the staff system efficiently against terrorist networks. Known to the public as the Penitence Law, Shriver Law or Pardon Law, the Law Concerning Sentences for Some Criminals No. 3419, dated 25 March 1988, stipulated that 'Those members of a terrorist organisation that took no part in terrorist attacks will be exempt from punishment, provided that they disarm and help prevent further crimes being committed by that organisation through their confessions.' It has been determined that this 'exemption' was an important factor in the success of the 'staff system,' because the PKK militants who wanted to benefit from the Penitence Law, shared their knowledge about the PKK with the JİTEM, and were eventually employed in regular jobs while maintaining their ties to the JİTEM. These personnel usually assisted as translators and scouts, and in the analysis of confiscated documents.[33] Moreover, due to the fact that the rural area was within the jurisdiction of the gendarmerie, that they had stations even in the smallest of residential areas and had close contact with the locals, then gendarmerie intelligence was in a position to be successful, particularly in comparison to the National Intelligence Organisation (MİT) and police intelligence.

The concept of the PKK shriver, first mentioned after the assassination in 1991 of Vedat Aydın, who was the Diyarbakır Provincial chair of the People's Labour Party (Halkin Emek Partisi), returned to the spotlight after the bombing of a

---

[33] Haşim Söylemez, 'İtirafçılar tetikte,' Aksiyon, 21 December 2005. See http://www.aksiyon.com.tr/detay.php?id=22875, [Access date: 3 February 2006]. [The term 'PKK Shriver' first came up after the People's Labour Party (Halkın Emek Partisi, HEP) member Aydın's body was found between Ergani and Maden. Shortly thereafter, it became a topic of debate with the unsolved murder of HEP Executive Remzi İl in Diyarbakır. According to one claim, the murders were committed by Hezbollah. But PKK argued that these murders were committed with the cooperation of the shrivers. HEP executives also thought that there was a shriver connection in these incidents. The murder of writer Musa Anter, and Democratic Labour Party (Demokratik Emek Partisi, DEP) Deputy Mehmet Sincar's shooting in Batman were among the unsolved murders that were committed during this time. (...) According to intelligence units, there were 1550 unsolved murders between 1990-2000. But PKK claims that the real number exceeds 2000. These murders were committed along the Diyarbakır, Mardin, Nusaybin, Şırnak, Cizre, Batman, Silvan, Şemdinli, Hakkâri and Yüksekova line. Most of these unsolved murders were committed in Diyarbakır. Serial murders were mostly attributed to Hezbollah. However, suspicions were raised as the modus operandi was unlike that of Hezbollah. According to PKK, there were shrivers within Hezbollah and they were working in coordination with JİTEM. PKK claims that 5000 people had left the organisation and they are defined as traitors. Those who were militants and later quit the organisation usually fled abroad. Again, according to the PKK's claims, at least 500 people work for JİTEM as shrivers. The organisation [i.e. PKK] has a list of these people and they are categorised as 'important enemies' of the organisation. JİTEM, or another governmental body, did not yet comment on how many shrivers they have. Nonetheless, it would be incorrect to put those militants who took refuge with the government and the shrivers in the same category.'

bookshop in Şemdinli on 9 November 2005. One of the suspects of the bombing, Veysel Ateş, was working for gendarmerie intelligence, and was a former PKK shriver. This reopened questions concerning the PKK shrivers' ties to governmental bodies.

Following the Şemdinli incident, a PKK shriver who introduced himself as Fırat, and claimed that he was on active duty but refused to name the unit he worked for, gave an interview to Aksiyon magazine and made some interesting points about the shriver organisation. Fırat was one of the first militants to join the PKK from Diyarbakır. After receiving his military training from Mahsun Korkmaz, who was one of the first people to lead the organisation's military wing and was killed in a battle in Gabar Mountain in 1986, Firat entered Turkey via Kandil in 1989. After taking part in many PKK activities, he surrendered to security forces in the Tunceli rural area in 1990 and voluntarily worked with the government. Firat stated that the word shriver was a rather vulgar term and should instead be replaced by 'a penitent person.' Fırat also told Aksiyon that not everybody was capable of becoming a shriver, and that the shrivers were chosen from amongst those who fought for the PKK, but who were later arrested or surrendered. Sound knowledge of the PKK organisation and solid strategic and military training were essential, and those who were single and without children or family bonds, stood a far a greater chance of being selected.

Shrivers were targets principally because they had fled from and turned against their organisation, and therefore they were provided with a new identity and some financial aid for their own protection. It was not enough for a militant to simply announce an intention to become a shriver or to work for the government. Those selected were tested and their activities were photographed and documented. Each shriver had to obey the superior to whom he was reporting and had to conduct his life according to the instructions he received.[34]

The Gendarmerie Intelligence's Legal Status

It took almost eight years work to legitimise gendarmerie intelligence, within an institution such as JİTEM or the Gendarmerie Intelligence Organisation (JİT). In 1998, the Draft Law for the Addition of Two Articles to the Law on the Establishment, Duties and Jurisdiction of Gendarmerie Tasks and Authority Resolution,' prepared by the Ministry of Internal Affairs, was sent to the TBMM Presidency (21st term), with the decision of the Council of Ministers dated 27 August 1998.[35] The legal grounds for the draft were 'to enable the gendarmerie to carry out intelligence activities and to employ additional units in case the local gendarmerie squads

---

[34] Ibid

[35] Prime Ministry General Directorate of Laws and Resolutions, Bill Concerning the Addition of Two Articles to the Law on the Establishment, Duties and Jurisdiction of Gendarmerie date 22 September 1998, Issue: B.02.0.KKG.0.11/101–1177/5368; Period and Legislation Year: 21, Keynote No: 1/572, Arrival to the Directorate: 22 September 1998; Arrival at the Internal Affairs Commission: 01 November 1999, Date of Release: 10 December 1999, Decision Date: 9 December 1999.

are insufficient.' This was, in a sense, the draft that would officially establish JİTEM. It was returned to the TBMM once again during the 22nd term on 13 January 2003 with the File Number 1/402. The draft was then sent to the Committee of Internal Affairs on 20 January 2003 and was returned following its retraction. The gendarmerie intelligence, previously known as 'JİTEM' or 'JİT', finally achieved legal status with the Law Concerning Amendments to Some Laws No. 5397. This law was accepted on 3 July 2005 and came into effect on 23 July 2005, and JİTEM thus became the Gendarmerie Intelligence Department within the General Command of the Gendarmerie. This law authorised the gendarmerie to carry out technical stakeouts.[36]

This law also brought about radical legal and institutional changes to the Technical Stakeout Law No. 5397, also known to the public as the 'Tele-Ear Law,' which drastically re-regulated communications tapping. The law stipulated that all kinds of telecommunications tapping should be monitored by a single body, and provisions were made for the establishment of a new structure which was called the Directorate of Telecommunications Communication.'[37]

In the event of a strong suspicion of crime where no other means of gathering evidence existed, this law regulated the authority to tap telephones, record and analyse the routing of a suspect or perpetrator's telecommunications during the course of a criminal investigation or prosecution. The tapping would be authorised by a judge or, in cases where time was of essence, by the Public Prosecutor's Office. The law stated that the prosecutor would immediately ask for permission from a judge and that he/she would have to make his/her decision within 24 hours. If a decision had not been reached by the end of the 24-hour period, or if the judge denied the request, then the prosecutor would immediately retract the orders.

Until 1 June 2005, the supervision of telecommunications and tapping of telephones, with the purpose of fighting terrorism and terrorist organisations, was regulated by the Law Concerning the Fight against Racketeer Influenced Crime Organisations No. 4422 and after this date, by the Law Concerning the Judgment of Crime No. 5271. The security forces' and intelligence units' authority for some of the precautions and methods used in the fight against terrorism came from the Law Concerning the Fight against Racketeer Influenced Crime Organisations No. 4422, as stated in Article 16. Since Articles 2-10 of this law regulated precautions and methods such as tapping of telecommunications, secret stakeouts, 'analysing records and data', 'use of secret agents' and 'use of witnesses and agents', then Article 16 was used by units involved in the fight against terror. Subsequently, when the new Turkish Penal Code (Türk Ceza Kanunu, TCK) No. 5237, and the Code of Criminal Procedures (Ceza Muhakemesi Kanunu, CMK) No. 5271 went into effect on 1 June

[36] For the Law Concerning Amendments to Some Laws No. 5397 see Resmi Gazete the (Official Gazette) dated 23 Juli 2005 No. 25884.

[37] In the provisional article added to Law No. 5397, it was stipulated that the Telecommunications Board be established within six months at the latest. Since the law went into effect after it was published in Resmi Gazete (Official Gazette) on 23 July 2005, the institution was officially and actively established on 23 January 2006.

2005, the crimes and precautions previously regulated by Law No. 4422 were re-regulated (CMK 135).

Hence, the tapping that would be carried out under the scope of Article 135 of Law No. 5271, would be overseen by the Directorate of Telecommunication Communication within the Telecom Company, who reported directly to the president of the company. This board would consist of one president and three experts, namely a technical, a legal and an administrative expert, and would have representatives from the National Intelligence Organisation, the Directorate General of Security and the General Command of the Gendarmerie.

An important change brought about by this law was the authority given to the undersecretary of the National Intelligence Organisation to give written orders to the Telecommunications Board for the , tapping, routing analysis and recording of telecommunications, in cases where time played an important factor. This authority was also afforded to his assistant, the director general of security or the president of its Intelligence Department Presidency, and the general commander of gendarmerie or chief of intelligence. This was limited to their relevant scopes of jurisdiction and the orders had to be submitted to the judge in charge within 24 hours, who in turn would have to make his/her decision within 24 hours.

Law No. 5397 stipulating the tapping of phones through a central authority, also contained rules concerning gendarmerie intelligence. An article was added to the Law on the Establishment, Duties and Jurisdiction of Gendarmerie No. 2803, to regulate the phone tapping activities of the gendarmerie. The article stated that the gendarmerie was authorised to request tapping and routing analysis of telecommunications in cases solely within their scope of authority, by a court order, or with the written orders of the gendarmerie general commander or the chief of intelligence, if time was an important factor.

The Law Concerning Amendments to Some Laws No. 5397,[38] stresses that intelligence is an essential tool in the fight against crime and criminality. However, since intelligence consists of the gathering and storing of information, it is closely linked to the issue of 'freedom to communicate' as intelligence covers private life, family life and the tapping of communications within those spheres. Depending on these grounds, it was stated that it was imperative to regulate intelligence activities by law, in compliance with the constitutional rights and freedoms in Turkey.

In the arguments used to justify the Law, the most striking one is that preemptive tapping for intelligence was not regulated, and that the new law aimed at filling this void. The Code of Criminal Procedure No. 5271 only regulates judicial tapping by the judicial police after a crime has been committed. The activities of intelligence agencies, however, are not directly linked to specific crimes, but instead are carried out with the aim of maintaining national security, ensuring a steady and systematic information flow and providing analysis regarding threats to the democratic rule of law.

The new regulations on the tapping of telecommunications arose out of the need for the timely prevention of terrorist threats against the democratic govern-

---

[38] This legal ground was prepared and presented by Yalova Deputy Şükrü Önder, who proposed the bill.

ment. Also significant were the efforts to redefine the authorities of the security forces in their fight against subversive, separatist and fundamentalist organisations who constantly changed their tactics and strategies. It was claimed that these new regulations would protect the citizen's individual rights and freedoms.

With this law, the Gendarmerie Intelligence Agency gained legal status, even though Prime Minister Recep Tayyib Erdoğan and TGNA President Bülent Arınç had raised the question of its existence. In the second article of this law, the term 'Gendarmerie Intelligence Presidency'[39] became an official part of the 'Law on the Establishment, Duties and Jurisdiction of Gendarmerie.'[40]

Basic Problems Concerning JİTEM

JİTEM, to quote Teoman Koman, is '[an institution] that never existed officially,' but one that was always influential and that had, for some, a frightening and for others a legendary reputation and power. This led to its name being abused by mafia-like criminal organisations. It developed to such an extent that news about people introducing themselves as JİTEM members and demanding extortion money, kidnapping for ransom and involvement in wrongful seizures, became a frequent occurrence.[41] For example, on 5 May 2005, the Radikal newspaper published an article about the PKK shriver Adil Timurtaş, who was caught red-handed trying to extort YTL 30'000 from DEHAP member Lezgin Bingöl. Timurtus claimed to be working for JİTEM and he is suspected of having been involved in many murders. There is currently a warrant out for his arrest. The article stated that Adil Timurtaş was arrested despite showing his JİTEM identity card, and was transferred to the Bureau of

39 For the Law on the Establishment, Duties and Jurisdiction of Gendarmerie No. 2803 see Resmi Gazete (Official Gazette) No. 17985 dated 12 March 1983. For additional Article 5 see Resmi Gazete (Official Gazette) dated 12 March 1983, No. 17985. 'The Gendarmerie, while carrying out duties stipulated in this Resolution's Article 7 subparagraph (a), in order to take preventive and protective measures, can, only within its own sphere of responsibility, determine communications made through telecommunication, eavesdrop, evaluate and record signal information with court order, or in matters where time is of essence, with the written order of the Gendarmerie Commander General or Chief of Intelligence, in order to prevent crimes that are stated in the Code of Criminal Procedure Number 5271, dated 4 December 2004, Article 250, Paragraph 1, Subparagraphs (a), (b) and (c), with the exception of crimes of espionage. The records obtained within the scope of this article cannot be used for purposes other than those stated in the first paragraph. The secrecy principle applies to the storage and preservation of the obtained information and records. Those who act against the dictum of this paragraph are subject to prosecution by the Republic Prosecutors, even if the act takes place during or due to the carrying out of a duty. Court orders and written orders are carried out by members of the Gendarmerie General Command Board of Intelligence. The beginning and end date and time of the act and the identity of the person carrying it out are recorded in a report of proceedings(...).'

40 For the Gendarmerie Organisation's Tasks and Authority Resolution No. 2803 see the Resmi Gazete (Official Gazette) dated 12 March 1983, No. 17985.

41 On interesting extortion and fraud activities where JİTEM and MİT's name were used, see Fuat Akyol, 'JİTEM hayaletiyle gasp terörü,' Aksiyon, 1 March 2004; Aydoğan Vatandaş, 'Kendisine JİTEM süsü veren mafya,' Zaman, 4 August 2002.

Organised Crime, along with Hacı İnan, Abuzer Gün, Abdulvahap Demir and three Macedonians who were accompanying him. The article also stated that Adil Timurtaş was decorated with the Superior Duty Medal, issued by the Land Forces Command's Special Operations Squadron.[42]

As mentioned above, the statements made by Ibrahim Babat during his interview with Necdet Açan in prison, make it clear that the authorisation given to state units in order to protect the security and welfare of the government, moved out of the government's control and were abused by organised crime units for personal gain and illicit business dealings.

> JİTEM groups, consisting of shriver soldiers with a license to kill, turned murder into amusement. Before each murder and bombing, they were playing word games to determine which organisation's they would name as responsible. Cem (Ersever), Abdülkadir (Aygan), the other shrivers and I would sit down and chat. Cem would say 'We have a job tomorrow, let's establish a new organisation.' A contest would start to find a name. One would say 'Iron Fist;' another would say 'T.I.T. (Turkish Avenger Brigade – Türk İntikam Tugayı),' and so on... That is how we would choose the name of the organisation that we use. It was really fun; we used to laugh a lot...[43]

Later, the rumour spread that some government officials were using shrivers to conduct illegal business. Although the issuing of penitence laws was aimed at bringing the PKK militants back from the hills and in order to damage the organisation and find shrivers, the number of shrivers increased. The shrivers took part in operations run with military squads, in special teams and village guards. The gendarmerie, the Democratic Council of Security and the MİT also began using the shrivers. Some of them even published their memoirs written during their time in the organisation, which revealed the personal weaknesses of the leaders, thus contributing to psychological warfare.[44]

Shrivers abused the opportunities they were given by the government and formed gangs and one of the most striking examples was that of Mahmut Yıldırım, alias 'Yeşil (Green).' To some, he was a shriver, and to some he was an 'intelligence agent,' and as such had worked with different intelligence units. In time he became a power centre of his own, however, he continued to use the name 'JİTEM' for his own purposes.

Several unsolved murders were attributed to JİTEM, and in the press JİTEM was described as 'a source of fear' which criminal organisations readily abused.

---

42 'İtirafçı Timurtaş yakalandı,' Radikal, 5 May 2005.

43 For this claim, see Açan, Yedig, Derin Devletin Peşinde, p. 23.

44 Sami Demirkıran, Kod Adı: Killer's of Mehmet's, (Ankara: Kipa Yayınları, 2002); Demirkan, PKK: Olaylar, Belgeler, Hatıralar!.. (İstanbul: Kipa Yayınları, 2001).

Latest Developments Concerning JİTEM and the Şemdinli Incident

If one takes into consideration the fact that JİTEM was an informal or semi-formal part of the gendarmerie, then the most important development to date is represented by the legitimisation of its intelligence activities with Law No. 5397, Addendum 5 on 3 July 2005.

Beside the legislative developments, the most significant events were the Şemdinli incident on 9 November 2005 and the Yüksekova incident that followed as these events brought JİTEM back into the spotlight.

The Şemdinli incident resulted in the deaths of two people. On 9 November 2005, the Umut Bookshop owned by Seferi Yılmaz, was bombed. Yılmaz was an alleged former PKK member, who is claimed to have served time for 15 years). One person (Mehmet Zahit Korkmaz) died and six were injured, and later that same day shots were fired into a crowd who were watching the prosecutor's investigations of the crime scene. These shots, which killed one bystander and injured four others, were said to have come from a car that belonged to Special Sergeant Tanju Çavuş.

This was, however, not the first explosion in the region. Between July and November, 14 explosions were reported, four of them in the centre, two in Şemdinli and eight in the Yüksekova district, killing eight soldiers and injuring many civilians. The placing of bombs in business centres, restaurants and buses caused much panic and unrest amongst the public.

According to the media, it is the way the event progresses that is symptomatic and exposes the offenders: Three people parked in front of a shopping arcade. One left the car, threw a bomb into the shop in a plastic bag and attempted to escape. The security forces opened fire and then after he was caught and harassed by the public, all three were handed over to security forces.

Found during the examination of the car were: three Kalashnikov rifles, 10 full cartridge chips, a few camouflage vests, materials used for making and destroying bombs, and three grenades produced by the [state-owned] Mechanical and Chemical Industry. The grenades were found in a black bag on one of the seats and four files were also found. One of these files consisted of six to seven pages and its contents were the vehicle registrations, consignment papers and official signatures, proving that the vehicle belonged to the gendarmerie. In another file, the names and addresses of various people were listed, including pictures and information about the owner of the bookshop as well as a layout of the shop and the shopping arcade. The name of the shop owner was crossed out with a red pen. The other files contained information about various people from Şemdinli, party executives and dignitaries, and their names were put into categories, such as potentially harmful and harmless. These files were recorded by the prosecutor.

The two special sergeants that had been released were re-arrested. The prosecutor's office wished to charge the offenders with: establishing a criminal organisation (TCK Article 220), crimes against the community (TCK Article 170), and crimes against life (TCK Article 82), and Articles 1 and 3 of the Anti-Terror Law.

The MİT and Gendarmerie Intelligence Presidency subsequently reported the Şemdinli incident to the TBMM Şemdinli Investigation Committee. In the 25-page intelligence report drafted by Brigadier General Mehmet Çörten, it was stated that the bombings in the Hakkari-Yüksekova-Şemdinli triangle were orchestrated by the PKK and that the two NCOs who were on a mission, had not been involved in the bombing. Furthermore, it was claimed that the PKK was preparing for street assaults, similar to those seen in France, and that 'the bombings and street assaults in the Hakkari-Şemdinli-Yüksekova triangle were in preparation for these assaults.' The presence of the two officers (Kaya and İldeniz) at the crime scene at the time of the bookshop bombing was described as a 'coincidence.'

In addition to the explosion on 9 November, the general strategy of the PKK in 2005 was explained, and statistics were included in the report. The explosions that had taken place in the regions of Hakkâri-Şemdinli and Yüksekova since 1 June 2005 were claimed to have been part of the organisation's strategy. The report accounted for 47 explosions between 1 June and 9 November 2005 and stated that the PKK's aim was to shift unrest to larger cities.

Whilst the general commander of the gendarmerie, General Fevzi Türkeri, referred to it as 'a a local incident', Prime Minister Erdoğan stated on 11 November that 'This does not seem to be a local incident as claimed. There is a mentality behind this. This mentality might be part of an ideological structure, or it could be the emotional reaction of a certain group of people. Once the evidence is solid, we are determined to investigate whatever is behind this.' The prime minister also made a statement about the future, confirmed that he had consulted the president and the chief of the general staff, and that they consented to go as far as it would take. He added that all government bodies were ready to act in harmony and do whatever was necessary.

When reminded that the Gendarmerie Intelligence Organisation (JİT) was suspected in the Şemdinli incident, Erdoğan stated, 'No, I do not recognise such an institution yet. Things such as that might have happened in the past or there might have been rumours, but no such thing has taken place during my term in office.' President of the TBMM Arınç requested an investigation of the Şemdinli incident, and also asked the government if JİTEM actually existed.

The question that should be answered at this point is why so many senior personnel, such as the prime minister and the head of the assembly, were not definitively informed about the existence of JİTEM. One of the main reasons why the existence of a separate intelligence organisation, working under the gendarmerie, was not officially acknowledged and was legally disputed until Code Number 5397 was the denial of the offices and officers accountable for the actions of such an institution. In the meantime, it can also be argued that this institution has, willingly or unwillingly, become a scapegoat for illicit dealings and therefore the government has chosen to claim ignorance of JİTEM's existence.

When the names of personnel from the Turkish Armed Forces were mentioned in the Şemdinli incident, the chief of the general staff, General Hilmi Özkök said, 'I do not accuse nor do I protect my personnel. Let us wait for the investigation to conclude.' Whereas the Republican People's Party Chairman (Cumhuriyet Halk Partisi, CHP) Deniz Baykal, attested that there were powers that used terrorism for other purposes, stating that 'what goes on in the region might be due to a conflict for profit. It is understood that some officials were involved in the incidents of 9 November. This is what the information suggests. There are undeniable signs.'

The willingness of the president, the president of the TBMM, the prime minister, the chief of the general staff and the leader of the opposition party, to investigate and clarify the background to these incidents showed promise in unveiling the affair. When the TBMM Ad-hoc Şemdinli Committee was formed, the public's desire for clarification was, once again, raised. However, differences of opinion among the Committee's members led to a deadlock, and, after approximately two months, the Committee was unable to complete its report, turning positive expectations into unresolved questions.

What led to these differences of opinion and to a deadlock were discussions concerning some military executives who were named in the report. The TBMM committee of Human Rights,[45] formed, in part, to assist the TBMM ad hoc committee, went to Şemdinli on 22 November 2005 to investigate further.

The draft report, containing research about the Şemdinli incident made by the subcommittee in Şemdinli and Yüksekova, was sent to the TBMM ad-hoc committee. The commander general of the land forces, Yaşar Büyükanıt, had publicly stated that he personally knew NCO Ali Kaya[46] and that he did not believe that he would commit a crime: 'I know that NCO. He worked under my command. He speaks Kurdish. He was with me in northern Iraq during the Swift Force Operation.' Büyükanıt made these comments officially, as a senior officer, without consulting documents or existing information. In the first excerpts of the draft that was leaked to the press, this statement was evaluated as 'unfortunate' and 'intervening with justice,' and reference was made to the Turkish Penal Code's Article against influencing the judiciary.

The draft report also contained the following statement: 'The General Command of Gendarmerie has to make the necessary explanations about the existence of units such as JİTEM and JİT, or lack thereof. Illegal organisations must be abolished, and those involved in such organisations must be prosecuted.' In this way, JİTEM/JİT's existence was therefore questioned.

It was later determined through the report that 'Yaşar Büyükanıt's statement to the press about knowing Ali Kaya and his belief in Kaya's innocence was unfortunate. Although he went on to say that he would not try to protect the person in question if he was involved in a crime, this statement can be perceived as intervening with justice.' Buyukanit's words were subsequently applied more generally: 'The statements made to the press by some officials can be perceived as intervening with justice.'[47]

Presumably, this was what left the Committee in a deadlock. It was alleged that military officials called on Mehmet Elkatmış to request that the information given to the Committee should not be leaked to the press and that members should

---

[45] This subcommittee consisted of the AKP Adıyaman Deputy Faruk Ünsal, CHP İzmir Deputy Ahmet Ersin and CHP Gaziantep Deputy Ahmet Yılmazkaya, under the presidency of AKP Nevşehir Deputy Mehmet Elkatmış.

[46] Aygan, who was a former PKK shriver and JİTEM member, wrote in his book İtirafçı that Kaya is JİTEM member 'Mutkili Ali.'

[47] 'Büyükanıt, Şemdinli Raporundan Çıkarıldı,' Haber 10, 17 December 2005. See http://www.haber10.com/haber/15700/ [Access date: 4 February 2006]

be warned to that effect. However, two of the Committee's members claimed that this was not how they perceived the situation, and that no such thing had been imposed on them. Another member, Faruk Ünsal, stated that he had not been requested to mention Büyükanıt or JİTEM in the report, but that he had intended to insert a more general statement along the lines of 'officials making statements that might influence the judiciary process.'[48] According to an article in Hürriyet, on 26 January 2006, subcommittee members Ahmet Ersin and Ahmet Yılmazkaya (from CHP) claimed that the judiciary was not so weak as to be influenced by such a sentence, and rejected its inclusion in the report. After pressure from CHP, the AKP wing accepted the removal of this sentence from the report.[49]

In conclusion, it can be said that there were four different approaches to the Şemdinli incident: the first was more of an official approach, accepting that the bombing was orchestrated by the PKK and that the presence of the gendarmerie intelligence was a coincidence. The second is the presumption that the intelligence members acted outside of the hierarchy and on their own initiative, and perhaps because of a personal conflict. The third views the bombing as a result of a Susurluk-like movement, in which PKK supporters are to be eliminated by counter-terrorist methods. This would mean that an illegal group remains active within the state and that the gendarmerie intelligence continues to use shrivers to accident that took place in Susurluk on 3 November 1996. Also worthy of consideration are 'the Parliamentary Investigation Committee's Report on Unsolved Political Murders accomplish their objectives. The fourth approach perceives the incident as an act of foreign secret services active in the region, aiming to incapacitate Turkey by creating domestic turmoil specifically on matters concerning northern Iraq.

Conclusion

The intricate web of relations that were unearthed after the Susurluk Crash of 3 November 1996, led to the questioning of some institutions and the structures within them. Although the ramifications were not as serious as the Susurluk incident, Şemdinli nonetheless reignited earlier suspicions.

Making the necessary arrangements for maintaining law and order and fighting threats is the most basic duty of a government, and the use of legally-defined secret operations and intelligence organisations are a part of the execution of this duty. One of the most important elements of a strong and stable state is to have strong security and intelligence organisations.

However, using the means and relations provided by the government in activities which are contrary to legal and constitutional principals, and establishing bonds and institutions to achieve this, is not something that should exist in a democratic state governed by the rule of law: it is also against the modern democratic tradition of civilian democratic oversight and control of the security bureaucracy. Prac-

---

48 'Şemdinli Komisyonu kilitlendi,' Haberextra, 30 January 2006. See http://www.haberextra.com/haber/9117/%C5%9Eemdinli/Komisyonu/kilitlendi. [Access date: 4 February 2006].

49 'Suçlamada geri adım,' Hürriyet, 26 January 2006.

tices and structures that do not comply with the rule of law and a democratic lifestyle and are not controlled by the parliament, civil society and the media, turn the fight against terrorism into a series of illicit activities, and these practices invariably lead to a distrust of the government and its institutions.

Naturally, the fine balance in the protection of democratic and legal principles should be preserved, the fight against terrorism must not be compromised for the preservation of these principles, and the fact that people and institutions make great sacrifices to fight terrorism should not be unjustly accused. However, to ensure that activities operate within a legal scope is an integral part of being a state governed by the rule of law, and as such, government officials are merely enforcers of the laws. Therefore, people employed by the government should not consider themselves entitled to operate outside these laws and legal principles. Moreover, no one should be allowed to see themselves as the sole owners of the state, breeding distrust among citizens of varying political opinions, beliefs and lifestyles. The government should also refrain, at all costs, from using illegitimate personnel.

In conclusion, some tactics used in the name of fighting effectively against terrorism have, at times, led to irreparable repercussions. One of the best examples known to the public is the use of shrivers by the gendarmerie. The public wants to know where and how shrivers are used. The Şemdinli incident might present a good opportunity for the gendarmerie intelligence to eliminate public suspicions on the matter. The time is right to repress defensive reflexes and shed light on significant claims. This also presents an important opportunity to demonstrate the power of the civilian authority and democracy in our country, especially during the course of the European Union (EU) membership process.

Non-Governmental Organisations

Ferhat Ünlü[*]

The Effect of Anti-Democratic National Security Practices on Civil Society: Civil Society Movements from the 1980s to 2000s

There is a direct relationship between the different conceptions of civil society, a people's 'civic consciousness' and the different notions of statehood.

If a person endowed with a sense of civic responsibility, considers that the authorities running his or her country do so for private gains, he or she can come together with link-minded individuals and form non-governmental organisations (NGOs).[1] In turn, these organisations can contribute to prevent the concentration and misuse of state authority[2]. It can be argued that the 'sacred state' or 'father state' tradition in Turkey has hindered the development of the concept of civil society. In its short history, the Republic of Turkey has witnessed three military coups: in 1960, in 1971 and in 1980. The legacy of these coups, and the fragile and often dysfunctional foundations of democracy, parliament and the press, have negatively impacted the development of an independent civil society until the adoption of the current Constitution in 1982.

Following the 1980 coup, all NGOs and political parties were banned and their properties were confiscated. In all, some 23'667 organisations were closed down.[3] However, as of 21 April 2005, there are 85'307 NGOs operating in Turkey.[4]

---

* Author in security-intelligence-terror, journalist.

1 In Aydın Uğur's, Yeni Demokrasinin Yeni Aktörleri: STK'lar, Merhaba Sivil Toplum Non-Governmental Organisations are defined as, 'the structures and activities that consist of organisations, foundations, civil enterprises, platforms, webs of connections, etc. that citizens form voluntarily out of a common viewpoint, common benefit, common sensitivities, common demand, etc., outside the legal, administrative, productive and cultural state organs.' Aydın Uğur, Yeni Demokrasinin Yeni Aktörleri: STK'lar, Merhaba Sivil Toplum (ed. Tacisel Ulaş) (İstanbul: Helsinki Yurttaşlar Derneği Yayınları, 1998) p. 69.

2 For the perception of state and consciousness of citizenship ingrained in the Turkish society, see Suavi Aydın, Amacımız Devletin Bekası, Demokratikleşme Sürecinde Devlet ve Yurttaşlar (İstanbul: TESEV Yayınları, 2006).

3 Some important data that displays the severity of the anti-democratic results of September 12 are as follows: 'Number of people tagged: 1,683,000. Number of trials and people tried: 230,000 people in 210,000 trials.

Number of death sentences and executions: 517 people were sentenced to death, 50 were executed. Number of people expelled from citizenship: 14,000. Number of recorded deaths through torture: 171 people.' Moreover, newspapers were not able to be published

The History Foundation (Tarih Vakfi) has established the most comprehensive NGO database in Turkey[5], aimed at improving ties between these organisations. According to Orhan Silier, President of the Foundation, there were approximately 50'000 NGOs in existence during the 1980s. Today, if one takes into account all of the organisations registered in public directories, there are approximately 1.3 NGOs in existence per 1'000 people.[6] These consist of the 82'000 organisations registered by the Ministry of Internal Affairs Organisations Chair, 4'200 foundations by the Foundations General Directorate and approximately 10'000 organisations from other networks. With a total of 13'731, Istanbul houses the highest number of NGOs, followed by Ankara and Izmir.

In the 1990s, despite low-intensity conflict in the eastern and south eastern provinces of Turkey, the idea of 'civil consciousness' gained momentum in the country, particularly in Istanbul, Ankara and Izmir. This was partly due to the 1995 Constitutional Amendment (Law No. 4121) which made it unlawful for organisations to 'have a political mission, carry out political activities, be supported by political parties, act together or share the same purposes as other NGOs.' Political parties were no longer permitted to organise meetings inside or outside Turkey and the constitutional freedoms of NGOs were restricted.[7] The final paragraph of Article 34 of the 1982 Constitution, for instance, regulates the right to organise meetings and demonstrations. It stipulates that organisations, foundations, unions and professional state organisations are not permitted to arrange meetings and demonstrations outside their specific areas of expertise.

Nonetheless, it is clear that NGOs cannot be forcibly removed from the political arena in modern democracies. NGOs serve an essential role, notably, monitoring of abuses of human rights, mobilising national and international public opinion against these abuses, and therefore the significance of these organisations for the democratic process is all the more important in more repressive environments.

After 1980, many of those that had suffered in the repressive environment that followed the coup, founded a number of NGO to address common problems, and in particular the issue of torture. The most well-known of these organisations are the Organisation for the Assistance to Families of Prisoners (Tutuklu Hükümlü Aileleri Yardımlaşma Derneği, TAYAD), founded in 1984[8], the Federation for the Assistance to Families of Prisoners (Tutuklu Aileleri Dayanişma Dernekleri Federasyonu, TUHAD-FED) and the Organisation for the Support to Families of Prisoners (Tutuklu Aileleriyle Yardımlaşma Derneği, TAYDER), which all carry out similar activities.

The most important issue that has influenced the NGO movement in Turkey after 1980, has been the low-intensity conflict in the eastern and south eastern prov-

---

for 300 days, and many cases of torture and suspicious death were witnessed. See http://www.memursen.org.tr/haberioku.asp?kategori=1&id=173.

4 Sevda Alkan, 'STK lar darbe yorgunu,' Yeni Şafak, 23 April 2005.

5 Available at http://www.stkrehberi.org (in Turkish)

6 Ibid.

7 http://www.tihak.org.tr/yaliefe1.html.

8 http://www.tayad.org

inces of the country. The anti-war discourse of some organisations, which criticised the war waged by the armed forces against the separatist organisation Kurdistan Workers' Party (Partiya Karkerên Kurdistan, PKK), was judged by the government and centralised media organisations to be supportive of terrorism. This was particularly true in the case of the Human Rights Organisation (İnsan Hakları Derneği, İHD). One of the organisation's founding members, novelist Adalet Ağaoğlu, criticised the İHD on similar grounds in 2000, at a time when the civilian situation in these regions had improved considerably in comparison to the 1980s and 1990s. Ağaoğlu had resigned from the organisation in the previous year, claiming that the İHD 'employs a one-sided, racist and nationalist approach.'[9] Ağaoğlu's resignation was a clear indication of the differences in perception of the PKK among the leftist intelligentsia.

However, there are other reasons that led the state and the centralised media to link the İHD to the PKK. The 'proof' of the ties between the İHD and the PKK was often linked to statements attributed to Şemdin Sakık.[10] It was claimed that Sakık said of the IHD's former president Akın Birdal: 'He is more of a PKK member than me.'[11] It was later revealed that these statements could not be attributed to Sakık and that their publication by the centralised media was done without authentication. This is one of the less elegant examples of the abuse of state power over the media.

Representatives of the İHD and of the Organisation for Human Rights and Solidarity for Oppressed People (İnsan Hakları ve Mazlumlar İçin Dayanışma Derneği, Mazlum-Der) were among the members of the delegation that visited the PKK camp in Northern Iraq and returned the imprisoned Turkish soldiers to Turkey in August 1998. The delegation also included Van Deputy, Fethulllah Erbaş, who was a member of the Welfare Party (Relah Partisi, RP), which was then a party in the ruling coalition. This good-willed attempt of the delegation was criticised by nationalist circles, and later by the centralised media. The focus of their criticism is perhaps best summarised by the following statement: 'they had pictures taken under the PKK flag.' An investigation was launched by the Ankara State Security Court and both the president of the İHD, Akın Birdal, and the president of Mazlum-Der, İhsan Arslan, were subsequently taken into custody.[12] Arslan later became a deputy for the government party, the AKP.

Activities undertaken by the group known as the Saturday Mothers (Cumartesu Anneleri) also generated widespread debate in the 1990s. The group's activities revolved around the symbolic protest against the unresolved murders in the 'state of emergency region' and the disappearances of individuals in custody. On 27 May 1995, friends and relatives of those who had disappeared, gathered in front of

---

9 Sefa Kaplan, 'İHD PKK cı, artık istifa ediyorum,' Hürriyet, 1 August 2005.

10 Sakık was handed over to Turkish security forces in northern Iraq on 14 April 1998.

11 'Birdal dan A Timi ne: Bilmem ne bereliler,' Hürriyet, 26 April 1998.

12 http://www.byegm.gov.tr/YAYINLARIMIZ/AyinTarihi/1996/eylul1996.htm

Galatasaray High School in Beyoğlu in a sit-down protest. After a year of police harassment, the protests ended on 13 March 1999.[13]

The Effects of the Susurluk Process and the Intervention of February 28 on Civil Society

The Susurluk accident of 3 November 1996[14] influenced civil society more than any other event during the period. The protest which drew much interest in the country was called 'One Minute of Darkness for Everlasting Enlightenment', and started on 1 February 1997 in response to the Susurluk accident. For one minute, an important portion of society turned off their lights at nine o-clock in the evening and protested by banging on various kitchen utensils. The RP Deputy and Minister of Justice of the time, Şevket Kazan mockingly described the event in the following way: 'They are blowing out the candles.'[15]

The 'One Minute of Darkness' protests, reported extensively by the centralist media, ended on 9 March 1997. Nonetheless, the 'anti-Susurluk' spirit, which was a reaction not only to the counter-guerrilla tactics of the 1990s in the east and south-east, but also to the state's anti-democratic practices before and after 1980, was maintained by both NGOs and other non-organised elements of society. The opinions expressed by Engin Cinmen, one of the leaders of the protests, and the legal spokesperson for Citizen Enterprise, should be viewed in this context.[16]

The National Security Council's (Milli Güvenlik Kurulu, MGK) decision of 28 February 1997 – described as a 'post-modern' military intervention - became yet another subject of interest for civil society. However, many NGOs failed to react adequately to this development. In particular, the reaction of NGOs positioned on the left of the political spectrum - whose existence has been based on protesting every anti-democratic practice – was far from constructive. This is certainly due to the fact that the intervention targeted the government coalition where the RP party, which is considered Islamist, was an important player. Ideological differences meant that a certain divide separated many NGOs during that period. Even cooperation between Mazlum-Der, the voice of religious minded organisations, and the left-wing İHD, working to free soldiers held captive by PKK, could not bridge the divide. Of significance, however, is that there have been very positive developments since 2000 in terms of cooperation between left wing and Islamist NGOs, in regard to human rights advocacy.

---

13 'Cumartesi Annelerinden 'Cumartesi',' Bianet, 17 May 2002. See http://www.bianet.org/2002/05/17/haber10036.htm

14 The accident, where police chief Hüseyin Kocadağ, civilian activist Abdullah Çatlı and his girlfriend Gonca Us died, and DYP Deputy Sedat Bucak was seriously injured, became the symbol of the 'deep government.'

15 The unfortunate declaration by the Minister of Justice was a send-up to the so-called Alevi tradition of putting out the candle.

16 Yasemin Varlık, 'Susurluk Kamu Vicdanında Bitmedi,' Bianet, 12 February 2001. See http://www.bianet.org/2001/09/07/728.htm

Similarly, Islamist circles did not develop a constructive approach to the Susurluk incident. An important reason for this was the RP's affiliation to the government and its Islam-friendly 'National View' (Milli Görüş). Islamists misjudged civil society and the centralist media's anti-Susurluk discourse and saw it as a conspiracy against their rule. Minister of Justice Şevket Kazan's scorn of the 'One Minute of Darkness' protests and Prime Minister Necmettin Erbakan's denigrating comments about the Susurluk protesters, contributed to create an inaccurate impression that Susurluk was only criticised by leftist politicians.

The 28 February decisions fragmented public dissent against practices that the Susurluk symbolised, largely because of the influence of the state-controlled media. The necessity to take a pro- or anti- 28 February stance divided the public, which previously had the potential to unite through the widespread disapproval of the Susurluk incident and its subsequant handling by state authorities.[17]

NGO's working for the Democratic Oversight of the Security Sector: TESEV

The Turkish Economic and Social Studies Foundation (Türkiye Ekonomik ve Sosyal Etüdler Vakfı, TESEV) is the leading NGO among those involved in security sector reform and issues related to the challenges of democratisation.

The history of TESEV, founded in 1994, date back as far as 1961 and the Economic and Social Studies Conference delegation, established by Dr. Nejat Eczacıbaşı.[18] In TESEV's current structure, cooperation between academia, civil society and bureaucracy plays a significant role. TESEV announced its foundation at a time when the impact of the 1980 coup had eased, and when NGOs were no longer viewed with suspicion and were, in essence, reborn. The foundation was established on 6 October 1994 and included amongst its 200 founding members academics, bureaucrats, businessmen, executives, industrialists, journalists, union leaders and various professionals. TESEV currently has 300 members.

TESEV's main objective is to convey economic, social and political recommendations to society and political circles, based on reliable scientific research, and thus contribute to the development of solutions to current problems.[19] TESEV does not want its studies to be merely research found on a library shelf, but rather aims to contribute to the political decision-making process for the public good. The foundation carries out studies in Turkey for the development of independent thinking, the establishment of the principle of transparency, the democratisation of the country as part of the process of European harmonisation and to help strengthen the country's role in the region.

TESEV, as the leading independent institute involved in the democratic oversight of the security sector, started research on civil-military relations in 2000. The

---

17 On the two different institutions' similar approach to February 28, see http://www.mazlumder.org/ana.php?konu=aciklama&id=465&lang=tr; http://www.memursen.org.tr/haberioku.asp?kategori=1&id=173

18 http://www.tesev.org.tr/tesev_tarihce.php

19 http://www.tesev.org.tr/tesev_misyon.php

foundations of TESEV's demilitarisation work were established in 2003.[20] At this time, it was decided that it was necessary to work in the areas of standardisation and democratisation of civilian-military relations. Its first initiative in this field was the publication of the handbook 'Parliamentary Oversight of the Security Sector' in Turkish. This handbook was prepared by the Geneva Centre for the Democratic Control of Armed Forces (DCAF) and the Inter-parliamentary Union (IPU), of which the Turkish Grand National Assembly (Türkiye Büyük Millet Mecilisi, TBMM) is also a member. The book was launched on 21 May 2004 in the presence of parliamentarians, high level bureaucrats, members of the press, and invited guests.

Another important area of work for TESEV in 2005, revolved around issues related to relations between civil society and the security sector. Work in this area has focused on institutions of the security sector such as the Police, National Intelligence Organisation (Milli İstihbarat Teşkilatı, MİT) the Directorate General of Security's Intelligence Department, as well as gendarmerie intelligence and paramilitary units.

The complex structure of relations between civilian and military authority, a structure unique to Turkey, has been seen not only as one of the most acute administrative problems since the founding of the Republic, but also an obstacle to the European Union (EU) harmonisation process. TESEV has done extensive research on relations between the security sector and political institutions and between the security sector and society at large. It has related developments in these fields to the democratisation process and issues of better governance.

Thus, the work of TESEV is not limited to narrow practical studies directed at fulfilling EU entry conditions or civil-military relations in Turkey. Additionally, TESEV carries out scientific research on other issues of importance to Turkish society and seeks to share its findings with the widest possible audience, in particular with bureaucrats of the security sector, parliamentarians, university students and representatives of the media and civil society. In other words, it seeks to encourage the development of openness and transparency in the security sector in order to assist the process of democratisation.

In the framework of democratisation of the security sector, TESEV organised a conference in Ankara on 3 February 2005, entitled 'Democratic Horizons in the Security Sector: Turkey and the European Security Sector Governance Experience.' The conference was attended by numerous parliamentarians, bureaucrats and experts from both Turkey and abroad, and was widely covered by the media.[21]

The book entitled 'Democratic Oversight of the Security Sector: Turkey and the World' was published by TESEV, in cooperation with DCAF.[22] The fact that most decisions in Turkey are taken and implemented by the state bureaucracy, and that civil society and even elected parliamentarians have little oversight over these decisions, is arguably one of the greatest obstacles to democratisation in Turkey.

20 http://www.tesev.org.tr/etkinlik/GSDA_TESEV.pdf
21 http://www.tesev.org.tr/basin/basin_tesev.php
22 http://www.tesev.org.tr/etkinlik/dcaf2.php

In this context, the TESEV Security Sector Work and Monitoring Group[23] is highly significant, because it questions the traditional function of state bureaucracy in Turkey and addresses ways in which a more civilised, more transparent administrative approach might be implemented.[24] The working group believes that security needs changed after the Cold War and became a 'social concept'. In turn, this 'socialised security concept' needs new provisions for it to be re-governed effectively.

Another of the 2005 TESEV publications investigating the security sector is the 'Turkish Human Rights Balance 2005 Monitoring Report' by Professor Baskın Oran.[25] Although this report does not aim to substitute the 2005 reports of NGOs such as İHD, the Turkish Human Rights Foundation (Türkiye İnsan Hakları Vakfı, TİHV), Mazlum-Der, BİANET or Antenna, it nevertheless contains important clues as to developments related to human rights issues in the West and in Turkey in 2005. It also unveils the negative impact that the United States' war on terror has had on democratic freedoms and is illustrated with concrete examples. Oran evaluated these developments by stating: 'panicking, Europe lost sense of how it has come to symbolise pluralistic democracy since 1215'.[26]

Indeed, in 2005, even EU countries enacted anti-democratic policies in the name of the so-called fight against terrorism. The French and Dutch 'no' to the EU Constitution in May and in June 2005, demonstrate that the number of people against expansion of the EU should not be underestimated.

TESEV's work on the security sector and problems of democratisation were met with a negative response by nationalist forces in Turkey. TESEV was the first institution subjected to some of the narrow-minded actions taken by the nationalist movement. Their actions target the bases of support of TESEV's research, rather than the content of its work. In fact, the only cause for debate is the fact that the Open Society Institute, financed by US investor George Soros, supports TESEV. In every TESEV study, all financial contributors are clearly stated. The question of

---

23 TESEV Security Sector/Bureaucracy Work and Monitoring Group consists of Prof. Ümit Cizre (Bilkent University), Associate Prof. Serhat Güvenç (Bilgi University), Dr. Hasan Ersel (Sabancı University), Associate Prof. Gencer Özcan (Yıldız Technical University), Dr. Ümit Kardaş (retired military judge and prosecutor, lawyer) and Prof. İbrahim Cerrah (Director of Police Academy Security Sciences Institute).

24 In the Work and Monitoring Group's president Prof. Ümit Cizre's article published in 'Radikal İki', it is stated that the democratic control of bureaucracy can only be carried out through the oversight of parliaments, ministries of defence, the media and non-governmental organisations. Cizre puts forth two solid suggestions in this context. The first is the clear separation of the spheres of duty and responsibility of the domestic and foreign security units which propagate and apply security and defense policies. The second is the implementation of the transparency and openness principle – which even includes the oversight of the secrecy principle – in the activities, tools, methods, policies and budgets of both civilian and military security bureaucracy. Ümit Cizre, 'Güvenlik Reformu, Ama Nasıl?,' Radikal 2, 5 June 2005.

25 Baskın Oran, Türkiye İnsan Hakları Bilançosu 2005 İzleme Raporu (İstanbul: TESEV Yayınları, 2006).

26 Ibid, p. 41-42.

why Soros backs social and political studies has already been addressed by TESEV officials.[27]

Some nationalist media went as far to say that 'TESEV is attempting to poison Turkish society and spread the claim that the concepts of martyrdom, war veterans and heroism are fallacies, in order to disincline Turkish youth from becoming soldiers.'[28]

The Yeniçağ newspaper headlined 'TESEV crosses the line',[29] when it reported on statements made by Bircan Akyıldız, Chairman of the Nationalist Unions' Federation (Turkish Kamu-Sen), during a visit by the Turkish War Veterans, Widows and Orphans of Martyrs Organisation, and on the documentary by Uz Ajans officials of the martyrs of the organisation.

The martyrdom and war veterans' debates reached such an extent that a court case was filed in the Şişli Criminal Court, against TESEV's Chairman of the Executive Board, Can Paker, for 'alienating the public from military service' in accordance with the Turkish Penal Code (Türk Ceza Kanunu, TCK) Article 155.[30]

ASAM

The Centre for Eurasian Strategic Studies (Avrasya Stratejik Araştırmalar Merkezi, ASAM), undoubtedly carries out the most extensive research on security issues in Turkey. In fact, perhaps the most important reason for the existence of ASAM is its capacity to produce strategic reports that reinforce the current dominant approach to security issues in Turkey. This is why Eurasia is one of the main research areas of the Institute, as it is seen as Turkey's National heartland by some nationalist circles due to the existence of the Turkish speaking republics in Central Asia. ASAM started its activities with the establishment of the Europe-Asia Union Turkish Eco-

---

27 TESEV's Chairman of the Board of Directors and President of the Open Society Institute Assistance Foundation Can Paker explains why Soros is financing the Open Society Institute in the following way: 'Soros is a businessman and supports such a philosophy. Why does a man who has a personal wealth exceeding 10 billion dollars do this? For a man who is 75 years old, where is the sense in making another 20 billion dollars? People can do a lot for some ideas, for some beliefs they create in their own heads. A lot of people in Turkey do this. There are a lot of people in Turkey who make sacrifices, spend money and effort for what they believe to be right.' 'Soros, Türkiye'de 'Açık Toplum'a 6 milyon dolar verdi,' Hürriyet, 27 May 2005. Can Paker's answer to the claims that Soros changed the regime in some Central Asian countries by using his financial power is also important in this context. Paker, after explaining that the Open Society Institute is active in 50 countries, spends 450-500 million dollars a year, half of this money goes to the country that is seen as the most problematic, the US, and that from the remaining 250-300 dollars, 5-6-7 million dollars are allocated per country, said: 'If you can change the regime with this amount, I think many holdings in Turkey are capable of regime change all over the world.' 'Soros'tan Türkiye'ye 6 Milyon $,' Ortadoğu, 28 May 2005.

28 Abdullah Akosman, 'Vatana İhanetin Adı Açık Toplum Oldu,' Önce Vatan, 30 May 2005.

29 'TESEV haddini aştı,' Yeniçağ, 19 May 2004.

30 Ümit Cizre, 'Güvenlik Reformu, Ama Nasıl?,' Radikal 2, 5 June 2005.

nomic, Social and Cultural Studies Foundation in 1993. It has made a name for itself through the publication of the magazine Avrasya Dosyası since 1994. In 1999, it expanded its staff and developed into its current status.

ASAM is the first strategic studies centre in Turkey and is an NGO that uses the methods of a think-tank as far as its working style and propagation of strategies and ideas are concerned. ASAM's research activities are divided into nine different departments each with a different geographical focus, and aim to establish an approach that focuses on foreign policy decisions rather than an analysis of the domestic 'strategy-intelligence' tradition employed by the state bureaucracy in Turkey.[31]

The majority of ASAM's staff are retired military personnel and civil servants, and this fact stands out immediately. The chairman of the Board, Edip Başer, is a retired general who was employed in a number of different positions in the Turkish Armed Forces (Türk Silahli Kuvvetleri, TSK). These positions included the post of Deputy Chief of Staff and Commander General of the Second Army. Başer was also reportedly considered for the post of MİT Undersecretary.[32] The President of ASAM, Gündüz Aktan, is a retired Ambassador. Another member of the Board, Ertuğrul Güven, is a retired intelligence officer who worked at senior levels in the MİT, however, this fact is not stated in his ASAM biography.[33] The remaining members of the board, Nüzhet Kandemir and İnal Batu, are also retired diplomats. ASAM's Vice-President, Armağan Kuloğlu, is a retired major general. The former president of ASAM, before Aktan, was Professor Ümit Özdağ, who occupied the post from 1999 to April 2004.[34] His father, Captain Muzaffer Özdağ, was a member of the group involved in the 27 May 1960 coup d'etat. Another member, Colonel Alpaslan Türkeş, later joined the National Union Committee (Milli Birlik Komitesi, MBK).[35] Ümit Özdağ, and the current president, Gündüz Aktan, are known for their nationalist sympathies.

If one analyses the reasons for its establishment, its working style, its professional pasts and the ideological stances of its members, ASAM inevitably seems to be an institution established for the purpose of strengthening the security sector and propagating the current dominant approach to security issues in the name of a stronger internal and external defence for Turkey.

The apparent discord that emerged during the 'Turkish Civil-Military Relations and the EU: Preparation for Continuing Convergence' research project is indicative of the current civil-military relations in Turkey. This project was carried out

---

31 These nine departments are Middle East, Russia, Ukraine, the Balkans, Caucasia, Turkistan, Europe, America, Far-East/Pacific and Turkey Study Departments.

32 'MİT'i 2.5 yıl önce önerdiler,' Hürriyet, 19 May 2005.

33 Güven's name was mentioned in the coup attempt in Azerbaijan. Azerbaijan President Haydar Aliyev accused Güven of cooperating with the revolutionaries during the coup attempt against Cevadov on 3 October 1994. 'Örtülüden kullanılan 45 milyon doların kaydı yok,' Hürriyet, 14 January 1998. For another article on the same subject, see Sedat Ergin, 'Yılmaz' ın zor kararı,' Hürriyet, 23 February 1998. Also, for detailed information about the Azerbaijan Coup, see Kutlu Savaş's Susurluk Report.

34 'ASAM'ın başkanlığına Gündüz Aktan atandı,' Zaman, 7 April 2004.

35 http://www.biyografi.net/kisiayrinti.asp?kisiid=2928

in cooperation with the Centre for European Security Studies (CESS) in Gröningen, Holland and the İstanbul Policy Centre (İstanbul Politikalar Merkezi, İPM).[36] However, ASAM members decided to withdraw from the research project in April 2005, upon CESS' insistence on recommending that the General Staff be under the command of the Ministry of National Defence, in order to increase civilian and democratic control over the security sector.[37] The report was made public on 14 November 2005, with a significantly toned-down language, and ASAM's criticisms had been taken into consideration. The report was also handed to the EU Council and the European Commission (EC). In the EC's Progress Report on Turkey of 9 November 2005, reference was made to TESEV and DCAF's cooperative reports.[38]

To contribute to the process of democratisation, the report suggests that the General Staff should be placed under the authority of the Ministry of National Defence, instead of the current framework which links it directly to the Prime Minister and Head of Government.[39] The report also states that the TSK would be more appropriately overseen by parliament due to the 'military guardianship' tradition which still remains strong in Turkey.[40]

The Chairman of the Board of ASAM, retired Major General Edip Başer, made the following statement about CESS and the İPM's report:

> What we say is this: if Turkey's security and threat assessments change in the future, authorised officials will make the necessary adjustments. What should guide us is not one or another EU guideline, but the security needs of Turkey. 60 years ago, the principle problem was the danger of the politicisation of the Turkish Armed Forces' top echelons. Some might say: Will Turkey's security problems change or be different in 10-15 years? Will politicisation concerns vanish

---

36 İPM was founded on 1 November 2001 as part of the Sabancı University.

37 In the related news article by Barkın Şık in Milliyet, the following was stated: 'The Final Report on the Civil-Military Relations in Turkey by the workgroup financed by the Dutch Ministry of Foreign Affairs, and consisting of retired soldiers and mostly civilians is completed. The president of the group, former Dutch Minister of Defence Wim Van Eekelen ignored the suggestions of the Turkish side in the final report and included the proposal of the Joint Staff being attached to MSB. ASAM, in its refusal of the proposal, stated 'there are issues that are not discussed and agreed upon, the sensitivities are not reflected. We cannot accept the report in its current state. This cannot be the report that we prepared in a joint effort.' 'Ankara'yı kızdıran rapor,' Milliyet, 10 May 2005.

38 Commission of the European Communities, Turkey 2005 Progress Report, Brussels, 9 November 2005, p. 14, For the full text, see http://europa.eu.int/comm/enlargement/report_2005/pdf/package/sec_1426_final_en_progress_report_tr.pdf

39 CESS, İPM, 'Türk Sivil-Asker İlişkileri ve Avrupa Birliği: Süregelen Buluşmaya Hazırlık,' p. 36. For a Turkish version of the report, see http://www.cess.org/publications/occasionals/pdfs/occasionals4.pdf

40 CESS, İPM, 'Türk Sivil-Asker İlişkileri ve Avrupa Birliği: Süregelen Buluşmaya Hazırlık.'

> through democracy and the growing maturity of the people, or not? I cannot say that we are politically mature enough. The EU's recommendations have nothing but ulterior motives.[41]

Co-chairman[42] of the working group, retired Major General Armağan Kuloğlu, said the following on the matter:

> It is believed that the report will be nothing but a one-sided document, that it will lead to unnecessary speculations that will be abused by certain circles, and that it will not guide the EU's policy-makers to the truth. That is why we resigned from the working group.[43]

ASAM President Gündüz Aktan claimed that the report's language was very aggressive.[44] When ASAM resigned from the working group because of comments and suggestions contained in the report, nationalist circles rejoiced.[45]

Additionally, ASAM did not comment – it did not approve nor did it criticise - nor did it prepare a report on one of the most important political developments of 2005, namely the entry into force of the new Turkish Penal Code. This is suggestive of ASAM's distinctiveness from other NGOs, of its focus on strategic matters, and of its role in the dissemination of policies for the benefit of the government. The following statement on its official website is suggestive of its tendency to offer policy recommendations and research for the benefit of the government: 'ASAM, in its structure, aims to define and analyse the opportunities and obstacles for the realisation of Turkey's national benefits, and understand the factors that threaten its security.'[46]

Not only is ASAM an atypical NGO, but some ASAM experts have made comments that suggest a cynical approach towards NGOs in general. One of ASAM's Central Asia experts, Gökçen Ekinci, states the following in an article entitled 'Foreign Civil Society Organisations and Civil Coups': 'public movements that result in a change of leadership and in the global balance of power, give way to a need to clearly define the trendy term 'non-governmental organisations' and for a better assessment of these organisations. The fact that these organisations have unlimited areas of activity

---

41 'Asker düğümü tartışması,' Milliyet, 11 May 2005.

42 In addition to Vice President Armağan Kuloğlu, European Desk Chief Dr. Mustafa Şahin and retired General Yılmaz Aklar, who later became Secretary General of ASAM, participated in the project on behalf of ASAM.

43 'Ankara'yı kızdıran rapor,' Milliyet, 10 May 2005.

44 'Paşalar rapordan imzalarını çekti,' Hürriyet, 27 June 2005.

45 http://72.14.203.104/search?q=cache:iqdQ9PLcFHAJ:www.cengizkan.com/html/ocaksistem.php%3Fname%3DHaber%26file%3Darticle%26sid%3D1456+%22Avrupa+G%C3%BCvenlik+Ara%C5%9Ft%C4%B1rmalar%C4%B1+Merkezi%22+(CESS)&hl=tr&ct=clnk&cd=30>

46 For more detailed information about ASAM's stance, see http://www.avsam.org/tr/giris3.asp

and that they have reached a potential to threaten political systems, has caused increased pressure and criticisms of foreign non-governmental organisations.'[47]

Another issue that should be pointed out is ASAM's aversion to Turkey's membership of the EU, which has even been described by ASAM experts as a strategic defeat.[48]

The articles that make it to the cover of ASAM's magazine Stratejik in 2005, provide a better idea of the institution's working style:

> The Turkish Report of Northern Cyprus is Looking for its Main Opposition Leader (November 2005), Elections in Azerbaijan (November - 2005), The Iraq Constitution and Turkey (October - 2005), Syria, Transformation and Turkey (September - 2005), Terrorism in London (August - 2005), Four Styles of Politics in the Turkish-American Relations (July - 2005), The Silk Road of the 21st Century: Baku-Tbilisi-Ceyhan (June - 2005), The Lausanne Peace Treaty and the Armenian Problem (May - 2005), Armenia; The Genocide Obstinacy and the Future that is Lost (April - 2005), Democracy Rehearsal in Iraq (March - 2005), Global Injustice in Energy (February - 2005), EU Membership Negotiations in the Shadow of Greek-Cypriot Veto Blackmails (January - 2005).[49]

Finally, the Istanbul Policy Centre (İstanbul Politikalar Merkezi,- İPM), which started its activities in December 2001 at Sabancı University, is involved in research in the areas of sociology, administration and public policy.[50] However, in 2005, the İPM did not undertake any research activities into the security sector, apart from 'Turkish Civil-Military Relations and the EU's project in cooperation with CESS.

Reactions of NGOs to the Legal Regulations and 'Deep State' Practices in 2005

In 2005, the İHD, Mazlum-Der, the TİHV, the Foundation for Social and Legal Studies (Toplum ve Hukuk Araştırmaları Vakfı, TOHAV), the Turkish Bar Association (Türkiye Barolar Birliğ), the Anti-War Organisation (Savaş Karşitali Derneği), the Initiative for Freedom of Expression (Düşünce Sucuna Karşi Girişim) and other NGOs, approached issues of human rights and the rule of law with great understanding. This is perhaps a reflection of the improvement of civil society consciousness in Turkey since 2000.

These organisations started their activities in the domain of human rights and legal affairs between the end of 1980s and the beginning of 2000, with the exception of the Turkish Bar Association that dates back to the 1930s. They are, therefore,

---

47 Gökçen Ekici, 'Yabancı Sivil Toplum Örgütleri ve Sivil Darbeler,' 20 April 2005. See http://www.avsam.org/tr/analizler.asp?ID=50

48 Prof. Dr. Ümit Özdağ, Avrupa Birliği'nin Türkiye Politikaları (Ankara: ASAM Yayınları, 2003). For the electronic version, see http://www.avsam.org/tr/asamcalismasi.asp?ID=1

49 http://www.avsam.org/tr/stratejikanaliz.asp?x_yil1=2005

50 http://www.erg.sabanciuniv.edu/ipm.htm

suggestive of the awakening of Turkish civil society following the coup of 12 September 1980.

The issues that attracted most attention for NGOs in 2005, were the new draft Anti-Terror Law (Terörle Mücadele Kanunu, TMK), the new Turkish Penal Code (Türk Ceza Kanunu, TCK) that went into effect on 1 June 2005, and the Kızıltepe-Şemdinli incidents. The TMK draft is seen by many NGOs as a step backwards for Turkey, in relation to the progress made towards the safeguard of human rights, the rule of law and the EU harmonisation process.

The Anti-Terror Law

Mazlum-Der's report on the new TMK criticised the fact that the draft text was not made public: 'Bills and draft laws should be published on the web for easy access and healthy public discussion.' According to Mazlum-Der, the TMK draft was intentionally brought into the spotlight at a time when terrorism and conflicts were on the rise, as an attempt to justify the measures of the draft law. In addition, it stated that the TMK contained many elements that are contrary to human rights law.[51]

The new TMK draft is presented as part of the larger 'war on terror' waged in response to the terrorist attacks of 11 September 2001. As many of the policies enacted in its name, it has infringed upon democratic freedoms. In Britain, for instance, the severe measures of the Anti-Terror Law drew condemnations from the media and NGOs alike.[52]

The Draft concerning Amendments to the Anti-Terror Law, which was accepted by the Commission formed by the Ministry of Justice, contains references to the British Anti-Terrorism law.[53] The expansion of the definition of what constitutes a terrorist was interpreted as a backwards step by Mazlum-Der, and in particular that of Article 8, which limits freedom of expression. However, amendment made through the Law Number 4928 of 19 July 2003 removed these provisions.

The Turkish Bar Association's appraisal of the new TMK was similar. The magazine Legal Life (Hukukla Yaşam), published by the lawyers of the Ankara Bar, argued that despite filling some important gaps, the draft law was 'almost like declaring a civilian state of emergency throughout the whole country.'[54]

The president of the Diyarbakır Bar Association, Sezgin Tanrıkulu, said: 'Current plans to amend TMK No. 3713 have new and wider implications. We be-

---

51 Mazlum-Der, 'Terörle Mücadele Kanunu Tasarısı Hakkında Değerlendirme Raporu,' 14 September 2005. For the full report, see http://www.mazlumder.org/ana.php?konu=rapor&id=1042&lang=tr

52 Ekrem Dumanlı, 'Terörle Mücadele Yasası işte böyle sorgulanır,' Zaman, 14 November 2005.

53 Mazlum-Der, 'Terörle Mücadele Kanunu Tasarısı Hakkında Değerlendirme Raporu.'

54 'Barodan TMK uyarısı: OHAL getirilmek isteniyor,' Zaman, 10 December 2005.

lieve that it should be abolished completely, as it is unacceptable in view of the supremacy of law and human rights.'[55]

One of the fiercest critiques of the new TMK draft law has been the Initiative for Freedom of Expression, of which Şanar Yurdatapan is the spokesperson. Yurdatapan declared that the two draft laws, although fundamentally different, both created new forms of crimes and annulled some of the positive developments contained in the Code of Criminal Procedure (Ceza Muhakemeleri Kanunu, CMK). Yurdatapan further stated that his group was preparing for acts of civil disobedience to protest to the draft law.[56]

Additionally, Turkey's leading NGOs declared that the government did not consult them in preparing the new TMK draft. The İHD, Mazlum-Der, the Human Rights Foundation, the Helsinki Citizens' Assembly and the Initiative for Freedom of Expression, stated that no one from the government had consulted or informed them; contrary to declarations of the Minister of Foreign Affairs Abdullah Gül who stated that the new TMK was prepared in consultation with various social institutions and NGOs.[57]

In 2004, NGOs did not make any demands regarding the shortening of periods of custody. This is because the duration of custody was lowered to 24 hours with the new TCK, introduced on 1 June 2005. However, the duration can be extended up to a maximum of four days for certain types of crimes.[58]

Police officials constantly express concerns, arguing that the new maximum period of custody is insufficient.[59] Istanbul Police Commissioner, Celalettin Cerrah, has requested that the maximum duration be extended to 15 days.[60]

In sum, the new draft Anti-Terror Law has not yet become law, because of the continuous and determined criticisms by NGOs and there is information that the draft was abandoned in April 2006. However, due to an augmentation of the number of demonstrations and the enduring conflict in the eastern and south eastern provinces since spring of 2006, the security sector has expressed the position that further adjustments need be added to the Anti-Terror law.[61]

---

55 'Diyarbakır Barosu: TMK tasarısıyla yapılmak istenenler,' 29 September 2005. See http://www.savaskarsitlari.org/arsiv.asp?ArsivTipID=6&ArsivAnaID=28810&ArsivSayfaNo=1

56 'Özgürlükleri savunmak için sivil itaatsizlik,' Bianet, 28 September 2005. See http://www.bianet.org/2005/09/28/67893.htm

57 'Hükümet yeni TMK taslağını hangi sivil topluma danıştı?,' January 10, 2006. See http://www.savaskarsitlari.org/arsiv.asp?ArsivTipID=9&ArsivAnaID=30627

58 http://tem.iem.gov.tr/cmk.php

59 'Gözaltı süresi yetersiz',' Sabah, 6 January 2006.

60 'Cerrah'tan 'olağanüstü' talepler,' NTV-MSNBC, 25 March 2006. See http://www.ntv.com.tr/news/366383.asp

61 For Minister of Justice and Government Spokesman Cemil Çiçek's statements on this issue, see 'Askerin istediği yasa çıkar sinyali, Hürriyet, 31 March 2006.

The Turkish Penal Code and Code of Criminal Procedure

One of the most important developments of 2005, in the legal and human rights sphere, is the introduction of Turkish Penal Code No. 5237 and the Code of Criminal Procedure No. 5271. These two laws, although criticised in some aspects, did not draw systematic or notable reactions from NGOs. Organisations known to adhere to Islamic values warned the government about the new TCK, stating in a joint declaration that 'although the [new] TCK brings some positive regulations, it is behind its predecessor in the articles concerning freedom of thought.'[62] These organisations included: Mazlum-Der, the Woman's Rights Association Against Discrimination (Ayrimciliğa Karşi Kadin Haklari Derneği, AK-DER), the Free Thought and Educational Rights Association (Özgür Düşünce ve Eğitim Haklari Derneği, Özgür-Der), all Theory Faculties and High Islam Institutes (Tüm İlahiyat Fakülteleri ve Yüksek İslam Enstitüleri Mezunlar Derneği, TİYEMDER), the Humanitarian Aid Foundation (İnsani Yardim Vakfi, İHH), and the Freedom to Veil Enterprise Group (Başörtüsüne Özgürlük Girşimi).

In its 2005 General Human Rights Report, the Human Rights Association assessed 2005 as 'a lost year as far as the improvement of rights and freedoms are concerned, [a year] when democracy and human rights wavered and sometimes receded'. It stated that the amendments to TCK were also a step backward.[63] Furthermore, the association declared that Articles 301, 216, 288 and 277 infringed upon freedom of expression.[64]

The Human Rights Foundation of Turkey made the following declaration on the results of the new CMK in practice: 'The cases that were filed against writers, journalists and human rights activists based on the TCK Articles 312 and 159 in previous years are now being filed principally based on articles 301 and 288. These trials now largely disfavour defendants.'[65] The Turkish Bar Association stated that the way the new TCK and CMK are interpreted and applied in practice do not correspond with their intended purpose.[66]

---

62 'Yeni TCK Tasarı'na Sivil Tepki,' İHH İnsani Yardım Vakfı, 17 September 2004. See http://www.ihh.org.tr/cgi-bin/index.pl?mod=news;op=news_id;id=1021

63 İnsan Hakları Derneği (İHD), '2005 Yılı Genel İnsan Hakları Raporu,' 28 February 2006. For the full report, see http://www.ihd.org.tr/ana.html

64 Ibid

65 Türkiye İnsan Hakları Vakfı (TİHV), '2005 Yılında İnsan Haklarının Genel Durumu.' See http://www.tihv.org.tr

66 Chair Özdemir Özok explained the Bar Association's views about TCK and CMK in a symposium in Mersin as follows: 'As you might remember, during the debates concerning these laws in TBMM General Meeting, a member of the parliament said 'this can only be stopped if a few people are sent to the gallows', and also our Minister of Justice stated that the authorities were not enough, and that if the authorities are expanded, he would be able to rip out the culprits' lungs. I leave you to assess how these statements comply with the legal grounds of Article 1 of the TCK. Besides those who do the legislation and those who put it into effect, how compliant are the actions of those who execute the law with the purpose defined in Article 1?' For a full transcript (in Turkish) see http://www.barobirlik.org.tr/tbb/baskan/konusmalar/051203_mersin.aspx.

The Initiative for Freedom of Expression called for 'civil disobedience' in protest of the TCK, just as it had done for the TMK.[67] The Foundation for Social and Legal Studies and the People's Law Office reacted insensitively to the new TCK and the proposed amendments to the CMK. The two institutions, in a joint declaration, stated that the proposed amendments were a blow to the presumption of innocence and the right to a fair trial.[68]

Practices such as phone monitoring, eavesdropping, the gathering of biased evidence on individuals - known to the public as 'profiling' [*] - which all fall under the mandate of the state intelligence services, attracted very little attention or examination from NGOs. Whilst experiencing setbacks in monitoring the legal area, NGOs fail to present an organised, systematic reaction to non-transparent, long-standing state practices, unless these practices are unveiled through a specific incident such as in Şemdinli. For instance, NGOs failed to adequately shed light on the Diyarbakır 6th High Criminal Court's decision in relation to the tapping of all phones in Turkey shortly after the new TCK took effect.

The Kızıltepe and Şemdinli Incidents

The Susurluk accident of 3 November 1996 is undoubtedly the event that had the most profound impact on the development of civil society's reaction to counter-terrorism, organised crime and the illegal activities of the state's security and intelligence services. From the point of view of efficiency, organisation and continuity, the success of the NGO's reaction to the Şemdinli bombing 9 years later, is attributable to the anti-Susurluk 'social consciousness'. The Şemdinli incident is widely seen by civil society as an extension of the Susurluk incident.

In 2005, NGOs demonstrated a much more systematic and powerful reaction to the Şemdinli incident than to the legal changes that impacted human rights, the principle of democratisation or practices such as phone monitoring or eavesdropping. In certain ways, an extrajudicial killing that took place in Kızıltepe-Mardin, a year before the Şemdinli incidents, had 'prepared' civil society to react to the Şemdinli incidents. The incident in question involved the killing of truck driver Ahmet Kaymaz and his 12-year old son Uğur Kaymaz, during an operation of the Special Forces. On 20 November 2004, a Special Forces unit surrounded the house in which it was claimed that a PKK member was hiding. As the father and son came out of the house, the Special Forces unit opened fire and killed them both.[69]

In their joint report on the killing of Yücel Solmaz in the Edremit district of Van, the Human Rights Foundation, Mazlum-Der Van Provincial Branch and the

---

67 http://www.ortakpayda.org/boxes.asp?foo=read&feox=139&ronin=5

68 'Yasa Teklifleri Savunma Hakkına Saldırı,' Bianet, 10 May 2005. See http://www.bianet.org/2005/05/10/60833.htm

* Editor's Note: 'Profiling' here refers to the illegal practice by the Turkish Government, which intends to keep track of and the file away information regarding citizens activities and affiliations, especially those of a political nature.

69 'Kızıltepe'deki operasyonda güvenlik kusurları belirlendi,' Zaman, 13 December 2004.

Health Social Services Workers Union (Sağlık Sosyal Hizmet Emekçileri Sendikası, SES) described the Kızıltepe raid as an 'extrajudicial killing.'[70]

The best organised and systematic responses in 2005 came after the Şemdinli incidents. The incidents started after gendarmerie intelligence officers Ali Kaya and Özcan İldeniz, and PKK double-agent Veysel Ateş threw grenades at the Umut Bookshop owned by Seferi Yılmaz, who had previously been in prison for 15 years for being a member of the PKK. In the explosion that ensued, Mehmet Zahir Korkmaz died and Metin Korkmaz was injured. Shortly after the explosion, Seferi Yılmaz gathered together the tradesmen and people who were in the vicinity and started following the three suspects. However, these three individuals, who were believed to be the perpetrators, were protected and later released by security forces.[71]

Not only did the gendarmerie intelligence assess the incident as 'provocative activity', it also incited reactions from the media, the public and NGOs. A report was published on the Şemdinli incidents on 12 November by a commission consisting of representatives of the following institutions: the İHD, Mazlum-Der, İnsan-Der, the Contemporary Legal Practitioners Association (Cağdaş Hukukcular Derneği, CHD) Van Provincial Branch, Hakkâri Tradesmen and Artisans Chamber, (Hakkâri Ensaf ve Sanatkârlar Odasi), Hakkâri Memur Sen, the Confederation of Public Employees Trade Unions (Kamu Emekçileri Sendikaları Konfederasyonu, KESK), Hakkâri Provincial Branches Platform, and the Hakkâri Student Parents Organisation (Hakkâri Öğrenci Velileri Derneği, ÖVDER). The commission had carried out investigations at the crime scene and interviewed witnesses. The report declared:

> Our commission concluded that as a result of the assault on civilians, the right to life was breached, human integrity was attacked, and property rights were disregarded. The people of Şemdinli lost their trust in public authorities when the security forces released the suspects involved in the incidents, and people are now in a state of indignation. To stem the tide and rebuild trust, the necessary mechanisms should be reinstated immediately. For this reason, our commission deems it appropriate to make two important recommendations: a Parliamentary Investigation Committee should be formed immediately by the TBMM to investigate this incident. Otherwise, the probability of obscuring evidence seems reasonably high, due to the nature of the incident. Due to [our] conviction that the Şemdinli Republic Attorney cannot solve this incident alone, it is recommended that a separate at-

70 İHD, Mazlum-Der Van provincial branch, SES Van provincial branch, 'Van İli Edremit İlçesinde Yücel Solmaz (35, SES Van Şb. Üyesi) İsimli Yurttaşımızın Yargısız İnfaz Sonucu Öldürülmesi İddialarını Araştırma-İnceleme Raporu,' 20 December 2004. For the full report, see http://www.ihd.org.tr/rapozel/vanedremit.html

71 Indictment dated March 3, 2006 and numbered 2006/32. Known as the Şemdinli indictment to the public, this indictment was debated for days and weeks because of the Van Republic Attorney Ferhat Sarıkaya's criticisms to high officials of the military, starting with Land Forces Commander General Yaşar Büyükanıt.

> torney be appointed for this incident by the Ministry of Justice. The prime minister, the minister of justice, the minister of internal affairs and the chief of the general staff must make declarations that will appease the public and demonstrate that the incident will be thoroughly investigated.'[72]

As suggested by the NGO Commission, an investigation committee was indeed established in Parliament and the prime minister and senior officials in the TSK made declarations. Notably, the declarations of the attorney's office on the Şemdinli incident had great repercussions.[73]

The Human Rights Joint Platform (İnsan Hakları Platformu - İHOP), TİHV, the Helsinki Citizens' Assembly and the Turkish branch of Amnesty International described the incident as a breach of law.[74]

NGO's reactions to the Şemdinli incident were not limited to the reports of organisations such as İHD and Mazlum-Der. In his statement about the Şemdinli indictment, the Chairman of Mazlum-Der Chair, Cevat Özkaya, warned that the debate was being politicised, and further emphasised the legal aspect of the matter, demanding punishment of those responsible.[75]

The President of İHD, Yusuf Alataş, assessed the debates of the indictment and stated that: 'Maybe one of the most basic problems of our democracy is that even civilians cannot accept the fact that a civilian public prosecutor can also prepare an indictment about a high-ranking military official'.[76]

In its 2005 General Report, İHD argued that the links between organised crime and the state, which had presumably gone into hiding after the Susurluk incident, resurfaced. The Şemdinli incident, the report argued, was an illustration of it.[77]

Determination to expose the individuals responsible was stressed in a brochure signed by the following: The Amargi Women's Cooperative, the Anti-Capitalist, Independent Revolutionary Class Platform, the Science-Education-Aesthetics-Culture-Art Studies Foundation (Bilim Eğitim Estetik Kültür Sanat Araştırmaları Vakfı, BEKSAV), the Democratic Rights Platform (Demokratik Haklar Platformu), the Democratic Society Party (Demokratik Toplum Partisi, DTP),

---

72 Mazlum-Der, '9-10 Kasım 2005 Şemdinli Olaylarını Araştırma-İnceleme Raporu,' 12 November 2005. For the full report, see http://www.mazlumder.org/ana.php?konu=rapor&id=1043&lang=tr

73 For Prime Minister Recep Tayyip Erdoğan's statements on the subject, see 'Başbakan Erdoğan: Olay Mutlaka Açıklığa Kavuşmalı,' Zaman, 11 October 2005. For the statements of Chief of Staff General Hilmi Özkök, Gendarmerie Commander General Fevzi Türkeri and Land Forces Commander General Yaşar Büyükanıt, see Şemdinli Indictment p. 48. When Büyükanıt said 'I know him, he's a good guy' for Petty Officer Ali Kaya who was involved in the incident, it led to debates.

74 İHD, 'Basın Açıklaması,' 12 November 2005. For the full text of the press release, see http://www.ihd.org.tr/basin/bas20051112.htm

75 For Mazlum-Der General President Cevat Özkaya's statement, see http://www.mazlumder.org/ana.php?konu=aciklama&id=472&lang=tr

76 http://www.ihd.org.tr

77 İHD, '2005 Yılı Genel İnsan Hakları Raporu.'

DİSK (Confederation of the Revolutionary Workers' Trade Unions)/Limter Trade Union, the Workers' Movement Party (Emekci Hareket Partisi EHP), Liberation of the Oppressed (Ezilenlerin Kurtuluşu), the Socialist Platform of the Oppressed, the Rights and Freedoms Front, the Peoples Cultural Centres, the Peoples Liberation Party (Halkin Kurtuluş Partisi, HKP), revolutionary magazines: Haziran, İşki Mücadelesi, Kara Kizil Notlar, Kaldirac, Odak, Partizan, Proleter Devrimci Duruş, Sinif Mücadelesi, KESK İstanbul Branches Platform, the Fight for Freedoms Platform, the Social-Democratic Party (Sosyalist Demokrasi Partisi) and the Socialist Solidarity Platform and the Social Freedom Platform.[78]

The Turkish Bar Association's Chair, Özdemir Özok, stated that utmost sensitivity was required in dealing with the incidents of the Şemdinli and Yüksekova districts of Hakkâri: 'We have been very sensitive about the issue since the beginning. We formed a commission to investigate the incidents in Hakkâri, Şemdinli and Yüksekova.'[79]

The spokesperson of the Initiative for Freedom of Expression, Şanar Yurdatapan, argued that the debates about indictment should not obscure the Şemdinli incident and warned: 'Do not let the result be the same as Susurluk.'[80] Nonetheless, reaction to the Şemdinli incident was not forthcoming due to the disagreement between the east and the west of the country. In contrast, the reactions to the Susurluk incident were equally vocal in eastern and western Turkey.

Conclusion

2005 was a defining year for NGOs working in the security sector and for those engaged in activities in the area of human rights and legal affairs. Security issues, terrorism and the 'democracy dilemma' were persistent issues of debate in Turkey.

It should be reiterated that the reaction of NGOs to the Şemdinli incident was systematic and resolute. However, this determination was not reflected in public opinion. Public outrage at the Şemdinli incidents was not as strong as the public outcry and the 'One Minute of Darkness' campaign that followed the Susurluk incident. Reactions were limited to demonstrations by society's more marginalised groups. While the people outside east and south eastern Turkey - with some exceptions - disapproved of the Şemdinli incident, they did not act upon it, as it was not considered to be 'their problem.'

The reactions of NGOs to the new draft Anti-Terror Law gives greater reasons to be optimistic about the future of civil society in Turkey. The TMK draft was put on hold because of the determined rejection of civil society. Although there have been attempts to restore the draft that would include additional anti-democratic regulations, the draft law has essentially lost all legitimacy in the eyes of the public, as a result of the efforts made by NGOs.

---

78 'Şemdinli'de yakalanan devletin ta kendisidir!-Rapor,' 25 January 2006. See http://www.savaskarsitlari.org/arsiv.asp?ArsivTipID=6

79 'Barolar Birliği Hakkari'ye Gidiyor,' Güncel Hukuk Haberleri, 20 November 2005. See http://www.hukuki.net/haber/detay.asp?id=525

80 Kezban Bülbül, 'İddianame Şemdinli'yi unutturmasın,' Yeni Şafak, 10 March 2006.

Given Turkey's geographical, historical and political reality, it is crucial that NGOs working on issues of democratisation and security sector reform be allowed to strengthen and increase in number. Resolving the Kurdish problem by economic, social and political means, and by limiting the 'deep bureaucracy' syndrome, will only be possible by building up civilian capacity. In fact, 'deep bureaucracy' undermines democratisation and is contrary to basic EU principles because it defines its own sphere of jurisdiction and regularly undertakes unlawful actions. Ultimately, NGOs certainly have the capacity to influence the public on basic issues such as human rights, democracy, the supremacy of law, civilian control of the security sector, as well as on the importance of civil society itself.

Media*

*Önder Aytaç**

Background

Democratisation and civilian oversight can only be achieved through the transformation of the security sector into a structure that is overseen and controlled by the parliament, civil service administration and the media. These mechanisms of control and oversight should not only be performed as adjustments on a vertical level by the appointed state institutions at the top, but should also be developed by establishing horizontal connections and by incorporating both the media and civil society.[1]

In Turkey, the relationship between the security sector and the media is perceived as one in which the former unilaterally makes use of the latter as an instrument to boost its own image. (?) However, the concept of an independent media has been developed in line with the liberalisation process, and was further strengthened by the establishment of private television channels whilst Prime Minister Turgut Özal was in power.[2] The relationship between the media and security — which operates within a context of changing balance between freedom of the press and the state authority— starting with the 1961 Constitution, has tilted towards the ideal of freedom of the press. The media and security actors have evolved in a country where a free press has coexisted with governmental control. Since 1961, however, the country has experienced ever greater press freedom.

However, at the start of the 1970s, this freedom, which had no social and cultural basis, was curtailed following the 1980 coup d'état when the restrictions placed on the media reached the highest level.

Beginning in 1983, and in line with the pro-free market economic policies implemented by the Özal government, freedom of the press was provided not only with a legal but also with a social, economic and cultural basis. Together with the founding of private television and radio channels, a liberalisation of the media sector reached its peak.

However, in 1997, along with the 28 February 'post-modern' coup d'êtat, new restrictions were initiated and a number of journalists were silenced after ficti-

---

* I owe special thanks to Emre Uslu, PhD candidate at the University of Utah, Middle East Centre.

* Police Academy, Faculty member (PhD), Faculty of Security Sciences.

1 See, http://www.tesev.org.tr/projeler/guvenlik_Sektoru_metin.pdf

2 Turgut Özal served as Prime Minister from 1983-1989 and as President of the Republic from 1989-1993.

tious security reports were leaked to the media. These reports were prepared by the intelligence unit of the general staff and referred to as 'memorandum' (andıç). Generals intervened in newspaper editorial meetings and applied restrictions through the system of accreditation, and some newspapers were even subject to discrimination. Due to these legal restrictions, journalistic work, especially in the field of security, was strictly monitored and journalists were handed over to public prosecutors by security organisations. These policies were maintained to some extent in 2005.

Media-Security Relations and Problems

In terms of democracy and good governance, the media not only has a right to gather and disseminate information for the public good on security-related issues, but also has a responsibility to report in accordance with the principles of accuracy, truth and objectivity. In this context, the media paves the way for the participation of civil society and contributes to its monitoring of the security sector.

In terms of civilian control, the media is responsible for disseminating the following information to the public:

- Strategically important documents, such as the National Security Policy Document (Milli Güvenlik Siyaseti Belgesi, MGSB);
- Annual budgets and the sources of each security unit;
- Significant parliamentary discussions and decisions, legal amendments regarding the security sector, as well as weekly press conferences held/scheduled by security units;
- Internet sites, including the minutes of meetings and discussions in parliament and related commissions that focus on the security sector and the National Intelligence Organisation (Milli İstihbarat Teşkilatı, MİT);
- Annual reports and publications on security issues;
- Examination/audit reports by the Supreme Court of Accounts (Sayıştay) regarding the security sector;
- Information regarding protocols on internal security which are assembled by security units, and bilateral or multilateral agreements with other countries' security units.

When the relationship between the media and security forces is evaluated in the context of the aforementioned points, the most significant question that emerges is whether the system within which the media functions is a liberal one, or one that is predominantly based on state control. If the structure of the media is subject to strict state control, it naturally presents Turkey's security sector as a perfect or even 'sacrosanct' model.

In Turkey, where elements of the liberal system are only partially incorporated and where the state is seen as sacred, reporting on the state's security forces is done within the framework of respecting that which is considered sacrosanct. It is therefore important to note that the reading of the abovementioned reports is carried out against such a cultural backdrop.

The Problem of the 'Sanctity' of the State

Despite the fact that news reports on the Susurluk incident were the most liberal in the history of the Turkish media, it seems apt to suggest that since the Susurluk (1997) and Şemdinli (2005) incidents, media reports on the security forces have been urged to uphold what is sacred. The power, position and standing of the state especially, conceptually determine the content of the news and the manner in which it is produced. For example, the news on Susurluk, while focussed on a less sacred institution, namely the police, the acceptable content of reports was established with the trilogy of 'police-mafia-politics' in mind. These are the three institutions thought to be the sources of corruption in Turkey. Take for instance news coverage of the Susurluk incident, which focused on a less sacred institution – the police: the only acceptable angle from which the media could cover the event was based on the 'police-mafia-politics' trilogy, the institutions believed to be the sources of corruption in Turkey.

The Deputy Chief of the Intelligence Department, Hanefi Avcı, from the Directorate General of Security (Emniyet Genel Müdürlüğü, EGM), stated that corruption is not limited to the police-mafia-politics triangle and that other units of the state are also guilty. A number of news reports and analyses intending to deceive the public were disseminated following Avcı's statement that many actions by hitherto unknown perpetrators were actually performed by Mahmut Yıldırım (a.k.a. 'Green' Yeşil) on behalf of the Gendarmerie Intelligence and Anti-Terrorism Organisation (Jandarma İstihbarat ve Terörle Mücadele Teşkilatı, JİTEM). News on the Susurluk incident consequently disappeared from the headlines altogether.

The Problem of Confidentiality

The concept of the inviolability of the state creates problems on many levels, specifically in relation to the issue of confidentiality. Public information is classified under three headings: unclassified, restricted and secret. By its very definition, unclassified information is not confidential. Restricted information can be circulated within the institution, but cannot be disseminated without permission and secret information should be protected. In the case of its disclosure without permission, such information has the potential to harm both the institution and the state.

However, the issue of who is to decide what information is unclassified, restricted or secret is a very important one. This particularly affects the security organisations, which perceive the state as sacred, and as such even common information is frequently listed as secret. Security issues may, indeed, logically be considered as falling within the definition of restricted or secret. However, in light of the fact that security personnel are generally reluctant to take risks and therefore prefer to err on the side of safety, means that practically any information, irrespective of how benign, is designated with a restrictive label which is justified by the security of the state. This problem serves to exacerbate the public perception that some subjects remain secret, untouchable and even taboo.

A telling example of how confidentiality affects the media and security organisations, was demonstrated by the lawsuit which was launched against Gökhan

Bozkurt, a reporter for CNN Türk. Bozkurt reported on the bargaining for tenders between Cemal Kaya, who subsequently resigned from the Justice and Development Party (Adalet ve Kalkınma Partisi, AKP), and the officials from the Ministry of Energy. The lawsuit was filed on the grounds that Bozkurt breached laws on the secrecy of investigation. With his programme called Night View (Gece Görüşü), which was broadcast on 15 February 2005, Bozkurt was accused of breaching Article 10 of Law No. 4422, on Combating Organisations Pursuing Illicit Gain and faces three years' imprisonment. The trial is ongoing.

Along with the classification of restricted information, procedures for declassification are rather arbitrary. Officials and institutions might leak confidential information to the media to settle personal grievances, and thus, this cultivation of a good relationship with the media represents a kind of insurance for security personnel. An example of this is the fact that the gendarmerie report on the Şemdinli incident was leaked to the media even though it should have remained confidential.

The Issue of Certain Media Outlets Esteemed by the Security Sector

It should be emphasised that relationships between the media and sources of information are very important within the context of security sector publications. Media bosses reserve the right to change their reporters at the whim of news sources, and Ankara representatives are frequently selected from among candidates who are accredited by the military, trusted by the police, close to the government and officials of the general staff and the EGM. As a consequence, media publications and broadcasts depend on good relations and mutual interest.

Another problem regarding the relationship between the media and security organisations is the latter's lack of confidence in media representatives. Most of the junior and middle-echelon security personnel mistrust media employees, except for those reporters and columnists who maintain good relationships with high-level officials. In their view, media employees are 'ravenously hungry for news' and publish any information that is unearthed, without regard for the consequences of the news source or other conditions. Therefore, security personnel believe that avoiding media representatives is generally advisable.

The Issue of Trials in Military Courts

Even though some legal regulations have attempted to ensure that civilians are no longer tried in a military court, journalists are still being tried in military courts as a result of their comments and reports on security. For example, the military court of the 3rd Army Corps Command within the Istanbul-Hasdal barracks, launched a case against Abdurrahman Dilipak in connection with his article: 'If the Generals Do Not Listen to Advice.' This article was published on 29 August 2003 in the weekly Friday (Cuma). Because Dilipak criticised the statements of some retired generals during the 2003 promotion period, he was charged under military penal code Article 169 with 'public action aimed at damaging the hierarchical structure, inciting insubordination towards superiors and commanders, and deriding and insulting the military.' The court decided to refer the case to a civilian court due to legislative change.

Yet by order of the commander of the First Army Corps, the court's decision was appealed and the Military High Court of Appeals ordered that the case remain in the military court.

Military courts should normally operate as a disciplinary body to hear cases of crimes committed by military personnel during the execution of their duties. However, the establishment of a multi-functional mandate, whereby civilians may also be tried, shows that a two-tiered legal system operates in the country.

In the context of the media's democratic control over security services, there is frequently a disparity between the information given to reporters' within security organisations and the particular approach of the newspaper editor toward the same security organisation. In these cases, reporters are trapped between their sources and editors. Such a case occurred when the former commissioner of the Istanbul Police Force stated that some operations had been crippled due to press reports. The commissioner's criticism sparked a backlash by the press. Police reporters (concerned that an escalation of tensions could harm both parties) acted as a moderating force and encouraged the commissioner to apply to the Press Council (Basın Konseyi) to settle the dispute.

The Issue of Accessing Sources

Security organisations tend to prohibit media representatives from visiting any office other than those of the principle clerks of the organisations. In this way, senior managers not only prevent uncontrolled statements by security personnel — which generally concern the problems associated with the institution — but also control the media by redirecting reports according to their own interests.

Although press conferences are held at the headquarters of the security organisations, and even though they are required to inform the media, reporters seek additional relationships with insiders so as to gain access to more detailed information. On the other hand, senior officials tend to cultivate relationships with journalists to create an avenue in which to tout their own success and increase their chances of being promoted.

Another point to emphasise is that the media can be exploited for political means depending on the power of the institution and the political views of the managers of the institutions. With headlines that read 'a high-ranking commander' or 'a high-echelon security authority,' it is clear that this news is not oriented to the public but rather intended for political purposes, related ministers, undersecretaries or general managers. The relationship between the journalists and the managers of such newspapers determines the method of the media's control over these institutions. This relationship is generally against the media.

As a result, the challenges faced by the media regarding the activities of security units can be listed as follows:

- To find a trustworthy news source;
- To publish the news from this source independently;
- To avoid threatening the security of the country in connection with the news;
- To avoid humiliating or damaging the security forces of the state;

- To submit evidence to court as a defendant during a trial in order to facilitate independent decisions by the court, taking into consideration that fact that security forces carry a great deal of weight in a court of law;
- To report news independent of the problems caused by the special institutional interests of media institutions and security organisations the problems caused by special institutional interests of the media or security actors.

Internet and Security Bureaucracy

The spread of the internet and satellite receivers has substantially increased access to information and fortified the trend toward transparency and accountability and the accessibility of official information. As a result, citizens are better informed, and this improves both the quality of discussions about important political matters and helps to establish a transparent and efficient security sector.

The internet has a much better chance than conventional media to influence security organisations, as it is resistant to legal and conventional pressures because it has no over-arching authority. In addition, the internet has changed the conventional reporter-news source relationship, as any employee uncomfortable or unhappy with the performance of their institution can themselves become a direct source of information on the internet.

The question here is how can the accuracy of the news be verified through a system of checks and balances. The posting of a news report on numerous web sites, the various tools for verification and denial of the information in question, and the attestation of the news by other means are all meaningful ways to verify the accuracy of internet news. Despite these issues, the internet remains the most effective medium to monitor closed bureaucratic structures such as the security organisations. For instance, news on corruption in the construction bidding for special forces facilities or the participation of some military and police special operations personnel in bank robberies, were found on the internet weeks, or even years, prior to their appearance in the official press. These internet reports were even responsible for the launching of an inquiry which was approved by the chief of the general staff and the general commissioner.

An internet search of the word 'Şemdinli', following the bookstore bombing on 9 November 2005, resulted in 941'000 hits from different websites reporting news verified by security personnel, citizens and media representatives in the area where the incident occurred. For example, a leaflet entitled To the Kurdish People ('Ey Kürt Halkı'), which was allegedly signed by the 'heroic Turkish police', intended to stir up sedition among the Kurdish population. It included defamatory anti-Kurdish statements and was distributed throughout Turkey's southeast before and during the Şemdinli incident. While the mainstream media did not report on the leaflet, it was posted on the website <www.aloihbar.org> and, as a result, was found to have been fraudulent. It was subsequently entered into police registries.

Thus, the internet can be an important tool that can help fulfil the requirements of democracy, transparency, accountability and monitoring. Essentially, because the internet is not bound by the restrictions arising from the relationship between the media and security organisations, websites can report news which cannot be published or broadcast by the mainstream media. This puts pressure on security organisations to become far more careful of their actions and to stay within the law, due to fear of disclosure.

Although security institutions have appealed to the courts to shut down certain websites, the requests have been rejected and the websites that were shut down have re-emerged under different names.[3]

Events of 2005

Media and the New Turkish Penal Code

As a result of the new penal code which went into effect on 1 June 2005, and as stated by the alternative media source <www.bianet.org>, members of the media have lived under the threat of imprisonment in accordance with Article 301 of the Turkish Penal Code (Türk Ceza Kanunu, TCK). Although the new TCK is prepared in line with the EU harmonisation process, Articles 301 and 305 of the law restrict free speech on security issues.

Article 301 states that: (1) Public denigration of Turkish-ness (Türklük), the Republic or the Grand National Assembly of Turkey, shall be punishable by imprisonment of between six months and three years. (2) Public denigration of the government of the Republic of Turkey, the judicial institutions of the state, the military or security structures shall be punishable by imprisonment of between six months and two years. (3) In cases where denigration of Turkish-ness is committed by a Turkish citizen in another country, the punishment shall be increased by one third. (4) Expressions of thought intended to criticise shall not constitute a crime.

According to the 2005 report by the Network for Monitoring and Reporting on Media Freedom and Independent Journalism, 29 journalists, columnists and publishers were put on trial due to Clause 1 of Article 301. Eight of these journalists were sentenced by local courts.

Article 305 of the same law states: (1) A citizen who either directly or indirectly accepts financial benefits for himself or for another person, from a foreign individual or organisation, in return for engaging in activities against fundamental national interests, shall be sentenced to imprisonment for a term of three to ten years. The same penalty shall be imposed on the person who provides the benefit or makes the promise. (2) If the act is committed during wartime, or if benefit has been given or promised in order to spread propaganda through the medium of the press and media, the penalty shall be increased by half. (3) Except in cases where the act is committed during wartime, the prosecution of the offence shall be subject to the

---

3 For example, the courts rejected the case brought by the general staff for closure of the site http://www.aloihbar.org. Unfortunately, http://www.yolsuzluk.com was not so fortunate. First, its domestic access was cancelled and then, as a result of pressure on the service provider in the United States, it was completely shut down. By the same token, http://www.ulusalihanet.com faced harsh criticism by the general staff. The site was banned at the headquarters of the Directorate General of Security.

authorisation of the minister of justice. (4) Within the meaning of the present article, fundamental national interests shall denote independence, territorial integrity, national security and the fundamental qualities defined in the Constitution of the Republic.

In both of the aforementioned articles of the Turkish Penal Code, crime can be defined by using concepts going beyond the general rule of constancy of crime. Within the context of media-security relations, the natural duty of the media is to criticise deficiencies of security implementations. Since the concept of 'public denigration' stated in Article 301 is not explained in detail, some criticisms that may be considered within the realm of freedom of speech, can be deemed 'public denigration' by security organisations that intend to bring them to court. Due to the ambiguity of the concept, musician Ferhat Tunç, and journalists Doğan Özgüden and Ersen Korkmaz have been charged with violation of Clause 1 of Article 301.

Again in Article 305 of the same law, the concept of national security was not clearly defined. Thus the decision regarding 'national security' can be rather subjective and can change at the whim of daily events.

The head of the Association of Turkish Journalists (Türkiye Gazeteciler Cemiyeti, TGC), Orhan Erinç stated that many journalists would have been imprisoned if the new TCK was implemented in line with the government's intention. Erinç added: 'Journalists save themselves from bad laws through good enforcement.'[4] Erinç is of the opinion that nearly 26 articles of the new code are undemocratic in terms of the penalties they impose and due to their dependence on interpretation. The head of the Izmir Journalists' Association, Erol Akıncılar, criticised the pressures on freedom of speech stating that 'Increased penalties for the crimes of the press and media aim at intimidating them and journalists and reporters cannot perform their duties.'[5]

Turkey paid a fine of YTL 224'000 in 2004 and YTL 540'000 in 2005 to ECtHR (The European Court of Human Rights) following its ruling related to freedom of speech and fair trial. Turkey has been obliged to pay YTL 764'000 in compensation since 2004, due to violations of Article 10 that protects freedom of speech, Article 6/1 that defines the right to fair trial and Article 2 regarding 'inadequate examination' in the death of a journalist. This clearly shows the importance of the role of the media in monitoring the security sector.

Doğan Özgüden, Emin Karaca and senior editor Mehmet Emin Sert were indicted for Özgüden's article 'After 30 Years' (Otuz Yul Sonra) and Karaca's article 'What Does the Thirtieth Year Remind Us Of?' (Otuzuncu Yilin Anımsattıkları) which were published in the review Literature in Turkey and Europe (Avrupa'da ve Türkiye'de Yazın) in April 2002. The journalists were accused of having insulted the Turkish Armed Forces (Türk Silahlı Kuvvetleri, TSK) according to Article 159 of the TCK in 2003. The court decided to separate Özgüden's file and to acquit Sert,

---

4 See, www.byegm.gov.tr/YAYINLARIMIZ/AyinTarihi/2005/agustos2005.htm

5 See, www.telehaber.com/haberler/haber-287453/

whilst Karaca was sentenced to a five-month term of imprisonment. The sentence was later reduced to a fine of YTL 900 and the case remains open on appeal.[6]

In 2005, local courts handed out fines of YTL 12'900, and a total of four years in prison, to radio employee Sabri Ejder Öziç, writer Karaca, journalist Hrant Dink, writer Zülküf Kisanak, publisher Fatih Taş, Çağrı magazine owner Aziz Özer and magazine reader Erkan Akay. However, YTL 900 and one and a half years from the four year sentence were deferred.

Seventeen journalists, who covered current human rights issues, such as the Kızıltepe case, the cancellation of the Ottoman Armenians Conference, and cases of torture, are being charged with 'Influencing the Court Decision,' and 'Attempting to Influence Fair Trial,' based on the Press Law and the Penal Code. The following journalists will face fines or prison sentences if found guilty in these trials: Ender Can Cevahir, Fehmi Koru, Mehmet Sucu, İlhan Selçuk, İbrahim Yıldız, İlhan Taşçı, Alper Turgut, Hrant Dink, Aydın Engin, Serkis Seropyan, Arat Dink, Hasan Cemal, Murat Belge, Haluk Şahin, Erol Katırcıoğlu and İsmet Berkan.

Twelve writer-journalists are charged with 'Disseminating Terrorist Propaganda' according to the TCK or the Anti-Terror Law. Among these journalists are Radikal reporter Neşe Düzel, Hürriyet reporter Sebati Karakurt, journalist Ertuğrul Mavioğlu and ATV producer Ali Kırca. Five journalists are standing trial in the high criminal courts for reports on the mafia. These will be filed in the basic criminal court following the amendments of criminal procedures and the penal code.

According to the Media Monitoring Report 2005 of the BIA (alternative news network) project, an appeals trial was held on 27 September in the 4th Judicial Office of the Court of Appeals involving the newspaper Anadolu'da Vakit which published an article entitled, 'The country where those who do not even have the ability to become Corporals, become Generals' (Onbaşi Bile Olamayacaklarin General Olduğu Ülke). The court is still deliberating on a verdict. Ankara's 20th Basic Criminal Court had accepted the generals' compensation claims on 20 May 2004 and sentenced representatives of the newspaper with a fine of YTL 624'000. With legal interest added, the amount has reached YTL 900'000. The criminal case is continuing in Bağcılar's 2nd Court.

Journalist Rahmi Yıldırım, from the website <www.sansursuz.com>, was sued for an article entitled 'The Qualified One Gets the Job Done' (İş Bilenin Kilic Kuşananin), on military and civilian state officials who are allegedly involved in corruption. Yıldırım stood trial on 7 September, facing up to three years' imprisonment. The case, brought to trial through a complaint made by the general staff for insulting the military, is ongoing in Ankara's 12th Criminal Court of General Jurisdiction. After the indictment was read in court, Yıldırım stated that some parts of the article had been altered in the text of the indictment and that he had been misquoted.

As a response to all of these curtailments, the TGC decided not to award a Press Freedom Prize at the anniversary of the Lifting of Censorship, which was

---

6 See, www.savaskarsitlari.org/arsiv.asp?ArsivTipID=8&ArsivAnaID=30187&ArsivSayfaNo=1 . Article 159 of former TCK, Article 301 of new TCK foresees sentence of imprisonment six months to three years.

celebrated on 25 July 2005. The selection committee protested against the TCK's restriction on the right to free speech, to inform and to acquire information, and took a solid vote to abstain from awarding the prize. The Turkish Union of Journalists (Türkiye Gazeteciler Sendikası, TGS) has asked for the amendment of the TCK which restricts the freedom of speech and threatens journalists with imprisonment.

Penalties by the Higher Council of Radio and Television (Radyo Televizyon Üst Kurulu, RTÜK)

Penalties imposed by RTÜK in 2005 were as follows:

- For violations of provision (e) of Article 4 of Law No. 3984 amended by Law No. 4756 which stipulates: 'Broadcasts shall not, in any manner, humiliate or insult people for their language, race, colour, sex, political opinion, philosophical belief, religion, particular sect, and any such considerations.' Warned: Haber Türk's Uyandırma Servisi programme, 15 June 2005 (30 June and 5 July);
- For violations of provision (e) of Article 4 of Law No. 3984 amended by Law No. 4756 which stipulates: 'Broadcasts shall not violate the national and moral values of the community or the Turkish family structure.' Requested defence: ATV's Yalnız Değilsin programme 28 April 2005 (30 June and 5 July 2005). Warned: Show TV's Serap Ezgü ile Biz Bize programme 14 April and 11, 12 May 2005; Kanal D's Ah Kalbim programme, 25, 26, 28 April 2005 (30 June and 5 July 2005); ATV's Harika Pazar, Elifnağme and Hande Ataizi ile En Çekici programmes, April 2005; CNN Türk's Evening News 12 May 2005 (30 June and 5 July 2005); Kanal Türk's foreign movie, 14 February 2005 (30 June and 5 July 2005);
- For violations of provision (g) of Article 4 of Law No. 3984 amended by Law No. 4756 which stipulates: 'Broadcasts shall serve for the improvement of the general objectives and basic principles of the Turkish national education system and the national culture:' Warned: Smart TV's Kemal Haluk Cebe ile Yorum programme, 3 March 2005 (30 June and 5 July);
- For violations of provision (l) of Article 4 of Law No. 3984 amended by Law No. 4756 which stipulates: 'Broadcasters shall respect the principles of impartiality, conformity and reliability in news programmes; broadcasts shall not prevent the free formation of opinions….' Warned: TV5's Evening News 26 April and 7-11 May 2005 (30 June and 5 July); STV's Evening News, 6 May 2005 (30 June and 5 July);
- For violations of provision (s) of Article 4 of Law No. 3984 amended by Law No. 4756 which stipulates: 'All the items of the program services shall respect human dignity and fundamental human rights.' Requested defence: Kanal D's Kadının Sesi programme, 10-12 May 2005 (30 June and 5 July 2005) Warnings: TGRT's İnci Ertuğrul Sizin Sesiniz programme, 11-13 April 2005 (30 June and 5 July 2005); Show TV's Serap Ezgü ile Biz Bize programme, 14 April and 11, 12 May 2005 (30 June and 5 July 2005); ATV's Özel Hat programme, 15 February and 12 April 2005 (30 June and 5 July 2005); Flash TV's Evening News, 7-8 May 2005 (30 June and 5 July 2005); One day off the air: Kanal D's İkinci Bahar Gönüllerde programme, 22, 27, 28 April 2005) (30

Conclusion

The problems between the media and the security sector ultimately derive from conventional bureaucratic approaches, organisational structures, the concept of confidentiality and the ambiguity of the law, and they can be considered as the reflection of general issues emerging with the democratisation of Turkey. The most remarkable incidents of 2005 involved the trials against media members in accordance with Article 301 of the new TCK.

Technological developments have turned the internet into an alternative and invaluable source within the context of media and security relations. As the internet is not subject to the obstacles which confront the mainstream media, it is used especially for airing criticism. Even though various state institutions have sued internet sites for exposing controversial issues, the fact remains that the internet is an alternative medium. Within this context, the internet will invariably continue to play a significant role, particularly in relation to the process of democratisation and civilian oversight of the security sector in Turkey.

List of Acronyms/Abbreviations

ACK	Military Criminal Code (*Askerî Ceza Kanunu*)
AK-DER	Woman's Rights Association Against Discrimination (*Ayrimciliğa Karşi Kadin Haklari Derneği*)
AKP	Justice and Development Party (*Adalet ve Kalkınma Partisi*)
Ar-De	Research and Assessment Presidency (*Araştırma Değerlendirme Başkanlığı*)
ATASE	Military History and Strategic Studies Board (*Askeri Tarih ve Stratejik Etüt Başkanlığı*)
ASAM	The Centre for Eurasian Strategic Studies (*Avrasya Stratejik Araştırmalar Merkezi*)
CHD	Contemporary Legal Practitioners Association (*Cağdaş Hukukcular Derneği*)
CHP	Republican People's Party Chairman (*Cumhuriyet Halk Partisi*)
CMK	Code of Criminal Procedures (*Ceza Muhakemesi Kanunu*)
DCAF	The Geneva Centre for the Democratic Control of Armed Forces
DGM	State Security Courts (*Devlet Güvenlik Mahkemeleri*)
DHKP/C	The Revolutionary People's Liberation Party/Front (*Devrimci Halk Kurtuluş Partisi/Cephesi*)
DKK	Turkish Naval Forces (*Deniz Kuvvetleri Komutanlığı*)
DTP	Democratic Society Party (*Demokratik Toplum Partisi*)
EGM	Directorate General of Security (*Emniyet Genel Müdürlüğü*)
EHS	Security Services Branch (*Emniyet Hizmetleri Sınıf*)
EMASYA	Security and Public Order Assistance Squads (*Emniyet, Asayiş Yardımlaşma Birlikleri*)
GATA	Gülhane Military Medical Academy (*Gülhane Askeri Tıp Akademisi*)
GKK	Temporary Village Guard System (*Geçici Köy Koruculuğu*)
GUSOD	Association of Security Systems and Oversight Organisations (*Güvenlik Sistemleri ve Gözetim Organizasyonları Derneği*)
İDB	Intelligence Department Presidency (*İstihbarat Daire Başkanlığ*)
IID	Important Issues Directorate (*Önemli İşler Müdürlüğü*)
IHD	Human Rights Organisation (*İnsan Hakları Derneği*)
İHH	Humanitarian Aid Foundation (*İnsani Yardim Vakfi*)
İHOP	Human Rights Joint Platform (*İnsan Hakları Platformu*)
İPM	İstanbul Policy Centre (*İstanbul Politikalar Merkezi*)
JCK	Gendarmerie General Command (*Jandarma Genel Komutanlığı*)
JİHİDEM	Gendarmerie Human Rights Evaluation Centre (*Jandarma İnsan Haklarını Değerlendirme Merkezi*)

JİT	Gendarmerie Intelligence Organisation (*Jandarma İstihbarat Teşkilatı*)
JİTEM	Gendarmerie Intelligence and Anti-Terrorism Organisation (*Jandarma İstihbarat ve Terörle Mücadele Teşkilatı*)
KADEK	Kurdistan Freedom and Democracy Congress
KDP	Kurdish Democratic Party's *(Partiya DEmokrata Kurdistanê)*
KESK	Confederation of Public Employees Trade Unions (*Kamu Emekçileri Sendikaları Konfederasyonu*)
KKK	Land Forces Command (*Kara Kuvvetleri Komutanlığı*)
KKTC	Turkish Republic of Northern Cyprus (*Kuzey Kıbrıs Türk Cumhuriyeti)*
KMYKK	Public Financial Administration and Control Law (*Kamu Mali Yönetimi ve Kontrol Kanunu*)
Mazlum-Der	Organisation for Human Rights and Solidarity for Oppressed People (*İnsan Hakları ve Mazlumlar İçin Dayanışma Derneği)*
MEB	Ministry of National Education (*Milli Eğitim Bakanlığı*)
MEH/MAH	National Security Service (*Milli Emniyet Hizmeti Riyaseti)*
MEH	National Security Service (*Milli Emniyet Hizmeti*)
MGK	National Security Council (*Milli Güvenlik Kurulu*)
MGSB	National Security Policy Document (*Milli Güvenlik Siyaseti Belgesi)*
MİKK	National Intelligence Coordination Committee (*Milli İstihbarat Koordinasyon Kurulu*)
MİT	National Intelligence Organisation (*Milli İstihbarat Teşkilatı*)
MKP	The Maoist Communist Party
MLKP	The Marxist Leninist Communist Party
MOBESE	Mobile Electronic System Integration (*Mobil Elektronik Sistem Entegrasyonu*)
MSB	Ministry of National Defence (*Milli Savunma Bakanlığı*)
MSYK	National Defence Higher Council (*Milli Savunma Yüksek Kurulu*)
ÖGHDK	Law Concerning Private Security Services (*Özel Güvenlik Hizmetlerine Dair Kanun*)
OHAL	State of Emergency Region (*Olağanüstü Hal*)
ÖHT	Special Operations Teams *(Özel Harekat Timleri*)
ÖGSİAD	Private Security Sector Businessman's Association (*Özel Güvenlik Sektörü İş Adamları Derneğ,*)
OYAK	Army Solidarity Institution (*Ordu Yardımlaşma Kurumu*)
ÖZGÜVDER	Private Security Social Assistance and Solidarity Association (*Özel Güvenlik Sosyal Yardımlaşma ve Dayanışma Derneği*)
PBK	TBMM Plan and Budget Committee (*Plan ve Bütçe Komisyonu*)
PIRA	Provisional Irish Republican Army
PKK	Kurdistan Workers' Party
PKK/CONGRA-GEL	Kurdistan Workers' Party/Democratic Congress of Kurdistan
PÖHT	Special Operations Police Teams (*Polis Özel Harekât Timleri)*

PVSK	Law on Police Duties and Powers (*Polis Vazife ve Selahiyet Kanunu,*)
RP	Welfare Party (*Relah Partisi*)
RTÜK	Higher Council of Radio and Television (*Radyo Televizyon Üst Kurulu*)
SAM	Crime Analysis Centre (*Suç Analiz Merkezi*)
SAS	Special Air Service
SASEM	Crime Investigation and Research Education Centre (*Suç Araştırma ve Soruşturma Eğitim Merkezi*)
SGK	Coast Guard General Command (*Sahil Güvenlik Komutanlığı*)
SSDF	Defence Industry Support Fund (*Savunma Sanayii Destekleme Fonu*)
SSM	Defence Industry Undersecretariat (*Savunma Sanayii Müsteşarlığı)*
TADOC	Turkish International Academy Against Drugs and Organised Crime
TAK	Kurdistan Freedom Falcons (*Teyrebazen Azadiye Kürdistan*)
TAYAD	Organisation for the Assistance to Families of Prisoners (*Tutuklu Hükümlü Aileleri Yardımlaşma Derneği*)
TBB	Turkish Bar Association (*Türkiye Barolar Birliği*)
TBMM	Turkish Grand National Assembly (*Türkiye Büyük Millet Meclisi*)
TCK	Turkish Penal Code (*Türk Ceza Kanunu*)
TESEV	The Turkish Economic and Social Studies Foundation (*Türkiye Ekonomik ve Sosyal Etüdler Vakfı*)
TGC	Association of Turkish Journalists (*Türkiye Gazeteciler Cemiyeti*)
TGS	The Turkish Union of Journalists (*Türkiye Gazeteciler Sendikası*)
TİB	Community Relations Presidency (*Toplumla İlişkiler Başkanlığı*)
TİHV	Turkish Human Rights Foundation (*Türkiye İnsan Hakları Vakfı)*
TKP-ML/ TIKKO	The Communist Party of Turkey-Marxist Leninist/Turkish Workers' and TIKKO Peasants' Liberation Army
TMK	Anti-Terror Law (*Terörle Mücadele Kanunu*)
TMYK	Anti Terror Higher Council (*Terörle Mücadele Yüksek Kurulu*)
TOHAV	Foundation for Social and Legal Studies (*Toplum ve Hukuk Araştırmaları Vakfı)*
TRT	Turkish Radio and Television Corporation (*Türkiye Radyo Televizyon Kurumu)*
TSK	Turkish Armed Forces (*Türk Silahlı Kuvvetleri*)
TSKGV	Turkish Armed Forces Strengthening Foundation (*Türk Silahlı Kuvvetleri Güçlendirme Vakfı)*
TÜBİTAK	Turkish Scientific and Technical Research Institution (*Türkiye Bilimsel ve Teknik Araştırmalar Kurumu*)
USK	National Strategic Concept (*Ulusal Stratejik Konsept*)
YAŞ	Supreme Military Council (*Yüksek Askeri Şura)*
YMM	Higher Defence Council (*Yüksek Müdafaa Meclisi*)
YÖK	Council of Higher Education (*Yükseköğretim Kurulu*)

Bibliography and Sources

Articles

Aytaç, Önder; Bal, İhsan, 'Medya ve Terörizm,' *Yeni Türkiye* 2 (12) (1996).

Ball, Nicole; Holmes, Malcolm, 'Integrating Defence into Public Expenditure Work,' Commissioned by UK Department for International Development (11 January 2002), http://www.grc-exchange.org/docs/SS11.pdf

Bayramoğlu, Ali, 'Asker ve Siyaset,' *Birikim* (August-September 2002).

Birinci, Ali, 'Türk Emniyet Teşkilatında İlkler,' *Polis Bilimleri Dergisi* 1 (3) (1999).

Cerrah, İbrahim, 'Sosyal Yapı ve Polis Alt-Kültürü,' İbrahim Cerrah, Emin Semiz (eds.) 21. *Yüzyılda Polis, Temel Sorunlar, Çağdaş Yaklaşımlar* (Ankara: EGM Yayınevi, 1998).

Cerrah, İbrahim, 'Bilişim Teknolojileri ve Etik: Bilişim Teknolojilerinin Güvenlik Hizmetlerinde Kullanımının 'Etik Boyutu' ve 'Sosyal' Sonuçları,' Tülin Günşen İçli, Fatih Karaosmanoğlu (eds.) *Uluslararası Polislik ve İç Güvenlik* (Ankara: Nobel Yayın Dağıtım, 2003).

Cerrah, İbrahim, 'Türkiye,' 'Türk Polisi' entries, *Encyclopedia of Law Enforcement* (California, ABD: Sage Publications, 2004-5).

Çoker, Fahri, 'Askerî Yargıtayın Tarihçesi,' *Askerî Adalet Dergisi* (1966).

Erol, Nuran, 'Söylem Olarak İdeoloji: New York Times Örneği,' *Toplum ve Bilim* (67) (Autumn1995).

MacFarlane, Leslie, 'Human Rights and the Fight Against Terrorism in Northern Ireland,' *Terrorism and Political Violence* 4 (1) (April 1992).

Ministry of Internal Affairs and United Nations Development Programme Research Project, 'Preparatory Assistance for Civilian Control of Security and Law Enforcement,' (unpublished article, 2005).

'Milli Güvenlik Kurulu Genel Sekreterliği Yönetmeliği,' *Humanite* (December 2003-January 2004).

Papers

Cerrah, İbrahim, 'Toplumsal Olayların Sosyal Yönü ve Medya,' Paper presented at the Criminal Justice and Police Symposium (Ankara, 6-8 May 1998).

Intelisano, Antonio, 'Independence of Military Judges, Judges Advocates and Public Prosecutors,' VIIIth International Conference (Ankara, 1979).

Uzun, Sabri, 'İç Güvenlik Hizmetlerinin İdeal Yapılanması,' Paper presented at the International Conference on Domestic Security (Ankara, 22-24 January 2004).

Books

Açan, Necdet; Yedig, Serhan, *Derin Devletin Peşinde* (İstanbul: Karakutu Yayınları, 2005).

Arcayürek, Cüneyt, *Darbeler ve Gizli Servisler* (Ankara:Bilgi Yayınevi, 1989).

Aydın, Suavi, *Amacımız Devletin Bekası, Demokratikleşme Sürecinde Devlet ve Yurttaşlar* (İstanbul: TESEV Yayınları, 2006).

Aytar, Osman, *Hamidiye Alaylarından Köy Koruculuğuna* (İstanbul: Medya Güneşi Yayınları, 1992).

Beşe, Ertan, *Terörizm, Avrupa Birliği ve İnsan Hakları* (İstanbul: Seçkin Yayıncılık, 2001).

Demirkıran, Sami, *PKK: Olaylar, Belgeler, Hatıralar!..* (İstanbul: Kipa Yayınları, 2001).

Demirkıran, Sami, *Kod Adı: Killer's of Mehmet's* (Ankara: Kipa Yayınları, 2002).

Duran, Ragıp, *Basın Güncesi* No: 9 (Ankara: Çağdaş Gazeteciler Derneği Yayınları, 1994).

Erdoğ, Fedai, *Türkiye Büyük Millet Meclisi (TBMM) Faili Meçhul Siyasi Cinayetleri Araştırma Komisyon Raporu* (İstanbul: Gizli Saklı Yayınevi, 2005).

Erman, Sahir, *Askerî Ceza Hukuku* (İstanbul: İ.Ü. Hukuk Fakültesi Yayınları, 1974).

Geleri, Aytekin; İleri, Hakan, *Organize Suçlarla Mücadelede Gizli ve Örtülü Yaklaşımlar* (Ankara: Seçkin Yayınları, 2003).

Golding, Peter; Elliott, Philip, *Making the News* (Londra: Longman, 1979).

İlter, Erdal, *Milli İstihbarat Teşkilatı Tarihçesi: Milli Emniyet Hizmetleri Riyaseti* (M.E.H/MAH) (1927/1965) (Ankara, 2002), http://www.mit.gov.tr/tarihce/giris_1.html

Kaya, Raşit, *Kitle İletişim Sistemleri* (Ankara: Teori Yayınları, 1985).

McQuail, Denis, *Mass Communication Theory*, (London: M. Joseph Ltd, 1987).

Mill, John Stuart, Özgürlük Üstüne (İstanbul: Belge Yayınları, 1985).

Mumcu, Ahmet, *Osmanlı Devletinde Siyaseten Katl* (Ankara: Birey ve Toplum Yayınları, 1963).

Mumcu, Ahmet; Üçok, Coşkun, *Türk Hukuk Tarihi* (Ankara: Savaş Yayınevi, 1982).

Oran, Baskın, *Türkiye İnsan Hakları Bilançosu 2005 İzleme Raporu* (İstanbul: TESEV Yayınları, 2006).

Özarpat, Hilmi, *Askerî Yargılama Usulü Hukuk* (Ankara, 1950).

Özdağ, Ümit, *Avrupa Birliği'nin Türkiye Politikaları* (Ankara: ASAM Yayınları, 2003), http://www.avsam.org/tr/asamcalismasi.asp?ID=1

Özdemir, Hikmet, *Rejim ve Asker* (İstanbul: Afa Yayıncılık, 1989).

Özkan, Tuncay, *Bir Gizli Servisin Tarihi: MİT* (İstanbul: Milliyet Yayinlari, 1996).

Seviğ, Vasfi Raşit, *Askerî Adalet* (Ankara, 1955).

Siebert, Frederick; Peterson, Theodore; Schramm, Wilbur, *Four Theories of the Press: The Authoritarian, Libertarian, Social Responsibility and Soviet Communist Concept of What the Press Should Be and Do* (ABD: University of Illinois Press, 1963).

Stalker, John, *Shoot to Kill and the Affair* (İrlanda: Harmondsworth, Penguin, 1988).

Şahan, Timur; Balık, Uğur, *İTİRAFÇI: Bir JİTEM'ci Anlattı* (İstanbul: Aram Yayıncılık, 2004).

Şenel, A. Turhan; Şenel, M., *İstihbarat ve Genel Güvenlik Konularımız No. 56* (Ankara: EGM İDB Yayınları, 1997).

Tunaya, Tarık Zafer, *Siyasi Müessesler ve Anayasa Hukuku*, Siyaset İlmi Serisi 9 (İstanbul, 1969).

Tuncay, Mete, *Türkiye Cumhuriyeti'nde Tek-Parti Yönetiminin Kurulması (1923–1931)* (İstanbul: Cem Yayınevi, 1992).

Uçak, H., *11 Eylül Sonrası ABD İç Güvenlik ve İstihbarat Çalışmaları* No. 89 (Ankara: EGM İDB Yayınları, 2005).

Uğur, Aydın, *Yeni Demokrasinin Yeni Aktörleri: STK'lar, Merhaba Sivil Toplum, Tacisel Ulaş* (der.) (İstanbul:Helsinki Yurttaşlar Derneği Yayınları, 1998).

Ünlü, Ferhat, *Eymür'ün Aynası: Eski MİT Yöneticisi Anlatıyor* (İstanbul: Metis Yayınları, 2001).

Yalçın, Soner, *Binbaşı Ersever'in İtirafları* (İstanbul: Kaynak Yayınları, 1994).

Genel Plan ve Prensipler Dairesi Başkanlığı, *Milli Savunma Bakanlığı Beyaz Kitap 2000*, http://www.msb.gov.tr

Jandarma Genel Komutanlığı, *Jandarma Genel Komutanlığı Tarihi* (Ankara, 2002).

Journals

TBMM Tutanak Dergisi, Period 18 (1988), Volume: 21, p. 200. [Legislative Year: 2, 19.12.1988, Meeting: 47, Sitting: 2].

Anayasa Yargısı, Volume: 17 (Ankara, 2000).

Yalova Milletvekili Şükrü Önder'in; Bazı Kanunlarda Değişiklik Yapılmasına Dair Kanun Teklifi ve İçişleri Komisyonu Raporu (2/546), *TBMM Tutanak Dergisi*, Period 22 (2005), Volume: 91, p.8 [Legislative year: 3, 3 July 2005, Meeting: 125, Number: 962], http://www.tbmm.gov.tr/develop/owa/tutanak_g_sd.birlesim_baslangic

Rules of Procedure

Türkiye Cumhuriyeti Anayasası ve Türkiye Büyük Millet Meclisi İçtüzüğü (Ankara, 2005), http://www.tbmm.gov.tr/ictuzuk/ictuzuk.htm

Laws

Constitution of Belgium of 1831.

Constitution of the Netherlands of 1887.

Constitution of Brazil of 1967.

Constitution of Republic of Turkey of 1982.

Law on the Establishment and Trial Procedure of Military Courts No. 353, http://www.msb.gov.tr/Birimler/AsAdIsB/AsAdIsB353Kanun.htm

Village Law No: 442, dated 18 March 1924.

Provincial Administration Law, No. 5442, dated 10 June 1949.

Law on the Supreme Court of Accounts, No. 832, dated 21 February 1967.

Law No. 3175, dated 26 March 1985.

The Law Concerning Sentences for Some Criminals No. 3419, dated 25 March 1988.

Public Bidding Law No. 4734, *Resmi Gazete* (Official Gazette) No. 24648, dated 22 January 2002.

Law Concerning the Transfer of Duties of Elimination and Pursuit of Smuggling to the Ministry of Internal Affairs for the Provision of Border, Coastal and Territorial Waters No. 6815, dated 16 July 1956, *Resmi Gazette* (Official Gazette), No. 9363, dated 24.07.1956.

Law on the Establishment and Duties of Supreme Military Council No. 1612, dated 17 July 1972, *Resmi Gazete* (Official Gazete), No. 14257, dated 26 July 1972.

Law on the Turkish Coast Guard Command No. 2692, dated 9 July 1982, *Resmi Gazete* (Official Gazette), No. 17753, dated 13 July 1982, http://www.basbakanlik.gov.tr

Law on the Establishment, Duties and Jurisdiction of Gendarmerie No. 2803, dated 10 March 1983, *Resmi Gazete* (Official Gazette), No. 17985, dated: 12 March 1983.

Law on the Protection and Security of Land Borders No. 3497, dated 10 November 1988, *Resmi Gazete* (Official Gazette), No. 1997, dated 22 November 1988.

Private Security Services Law No. 5188, dated 10 June 2004, *Resmi Gazete* (Official Gazette), No. 25504, dated 26 June 2004.

Law Concerning Amendments to Some Laws No. 5397, date 3 July 2005, *Resmi Gazete* (Official Gazette), No. 25884, dated 23 July 2005.

Prime Ministry Directorate General of Laws and Resolutions, Bill Concerning the Addition of Two Articles to the Law on the Establishment, Duties and Jurisdiction of Gendarmerie dated 22 September 1998, Issue: B.02.0.KKG.0.11/101–1177/5368; Decision Date: 9 September 1998.

General and Supplementary Budget Final Account Law Drafts for the Financial Year 2003.

Village Guards Resolution, Official Gazette, No. 24096, dated 1 July 2000, http://www.mevzuat.adalet.gov.tr/html/20524.html

Information Notes

Tuncer, Naciye Aslıhan; Kuşoğlu; Baran, 'Eğitim, Sağlık ve Güvenlik Harcamalarının Bütçe Payları,' TBMM Araştırma Servisi Bilgi Notu, October 2005.

Indictment

'Şemdinli Indictment,' No. 2006/32, dated 3 March 2006.

Summary of Investigation

İstanbul National Security Court General Prosecutor, 'Susurluk Fezlekesi,' Prep. No. 1997/221, Summary No. 1997/1 (30.01.1997).

Minutes

2003 Mali Yılı Genel ve Katma Bütçe Kesin Hesap Kanunu Tasarılarının Plan ve Bütçe Komisyonu Görüşme Tutanakları, Printed Minutes.

Türkiye Büyük Millet Meclisi (TBMM) Genel Kurul Tutanağı, 22nd Period, 3th Legislative year, 101th Meeting (24 May 2005).

Plan and Budget Committee, Milli Savunma Bakanlığı Bütçe Görüşme Tutanakları, 11 November 2005.

Plan ve Bütçe Komisyonu Mali Yılı Bütçe Görüşmeleri Tutanakları, Date: 24 November 2005, http://www.tbmm.gov.tr

Reports

'Ülkemizin Çeşitli Yörelerinde İşlenmiş Faili Meçhul Siyasal Cinayetler Konusunda Meclis Araştırma Komisyonu Raporu,' No: 10/90, Issue No: A.01.1.GEÇ/300–554, Decision No: 10 (12.10.1995)

Kutlu Savaş, Susurluk Raporu, m.0001 (10.01.1997).

Kutlu Savaş, Susurluk Raporu, Aktüel-Ek, 5 February 1998.

Kutlu Savaş, Susurluk Raporu (internet edition), http://siyaset.bilkent.edu.tr/susurluk/kutlu/p3.html

Turkish Human Rights Movement Conference, 25–26 November 2000, Nihai Rapor ve Sonuç Bildirisi, http://www.turkeiforum.net/konf/conf3-tr.html

World Trade Organization, Working Group on the Relationship between Trade and Investment, 'Transparency,' WT/WGTI/W/109, (02-1561), 27 March 2002, http://www.dfait-maeci.gc.ca/tna-nac/documents/W109-e.pdf

Türkiye İnsan Hakları Vakfı (TİHV), 'Ağustos 2004 Raporu,' http://www.tihv.org.tr/rapor/2004_08/agukurtsorunu.html

İnsan Hakları Derneği (İHD), Mazlum-Der Van Şubesi, SES Van Şubesi, 'Van İli Edremit İlçesinde Yücel Solmaz (35, SES Van Şb. Üyesi) İsimli Yurttaşımızın Yargısız İnfaz Sonucu Öldürülmesi İddialarını Araştırma - İnceleme Raporu,' 20 December 2004, http://www.ihd.org.tr/rapozel/vanedremit.html

Füsun Üstel, 'Zorunlu İç Göç Sonrası Köye Dönüş (ön) Raporu,' TESEV, 2004.

Mazlum-Der, 'Terörle Mücadele Kanunu Tasarısı Hakkında Değerlendirme Raporu,' 14 September 2005, http://www.mazlumder.org/ana.php?konu=rapor&id=1042&lang=tr

Mazlum-Der, '9-10 Kasım 2005 Şemdinli Olaylarını Araştırma-İnceleme Raporu,' 12 November 2005, http://www.mazlumder.org/ana.php?konu=rapor&id=1043&lang=tr

İnsan Hakları Derneği (İHD), 'Mardin İli Kızıltepe İlçesinde Ahmet Kaymaz ve 12 Yaşındaki Oğlu Uğur Kaymaz'ın Yaşam Hakkının İhlal Edildiği İddialarını Araştırma-İnceleme Raporu,' 25 November 2004, http://ihd.org.tr/rapozel/kiziltepekaymaz.html

Center for European Security Studies (Avrupa Güvenlik Araştırmaları Merkezi, CESS), İstanbul Politikalar Merkezi (İPM), 'Turkish Civil-Military Relations and the EU: Preparation for Continuing Convergence,' November 2005, http://www.cess.org/publications/occasionals/pdfs/occasionals4.pdf

Önder, Şükrü, Bazı Kanunlarda Değişiklik Yapılmasına Dair Kanun Teklifi ve İçişleri Komisyonu Raporu, 2005, http://www.tbmm.gov.tr/sirasayi/donem22/yil01/ss962m.htm

Aker, Tamer; Çelik, A. Betül; Kurban, Dilek; Ünalan, Turgay ve Yükseker, Deniz, 'Türkiye'de Ülke İçinde Yerinden Edilme Sorunu: Tespitler ve Çözüm Önerileri,' TESEV, 2005, http://www.tesev.org.tr/etkinlik/TESEV_UYE_Grubu_Raporu.pdf

İnsan Hakları Derneği (İHD), '2005 Yılı Genel İnsan Hakları Raporu,' 28 February 2006, http://www.ihd.org.tr/ana.html

Türkiye İnsan Hakları Vakfı (TİHV), '2005 Yılında İnsan Haklarının Genel Durumu', http://www.tihv.org.tr

Newspaper Articles–Columns

Gönensin, Okay, 'Gazetecinin Anayasası,' Cumhuriyet, 27 August 1990.

Dündar, Can, 'Dikkat...! Haber Öldürücü Bir Silahtır...' Aktüel, 24 August 1995.

Süsoy, Yener, 'ABD'liler isim vermedi ama tarif Şahinkaya'ydı,' Hürriyet, 12 November 2001.

Vatandaş, Aydoğan, 'Kendisine JİTEM süsü veren mafya,' Zaman, 4 August 2002.

Yetkin, Murat, 'Bayramdan sonra sivil MGK geliyor,' Radikal, 28 November 2003.

Ergin, Sedat, 'Sivil darbe mi, askeri tasfiye mi,' Hürriyet, 7 December 2003.

Ergin, Sedat, 'Ordu ile oynamak,' Hürriyet, 9 December 2003.

Akyol, Fuat, 'JİTEM hayaletiyle gasp terörü,' Aksiyon, 1 March 2004.

Düzel, Neşe, 'Bayramoğlu: İzleniyoruz,', Radikal, 12 April 2004.

Tayman, Enis, 'Korucular için 'çıkış yolu' aranıyor,' Tempo, 30 August 2004.

Kaçar, Hüseyin, 'Süryani köyündeki korucular jandarma tehdidiyle çıkarıldı,' Sabah, 13 September 2004.

Zeyrek, Deniz; Demirtaş, Serkan, 'Yeni MGK'dan ilk icraat: Fişler imha,' Radikal, 18 November 2004.

Yetkin, Murat, 'Kuşlar nereye uçtu?,' Radikal, 19 November 2004.

Bila, Fikret, 'Milli Güvenlik Siyaseti Belgesi,' Milliyet, 25 November 2004.

Köylü, Hilal, 'Patrikhane tehdit değil,' Radikal, 28 November 2004.

Mercan, Faruk, 'Kırmızı kitaplar yenileniyor,' Aksiyon, 6 December 2004.

Akyol, Fuat, 'Mardin'de şehven infaz,' Aksiyon, 13 December 2004.

Çakırözer, Utku, 'MGK'da kadın yönetici devri,' Milliyet, 21 February 2005.

Alkan, Sevda, 'STK'lar darbe yorgunu,' Yeni Şafak, 23 April 2005.

Ergan, Uğur, 'Heybeli açılmasın,' Hürriyet, 28 April 2005.

Hiçyılmaz, Ufuk, 'Başbakanlık krize talip,' Aksiyon, 2 May 2005.

Akosman, Abdullah, 'Vatana İhanetin Adı Açık Toplum Oldu,' Önce Vatan, 30 May 2005.

Cizre, Ümit, 'Güvenlik Reformu, Ama Nasıl?,' Radikal 2, 5 June 2005.

Kaplan, Sefa, 'İHD PKK'cı, artık istifa ediyorum,' Hürriyet, 1 August 2005.

Yetkin, Murat, 'Konuyu kim açar,' Radikal, 15 August 2005.

Yetkin, Murat, 'Geniş açıdan bakınca,' Radikal, 25 August 2005.

Yetkin, Murat, 'Terörle mücadelenin başına Dışişleri Bakanı,' Radikal, 27 September 2005.

Şık, Barkın, 'Albaylık zorlaşıyor,' Milliyet, 18 October 2005.

Sali, Ali, 'MGSB'de ilk tehdit yine terör,' Yeni Şafak, 24 October 2005.

Yılmaz, Turan, 'Aşırı sağ artık tehdit değil,' Hürriyet, 25 October 2005.

Şık, Barkın, 'Aşırı sağ tehdit değil,' Milliyet, 26 October 2005.

Zeyrek, Deniz, 'Gerekirse asker yine 'göreve,' Radikal, 28 October 2005.

Saydamer, Kemal, 'Dülger: Water strategy vital to Turkey,' Turkish Daily News, 30 October 2005.

Donat, Yavuz, '35'inci Madde Kalkmalı,' Sabah, 31 October 2005.

Özkök, Ertuğrul, 'O haber niye Hürriyet'e 'sızdırıldı,' Hürriyet, 1 November 2005.

Aksoy, Ergun, 'Kırmızı kitabı kim medyaya sızdırdı?. Erdoğan: MGK Genel Sekreterliği
çalışanları,' Sabah, 2 November 2005.

Donat, Yavuz, 'Demokrasi'de ordunun yeri,' Sabah, 3 November 2005.

'Başbakan Erdoğan: Olay Mutlaka Açıklığa Kavuşmalı,' Zaman, 11 November 2005.

Dumanlı, Ekrem, 'Terörle Mücadele Yasası işte böyle sorgulanır,' Zaman, 14 November 2005.

Yedig, Serhan, 'Bir var bir yok! Hem var hem yok JİTEM,' Hürriyet, 21 November 2005.

Özkök, Ertuğrul, 'MİT Müsteşarı gölgeden çıktı,' Hürriyet, 24 November 2005.

Ergan, Uğur, 'En az ihraç,' Hürriyet, 2 December 2005.

Özkök, Ertuğrul, 'İmralı'da ilk sıradışı ziyaret,' Hürriyet, 6 December 2005.

Tosun, Resul, 'Daha sivil bir görüntü,' Yeni Şafak, 7 December 2005.

Öneş, Cevat, 'Terör-kimlik-türban... Güvenlikte yeni arayışlar,' Radikal, 7 December 2005.

Bayramoğlu, Ali, 'Şu JİTEM dedikleri ve Şemdinli,' Yeni Şafak, 15 December 2005.

Gökçer Tahincioğlu, 'Yemin gibi İlkeler,' Milliyet, 20 December 2005.

Söylemez, Haşim, 'İtirafçılar tetikte,' Aksiyon, 21 December 2005, http://www.aksiyon.com.tr/detay.php?id=22875

Yetkin, Murat, 'Irak ve Kürt federasyonu MGK'da,' Radikal, 25 December 2005.

Yetkin, Murat, '29 Aralık MGK'sının önemi,' Radikal, 31 December 2005.

Yetkin, Murat, 'PKK'yla mücadelede yeni patron,' Radikal, 4 January 2006.

Bülbül, Kezban, 'İddianame Şemdinli'yi unutturmasın,' Yeni Şafak, 10 March 2006.

'Örtülüden kullanılan 45 milyon doların kaydı yok,' Hürriyet, 14 January 1998.

'Yılmaz'ın zor kararı,'Hürriyet, 23 February 1998.

'Birdal'dan A Timi'ne: Bilmem ne bereliler,' Hürriyet, 26 April 1998.

'Korucular yakalandı,' Radikal, 29 September 2002.

'Askerler istemese AWACS'lar alınmazdı,' Milliyet, 9 May 2003.

'AWACS ihalesi sorun oldu,' Radikal, 11 May 2003.

'Polis'ten Jandarma'ya sitem,' Hürriyet, 3 December 2003.

'Üskül: 'Yetkisi yok,' Milliyet, 11 March 2004.

'Erdoğan: TSK'nın görevi değil,' Cumhuriyet, 15 March 2004.

'ASAM'ın başkanlığına Gündüz Aktan atandı,' Zaman, 7 April 2004.

'TESEV haddini aştı,' Yeniçağ, 19 May 2004.

'Jandarma, Süryanilerin boşalttığı köydeki korucuları zorla çıkarttı,' Zaman, 13 September 2004.

'CHP'li Elekdağ'dan 'TSK yeniden yapılandırılsın' çağrısı,' Anadolu Ajansı, 8 November 2004.

'Sivil MGK perdelerini açıyor,' Hürriyet, 25 November 2004.

'Adli kolluk' resmi görüşe rağmen geçti,' Sabah, 28 November 2004.

'Adli kolluk komisyondan geçti,' Zaman, 28 November 2004.

'Şeffaflaştık,' Hürriyet, 1 December 2004.

'Açıklamaya Dikkat,' Hürriyet, 1 December 2004.

'Terörist değillerdi,' Radikal, 1 December 2004.

'Kızıltepe'deki operasyonda güvenlik kusurları belirlendi,' Zaman, 13 December 2004.

'Tokat Paşa: Suçlular cezalandırılsın, ordu yıpratılmasın,' Zaman, 29 December 2004.

'Silahsız kuvvetlerin maaşı da çok düşük,' Milliyet, 28 January 2005.

'MİT telefonunu istiyor,' Milliyet, 10 March 2005.

'New Gendarmerie controversy sparked,' Turkish Daily News, 17 March 2005.

'Özel timciler genel müdürlükten olumlu not aldı,' Zaman, 27 March 2005.

'MİT'ten dinleme ısrarı,' Milliyet, 31 March 2005.

'İtirafçı Timurtaş yakalandı,' Radikal, 5 May 2005.

'Ankara'yı kızdıran rapor,' Milliyet, 10 May 2005.

'Asker düğümü tartışması,' Milliyet, 11 May 2005.

'Tek soruda aklandı,' Milliyet, 17 May 2005.

'MİT'i 2.5 yıl önce önerdiler,' Hürriyet, 19 May 2005.

'Kızıltepe Olayı'nda Baro Raporu: Baba Kaymaz PKK milisi,' Milliyet, 22 May 2005.

'Soros, Türkiye'de 'Açık Toplum'a 6 milyon dolar verdi,' Hürriyet, 27 May 2005.

'Soros'tan Türkiye'ye 6 Milyon $,' Ortadoğu, 28 May 2005.

'Türkiye'yi sarsacak belge,' Vatan, 1 June 2005.

'MİT izlemesi Bakanlar Kurulu'nda,' Milliyet, 2 June 2005.

'Güvenlik Anayasası masada,' Cumhuriyet, 21 June 2005.

'Savcı: Dinleme yasal,' Milliyet, 25 June 2005.

'Paşalar rapordan imzalarını çekti,' Hürriyet, 27 June 2005.

'MİT Müsteşarı Şenkal Atasagun'un neden emekliliğinin istendiğini açıklıyoruz,' Haftalık, 29 June-5 July 2005.

'Tolon: Terör konusunda Türkiye'ye çifte standart uygulandı,' Anadolu Ajansı, 24 July 2005.

'Gizli yönetmelik, soru önergesiyle ortaya çıktı,' Zaman, 25 July 2005.

'Koruculara 'gizli' yönetmelik,' Yeni Şafak, 14 August 2005.

'Genelkurmay, JİTEM bizi bağlamaz,' Milliyet, 16 September 2005.

'Bucak gizliliğe sığınıyor,' Cumhuriyet, 1 October 2004.

'Meclis'teki taburu kaldırma gücüm yok,' Hürriyet, 7 October 2005.

'Uğur Kaymaz davasında avukat protestosu,' Hürriyet, 24 October 2005.

'Özkök cool towards YÖK stance,' Turkish Daily News, 31 October 2005.

'Canan: Susurluk'tan beter,' Milliyet, 11 November 2005.

'MİT bütçesi sessiz geçti,' Milliyet, 11 November 2005.

'Ecevit: Türkiye'de derin devlet hep var,' Ajanslar, 21 November 2005.

'Evlerin alımı hukuken ve ahlaken mümkün değil,' Hürriyet, 24 November 2005.

'Savunmada yerli üretim artmalı,' Cumhuriyet, 25 November 2005.

'Welcome to Kürdistan,' Tempo, 2 December 2005.

'MİT Müsteşarı ile Barzani ne konuştu?,' Haftalık, 2-8 December 2005.

'Genelkurmay'dan tepki: Muhafız alayı teklifi hezeyan,' Radikal, 9 December 2005.

'Türkiye laiklikten uzaklaştırılıyor,' Cumhuriyet, 10 December 2005.

'Barodan TMK uyarısı: OHAL getirilmek isteniyor,' Zaman, 10 December 2005.

'FBI Başkanı MİT'e de gitti,' Radikal, 10 December 2005.

'Kaymaz'ın sırtındaki 9 kurşun da ölümcül,' Milliyet, 18 December 2005.

'Yemin gibi ilkeler,' Milliyet, 20 December 2005.

'Gül: TSK yetmez,' Milliyet, 26 December 2005.

'Şemdinli patlamalarına JİT ve MİT savunması,' Sabah, 27 December 2005.

'Commission deliberates axing state secret shield,' Turkish Daily News, 28 December 2005.

Cevat Öneş, 'Güvenlik ve demokrasi,' Radikal, 28 December 2005.

'Şemdinli Komisyonu'nda Tuğgeneral gerginliği,' Milliyet, 29 December 2005.

'Hakkari ve Şemdinli'nin Mülki Amirleri komisyonda dinlendi: 'Astsubayları tanımıyoruz,' Milliyet, 29 December 2005.

'Gül: Terörle mücadelede direktifi hükümet verir,' Milliyet, 4 January 2006.

''Gözaltı süresi yetersiz,' Sabah, 6 January 2006.

'Tümgeneral Beştepe'den OMÜ'ye destek ziyareti,' Cumhuriyet, 21 January 2006.

'Kritik diyalog,' Bugün, 23 January 2006.

'Yeşil'in yargılandığı JİTEM davası başlıyor,' Zaman, 24 January 2006.

'Suçlamada geri adım,' Hürriyet, 26 January 2006.

'Şemdinli raporu sonunda rafa kalktı,' Sabah, 31 January 2006.

'Evleri, kılıcı ve apoleti gitti,' Hürriyet, 8 February 2006.

'Askerin istediği yasa çıkar sinyali,' Hürriyet, 31 March 2006.

Press Release

MİT Basın Açıklaması, 2 June 2005, http://www.mit.gov.tr/basin23.html

Memur-Sen Basın Açıklaması, 12 September 2005, http://www.memursen.org.tr/haberioku.asp?kategori=1&id=173

İnsan Hakları Derneği (İHD) Basın Açıklaması, 12 November 2005, http://www.ihd.org.tr/basin/bas20051112.htm

MİT Basın Açıklaması, 2 December 2005, http://www.mit.gov.tr/basin24.html

Progress Reports

Avrupa Komisyonu, Türkiye 2005 İlerleme Raporu, 9 November 2005, http://www.abgs.gov.tr

Commission of the European Communities, Turkey: 2004 Progress Report, Brussels, 6 October 2004, SEC (2004) 1201.

Commission of the European Communities, Turkey: 2005 Progress Report, Brussels, 9 November 2005, SEC (2005) 1426. http://europa.eu.int/comm/enlargement/report_2005/pdf/package/sec_1426_final_en_progress_report_tr.pdf

Internet News

Varlık, Yasemin, 'Susurluk Kamu Vicdanında Bitmedi,' Bianet, 12 February 2001, http://www.bianet.org/2001/09/07/728.htm

Ulusoy, Kemal, 'Askerin Yetkisi Az Değil Fazla Bile!,' Aktif Haber, 12 August 2005, http://www.aktifhaber.com

Öztürk, Saygı, 'Komutan 'JİTEM' Gerçeğini Açıklıyor!,' Medya24, 14 November 2005.

'Analiz 06: MAH'tan MİT'e,' Anadolu Türk İnterneti (ATİN), 1 August 1991, http://www.atin.org/detail.asp?cmd=articledetail&articleid=115

'Analiz 07: Gehlen ve İstihbarat,' Anadolu Türk İnterneti (ATİH), 1 August 1991, http://www.atin.org/detail.asp?cmd=articledetail&articleid=116

'Cumartesi Annelerinden 'Cumartesi',' Bianet, 17 May 2002, http://www.bianet.org/2002/05/17/haber10036.htm

'Yeni TCK Tasarısı'na Sivil Tepki,' İHH İnsani Yardım Vakfı, 17 September 2004, http://www.ihh.org.tr/cgi-bin/index.pl?mod=news;op=news_id;id=1021

Ekici, Gökçen, 'Yabancı Sivil Toplum Örgütleri ve Sivil Darbeler,' 20 April 2005, http://www.avsam.org/tr/analizler.asp?ID=50

'Yasa Teklifleri Savunma Hakkına Saldırı,' Bianet, 10 May 2005, http://www.bianet.org/2005/05/10/60833.htm

'Telefon dinleme yetkisinde son nokta,' CNN Turk, 4 July 2005, http://www.cnnturk.com/HABER/haber_detay.asp?PID=318&HID=1&haberID=108432

'5 bin köy korucusu suç işledi,' NTV-MSNBC, 28 September 2005.

'Özgürlükleri savunmak için sivil itaatsizlik,' Bianet, 28 September 2005, http://www.bianet.org/2005/09/28/67893.htm

'Diyarbakır Barosu: TMK tasarısıyla yapılmak istenenler,' 29 September 2005, http://www.savaskarsitlari.org/arsiv.asp?ArsivTipID=6&ArsivAnaID=28810&ArsivSayfaNo=1

'Barolar Birliği Hakkari'ye Gidiyor,' Güncel Hukuk Haberleri, 20 November 2005, http://www.hukuki.net/haber/detay.asp?id=525

'Büyükanıt, Şemdinli Raporundan Çıkarıldı,' Haber 10, 17 December 2005, http://www.haber10.com/haber/15700/

'Kaymaz'ın çatışmaya girmesi imkânsız,' CNN Turk, 19 December 2005.

'Hükümet yeni TMK taslağını hangi sivil topluma danıştı?,' 10 January 2006, http://www.savaskarsitlari.org/arsiv.asp?ArsivTipID=9&ArsivAnaID=30627

'Şemdinli'de yakalanan devletin ta kendisidir!-Rapor,' 25 January 2006, http://www.savaskarsitlari.org/arsiv.asp?ArsivTipID=6

Şemdinli Komisyonu kilitlendi,' Haberextra, 30 January 2006, http://www.haberextra.com/haber/9117/%C5%9Eemdinli/Komisyonu/kilitlendi

Cerrah'tan 'olağanüstü' talepler,' NTV-MSNBC, 25 March 2006, http://www.ntv.com.tr/news/366383.asp

Websites

http://72.14.203.104/search?q=cache:iqdQ9PLcFHAJ:www.cengizkan.com/html/ocaksis-tem.php%3Fname%3DHaber%26file%3Darticle%26sid%3D1456+%22Avrupa+G%C3%BCvenlik+Ara%C5%9Ft%C4%B1rmalar%C4%B1+Merkezi%22+(CESS)&hl=tr&ct=clnk&cd=30
http://www.anap.org.tr/anap/genelbaskanlar/YILMAZ/konusmalar/1998/ocak98/22ocak98.htm, 22 Ocak 1998
http://www.avsam.org/tr/giris3.asp
http://www.avsam.org/tr/stratejikanaliz.asp?x_yil1=2005
http://www.barobirlik.org.tr/tbb/baskan/konusmalar/051203_mersin.aspx
http://www.biyografi.net/kisiayrinti.asp?kisiid=2928
http://www.bumko.gov.tr
http://www.bumko.gov.tr/chart/data.htm
http://www.bumko.gov.tr/proje/proje1/fonksinif.mht
http://www.byegm.gov.tr/YAYINLARIMIZ/AyinTarihi/1996/eylul1996.htm
http://www.byegm.gov.tr/YAYINLARIMIZ/AyinTarihi/2005/ agustos2005.htm
http://www.danistay.gov.tr
http://www. egmidb.gov.tr
http://www.erg.sabanciuniv.edu/ipm.htm
http://www.ihd.org.tr
http://www.jandarma.gov.tr
http://www.korkuteken.com/kimdir.htm
http://www.mazlumder.org/ana.php?konu=aciklama&id=465&lang=tr
http://www.mazlumder.org/ana.php?konu=aciklama&id=472&lang=tr
http://www.memursen.org.tr/haberioku.asp?kategori=1&id=173
http://www.mgk.gov.tr/sss.html
http://www.mit.gov.tr/merak-Cevap17.html
http://www.mit.gov.tr/stat_butce.html
http://www.msb.gov.tr
http://www.ortakpayda.org/boxes.asp?foo=read&feox=139&ronin=5
http://www.tayad.org
http://www.tbmm.gov.tr
http://tem.iem.gov.tr/cmk.php
http://www.savaskarsitlari.org/arsiv.asp?ArsivTipID=8&ArsivAnaID=30187&ArsivSayfaNo=1
http://www.telehaber.com/haberler/haber-287453/
http://www.tesev.org.tr/basin/basin_tesev.php
http://www.tesev.org.tr/etkinlik/dcaf2.php

http://www.tesev.org.tr/etkinlik/GSDA_TESEV.pdf
http://www.tesev.org.tr/projeler/guvenlik_Sektoru_metin.pdf
http://www.tesev.org.tr/tesev_misyon.php
http://www.tesev.org.tr/tesev_tarihce.php
http://www.tihak.org.tr/yaliefe1.html
http://www.tsk.mil.tr
http://www.yargitay.gov.tr
http://www.yenisafak.com.tr/diziler/mgk/mgk2.html

List of Contributors

Zühtü Arslan

Dr. Zühtü Arslan, Associate Professor of Constitutional Law, teaches at the Faculty of Security Sciences, Ankara. He graduated from the Faculty of Political Sciences at Ankara University, and received his MA and PhD degrees from the Law Faculty of Leicester University in England. His research interests include constitutional justice, politics of law, freedom of expression, political parties, and civil-military relations. Among his recent publications are; Constitutional Law of Turkey (co-author) (Kluwer Publication, 2004); 'Conflicting Paradigms: Political Rights in the Turkish Constitutional Court,' Critique: Critical Middle Eastern Studies, 11/1 (2002), p. 9-25; 'Taking Rights Less Seriously: Postmodernism and Human Rights,' Res Publica, 5/2 (1999), p.195-205.

Önder Aytaç

Dr. Önder Aytaç is an Assistant Professor and Vice Dean of Faculty of Security Sciences, Police Academy. He graduated from Faculty of Law at Ankara University (LLB), received a certificate for law from Ankara Bar Association, received his MSc degree in Criminology and Criminal Justice Department at Loughborough University and completed his PhD in Sociology at Middle East Technical University. He is lecturing on 'media,' 'public relations,' 'terror and terrorism' and 'policing' matters at undergraduate and postgraduate levels. He conducts research and writes on media, public relations, policing and related matters. He is the author of five books and several articles in Turkish and English. In addition to this, he is Vice President of International Police Association's (IPA) Turkish Section and he is a columnist at daily English-language newspaper The New Anatolian.

Volkan Aytar

Volkan Aytar is a Program Officer for the Turkish Economic and Social Studies Foundation (TESEV), (2004-present) and an advanced doctoral candidate in sociology at the State University of New York-Binghamton. He formerly worked as an Assistant Editor for the Political Handbook of the World in New York. He received; BA in Political Science & Public Administration from Bilkent University, Ankara; MA in Sociology and Certificate in Global Studies from the State University of New York-Binghamton. His publications include: 'Caterers of the Consumed Metropolis: 'Ethnicized' Tourism and Entertainment Laborscapes in Istanbul,' in Jan Rath (ed.) Tourism, Ethnic Diversity and the City, Forthcoming in 2006; (Editor) Democratic Oversight of the Security Sector: Turkey & the World, 2005; (Author) Metropol,

2005; (Author) (Co-Author with Ayşe Betül Çelik) 'Gender: Feminism and Women's Studies,' in Immanuel Wallerstein & Richard Lee (eds.) Overcoming the Two Cultures: Science versus the Humanities in the Modern World-System, 2004; (Co-Author with Azer Keskin) 'Scuffling and Intermingling Sounds in a Fragmented Metropolis: Constructions of Spaces of Music in Istanbul,' Géocarrefour: Revue de Géographie de Lyon, 2003.

Ertan Beşe

Dr. Ertan Beşe studied Public Administration at İstanbul University, Faculty of Political Sciences where he received his BA degree (1989). In 1991 he became a research assistant at the Police Academy. In 1994 he received a Master's degree (LLM) in Public Law at the University of Wales, Aberystwyth Law Department (The UK). His dissertation was entitled 'General Aspects of Contemporary Political Terrorism and State Responses.' He obtained his first PhD from İstanbul University with his thesis titled 'Fighting against Terrorism and Human Rights from the Perspectives of the European Union' in 2002, and then he had a position as an Assistant Professor of Criminology at the Faculty of Security Sciences, Police Academy. He also completed a second PhD from the Sociology department at Middle East Technical University in March 2005. The title of his dissertation is 'Sociological Analysis of Organized Criminality in Turkey.' Ertan Beşe is currently a member of the teaching staff at the Faculty of Security Sciences, Police Academy.

İbrahim Cerrah

İbrahim Cerrah completed his Master's and PhD degrees in England between 1990 and 1995. Following his graduation, he worked as a university lecturer at Police Academy, Ankara since 1995. As a Fulbright lecturer, he gave various lectures such as 'introduction to police sciences,' 'police administration,' and 'comparative police systems' at New York University. He has studies in the fields of 'police ethics,' 'police sub-culture,' 'police education,' 'civilian participation in security sector,' 'oversight and control of security sector,' and 'security sector reform' together with several researches and publications in domestic security issues. Dr. Cerrah is also the member of the Security Sector Working and Monitoring Group established by TESEV. In 2005, he worked in the project entitled 'Preparatory Assistance for Civilian Control of Security and Law Enforcement' which was run by the support of the Ministry of Internal Affairs and the United Nations Development Program, as national advisor. He was the founder and editor of the Turkish Journal of Police Studies. His books and articles published both in Turkey and abroad include Turkish Yearbook of Human Rights; Intsec: The Journal of International Security; Security Journal; LA Gazetta: Une Publication De La Gendarmerie Royale Du Canada; Turkish Public Administration Annual and Turkish Journal of Police Studies. He became an Assistant Professor in 2001 and Professor in 2006. Since 2001, he is the Director of Institute of Security Sciences at the Police Academy.

Ümit Cizre

Ümit Cizre, Professor of Political Science, Bilkent University, Ankara-Turkey; former Fulbright Research Scholar (Princeton University) and Jean Monnet Research Fellow (RSC, European University Institute, Florence). Her research interests are centered on democratic governance of civil-military relations; politics of national security; security sector reform; politics of ethnicity and nationalism. Some of her publications have appeared in European Journal of Political Research; Comparative Politics; Middle East Journal; Human Rights Review; History of European Ideas; Journal of Muslim Minority Affairs; International Journal of Middle Eastern Studies; Development and Change, The South Atlantic Quarterly. She has contributed to such edited volumes as Middle Eastern Armies: Politics and Strategy (Frank Cass, 2002); Rightsizing the State: The Politics of Moving Borders (Oxford University Press, 2002); Turkey: Identity, Democracy, Politics (Frank Cass, 1996).

Mesut Bedri Eryılmaz

Associate Professor M. Bedri Eryılmaz is a lecturer of law at Police Academy. He graduated from Dokuz Eylül University, Law Faculty in 1988. He completed his LLM and PhD in England, University of Leicester, Law Faculty between 1989 and 1995. His areas of specialization are 'police law,' 'criminal law' and 'international human rights law.' He gives lectures on 'criminal law,' 'criminal procedures law,' 'police powers,' 'European Court of Human Rights (ECtHR)' and 'police' at Police Academy, Faculty of Security Sciences and Institute of Security Sciences. He also gives lectures on 'criminal procedural law' at Başkent University, Faculty of Law. He has two books published, namely, Arrest and Detention Powers in English and Turkish Laws and Practice in the Light of the European Convention on Human Rights (Kluwer Law Interenational, the Hague, 1999) and Stop and Search Powers in English and Turkish Laws and Practice (Seçkin, Ankara, 2003). He has also published many translated and edited books and articles on police law and rights of individuals.

Ümit Kardaş

Dr. Ümit Kardaş has worked as legal counsel, attorney general and adjudicator in the Turkish Armed Forces for 22 years and currently he is working as a legal practitioner. He received his PhD in law in 1985. He is a member of the Security Sector Working and Monitoring Group established by TESEV. In addition to his articles and interviews that were published in several newspapers and reviews, he has several books such as Hâkim Bağımsızlığı Açısından Askerî Mahkemelerin Kuruluşu ve Yetkileri, Askerî Ceza ve Ceza Yargısı, Disiplin Mahkemeleri ve Yarglama Usulü, and Türkiye'nin Demokratikleşmesinde Öncelikler.

Gencer Özcan

Gencer Özcan graduated from Ankara University, Faculty of Political Sciences and received his PhD from Boğaziçi University. He has been teaching at Yıldız Technical University, Department of Politics and International Relations since 1999. His research interests are 'diplomatic history,' 'Turkey's foreign policy making process,' 'the military's role in the making of Turkey's foreign and security policy decisions,' 'Turkey's policy towards the Middle East,' and 'Turkish-Israeli bilateral relations.' His publications include, (with Ofra Bengio) 'Old Grievances, New Fears: Arab Perceptions of Turkey and Its Alignment with Israel,' Middle Eastern Studies (April 2001); (with Ofra Bengio) 'Decade of the Military: The Case of the Alignment with Israel,' International Journal of Turkish Studies (Spring 2001); 'The Military and Foreign Policy Making in Turkey,' Barry Rubin and Kemal Kirişçi (eds.) Turkey in World Politics (New York:Lynn Ryneer Publishers, 2001); 'Türkiye'de Siyasal Rejim ve Güvenlikleştirme Sorunsalı,' Burak Ülman and İsmet Akça (eds.) Prof. Dr. Kemâli Saybaşılı'ya Armağan (İstanbul: Bağlam, 2005). He also co-edited with Şule Kut, En Uzun Onyıl, Türkiye'nin Ulusal Güvenlik ve Dış Politika Gündeminde Doksanlı Yıllar, (İstanbul: Boyut, 1998). His latest publication is Türkiye-İsrail İlişkilerinde Dönüşüm: Güvenliğin Ötesi (İstanbul: TESEV, 2005).

Lale Sarıibrahimoğlu

Lale Sarıibrahimoğlu has been working for the UK-based Jane's Defence Weekly (JDW) as Turkey Correspondent since 1991 as well as daily Bugün as a columnist and senior correspondent. Starting her journalism career in 1979, she has been covering military issues as well as foreign policy and energy related topics. Her yearly surveys on the Turkish military and Turkish defence industry have been published in JDW. She is a fellow of the 21st Century Trust, a UK-based think tank. She earned Diploma in World Politics in 1991 from the U.K. based London School of Economics and Political Science. She has two books published. She received a national journalism award for her book on Baku-Tbilisi-Ceyhan oil pipeline, published in 1997. 'Turkish Defence Procurement, Joint Ventures and Offset Agreements…The International Guide to the Turkish Defence Industry,' was published in 1999 by the UK-based SMI.

Itır Toksöz

Itır Toksöz received her BA degree from Marmara University, Department of Public Administration as 1st in rank in her class. She has received a French Government Scholarship and obtained a DEA degree on Strategy and Politics in International Relations at Université Paris I Panthéon-Sorbonne. She then obtained an MA degree in International Relations from Northeastern University in Boston. Currently, she is completing her PhD dissertation on Turkey's Security Dilemma in the Light of Turkish Military's Threat Perceptions as a PhD Candidate in International and Public Affairs Program at Northeastern University, Department of Political Science. Toksöz resides in Turkey on dissertation field research for the last two years and has been working as an instructor at Koç University, Department of History. Since March 2005, she was involved in TESEV Security Sector Working and Monitoring Group as an observer and consultant. Her areas of research interest include 'threat perceptions,' 'civil military relations,' 'national security,' 'science-technology and politics' and 'international humanitarian law.'

Ferhat Ünlü

Ferhat Ünlü has started his career in journalism in 1995, while he was studying at İstanbul University, Faculty of Communication. He has published numerous news stories and studies on the issues of security, intelligence and terrorism published. Those publications also include Susurluk Gümrüğü (Birey, 2000); Eymür'ün Aynası and Sadettin Tantan (Metis). Ünlü also published fiction books including, Buzdan Gözyaşı (Bakış, 2002); Bir Gölgenin İntikamı (Everest, 2003); as well as crime fiction entitled, Münasebetsizleri Ayıklama Teşkilatı (MAT) (Everest, 2006). Currently, he works for the weekly newsmagazine Haftalık, while completing his new novel. Ünlü has also published articles in numerous literary journals and reviews.

Ahmet Yıldız

Dr. Ahmet Yıldız is the Director of the Research Centre of the Turkish Grand National Assembly. Before, he produced various research reports as political science subject specialist. His research interests lie in the 'politico-religious discourse of political parties representing the National Outlook (Milli Görüş) Movement,' 'the source of Islam-oriented parties in Turkey,' 'the ethno-secular boundaries of Turkish nationalism,' and 'the Turkish political thought.' For his comparative study on the management of ethnic violence, he received the social science award from daily Milliyet in 1996. He authored two books in Turkish: 'Ne Mutlu Türküm Diyebilene!' Türk Ulusal Kimliğinin Etno-seküler Sınırları (1919-1938) (İstanbul: İletişim, 2001) and İktidar Herşey Değildir (İstanbul: Karakalem, 2004). His articles have been published in Turkish and English in several books, and academic journals including, The Muslim World, Tezkire and Liberal Düşünce.

Geneva Centre for the Democratic Control of Armed Forces (DCAF)

Heiner Hänggi;
Theodor H. Winkler (Eds.)
Challenges of Security Sector Governance
2003, 312 pp., 23,90 €, br.,
ISBN-DE 3-8258-7158-4, ISBN-CH 3-03735-018-0

Marina Caparini; Otwin Marenin (Eds.)
Transforming Police in Central and Eastern Europe
Process and Progress
2004, 376 pp., 29,90 €, br.,
ISBN-DE 3-8258-7485-0, ISBN-CH 3-03735-005-9

Alan Bryden; Heiner Hänggi (Eds.)
Reform and Reconstruction of the Security Sector
2004, 296 pp., 29,90 €, gb.,
ISBN-DE 3-8258-7770-1, ISBN-CH 3-03735-019-9

Bernardo Arévalo de León;
José Beltrán Doña;
Philipp H. Fluri (Eds.)
Hacia una Política de Seguridad para la Democracia en Guatemala
Investigación Acción Participativa (IAP) y Reforma del Sector Seguridad
2005, 352 S., 34,80 €, br.,
ISBN-DE 3-8258-8692-1, ISBN-CH 3-03735-022-9

Alan Bryden; Heiner Hänggi (Eds.)
Security Governance in Post-Conflict Peacebuilding
2005, 304 pp., 29,90 €, br.,
ISBN-DE 3-8258-9019-8, ISBN-CH 3-03735-023-7

Marina Caparini; Philipp Fluri;
Ferenc Molnar (Eds.)
Civil Society and the Security Sector
Concepts and Practices in New Democracies
2006, 264 pp., 29,90 €, br.,
ISBN-DE 3-8258-9364-2, ISBN-CH 3-03735-024-5

Marina Caparini; Otwin Marenin (Eds.)
Borders and Security Governance
Managing Borders in a Globalised World
2006, 320 pp., 29,90 €, br.,
ISBN-DE 3-8258-9438-X,
ISBN-CH 3-03735-005-9

Alan Bryden; Marina Caparini (Eds.)
Private Actors and Security Governance
The privatisation of security –understood as both the top-down decision to outsource military and security-related tasks to private firms and the bottom-up activities of armed non-state actors such as rebel opposition groups, insurgents, militias and warlord factions – have profound implications for the state's monopoly on the legitimate use of force. Both top-down and bottom-up privatisation have significant consequences for effective, democratically accountable security sector governance as well as on opportunities for security sector reform across a range of different reform contexts. This volume situates security privatisation within a broader policy framework, considers several relevant national and regional contexts and analyses different modes of regulation and control relating to a phenomenon with deep historical roots but also strong links to more recent trends of globalisation and transnationalisation.
2006, 336 pp., 29,90 €, gb.,
ISBN-DE 3-8258-9840-7, ISBN-CH 3-03735-017-2

David M. Law (Ed.)
Intergovernmental Organisations and Security Sector Reform
2007, 320 pp., 29,90 €, br.,
ISBN-DE 978-3-8258-0752-8,
ISBN-CH 978-3-03735-187-1

LIT Verlag GmbH & Co. KG Wien – Zürich
Auslieferung Österreich: Medienlogistik Pichler-ÖBZ GmbH & Co KG
IZ-NÖ Süd, Straße 1, Objekt 34, A-2355 Wiener Neudorf, Postfach 133
Tel. +43 (0) 2236 / 63 535 - 236, Fax +43 (0) 2236 / 63 535 - 243, e-Mail: bestellen@medien-logistik.at
Auslieferung Deutschland: Fresnostr. 2 48159 Münster
Tel.: 0251 / 620 32 22 – Fax 0251 / 922 60 99
e-Mail: vertrieb@lit-verlag.de – http://www.lit-verlag.de